D0122403

The Frodo Franchise

*The publisher gratefully acknowledges the
generous contribution to this book provided
by the General Endowment Fund of the
University of California Press Foundation.*

The Frodo Franchise

The Lord of the Rings
and Modern Hollywood

KRISTIN THOMPSON

UNIVERSITY OF CALIFORNIA PRESS

BERKELEY   LOS ANGELES   LONDON

University of California Press, one of the most distinguished university presses in the United States, enriches lives around the world by advancing scholarship in the humanities, social sciences, and natural sciences. Its activities are supported by the UC Press Foundation and by philanthropic contributions from individuals and institutions. For more information, visit www.ucpress.edu.

This book is an independent work of scholarship. It is based on the author's own research, which included interviews with many of the artists, writers, and business people who participated in the making of *The Lord of the Rings* motion pictures and related projects. The author has attempted to verify the factual accuracy of the information presented here; nothing is made up or imagined. Many people involved with *The Lord of the Rings* motion pictures have assisted the author's research on this book by providing information and materials to her. However, no person or entity associated with the producers of *The Lord of the Rings* motion pictures has sponsored the research or writing of the book or endorsed the final product.

University of California Press
Berkeley and Los Angeles, California

University of California Press, Ltd.
London, England

© 2007 by The Regents of the University of California

Some of the topics in this volume appeared in "Fantasy, Franchises, and Frodo Baggins: *The Lord of the Rings* and Modern Hollywood," in *The Velvet Light Trap* 52 (Fall 2003): 45–63, published by the University of Texas Press.

An early version of the discussion of the buildup of the filmmaking infrastructure in Wellington was delivered as a paper at a symposium in Bremen and subsequently published in German in the proceedings of the symposium, as follows: "Hollywood, Wellywood und Peter Jackson," in *Experiment Mainstream? Differenz und Uniformierung im Populären Kino,* ed. Imbert Schenk et al. (Berlin: Bertz + Fischer, 2006), 85–96.

Library of Congress Cataloging-in-Publication Data

Thompson, Kristin, 1950–
    The Frodo franchise : *The Lord of the Rings* and modern Hollywood / Kristin Thompson.
        p. cm.
    Includes bibliographical references and index.
    ISBN: 978-0-520-24774-1 (cloth : alk. paper)
    1. Lord of the Rings films—History and criticism.   I. Title.
    PN1995.9.L58T46   2007
    791.43'75—dc22   2007000109

Manufactured in the United States of America

16 15 14 13 12 11 10 09 08 07
10 9 8 7 6 5 4 3 2 1

The paper used in this publication meets the minimum requirements of ANSI/NISO Z39.48–1992 (R 1997) (*Permanence of Paper*).

For Barrie Osborne,
who trusted me and thus made this book possible

This is just the overture, as the sweeping arms of popular culture embrace the Professor and his works.

CLIFF BROADWAY (QUICKBEAM)
TheOneRing.net, 2001

CONTENTS

LIST OF ILLUSTRATIONS   xi

PREFACE AND ACKNOWLEDGMENTS   xiii

LIST OF INTERVIEWS   xvii

ABBREVIATIONS   xxi

INTRODUCTION: SEQUEL-ITIS   I

PART ONE

THE FILM

1 / Prudent Aggression   17

2 / Not Your Father's Tolkien   53

3 / Handcrafting a Blockbuster   75

PART TWO

BUILDING THE FRANCHISE

4 / Flying Billboards and FAQs   105

5 / Click to View Trailer   133

6 / Fans on the Margins, Pervy Hobbit Fanciers,
and Partygoers   165

PART THREE

BEYOND THE MOVIE

7 / Licenses to Print Money   193

8 / Interactive Middle-earth   224

PART FOUR

THE LASTING POWER OF THE RINGS

9 / Fantasy Come True   257

10 / Right in Your Own Backyard   282

NOTES   333
INDEX   371

ILLUSTRATIONS

Plates follow page 234

FIGURES

1. Some book-related franchise products — 11
2. The genealogy of *The Lord of the Rings* — 21
3. Harvey and Bob Weinstein's credits in *The Return of the King* — 36
4. Galadriel's boat on the swimming pool, New Line's Cannes party — 47
5. Bruce Lee in *Fist of Fury* — 62
6. Legolas during a skirmish in the Golden Hall in *The Two Towers* — 62
7. A white-bearded master in *Executioners from Shaolin* — 64
8. Gandalf "flying" during the fall with the Balrog (*The Two Towers*) — 66
9. Sam confronts Shelob (*The Return of the King*) — 66
10. *Fox Trot,* 8 February 2001 (by Bill Amend) — 69
11. A jug in the *palantír* scene (*The Return of the King*) — 78
12. Bob Shaye with Ian Holm and Ian McKellen, Wellington (2000) — 80
13. Intriguing clutter in Saruman's study (*The Fellowship of the Ring*) — 93
14. Legolas's arrows (*The Return of the King*) — 94
15. Digital doubles on the bridge in Moria (*The Fellowship of the Ring*) — 99

16. Digital doubles fighting on the causeway at Helm's Deep (*The Two Towers*) 99

17. The electronic press kit: the "Characters" category 122

18. News on fan sites: popcorn-bag designs 137

19. The four founders of TheOneRing.net 156

20. Lilith of Sherwood in Wellington 168

21. Home page of Figwit Lives! 171

22. The Fellowship in The Lord of the Peeps 173

23. Home page of Figpeep Lives! 175

24. Shop outside *The Lord of the Rings* Motion Picture Trilogy—The Exhibition, Museum of Science, Boston (2004) 199

25. Sideshow Weta's display, One Ring Celebration (2005) 202

26. Elijah Wood and fan, One Ring Celebration (2005) 203

27. Electronic Arts' "The Two Towers" video game 236

28. Electronic Arts request form (2003) 239

29. Victor Juhasz, caricature of Frodo, *Hollywood Reporter* (2003) 266

30. SF Film's new headquarters, Copenhagen 270

31. Robert Rutherford and Glenorchy Air plane 286

32. Two new "Safari of the Scenes" Land Rovers 287

33. Kaitoke Regional Park sign for Rivendell 289

34. Three Foot Six's offices, Wellington 294

35. Studio A, Stone Street Studios, with the last standing set for *The Lord of the Rings* (2003) 296

36. Tourism New Zealand billboard, outside Los Angeles Airport (2004) 314

37. Street in front of the Embassy Theatre, Wellington (2003) 323

38. Miramar North School banner, Wellington (2004) 324

MAP

Several filmmaking facilities, Wellington's Miramar suburb 292

The *Lord of the Rings* film franchise is not over, nor will it be for years. I originally intended to end this book's coverage shortly after the extended-version DVD of *The Return of the King* was released. The extensive cooperation I received from the people I interviewed, however, entailed more travel than I expected, and as time went on, my files swelled with more notes, clippings, photocopies, and printouts on a huge variety of related topics. The flow of information has slowed but definitely not stopped, and there is always the temptation to go on and describe the next video game or tie-in book. Certainly new signs of the trilogy's influence on the film industry surface regularly, and some seem to be important examples that would bolster my claim that *Rings'* broad impact makes it one of the most important films ever made.

The coverage of even an ongoing phenomenon must end, however, and I find myself with a complete manuscript at the end of April 2006. I may be able to update here and there during the copyediting process, but essentially this book can claim to cover events only up to that date.

Once in a lifetime: I encountered this phrase again and again, in print and in my interviews. Even people who played nonspeaking roles or made promotional documentaries feel that they experienced something unique. Perhaps Cate Blanchett sums the attitude up most succinctly: "It's something that will be passed on from generation to generation. So many people have said how they wanted to be part of this because it is historic. They know it's a once-in-a-lifetime experience."

While researching and writing this book, I have felt the same way—that I have participated, albeit on the sidelines, in an extraordinary event that is indeed historic—so much so that I felt it deserved a more in-depth examination than the many licensed making-of coffee-table books could give it.

The cooperation I received from the filmmakers and the people at the many agencies and companies somehow connected with the trilogy makes this an extraordinary, unprecedented kind of book. No academic film historian has ever been able to witness part of the making of a blockbuster and talk to those working on it. The result examines not just the film but the franchise it spawned, and through that franchise, we can also look behind the scenes at some of the key ways in which Hollywood creates the big films that play so great a part in our lives.

This book is not a part of that franchise. It was not commissioned by anyone. I wrote it simply because the topic fascinated me, and I sought a publisher only after it was substantially finished. I have paid no licensing fees to New Line or anyone else (except a few of the photographers whose work illustrates this volume). No doubt in some small way I am publicizing the film and many other aspects of the franchise that I have discussed in these pages. Still, so have fans on their websites, moviegoers who recommended the film to friends, and the other film scholars who write on the subject. And, in the sea of public attention of all sorts, *The Lord of the Rings* hardly needs boosting from me.

I could not have told that story anywhere nearly as thoroughly as it deserves had it not been for the help of many people. Foremost among them are the seventy-seven wonderful interviewees, many of them actively involved in film projects or other work, who found the time to talk with me. They are listed in the "Sources" section at the beginning of the book. Special thanks to those who took additional time to guide me around facilities, to answer my follow-up e-mail queries, to read and comment on draft chapters, and to supply illustrations.

People directly associated with the making of *Rings* gave generously of their time and assistance. Peter Doyle hosted me at the PostHouse and gave me a lengthy demonstration of the selective digital grading process he had helped to invent. Rose Dority and Janna Roash were particularly helpful during my visits to The Film Unit. Mel Turner and Sarah Spurway, of Three Foot Six, graciously gave advice and passed on requests, and Jan Blenkin patiently handled one of those requests, resulting in a brief chance to watch Peter Jackson at work. Jenny Williams facilitated my correspondence with Richard Taylor.

Special thanks to John Howe (along with Chris Smith of HarperCollins) and Victor Juhasz for allowing me to reproduce their artworks.

I am grateful to Christopher Tolkien, Cathleen Blackburn of Manches LLP, and David Brawn of HarperCollins for clarifying the rights situation of my project in relation to their own interests, thus clearing the way for my gaining access to the filmmakers. Their kindness in no way implies any endorsement of my book.

I regret that ultimately New Line Cinema decided not to allow me to interview any of its executives for this book, but I thank David Imhoff and Marianne Dugan for making it possible for me to talk with many of the filmmakers and to observe the filmmaking facilities of Wellington in action.

I am also grateful to Gary Berman and Monica Gillen of Creation Entertainment for giving me the opportunity to observe the One Ring Celebration, as well as to Garfiemao of TheOneRing.net for helping to arrange that and to Emma Abraham and Kim Bissell for sharing their room with me when the convention hotel was booked solid. Edwina Mizzler helped me obtain a ticket for *The Lord of the Rings* Motion Picture Trilogy—The Exhibition. Professor Henry Jenkins III of MIT facilitated my interview with Neil Young at Electronic Arts. Jonathan Frome vetted the video games chapter. Genevieve Baillie of Lord of the Peeps and Iris Hadad and Sherry de Andres of Figwit Lives! generously provided information and permission to reproduce images from their websites.

Thanks also to others who aided me in a variety of ways: Mike Maser of Electronic Arts; Tom Williams and Melissa Bernstein of Gran Via Productions; Robert Walak of Alliance Atlantis; Professor Andy Horton of the University of Oklahoma; Anita Wolfgram of Tourism New Zealand (Los Angeles); Gill and Kel of Chalet Queenstown; Nancy and Kevin Crowther of the Victoria Court Motor Lodge; Sharon Williams, Jo Kirk, and Alick Shaw of the Office of the Mayor (Wellington); Josie Brennan and Gill Lockhart of Tourism New Zealand (Wellington); Louise Baker, Gareth Ruck, and Julia Bartley of Park Road Post; Melanie Marquez of BB Planet; René van Rossenberg of the Tolkien Shop; Don Badman, of the Office of Hon Pete Hodgson; Douglas A. Anderson, Tolkien scholar; and James Peterson of LaFollette, Godfrey & Kahn.

The staffs of Wingnut Films, Three Foot Six, The Film Unit, Weta Digital, Weta Workshop, the PostHouse, Nomad Safaris, Glenorchy Air, Dart River Safaris, Wellington Rover, Lamp-Post Productions (*The Lion, the Witch and the Wardrobe*), the American Film Market, Electronic Arts, and AT&T Global Network Services International in Wellington were most helpful. Diane Pivac and Kristen Wineera facilitated my visits to the New Zealand Film Archive. Professor Harriet Margolis of Victoria University of Wellington extended hospitality, showed me *Rings* locations, and generously discussed her own project on the trilogy.

Very special thanks to Annabelle Sheehan, who launched this project by introducing me to Barrie Osborne, who supported my project from day one. Without his support, this book might not have gone forward.

Two people gave me invaluable help in setting up interviews and facilities tours: unit publicist Melissa Booth, who as my point person during my first visit to Wellington provided valuable advice and aid, and Matt Dravitzki, who somehow found time in his busy schedule as Peter Jackson's assistant on *King Kong* to deal amiably and efficiently with my various requests on subsequent visits.

I am grateful to my agent, Sydelle Kramer; to my editors at the University of California Press, Mary Francis, Kalicia Pivirotto, and Rachel Berchten; and to copy editor Susan Ecklund. Jake Black and Kristi Gehring provided invaluable help in preparing the illustrations.

Versions of some chapters were read to groups at the University of Wisconsin–Madison that kindly offered comments and suggestions: members of the Tolkien and Fantasy Society, the film studies faculty and graduate students of the Department of Communication Arts, and those attending the symposium "Film Style in Question: An International Symposium in Honor of David Bordwell." Other occasions when I received similar feedback were at the "'Experiment Mainstream?' 10. Internationales Bremer Symposium zum Film" in Bremen and a lecture for the "Humanities Center Cinema Roundtable," at the University of Georgia.

Finally, heartfelt thanks to David Bordwell, who survived Trilogy Tuesday with me and probably thought at times during this project that the Road really *did* go ever on. His sage advice and keen editorial eye have helped give shape and style to this vast topic.

NOTE ON SOURCES

The URLs that appear in this book are current as of April 2006.

INTERVIEWS

Unless otherwise attributed, all quotations from and information concerning the following people are based upon the interviews listed below. Titles and positions are as of the time of the interviews.

Aitken, Matt. Digital models supervisor for *Rings,* Weta Digital. Wellington, 22 October 2003; Wellington, 1 December 2004.

Alley, Judy. Merchandising coordinator, *Rings,* and assets manager, *King Kong.* Wellington, 30 September 2003; Wellington, 5 December 2004.

Alley, Stan. Props standby assistant, *Rings;* coproducer, codirector, and cinematographer, *Frodo Is Great . . . Who Is That?!!* Wellington, 26 June 2004.

Anderson, Gregg. Regional manager, United States and Canada, Tourism New Zealand. Los Angeles, 2 September 2004.

Arden, Dan. Arden Entertainment, producer of *Rings* and *King Kong* documentaries for cable and DVD supplements. Los Angeles, 31 August 2004. www.arden entertainment.com.

Booth, Melissa. Publicist, *Rings,* and unit publicist, *King Kong.* Wellington, 23 October 2003.

Botes, Costa. Director, *The Making of "The Lord of the Rings"* (three films). Wellington, 3 October 2003.

Boyens, Philippa. Screenwriter, *Rings* and *King Kong.* Wellington, 2 July 2004.

Bragg, Jason. Owner, Wellington Rover, offering a "Rover Rings" tour. Wellington, 2 December 2004. www.wellingtonrover.co.nz.

Bridger, Sue. Business development manager, AT&T; formerly corporate sales account manager for the media, Telecom NZ, and contractor, Three Foot Six. Wellington, 22 June 2004.

Broadway, Cliff (Quickbeam). Contributor to TheOneRing.net; writer/producer, *Ringers: Lord of the Fans.* Los Angeles, 3 September 2004.

Caddington, Tim. Production manager (New Zealand), *The Chronicles of Narnia: The Lion, the Witch and the Wardrobe.* Auckland, 17 June 2004.

Cañizares, Alberto G. General manager, Aurum (Spanish distributor of *Rings*). Los Angeles, 7 November 2005.

Challis, Erica (Tehanu). Cofounder, TheOneRing.net; consultant, Red Carpet Middle Earth Tours. Auckland, 18 June 2004; Auckland, 23 November 2004. www.red-carpet-tours.com/index.cfm.

Cordova, Carlene (Asfaloth). Contributor to TheOneRing.net; producer/writer/director, *Ringers: Lord of the Fans.* Los Angeles, 3 September 2004.

Cossar, Tim. CEO, Positively Wellington Tourism. Wellington, 6 December 2004.

Crowley, James. Supervising location manager, *The Chronicles of Narnia: The Lion, the Witch and the Wardrobe.* Auckland, 17 June 2004.

Dickson, Ngila. Costume designer, *Rings.* Lower Hutt, 15 October 2003.

Dobner, Nina. Director of partner relations, Electronic Arts. Los Angeles, 10 November 2005.

Ebert, Roger. Film critic, *Chicago Sun-Times.* Madison, Wisconsin, 2 April 2006.

Falconer, Daniel. Weta Workshop, designer/sculptor for *Rings.* Wellington, 7 October 2003.

Finnie, Hilary. Dart River Safaris. Queenstown, 11 December 2002. www.dartriver.co.nz.

Flight, Simone. Formerly public relations manager, United States and Canada, Tourism New Zealand, Los Angeles office. Wellington, 3 December 2004.

Forbeck, Matt. Coauthor and developer, Decipher's *Rings* role-playing games. Madison, Wisconsin, 10 April 2005.

Funke, Alex. Visual effects director of photography, *Rings* and *King Kong.* Wellington, 10 December 2004.

Gatward-Ferguson, David and Amanda. Co-owners, Nomad Safaris, offering "Safari of the Rings" tours. Queenstown, 10 December 2002; second interview just with David, 18 November 2004. www.nomadsafaris.co.nz/sotr.htm.

Harley, Dr. Ruth. CEO, the New Zealand Film Commission. Wellington, 8 October 2003; Los Angeles, 5 November 2005.

Hennah, Chris. Art department manager, *Rings* and *King Kong.* Wellington, 8 December 2004.

Hennah, Dan. Supervising art director/set decorator, *Rings* and *King Kong.* Wellington, 8 December 2004.

Hickton, George. CEO, Tourism New Zealand. Wellington, 6 October 2003; Wellington, 30 November 2004.

Hodgson, Pete. Member of Parliament for Dunedin North, aka "The Minister of *The Lord of the Rings.*" Wellington, 13 October 2003.

Jackson, Peter. Coproducer, director, co-screenwriter, *Rings* and *King Kong.* Wellington, 2 July 2004.

James, Az. Touring exhibition manager, Te Papa (Museum of New Zealand). Wellington, 6 December 2004.

James, Sharon. Motion-capture combat choreographer, *Rings.* Wellington, 11 December 2004.

Johnson, Mark. Producer, *The Chronicles of Narnia: The Lion, the Witch and the Wardrobe.* Auckland, 17 June 2004.

Johnston, Jean. Manager, Film Wellington. Wellington, 21 June 2004.

Kamins, Ken. Cofounder, Key Creatives; formerly with ICM. Agent for Peter Jackson, Fran Walsh, and Philippa Boyens. Los Angeles, 1 November 2005.

Knowles, Harry. Webmaster, Ain't It Cool News. Austin, 29 December 2004.

Lilith of Sherwood. Webmaster, Lilith's *Lord of the Rings* Fan Site. Chicago, 7 August 2004.

Major, Grant. Production designer, *Rings* and *King Kong.* Wellington, 23 June 2004.

Malik, Ernie. Unit publicist, *The Chronicles of Narnia: The Lion, the Witch and the Wardrobe.* Auckland, 17 June 2004.

Maxwell, Kirk. New Zealand stunt coordinator, *Rings.* Wellington, 11 December 2004.

McFetridge, Susan. Investment director—screen production, Investment New Zealand. Auckland, 22 November 2004.

McKellen, Ian. "Gandalf"; owner, www.mckellen.com. London, 21 February 2005.

McRae, Alyson. Former merchandising coordinator, *Rings.* Wellington, 13 October 2003.

Mullane, Liz. Casting director (New Zealand), *Rings* and *The Chronicles of Narnia: The Lion, the Witch and the Wardrobe.* Auckland, 17 June 2004.

Nedergaard, Mads. Label manager, SF Film (Danish distributor of *Rings*). Copenhagen, 28 January 2005.

Ngan, Milton. Digital operations manager, Weta Ltd. Wellington, 1 July 2004.

Nimmo, Duncan. IT, *Rings* and *The Chronicles of Narnia: The Lion, the Witch and the Wardrobe.* Auckland, 19 June 2004.

Ord, Susan. Projects manager, Film New Zealand. Wellington, 9 October 2003; Wellington, 1 December 2004.

Osborne, Barrie M. Producer, *Rings.* Wellington, 15 October 2003; 2 December 2004.

Pellerin, Michael. Pellerin Multimedia, Inc., producer/director, *Rings* extended-version DVD supplements and *King Kong* supplements. Wellington, 23 October 2003.

Pirrotta, Chris (Calisuri). Cofounder, TheOneRing.net; webmaster, Sideshow Weta. Los Angeles, 29 August 2004.

Porras, Rick. Coproducer, *Rings.* Los Angeles, 14 June 2005.

Powell, Lucy. Communications manager, the Americas, Air New Zealand. Los Angeles, 30 August 2004.

Prendergast, Kerry. Mayor of Wellington. Wellington, 22 October 2003.

Quint. Contributor, Ain't It Cool News. Austin, 30 December 2004.

Rutherford, Robert and Janet. Owners, Glenorchy Air, offering a "trilogytrail" tour. Queenstown, 11 December 2002; Queenstown, 20 November 2004. www.trilogy trail.com.

Salo, David. Tolkien linguist, *Rings*. Madison, Wisconsin, 28 September 2004.

Saville, Ken. Sound recordist, *Rings;* head of Wellington branch, New Zealand Film and Video Technicians Guild. Paraparaumu, 27 June 2004.

Selkirk, Jamie. Coproducer and supervising editor, *Rings;* editor, *Return.* Wellington, 7 December 2004.

Simpson, Jenny. Sponsorship manager, Air New Zealand. Auckland, 23 November 2004.

Skaggs, Mark. Executive producer, "The Lord of the Rings: The Battle for Middle-earth" (EA Games, 2004). Los Angeles, 1 September 2004.

Stern, Keith. Owner, CompuWeb, Inc.; webmaster, www.mckellen.com. Los Angeles, 15 June 2005. www.cucare.com.

Taylor, Hayden. Systems manager, Film New Zealand. Wellington, 9 October 2003.

Taylor, Richard. Co-owner, Weta Ltd.; designer, *Rings, The Chronicles of Narnia: The Lion, the Witch and the Wardrobe,* and *King Kong.* Wellington, 7 October 2003; Wellington, 7 December 2004.

Thomas, William (Corvar). Cofounder and co-webmaster, TheOneRing.net. Milwaukee, 12 June 2004.

Thompson, Sue. CEO, Park Road Post (formerly The Film Unit); ex-chairperson, Film New Zealand. Lower Hutt, 15 October 2003; Wellington, 9 December 2004.

Voigt, Paul. Investment director—screen production industry, Investment New Zealand. Auckland, 22 November 2004.

Walker, Kerry. Sales and marketing manager, Dart River Safaris. Queenstown, 19 November 2004. www.dartriver.co.nz.

Weaver, Rebecca. Manager, partnership marketing, The Americas, Air New Zealand. Los Angeles, 30 August 2004.

Wolf, Jonathan. Executive vice president, Independent Film and Television Alliance; Managing Director, American Film Market. Los Angeles, 13 June 2005.

Wootten, Ben. Weta Workshop, designer/sculptor for *Rings.* Wellington, 7 October 2003.

Young, Neil. Vice president, Electronic Arts; Executive Producer, "The Lord of the Rings" video games. Redwood City, 26 August 2004.

ABBREVIATIONS

AICN	Ain't It Cool News
EA	Electronic Arts
EE DVD	Special Extended Edition DVD
EW	*Entertainment Weekly*
HR	*Hollywood Reporter*
LotRFCOMM	*"The Lord of the Rings" Fan Club Official Movie Magazine*
SD	*Screen Digest*
SI	*Screen International*
TORN	TheOneRing.net
VDM	*Variety Deal Memo*

——————

Sequel-itis

Get ready to write a sequel.

GANDALF TO BILBO
(in Tolkien's *The Fellowship of the Ring*)

AT AGE TEN, RAYNER UNWIN was probably the youngest paid editorial consultant in the history of publishing. His father, Stanley, gave him a shilling each to comment on manuscripts of prospective children's books. In 1936, a fantasy novel was submitted to Allen & Unwin by an Oxford professor of Anglo-Saxon, J. R. R. Tolkien. Rayner declared it "good" and added with the confidence of youth that "it should appeal to all children between the ages of 5 and 9." *The Hobbit* appeared in 1937 and was immediately successful. Since then it has been translated into at least thirty-eight languages and has sold upwards of thirty-five million copies.

Naturally, Allen & Unwin pressed Tolkien for a follow-up. *The Hobbit* had been based on bedtime stories he told his children, but the sequel proved harder to compose. His faculty duties delayed him, but there was an inner drive as well. Tolkien felt compelled to chart an entire, densely populated world in which Hobbits manifest humble heroism in the face of horrendous dangers. "This tale," as Tolkien put it in his "Foreword to the Second Edition," "grew in the telling" over the twelve years he took to write it. When in 1950 he sent the manuscript of *The Lord of the Rings* (hereafter *Rings*) to the publisher, it was no longer a children's book. It was an epic.

Rayner Unwin had grown up in the meantime and as an editor at Allen & Unwin was again asked to evaluate Tolkien's manuscript. When printed, it would run to around a thousand pages. Rayner Unwin calculated that with a "moderate success," the book would probably lose one thousand pounds—

a considerably greater sum at the time than it is now. It was, he reckoned, "a big risk." His father wrote to him, "*If* you believe it is a work of genius, *then* you may lose a thousand pounds." Though Tolkien considered *Rings* one large novel (as I shall here), Rayner insisted on printing it in three volumes to cover the high costs. *The Fellowship of the Ring* (hereafter *Fellowship*) and *The Two Towers* (hereafter *Towers*) appeared in 1954 and *The Return of the King* (hereafter *King*) in 1955.[1] *Rings* became the firm's greatest publishing success, with more than eighty million copies sold and no end in sight. Like its predecessor, it has been translated into dozens of languages.

The Unwins had gambled on the novel and won spectacularly. Despite the worldwide popularity of the books, though, a film version was seen as a nearly impossible project. *Rings* was simply too long and the monsters and creatures depicted too difficult to create with special effects. A number of projects to film it died in the planning stages, and a 1978 animated version of the first half failed to please critics or audiences.

Some years later the digital revolution occurred, and special-effects technology reached a point where Jurassic dinosaurs or morphing Terminators could be convincingly portrayed on the screen. Sequels and series gave Hollywood some of its biggest hits as the age of the franchise film arrived. Peter Jackson, a New Zealand director known mainly to fans of low-budget splatter movies, decided that Tolkien's novel was the ideal way to indulge his passion for fantasy and special effects. Through a remarkable combination of determination and luck, that decision resulted in a film released, like the book, in three parts (*Fellowship,* 2001; *Towers,* 2002; *Return,* 2003). No Hollywood film had ever been conceived on such a grand scale, and no producer had ever taken the risk of making all the parts of a series at once, without waiting to gauge the success of the first one. *Rings'* enormous success meant that, like a great rock falling into a lake, the ripples that it caused spread far, and they will continue to do so for years to come.

RECYCLING, HOLLYWOOD-STYLE

It's a familiar complaint. An expensive sequel or remake or adaptation comes out and disappoints critics and audiences. It adds to a sense of barrenness in recent cinema. Commentators, professional and amateur alike, accuse Hollywood of having lost its imagination. Scriptwriters have run out of original ideas, studio bosses have lost their nerve. The symptoms seem to be everywhere. French, Japanese, and Korean films are purchased not for distribution but to be remade in English-language versions. Studios resort to recycling material from older movies, TV series, and comic books.

Sequels have actually been around since nearly the beginning of the cinema. The success of the 1911 Danish crime thriller *Dr. Gar el Hama* led to *Dr. Gar el Hama flugt* (1912). The great Finnish director Mauritz Stiller followed his hit *Thomas Graal's Best Film* (1917) with *Thomas Graal's Best Child* (1918). Matinee idol Rudolph Valentino was particularly popular in *The Sheik* (1921), and the producers followed it with *Son of the Sheik* (1926). Such attempts to capitalize on success have continued up to the present, with profitable sequels leading to series, as with MGM's popular Andy Hardy films in the 1930s. In the last few decades, however, sequels and series have become more common and gained a higher profile.

Until the end of the 1990s, it was a rare Hollywood sequel that made more than the original film. Sequels and series often were continued so long that they outstayed their welcome. The Batman films began in 1989 with Tim Burton's popular *Batman,* but eventually audiences watched *Batman and Robin* (1997) crash and burn, apparently killing the franchise—until another entry, *Batman Begins* (2005), revived it to the sort of acclaim that had greeted Burton's original. *Speed 2* (1997) recaptured none of the excitement of the 1994 original. With *The Avengers* (1998) and *Bewitched* (2005), Hollywood sank to scavenging old TV programs, and scriptwriters could not even match the level of the originals. Successful series based on original ideas, such as the *Halloween* and Freddy films, became increasingly clichéd in their premises as the producers attempted to exploit them beyond what their underlying ideas would sustain.

There are plenty of clever, original screenplays being written, critics point out. Why can't the studios put more support behind quirky films like *Memento* (2000) or *Being John Malkovich* (1999) or *Election* (1999)? But then, if the bosses do manage to recognize the talent behind these films, their directors often end up assigned to blockbusters, as *Memento*'s Christopher Nolan was with *Batman Returns.* The same happens with talented foreign directors. Lee Tamahori (*Once Were Warriors,* New Zealand, 1994) makes a James Bond movie (*Die Another Day,* 2002) and an action sequel (*XXX 2: The Next Level,* 2005). Alfonso Cuarón (*Y Tu Mamá También,* Mexico, 2001) is recruited for the third entry in the *Harry Potter* series.

All these factors indicate that the studio decision makers are looking for something beyond the individual film, however successful. They want franchises.

People use the term "franchise" rather loosely in relation to films. Essentially it means a movie that spawns additional revenue streams beyond what it earns from its various forms of distribution, primarily theatrical, video, and television. These streams may come from sequels and series or from the production company licensing other firms to make ancillary products: action figures, video games, coffee mugs, T-shirts, and the hundreds of other items that licensees conceive of. In the ideal franchise, they come from both.

Film franchises are not new. Back in the 1920s, the popular Felix the Cat cartoons led to stuffed toys and other tie-in products. When Mickey Mouse rose to stardom late in the same decade, Walt Disney licensed numerous items on a far larger scale. For decades Disney's was the only Hollywood studio that essentially ran on the franchise principle—not only creating tie-ins but also rereleasing his classic animated features regularly, so that in a pre-home-video age, audiences could see them again and again. The merchandising around them remained perpetually current and desirable.

The blockbuster franchises of modern Hollywood did not begin until the late 1970s. Steven Spielberg's *Jaws* (1975) may have set the pattern of the blockbuster event film that spawns sequels (in 1978, 1983, and 1987), but it did not generate much of a franchise on the merchandising front. George Lucas took the next step. He persuaded 20th Century–Fox to compensate him for his direction of *Star Wars* (1977) by granting him the licensing rights. He became a rich independent producer/director and built a sophisticated production facility in the Bay Area. The *Star Wars* series became the model of how to create a franchise by linking films and related merchandise. The first *Star Trek* movie followed two years later, in 1979, and *Raiders of the Lost Ark* in 1981. *Superman* (1978) pioneered the elevation of a familiar superhero from comic books, movie serials, and TV series into a big-budget screen franchise. Less prestigious franchises were gearing up at the same time, as when *Halloween* (1978) kicked off the seemingly endless teen-oriented slasher cycles.

All this was not happening by coincidence, nor did it signal a withering of scriptwriters' inspiration. It came about largely because the Hollywood studios were in the process of being bought up by large corporations and then by multinational conglomerates. The process began in 1962, when MCA (Music Corporation of America) bought Universal. By the end of the decade, Gulf + Western owned Paramount, Seven Arts had purchased Warner Bros., and Transamerica Corporation had acquired United Artists. After a lull, the process revived and accelerated in the 1980s: Coca-Cola bought Columbia in 1982; 20th Century–Fox became part of Rupert Murdoch's global media giant, News Corporation (1985); Sony purchased Columbia (1989); and Time merged with Warner Bros. to create Time Warner (1989). Smaller firms like MGM changed hands as well. The entire process has continued to the present.

As a result of this absorption of the studios into much bigger companies, a greater emphasis on the bottom line became central. Indeed, with accelerating costs—star salaries and digital special effects being primary among them—Hollywood came to a point where most big-budget movies were not really making money in theatrical release. Profits came only when ancillaries like home video, television screenings, and licensed products were reckoned in. Nowadays a really high budget almost automatically raises the question of whether a film can generate a franchise. As Mark Johnson, the producer of *The Chronicles of Narnia: The Lion, the Witch and the Wardrobe,* told me, "When it gets to a certain figure costwise, it has to have that kind of potential." The studios also sought to bring some predictability to the business of making movies. Franchises offered an obvious method for increasing ancillaries. A continuing series brought with it automatic name recognition once its characters and story gained wide currency.

Essentially franchising allows film companies to create a brand that carries across multiple products. Of course, studios are brands. A film begins with logos for the various companies involved in making and distributing it. Audiences do not, however, attend a film because it was made by Paramount or Warner Bros.

Back in the days before television and all the other leisure activities that have grown up since the 1940s, branding was not so important. Hollywood used to depend on people loving movies in general and going to them every week or two. Viewers had favorite films, but they seldom became really caught up with them. They couldn't expect ever to see them again, except when some of the biggest successes got rereleased. What they could see again was the stars. Stars, somewhat paradoxically, meant more than they do now, because people went to see their favorites over and over, often in a wide variety of roles.

Now most people don't go to films so often or regularly. They go to big event films or those quirky independent films or feel-good ensemble-cast films or raunchy comedies, depending on their tastes. Star power is still important, but these days virtually no star is guaranteed to be able to "open" a film, and even the biggest names in Hollywood have flops among their credits.

Certain films, though, the mass audience—especially young people—falls thoroughly in love with. The follow-ups to those films create a franchise, and the franchise creates a brand. Just as kids dress in certain brands of clothes and carry certain brands of cell phones and drink certain brands of soda, they identify with certain movie franchises. They buy the films on DVD and watch them over and over. They play them as video games and read fan magazines and the Internet to get updates on the next sequel.

Today the franchise is often the star. People have continued to go to James Bond and Batman films even though different actors have played their central characters. *Star Trek* goes on regardless of what generation of the crew features in any given entry. *X-Men* may be the ultimate franchise because it can circulate characters in and out of the story, bringing minor ones forward and pushing major ones to the background—and there is a huge set of characters from the comic books for filmmakers to draw upon. (Although *X-Men: The Last Stand* is supposedly the last film of the series, Twentieth Century Fox would have the option to make more sequels, and it is planning spin-offs dealing with individual characters.) Similarly, big movies that spawn franchises often have no actors with major name recognition—though those actors may gain stardom by being in such films, as happened with Viggo Mortensen, Orlando Bloom, and others in *Rings*.

Not just any movie can generate a franchise. Musicals, biopics, and adaptations of most literary classics don't offer much potential for follow-ups and video games. Instead, Hollywood has turned increasingly to popular genres, especially those aimed largely at youngsters or at family audiences: adventure and science fiction, and now also fantasy of various stripes, from comic-book-based superhero sagas to children's book series. Such films have come to dominate the annual lists of top grossers.

Commentators decrying the decline of Hollywood cinema into crass commercialism turn up their noses at the prevalence of sequels, series, remakes, and other kinds of recycling that form the bases for franchises. Yet such borrowings and repetitions have been common in the history of all art forms. Indeed, there is plenty of evidence that they can result in great artworks. *The Adventures of Huckleberry Finn* was a sequel to *The Adventures of Tom Sawyer*. The second part of *Don Quixote* was originally a second novel published fifteen years after the first half. Tolkien wrote *The Lord of the Rings* as a sequel to *The Hobbit*. (Gandalf himself sanctions the writing of sequels in his advice to Bilbo.) Shakespeare turned Sir John Falstaff into the Renaissance equivalent of a franchise. Many operas take their plots from existing books or plays. Few bodies of work can be as formulaic as the exquisite reliefs carved on the walls of ancient Egyptian tombs (and probably copied from pattern books). Painting studios run by Rubens and Rembrandt turned out multiple versions of the same composition, mostly executed by assistants. In one common genre of classical music, one composer writes a set of variations on a theme by another. The impulse to reuse or develop successful material is far from new.

The possibility for originality in repetition exists in film as well. *The Godfather II* demonstrated that a sequel could live up to its highly admired original. Warner Bros. adapted the novel *The Maltese Falcon* three times in one decade, culminating in the definitive John Huston version in 1941. The comic duo of Wallace and Gromit started life in three shorts made for television before arriving on the big screen in *The Curse of the Were-rabbit* in 2005. The three *Back to the Future* films, comic science fiction though they be, contain some of the most complex, skillful storytelling of recent decades, with the second and third entries playing elaborate variations on the first. Hollywood's recycling does not necessarily lead to repetition and cliché, nor does it reflect the disappearance of inspiration among writers.

Peter Jackson's three-part film adaptation of *Rings* became one of the most successful film franchises of all time. The *Star Wars,* James Bond, and *Star Trek* series were more extensive, but *Rings* appeared over such a short period of time—three long films in twenty-four months—that its earning power was concentrated. The enormous affection that its fans felt for the film meant that the franchise will live on well after *Return*'s departure from theaters. In a way, *Rings* is the perfect franchise—strong enough to maintain its commercial potential and yet self-contained enough as a narrative not to beget a series that outstays its welcome.

WHY *LORD OF THE RINGS?* A TRILOGY OF REASONS

In the mid-1960s, like so many soon-to-be Tolkien fans, I was in high school. The Ballantine paperback editions of *The Hobbit* and *The Lord of the Rings* were just coming out. Although both *The Hobbit* (1937) and *The Lord of the Rings* (1954–55) had achieved immediate popularity, these paperbacks brought them an immensely broader audience. At the recommendation of my best friend's mother, and being a bit of an Anglophile, I read *The Hobbit* and then quickly devoured the trilogy. Though never a hippie myself, I witnessed how the flower-child generation in particular made Tolkien's books part of their culture. I didn't dress up as a Hobbit or learn Elvish, but I bought a few calendars and upgraded to hardback copies of the novels when my income permitted.

My love for Tolkien never left me, though I "only" read the trilogy on average every seven years or so. While in college, I discovered film studies and spent a lot of my time exploring the classics of world cinema—a time-consuming process. I knew that many others were rereading the novels, attending Tolkien Society meetings in various cities and universities, and providing enough of a market that Christopher Tolkien could edit and publish an unprecedented twelve-volume set of annotated rough drafts of most of his father's Middle-earth texts.

Shortly after I got my Ph.D. and set out on a career of studying and writing about cinema, Ralph Bakshi, of *Fritz the Cat* fame, made an animated film of part of *Rings* (1978). Based on reviews and word of mouth, I did not see it. Much later, in August 1998, New Line Cinema announced that it was producing the trilogy in three feature-length parts, to be directed by someone whose name I recognized only from favorable reviews I had read of the film *Heavenly Creatures* (1994). I reserved judgment, initially paying little attention to the Tolkien fans' excitement or indignation about the project—partly because much of their discussion took place on the Internet, onto which I had not yet ventured, and partly because (like many others, as I later discovered) I feared having my hopes raised and dashed.

At times I heard bits of news. During the period from August to October 1999, I read announcements that Ian McKellen would play Gandalf and Cate Blanchett would play Galadriel. Very intelligent casting, I thought. If everything else about this production is done with that sort of intelligence, the film will be a huge hit. I never ceased to believe that, even though I was still dubious about whether I myself would like the film. In May 2001, I read reports that a twenty-minute preview of the trilogy had been shown at Cannes to a rapturous response. With no specific goal in mind, I started clipping news items from magazines like *Variety* and *Entertainment Weekly*.

As the publicity machine started working over the next months, popular anticipation grew. It exploded with the release of the first film and, if anything, had grown considerably by the release of the third (plate 1). This all seemed very familiar from the days back in the 1960s when the first tidal wave of Tolkien enthusiasm had struck. It was happening again, but on a vastly grander scale. Abruptly, stories that I had loved for years and thought of as a cult taste were attracting attention and excitement around the world. It was a fascinating process to witness, and gradually the idea of recording it in a book-length history emerged.

A second reason for writing about *Rings* is that, quite apart from what fans or detractors may think of the movie, it can fairly claim to be one of the most historically significant films ever made. It is difficult to grasp the overall impact that it has had and will go on having. Conveying the scope and diversity of that impact will be one of my main goals in this book.

Once the film's first part had appeared, the fan base turned out to be broader than most people had expected: not just teenage boys and young men, but girls and young women, as well as the older generation who had read the books in the 1960s and 1970s. Ignorance of the novel proved not to impede viewers from becoming passionately devoted to *Rings.* Fans looked forward to the annual Christmas releases, and there was widespread regret expressed in both the popular and the trade press in late 2004 at the prospect of a year without another part of *Rings* appearing. In late 2004, in a lukewarm recommendation of a TV miniseries, *Legend of Earthsea, Entertainment Weekly* remarked, "At this point we'll take anything to fill the *LOTR* void."[2] There were even traces of *Rings* nostalgia lingering in the press during the lead-up to the 2005 Christmas season.

The entire franchise earned staggering amounts of money. Most people think primarily in terms of the three parts' remarkable gross box-office income: nearly $3 billion internationally. Consider, however, that the DVDs and the video games might each make something close to that figure. Licensed products have probably brought in more than a billion dollars by now, and the end is not in sight. For a long time there will remain the potential for such products as DVDs of documentaries about the film and professionally organized annual fan conventions. Pinning down precise figures is impossible, especially since the franchise is ongoing, but I would not be at all surprised if *Rings*' gross income ultimately went well over $10 billion. There are additional types of income that will not go to the filmmaking companies or their licensees, such as royalties on the memoirs that will be written by cast and crew members, the money made by tourism companies in New Zealand, and the flow of payments to eBay sellers of many thousands of film-related items. *Rings* has become a small industry in itself.

Rings has affected the film industry in general, too. Most significant is a little-known story: how the trilogy's revenues speeded the foreign-language and independent film markets' recovery from a significant international downturn that occurred during the years in which the three parts were released. Beyond that, *Rings,* appearing as it did alongside the first three Harry Potter films, helped raise fantasy from its status as box-office poison to a position at the core of current popular filmmaking.

And the franchise is not nearly over. Middle-earth-themed video games continue to appear. Additional licensed toys and collectible items are still being brought out. Fan activity remains lively in cyberspace and the real world.

The phenomenon has reached into international culture in ways that go far beyond the commercial confines of the franchise. Politics, education, sports, and religion all reflect the influence of the film. An extinct race of tiny people discovered on a Pacific island was instantly dubbed "hobbits" by headline writers and even the scientists who discovered them.

Rings was made over a stretch of years in which new technologies were having a huge impact on the ways in which films are made and marketed and in the types of ancillary products tied to them. In almost every case, whether it be the Internet campaign, the DVD supplements, or the video games, *Rings* was on the cutting edge. So quickly does that cutting edge move on that within a few years it will be easy to forget how innovative and influential *Rings* has been. Not just as a film trilogy but as a larger phenomenon, *Rings* reveals a great deal about the changes going on in Hollywood in this transitional era of globalization and new media.

For those who view the film as a giant income-generating machine that exploits the original novel, I should point out that Tolkien's masterpiece had long been the basis for a more modest franchise. Tolkien's publishers have created and licensed tie-in products since the two Hobbit novels became such an enormous hit in the mid-1960s. HarperCollins and Ballantine issued numerous calendars starting in 1973, resulting in many illustrations by such key Tolkien-related artists as Ted Nasmith, Alan Lee, and John Howe. Howe has recalled this era: "I eventually sent some colour transparencies to the editors and got a commission to do a couple of pictures for the 1985 calendar, and went on from there. Because there's no new text for *Lord of the Rings* and Tolkien, their idea was to publish spin-off things like calendars, diaries and posters to renew people's interest in the books, and to have covers redone."[3] There were puzzles, Royal Doulton ceramic figurines, and even early video games (figure 1).

As an undergraduate, I adorned my dorm wall with a poster-map of Middle-earth. There were board games, stamps, and action figures. There were recordings of the author reading excerpts from his own work. With Tolkien's co-operation, in 1967 Donald Swann composed a cycle of songs from his poems, and it was recorded and brought out in book form.[4] Ever since the 1960s, the publishers have issued and reissued *Rings* (and *The Hobbit*) in numerous editions, hardbound and paperback, sets of three volumes in boxes or large single volumes in slipcases. Anniversaries of the original publications have seen new editions illustrated by prominent artists, and the film led to numerous cheaper copies sporting publicity photos on their covers. Harper-Collins (United Kingdom) and Houghton Mifflin (United States) have pub-

Figure 1. Some book-related franchise products: puzzle (1973), video game (1989), calendar (1998), Gandalf action figure (2000), and board game (2004). (Photograph by Mark Ambrose.)

lished Tolkien-related books, including scholarly studies and collections of illustrations.

The success of *Rings* in the 1960s made possible the publication of other Tolkien drafts that probably would otherwise never have reached the public. Immediately after that success, *The Tolkien Reader* (1966), containing poetry and short prose pieces, appeared, followed by a brief novella, *Smith of Wootton Major* (1967). Subsequently Christopher Tolkien has dedicated much of his own career to sorting through the disorganized and often nearly illegible drafts that his father left at his death in 1973. He began by editing an unfinished epic covering earlier eras of Middle-earth's history: *The Silmarillion* (1977), a dense and demanding book quite unlike the sprawling quest tale of *Rings*. Children's books illustrated by Tolkien appeared: *The Father Christmas Letters* (1976, expanded as *Letters from Father Christmas* in 1999), *Mr. Bliss* (1983), and *Roverandom* (1998). In September 2006, Houghton Mifflin and HarperCollins startled fans by announcing that Christopher had again edited numerous drafts and fragments into another Middle-earth novel, *The Children of Húrin*, to be released in April 2007.

Saul Zaentz, the American entertainment entrepreneur who has owned the trademarks for *The Hobbit* and *Rings* since the mid-1970s, licenses products through his Tolkien Enterprises. The firm has authorized many games, puzzles, stage productions, and other tie-in products over the years—many of them before the films were conceived. (Some of these stem from the unsuccessful Ralph Bakshi version of *Rings* [1978], as a glance through eBay demonstrates.)

Peter Jackson even used the existing franchise to considerable advantage in selling his project to New Line Cinema. In the pitch tape that he showed studio executives, he strongly stressed the rich visual design that was being created: "We're very fortunate with *Lord of the Rings,* because of the fact that it's been around for 45 years. There's a huge amount of visual material available. There's books, there's calendars, posters. In fact, this is a case where the merchandising has preceded the film by 30 or 40 years." Whether the new merchandising around the film will last that long is anyone's guess, but I would not be surprised if decades from now people are still buying *Rings* on whatever new format is then in use for viewing movies at home.

Such things, as Ethan Gilsdorf pointed out in an article about the commercialization of Tolkien's work, are inevitable with very successful works of art. Commenting on both the book and film franchises, Gilsdorf rightly pointed out: "Perhaps Tolkien deserves better, but he's powerless to shape his legacy now. By conjuring for the public an imaginative space with such broad and far-reaching appeal, the Oxford don unintentionally became the author of not only a book but of its unimaginable consequences."[5] This book deals with some of those consequences.

The third reason for centering this book around *Rings* is simply because it was possible. No book has ever been written about a significant Hollywood movie by an academic film historian who was given access to a part of the production process and numerous interviews by people involved. If I had tried to tackle such a book on virtually any other big film franchise, the project probably would have never left square one.

Most of the people who made *Rings* are New Zealanders, and New Zealanders must be among the world's friendliest and most hospitable people. For four weeks in October 2003, I was able to visit Wellington, where I toured facilities and watched some of the postproduction work—including a few shots being made in the very late pickups. Some of the filmmakers made time in their packed schedules to give me the sort of information that I never could have gleaned from the trade papers, the popular press, or the Internet. Two subsequent trips to New Zealand led to further interviews. The people involved in *Rings* cooperated in this way, I believe, because they realize that they were part of an immensely important project, and as it was ending, they sensed that its history should be written on a scale that reflected that importance. At the ends of the interviews, a number of them expressed their gratitude to me, clearly believing that the film deserved such a book. It does, and I hope that the result conveys a sense of just how much they achieved.

PART ONE

The Film

CHAPTER I

Prudent Aggression

I always got the impression that, as far as studios go,
New Line definitely had a tradition of allowing the
filmmaker to run with it.

RICK PORRAS
Coproducer, *The Lord of the Rings*

THE STORY HAS A CHARMING David-and-Goliath quality. A Hollywood studio entrusts hundreds of millions of dollars to an eccentric, largely unknown director from a distant country where film production barely exists. He undertakes to adapt a beloved classic book with a devoted cult following—a large cult, certainly, but hardly enough to ensure box-office success for such an expensive venture. The director refuses to leave the little country, instead building a world-class filmmaking infrastructure in his neighborhood. He shoots three long features simultaneously and creates the biggest box-office franchise in history. To top it off, despite being in the despised fantasy genre, the three parts of *The Lord of the Rings* win a total of seventeen Oscars.

These days, any expensive Hollywood feature that actually makes it to the screen relies on considerable luck and travels a circuitous path to completion. That said, *Rings* needed—and had—more lucky breaks than most, and its path was circuitous indeed. Peter Jackson has pointed out just how unlikely success might have seemed at the outset:

> If you were entrusting $270 million to someone making three movies, you wouldn't choose me. You would not choose a little New Zealand digital effects company to do your digital effects, either. And you wouldn't choose Philippa Boyens, who's one of our co-writers, to write the screenplay, because she has

never written a script before in her life [laughs]. I like the way that this project has, somehow, against all common sense, gotten itself made.[1]

True in a way, but we should probably amend this to "against all apparent common sense." Hollywood studios do not make such important decisions on whims, and the executives at New Line Cinema and the many other companies that invested in and ultimately made large amounts of money on *Rings* had solid reasons for thinking that there was a decent chance of success.

Despite the high budget and his own lack of a track record, Jackson was able to keep a remarkable degree of control over the *Rings* project, partly by making the film far from New Line headquarters, partly by having sympathetic producers working with him, and partly by sheer stubbornness. (Ian McKellen described him as "a terrier" when it came to disputes with the studio.) The proof was also in the pudding. Even during the early design and shooting stages of production, Jackson and his team were able to show visiting New Line officials props, sets, costumes, and computer images that convincingly displayed the high quality of the work that was going into the films.

So it was common sense, although of a very high order, that brought *Rings* along its convoluted path from cult fantasy to major international franchise.

ZAENTZ AND ZAENTZ ABILITY

Projects to adapt *Rings* into a film began within a few years of the three volumes' original publication in 1954 and 1955. On 4 September 1957, Forrest J. Ackerman, then a literary agent, visited Tolkien and presented him with some sample pictures and a treatment for a proposed animated film based on the novel. Although Tolkien was impressed by the images, he heartily disliked the synopsis and in June of the following year wrote a lengthy critique of it ("[Morton Grady] Z[immerman] may think that he knows more about Balrogs than I do, but he cannot expect me to agree with him").[2]

Yet Tolkien was pragmatic. For many years before the royalties for *Rings* started to appear, he had supplemented his modest professor's income by drudging at exam grading during the summer. Fearing that the royalties from the trilogy would decline, Tolkien was willing to talk terms: "[Publisher] Stanley U[nwin] and I have agreed on our policy: Art or Cash. Either very profitable terms indeed; or absolute author's veto on objectionable features or alterations."[3] Rayner Unwin soon succeeded his father as Tolkien's editor at Allen & Unwin. Inexperienced in coping with movie rights, the firm hired a Hollywood agent—who ultimately proved of little assistance. In 1959, Ackerman abandoned his project. During the previous year he had founded the magazine *Famous Monsters of Filmland.* As part of his subsequent role as the guru of horror fandom, he would also appear in cameo roles in numerous films, including Peter Jackson's *Braindead* (1992).

In 1967, two producers, Gabe Katzka and Sam Gelfman, set out to obtain the film rights to *Rings,* intending to make a feature for United Artists. Unwin writes that their inquiries started "a negotiation of nearly two years' duration that was eventually consummated in a fifty-page contract, the complexities and uncertainties of which have dogged the publishers and the author's estate ever since." In October 1969, the contract was finally signed, and "what seemed substantial sums of money" were paid.[4] "Complexities and uncertainties" may refer to the fact that the contract granted the film rights in perpetuity, rather than the normal arrangement of a limited period of time. The lapse would prove crucial to Jackson's project.

During the two years of negotiations, Apple Films, the Beatles' production company, also became interested in adapting *Rings,* to star the Fab Four. Apple discovered that the rights to the novel were apparently soon to belong to United Artists. Given that the group's first two films, *A Hard Day's Night* (1964) and *Help!* (1965), had been distributed in the United States by United Artists, a relatively straightforward arrangement for a *Rings* project seemed not impossible, and indeed the *Hollywood Reporter* stated that United Artists was in talks to involve the Beatles.[5] Not surprisingly, Apple's inquiries to David Lean, Stanley Kubrick, and Michelangelo Antonioni failed to secure a director for the project, which went no further. Instead United Artists commissioned a script—not intended for the Beatles—from John Boorman, but that project also came to nothing. The rights sat with United Artists.

Producer Saul Zaentz, whose main source of income at the time was Fantasy Records, was also moving into film production in the 1970s. Fantasy Films' first significant release was *One Flew over the Cuckoo's Nest* (1975), which won a Best Picture Academy Award. (Zaentz has also produced two other Best Picture winners: *Amadeus* in 1984 and *The English Patient* in 1996.) Zaentz acquired the film rights to *Rings* from United Artists in 1976. He also obtained from the Tolkien Estate the trademarks for the names of all the characters, places, and objects in the novels. According to Unwin, however, "The 1969 contract, a complicated and ambiguous document especially in its definition of merchandising rights, has been a perpetual source of trouble, and although efforts are spasmodically made to redefine areas under dispute in the light of the new technologies that are now evolving, the [Tolkien] Estate and Fantasy Films have tended to block each other's actions and have consequently exploited very few non-book rights."[6] Zaentz set up Tolkien Enterprises in 1978; the company licenses "dramatizations, musicals, puppet performances, services and merchandise using the Tolkien trademarks."

Zaentz produced one film based on the *Rings* rights: Ralph Bakshi's animated *J. R. R. Tolkien's The Lord of the Rings* (1978), which covered the trilogy's first half. Its critical and commercial failure meant that the intended second part wasn't made.[7] There matters concerning the film rights to *Rings* sat for nearly two decades. (Figure 2 provides an outline of the convoluted path *Rings* took before reaching the screen.)

About ten years after Bakshi's film appeared, a young filmmaker in New Zealand was struggling to make his first feature. Peter Jackson had been born in 1961 in the small town of Pukerua Bay, a short way up the western coast of New Zealand's North Island from the capital city of Wellington. Jackson's fascination with film had been fired at the age of nine, when he saw *King Kong* (1933) on television, and he began shooting his own version of *Kong* and other films on 8mm, using homemade models and prosthetics. Upon getting out of school in 1978, he was rejected for a job in the government's postproduction company, The Film Unit. Twenty years later he would buy The Film Unit and transform it into one of the world's most sophisticated postproduction facilities.

Jackson instead got a job as a photoengraver at a newspaper. On weekends he worked with friends on more 8mm films. In 1983 he bought a used 16mm camera and began a planned ten-minute short, *Roast of the Day.* The next year the success of Sam Raimi's microbudget film, *The Evil Dead,* convinced Jackson that it was possible to shoot a commercially successful horror film on 16mm, and the short quickly evolved into the feature-length *Bad Taste.* In 1986, Jackson applied to the government's funding body, the New Zealand Film Commission, for money to complete his project.

The Film Commission was understandably puzzled by the footage of Jackson's cheerfully gory tale of space aliens invading earth and slaughtering people to supply meat for fast-food restaurants—a puzzlement no doubt compounded by the fact that *Bad Taste* had been shot silent. The commission asked veteran film editor Jamie Selkirk for his opinion. Selkirk was a bit puzzled himself, but he saw signs of a good eye and distinct talent. He recommended that it be funded and ended up serving as editor for *Bad Taste* and nearly all of Jackson's subsequent films—culminating in a Best Editing Oscar for *The Return of the King.* Selkirk also became one of Jackson's business

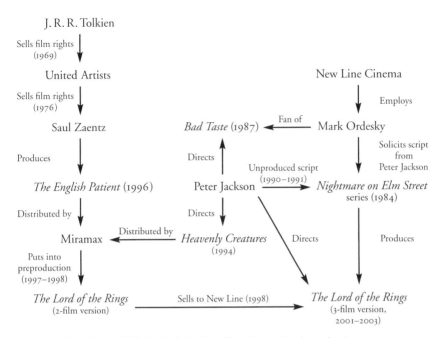

Figure 2. Genealogy of *The Lord of the Rings* film trilogy. (By the author.)

partners in building Weta Ltd., the special-effects company at the core of Wellington's growing filmmaking infrastructure.

Upon receiving NZ$30,000 from the Film Commission, Jackson quit his newspaper job and finished *Bad Taste,* which was released in 1988 and distributed in thirty territories internationally.[8] He cemented his reputation as a director of eccentric, blood-drenched films with *Meet the Feebles* (1989), a perverse tale of Muppet-like creatures involved in the behind-the-scenes intrigues of a popular television program that lead to mass murder. His next feature, *Braindead* (1992; aka *Dead Alive*), was a comic zombie film with a notoriously sanguinary finale.

Jackson's tongue-in-cheek splatter films, screened at various horror and fantasy festivals, spawned a cult following. His next film, however, brought him a new audience. With partner Fran Walsh, he wrote *Heavenly Creatures* (1994), a psychological drama based on the true story of two teenagers who develop an obsessively close relationship and murder the mother of one of them when she threatens to separate them. The film was a critical success and played widely in art cinemas. It even earned an Oscar nomination for its script. Ultimately, though, it grossed only $3 million on a $5 million budget.

Although it was far from apparent at the time, *Heavenly Creatures* also created two factors that would enable Jackson to make *Rings*. First, the American distributor of *Heavenly Creatures* was Miramax, a prestigious art-film distribution company that would later acquire the rights for *Rings* from Zaentz and launch Jackson's production. Second, in 1993 Jackson had seen Steven Spielberg's *Jurassic Park* and realized that the future of special effects lay in computer-generated imagery (CGI). He and Walsh added some psychological-fantasy sequences to *Heavenly Creatures,* using the creation of these shots as the justification for acquiring Weta Ltd.'s first computer.

Also in 1993, Jackson and Walsh submitted a ghost story script for a proposed *Tales from the Crypt* film series, to be made by major directors like Robert Zemeckis. Instead, Zemeckis offered to produce *The Frighteners* for Universal, to be directed by Jackson, who persuaded Zemeckis to let him make the film in New Zealand. Weta's computing power rose from one computer to around fifty, and 570 effects shots were done for *The Frighteners.* (*Jurassic Park,* made two years earlier, had about fifty computer-generated shots.)[9]

At the same time that he was making *The Frighteners,* Jackson codirected another project with his longtime friend Costa Botes (who would later film extensive candid footage of the making of *Rings*). A TV mockumentary called *Forgotten Silver* (1996), it purportedly told the story of Colin McKenzie, an overlooked New Zealand film pioneer. *Forgotten Silver* featured convincing "talking heads" interviews, simulated footage from McKenzie's silent films, and a framing story of Jackson's earnest search for the remains of the great man's work. Many viewers took *Forgotten Silver* for an actual documentary, and controversy erupted when the public learned that their patriotic fervor over a neglected national genius had been aroused for nothing. Apart from being a clever film, *Forgotten Silver* gave Jackson experience with directing two overlapping productions: "Jackson swore he'd never again make two films at the same time. 'Ultimately it proved to be good training,' he says with a grin."[10]

The terms of the *Heavenly Creatures* distribution deal had left Miramax with a first-look option on Jackson's future projects. Any film property that he owned or controlled would have to be offered to the company, and if he didn't control the rights, Miramax would have to try and obtain them. When Zemeckis offered Jackson *The Frighteners,* Miramax had nothing for him to direct, so it agreed to a standard "suspend and extend" arrangement, whereby Miramax's first-look deal would be lengthened by the amount of time Jackson spent on *The Frighteners.*

By the autumn of 1995, the CGI work for *The Frighteners* was going so well that Jackson and his colleagues decided to seek another, even more effects-heavy, project. In late September or early October, Jackson asked his agent, Ken Kamins, to track down the film rights for *Rings*. Kamins quickly discovered that Zaentz owned them. Because of the first-look deal with Miramax, Jackson and Kamins contacted the firm's president, Harvey Weinstein. Jackson's initial pitch was to make *The Hobbit* first and then, if it was successful, to go on to *Rings*, filming it in two parts, back-to-back.

Weinstein was excited about the idea and revealed that, by a happy coincidence, he had recently come to Zaentz's rescue when his project to produce *The English Patient* had nearly fallen through. Twentieth Century Fox had been set to produce the film with Zaentz, but disputes over casting led it to pull the plug about five weeks before shooting was due to start. Miramax stepped in and financed the film. Apart from its six Oscars, including Best Picture, *The English Patient* was Zaentz's top-earning film, with a $228 million worldwide gross. Zaentz definitely owed Miramax a favor.

The problem was that, although Zaentz owned the production rights to *The Hobbit,* its distribution rights had somehow stayed with United Artists. For *Rings,* however, he had a full set of rights. By 1995, United Artists had merged with MGM to form MGM/UA. Weinstein approached the company about the rights, but since MGM/UA was up for sale, it was not about to let any of its assets go. (Sony's purchase of United Artists in 2004 further delayed any negotiations over *The Hobbit*'s distribution rights.) In early 1996, Weinstein told Jackson that they should start with *Rings* rather than *The Hobbit.* Despite Zaentz's debt of gratitude to Weinstein, the negotiations dragged on for nearly a year.

In the spring of 1996, Zemeckis got wind that one of Universal's planned summer films would not be finished in time. He suggested that Jackson put together a reel of clips from *The Frighteners* to show Universal. The studio was excited by the footage and decided to move the film from its planned Halloween slot and plug it into its June gap. The buzz in Hollywood was that, just as Steven Spielberg had mentored Zemeckis as a director, Zemeckis was now doing the same for Jackson. Jackson began to receive other directing offers. Universal wanted him to do a remake of *King Kong,* a prospect he found just as exciting as *Rings*. Fox came to him with a remake of *Planet of the Apes,* at that time with James Cameron attached as producer and Arnold Schwarzenegger as star. There was still some hope that Weinstein's negotiations with Zaentz would end soon. Jackson found himself with three potential blockbusters on his plate.

On Monday, 1 April, Kamins got home at 11:00 P.M. and found an urgent message to call Jackson. It turned out that as work on *The Frighteners* was ending, headhunters from the big special-effects companies in the United States, who had heard rumors about the film's technical sophistication, were trying to lure away his staff of CGI animators. To keep them on, Jackson had to offer them a project. He needed to know by the end of the week which of the three films he would be making. Kamins requested that the three companies make specific offers immediately, and they did so.

On the *Apes* deal, Jackson was worried about working with two such powerful personalities as Cameron and Schwarzenegger. As Kamins puts it, "There was no way that he wasn't going to be the caboose on that train." Jackson passed on it. (Ironically, in 2001 it ended up being directed by Tim Burton, without either Cameron or Schwarzenegger being involved.) Weinstein still didn't have the rights to *Rings,* but he was furious at the possibility of having to suspend and extend his contract with Jackson again while the director made *Kong.*

Ultimately Jackson proposed a compromise. Universal would own domestic rights on *Kong,* with Miramax taking the foreign rights. For *Rings,* Miramax would distribute in the United States, and Universal would take it abroad. Weinstein complained that he would be trading two films (since *Rings* was still planned for two parts) for one from Universal. Universal agreed to throw in the rights for a project called *Shakespeare in Love,* and the deal was settled.

When *The Frighteners* came out in June, Jackson's team was at work on *Kong's* script and design. In the meantime, Weinstein continued the difficult negotiations with Zaentz over the *Rings* rights. By early 1997, Universal was getting cold feet. *The Frighteners* had opened on the first weekend of the summer Olympics rather than at Halloween, and it had not done well. Moreover, other studios' projects for films about Mighty Joe Young and Godzilla might steal *Kong's* thunder. Universal decided to pull the plug. Jackson and Walsh were devastated at having to tell their crew that all their work had been for nothing.

Fortunately, at about the same time, on 22 January 1997, Weinstein had officially acquired the rights to *Rings.*[11] Kamins gives him credit for sticking by Jackson when the *Kong* deal fell through: "Harvey could have looked at this situation with *The Frighteners* and used it as an opportunity either to attempt to alter Peter's deal, because Peter was in a weakened position—he didn't do that—and he could have used it as a opportunity to lose faith in Peter altogether and simply say, 'You know what, I do have these rights, but I don't want to do this movie with you anymore.' And he didn't do that either." Jackson's team finally had a big, effects-heavy project that it would be able to finish—though not without further disappointments and deals.

THE MIRAMAX PERIOD

As planning on *Rings* began, Weinstein sat Jackson down in the Miramax screening room to watch Bakshi's animated film. The truncated version was exactly what they did not want to end up with and confirmed the wisdom of proceeding with two feature-length parts shot simultaneously. They were to be tentatively budgeted at $70 million for both, which seems absurdly small in retrospect but was a departure from the company's typical modest projects.

Working in Wellington, Jackson and Walsh began by writing one long script, planning to figure out later how to divide it into two films: *The Fellowship of the Ring* and *The War of the Ring*. In August 1997 Walsh's friend Philippa Boyens, a writer and longtime Tolkien fan who had never done a film script, came on board. Steven Sinclair, who had scripted *Braindead* and coscripted *Meet the Feebles,* participated in the writing for a time and received credit on *Towers*. While they wrote, Weta worked intensively on the designs, construction, miniature building, and R & D for the special-effects programs. *Rings* spent about eighteen months in preproduction.

As the script progressed, it became apparent that the film would cost more than the announced budget. Bob Weinstein, Harvey's brother, was in charge of Dimension, a division of Miramax that was coproducing *Rings*. By early 1998, he was concerned about the rising costs and disinclined to continue the project. There were rumors that the company might put the film into turnaround.[12] ("Turnaround" means that a project already in progress is halted and put on the market to find a new producer.) Harvey was, however, keen to carry on, seeking ways to reduce costs. Boyens recalls the scriptwriters receiving a note that read, "What do you need four Hobbits for? Why not two?" and Jackson says: "Harvey was giving us notes, and he sounded like a guy from the mafia and says, 'Look, ya gotta kill one of the Hobbits. One of the Hobbits has to die.'"[13]

In June 1998, when the two scripts were nearing completion, it became apparent that the project would cost close to $140 million. Harvey Weinstein took his case to Disney's studio chairman, Joe Roth, who in turn took it to the chairman and CEO, Michael Eisner. Eisner, who had recently demanded cost-cutting measures, refused, saying that the budget cap for Miramax was $75 million. The company was not supposed to be making big-budget films that would compete with Disney's own. Besides, Eisner had no faith in the project.[14]

Eisner's refusal meant reducing *Rings* to a single two-hour feature. Weinstein met with Jackson and Walsh to give them the bad news. Miramax owned the rights, the company had sunk about $10 million into preproduction, and Weinstein had no intention of simply abandoning the project. Jackson and Walsh returned to Wellington and discussed whether they could settle for doing one film. Jackson recalls, "We got home, decided this was not something that we wanted to do. We knew that decision could end our careers, but we thought, We could do TV films." If they abandoned the project, all the designs, models, weapons, and other work already accomplished by Weta would belong to Miramax. According to Jackson, Weinstein's plan was to turn the film over to long-established television director John Madden, who had recently moved into filmmaking with *Mrs. Brown* (1997), a biopic that had been distributed by Miramax. His most famous film, *Shakespeare in Love,* which Universal had traded away to make *Kong* possible, was to be released in December of that year.[15]

Had Jackson's team been able to stay with Miramax and make *Rings* in two parts, the result would probably have been fundamentally different from the film that ultimately got made. Possibly Weinstein would have steered the film more toward a middlebrow "quality" literary adaptation of the *English Patient* variety and less toward the genre film that it became. Jackson emphasizes that the Miramax period had very little influence on the finished film, since the casting was crucial and he never even got to the stage of discussing it.

LAST DITCH FOR PJ PITCH

It was a great idea on Peter's part. Let's come up with
a making-of of a movie that hasn't been made yet.

RICK PORRAS
Coproducer, *Rings*

In June, shortly after Harvey Weinstein's ultimatum, Kamins convinced him to give Jackson one last chance by putting *Rings* into turnaround. Such sales of in-progress films are not uncommon, and some have become major hits for their new owners. Warner Bros. decided it did not want *Home Alone,* and the project was snapped up by Twentieth Century Fox—which also bought *Speed* and *There's Something about Mary* in turnaround. Miramax and New Line have been credited as the most successful firms at plucking winners from the ranks of films abandoned by other studios. Miramax obtained *Pulp Fiction* after TriStar put it into turnaround, and it took over *Good Will Hunt-*

ing from Castle Rock.[16] Like *Rings,* both *Rush Hour* and *Elf* were put into turnaround by Disney and picked up by New Line—two more instances of Eisner's misjudgments redounding to the advantage of New Line founder and copresident, Bob Shaye.

Weinstein has spoken bitterly of Eisner's decision to radically cut the project's budget: "Disney didn't believe in it, wouldn't give me the money to make the film. I gave Peter the worst turnaround in the history of turnarounds, because I didn't want to lose it. I gave him three weeks to find another taker. I said, 'Nobody's gonna buy it.'"[17] The terms that Weinstein formulated were draconian. The time allotted for the search was short. Any company that wanted *Rings* would have to pay within twenty-four hours a lump sum of around $12 million: $10 million for all preproduction costs incurred thus far and $2 million for the New Zealand currency Miramax had bought forward. (Ordinarily only 10 percent of the total would be paid up front, and the rest after the film was finished.) That studio would then own all the designs, props, and technology so far devised by Weta. Miramax would not help sell the project; Jackson himself would have to find a buyer.[18] Harvey and Bob Weinstein would be credited as executive producers, and Miramax would receive 5 percent of gross international box-office receipts. Zaentz would also receive a significant percentage of the gross.

Jackson quickly returned to Wellington and at his own expense put together a thirty-six-minute VHS tape about the project to use in potential pitch sessions with Hollywood executives. It was basically a making-of documentary about a film that hadn't yet been made, designed to show that special-effects technology could cope with Tolkien's story, that the money spent so far had gone for worthwhile film elements, and that Jackson was capable of directing the project. The result contained a few dramatized scenes using storyboard images and local actors' voices. These scenes were interspersed with dramatically lit images of maquettes (high-quality models) of monsters and Orcs, drawings by noted Tolkien illustrators Alan Lee and John Howe, and talking-head interviews with Jackson, Lee, Howe, and various Weta Digital technicians explaining their early experiments with the Massive program for generating realistic crowd scenes. In the tape, Jackson betrays no sense that the production was most likely coming to an end as far as he was concerned. Instead, he appears utterly confident, even though all the preproduction work had halted abruptly when the film went into turnaround.

Meanwhile, Kamins contacted all the main production firms in Hollywood. Only two were interested enough to make appointments to allow Jackson and Walsh to pitch their project: PolyGram and New Line. PolyGram was a

Dutch company, the world's third-largest producer of recorded music, that had released several successful independent films in the United States during the mid-1990s: *Four Weddings and a Funeral, Shallow Grave* (both 1994), *The Usual Suspects* (1995), *Trainspotting, Fargo* (both 1996), and *Bean* (1997). When Turner Broadcasting System and Time Warner had merged in 1996, Time Warner tried to sell its subsidiary, New Line, hoping to use the proceeds to help pay down debt. PolyGram was briefly interested, but ultimately no buyer wanted to pay the $800 million to $1 billion asking price. (Turner had paid $550 million for New Line in 1994.)[19] By mid-1998, PolyGram's costly failures had outweighed its hits, and it was about to be sold and split up, with its film division going to USA Films. When *Rings* was in turnaround, Poly-Gram could hardly take on any projects, let alone a pricey epic.

New Line's interest in *Rings* initially came from the president of the firm's art-house subsidiary, Fine Line. Mark Ordesky had been a fan of Jackson's ever since *Bad Taste,* and in 1990 he had gotten the director a job writing a script for an entry in the *Nightmare on Elm Street* series. The script was never produced, but the two had remained friends. Ordesky informed Shaye of the availability of the *Rings* project and convinced him to listen to Jackson's pitch. Kamins, Walsh, and Marty Katz, Miramax's line producer for *Rings,* were also present at that meeting. This crucial moment in the history of the film has been reported and interpreted by several of the people present. What happened is well known, but why did it happen?

Before the actual pitch session started, Shaye drew Jackson aside. According to Ordesky, Shaye wanted to assure Jackson that he admired *Heavenly Creatures* and hoped to work with him one day even if he decided not to undertake *Rings.* Jackson apparently saw the little exchange as a sign of Shaye's honesty: "The first thing Bob said was, 'I liked "Heavenly Creatures," but I didn't like "The Frighteners."' I thought this was the most amazing thing: In Hollywood, someone is telling you they don't like your film. I just thought, 'cool.'"[20]

Jackson began with a verbal presentation, explaining why it was the right time to make *Rings.* He showed off art-department sketches and stressed that the novel was an epic drama, not a fantasy. According to Ordesky, "We talked about the two scripts and how Miramax only wanted to make one film, and that was why they had this three-week window to set LOTR up elsewhere. I had already read the two scripts; Bob had not."[21]

This introduction led into the pitch videotape. Ordesky had warned Jackson, Walsh, and Kamins that Shaye might simply turn off the tape after several minutes if he sensed that the project was not for him. As the tape ran, they nervously waited for Shaye to hit the stop button, but he did not. Instead, after the presentation ended, Shaye changed the trajectory of the project dramatically.

Exactly what he said has been reported in different ways. An account based on Shaye's own recollections has it this way: "Finally Shaye had heard enough. 'It's not two movies,' he said. Jackson's heart sank—he'd already heard this at Miramax. Then Shaye said the magic words. 'Tolkien did your job for you. He wrote three books. You should make three movies.'"[22] In an interview in early 2002, Jackson recalled the event:

> As the tape comes to an end, he says, "I don't get it," and I thought [sighs], "Oh, OK." And he turns and he says, "I don't get it. Why would you be willing to do two *Lord of the Rings* films? It's three books, isn't it? Shouldn't it be three films?" And I thought, "What's he saying here?! What's he saying here?" and he said, "Look, we're interested, but we're basically interested in three movies."[23]

Although Shaye did not make a commitment that same day, he apparently believed that there was competition for *Rings* and urged Jackson not to promise the project to another studio. Ordesky recalls Shaye telling him, "Get into it. Find out what the parameters are, get Michael Lynne up to speed—I want him to see this tape." (Lynne was copresident of New Line.) As Jackson said later, the pitch tape was "probably the most important 30 minutes that I've ever shot in my life."[24]

Shaye's response—urging Jackson to make the project even more ambitious—may seem strange, and it certainly came as a surprise to others present at the meeting. Yet a look at the pitch tape allows insight into Shaye's reasoning. On a simple level, the tape itself might easily prompt a viewer to think Jackson wanted to make three films. Near the beginning, a montage slowly shows shots of each volume of Tolkien's book while Jackson's narrating voice-over emphasizes how popular and admired *Rings* is. Whether by intention or not, the tape contains no reference to a two-film version—or a three-film version or a one-film version. Instead, Jackson consistently refers to the proposed adaptation as "the film" (and he has continued to insist that, like Tolkien's novel, his version is one story told serially). Simply watching the tape without much knowledge of the two-film project at Miramax, a viewer might well expect that the pitch is for one feature for each Tolkien volume.[25] Shaye of course did know about that background—but his suggestion that Jackson make three films was not just a whim.

NEW LINE'S "GAMBLE"

If I really want to shoot craps, I generally go to Las Vegas.

BOB SHAYE

To Jackson and his colleagues, Shaye's decision must have seemed like a miraculous reprieve. The project that the scriptwriters and Weta Ltd. had worked on for eighteen months would not be taken out of their hands and produced by Miramax in a self-evidently inadequate single feature film with a $75 million budget.

Certainly Shaye's inquiry about making three films has usually been portrayed to the public in this way—as a quirky, risky $270 million throw of the dice. No doubt there was a risk involved, but Shaye's view of the odds would have been very different from those of the filmmakers. A sign in his office reads "Prudent Aggression," a phrase that acts as an unofficial motto for New Line, often quoted by its employees in interviews.

There were obvious disadvantages in producing *Rings.* Jackson was a relatively unknown filmmaker with not one financial success to his credit. The films would have to be mounted on a scale commensurate with the epic novel, and the fantasy elements would require expensive CGI work, as the pitch film made abundantly clear. Expanded to three parts, the undertaking would require a huge budget. New Line, although a wholly owned subsidiary of Time Warner, operated independently and would have to come up with the financing itself, and it had never made such a major project.

Yet the potential rewards were enticing. *Rings* could obviously become a franchise. New Line's growth from a tiny 16mm film-rental firm that Shaye founded in 1967 to one of the biggest independent production/distribution companies in Hollywood had come primarily through two wildly successful series. In 1984, *Nightmare on Elm Street,* made for $1.8 million, grossed $25.5 million domestically. Five more cheaply produced entries in this series appeared, the last in 1991 (with two later spin-offs, *Wes Craven's New Nightmare,* 1994, and *Freddy vs. Jason,* 2003), and a TV show based on the same material ran for two seasons. Just as the *Nightmare* films were losing steam, New Line paid $3 million for a comic-book-derived item called *Teenage Mutant Ninja Turtles* (1990), which then grossed more than $200 million worldwide. Two sequels followed (in 1991 and 1993). The spectacular success of the Turtles (played in that pre-CGI age by Jim Henson creations) overshadowed the more modest but distinctly profitable *House Party,* also released in 1990 and also leading to two sequels (1991 and 1994; in 2001, the fourth went straight to video).

By 1998, all three series were moribund. The biggest one-off hits that the studio had produced, *Dumb and Dumber* and *The Mask* (both 1994), had so far failed to spawn sequels, since Jim Carrey's fee had rocketed beyond New Line's price range. *Austin Powers: International Man of Mystery* (1997) had been a surprise hit, but the release of its sequel was still a year away when Jackson made his pitch.

During the pitch session, Shaye told Kamins that New Line had eagerly been seeking another franchise. The firm had spent around a year developing a project based on Isaac Asimov's "Foundation" book series. Finally, unable to come up with a viable script, New Line had let its option on the books lapse. That happened only weeks before Jackson's pitch. Shaye saw *Rings* as another chance for a franchise.[26] Asked later why he had wanted a three-film version, he said, "It was so wonderfully presold. It was like *Superman* or *Batman*."[27] Like those franchises, *Rings* potentially could generate enormous income from ancillary products.

Ordesky's account of Shaye's famous "three-film" remark suggests that such factors were on his mind:

> The lights came up, Bob was sitting there, and we were all watching him. Bob said, "Why two movies?" Then Bob said, "There are three books. Why aren't you making three movies?" Peter gives me this sidelong glance like "Dare I hope this is actually being said?" Peter was saying, "Well, Bob, that would be great, of course!" He didn't want to scare it away. Bob was saying, "Well, it makes sense. Artistically, you could follow the books. Then there are three theatrical windows, three video releases." Bob is talking about the fusion of art and commerce . . . brilliant.[28]

The leap from inexpensively made horror films or comedies to a huge, fairly prestigious literary adaptation was, however, a considerable one. Shaye had always run New Line as a studio that economized as much as possible. Despite the huge potential outlay on *Rings,* Shaye would have foreseen ways to cut costs and minimize risk. As he said, gambling is for Las Vegas.

To begin with, making three films simultaneously in New Zealand saved an enormous amount of money. Not having to start up three separate films reduced expenditures on set building, transport of cast and crew members to and from New Zealand, and so on. One consideration was that many of the pristine landscapes used as locations were in parks, where the filmmakers were required to leave the area exactly as they found it. Crews had to dig up and later replace rare plants, put down sod on damaged lawns, and build roads that had to be removed after filming was done. Repeating all this for those locales that appeared in two or three parts of *Rings* would have been monumentally inefficient. In 2001, at a press conference in Cannes, Ordesky claimed, "By shooting all three at once, the studio may have saved up to $100 million."[29]

These cost savings alone, however, would not be enough to cause New Line to attempt simultaneous productions. If they were, other films would be made this way. Even after the success of *Rings,* studios are not eager to attempt ambitious simultaneous shoots on potential franchise films. Few, if any, are as "wonderfully presold" as Shaye perceived *Rings* to be. Nevertheless, there have been other franchises where the studio cautiously waited to see if a film was successful and then cut costs by doing two sequels at once. While editing *Back to the Future II,* Zemeckis was shooting the third film, and the second and third films of the *Pirates of the Caribbean* franchise were shot simultaneously. The original *Back to the Future* and *Pirates of the Caribbean* films' narratives were self-contained. *Fellowship* was only one-third of a story. Shaye presumably trusted that its "presold" nature made treating it as a single three-part film reasonably safe.

Certainly shooting entirely in New Zealand offered many sorts of savings. Most of the crew were Kiwis, and the New Zealand film industry has no unions. Of the 1,200-plus people listed in *Rings'* credits, most would be working for considerably less than Hollywood scale. Although the exchange rate of the New Zealand dollar fluctuated through the long shoot, it typically remained around fifty cents or less to the American dollar. As of the spring of 2002, about 74 percent of the film's budget had been spent in New Zealand, so the exchange rate alone would have cut costs by a very substantial amount (though of course transportation expenditures were higher).[30] Tax benefits for filmmaking in New Zealand saved additional tens of millions of dollars.

Given the wild success of *Fellowship,* including the rise to stardom of some of its cast members, a single lengthy shoot bestowed another benefit. Shaye describes the project's savings in the era of ballooning celebrity salaries: "I realized that I could have one of those films in each of the next two years, and we wouldn't have the aggravation of renegotiating with talent, having to have costs go up astronomically from the first to the second to the third. All of this really appealed to me from a corporate perspective."[31] Doubtless Shaye would vividly recall Jim Carrey's departure after *Dumb and Dumber* four years earlier to a higher salary at Warner Bros. for *Batman Forever.* The eventual sequel, *Dumb and Dumberer: When Harry Met Lloyd* (2003), failed at the box office largely because it lacked the original stars, Carrey and Jeff Daniels.

It's difficult to estimate what *Rings* would have cost if it had been made one film at a time in the United States. We shall never know what such overnight stars as Orlando Bloom, Elijah Wood, Viggo Mortensen, and Ian McKellen might have demanded for the second and third installments. Moreover, Jackson estimates that the nearly 1,500 CGI shots for *Return* alone cost around $47 million to create at Weta and would have been more than $100 million in the United States: "Making them in the States would have been too expensive—and they probably would never have gotten made in the first place."[32]

On a cost-per-minute basis, *Rings* stacks up favorably against James Cameron's *Titanic* (1997), which made a record $1.8 billion worldwide. *Titanic* was another long, enormously successful CGI-heavy epic that involved no renegotiations of actors' salaries. Its estimated budget was $200 million, meaning that it cost on average $1.03 million for each of its 194 minutes. Final budget estimates for *Rings* are inconsistent, running from $310 to $350 million.[33] Taking a figure in the middle, $330 million, the 557 minutes of the trilogy's theatrical versions average out to just under $600,000 each (with the 677 minutes of the extended versions averaging less than half a million each). To get a vague sense of what *Rings* might have cost to make in the United States (or, more properly, North America, since *Titanic* was shot partly in Mexico and Newfoundland), let's multiply the number of minutes in it by the average cost per minute of Cameron's film. By such a measure, the theatrical versions would have cost about $544 million, the extended versions about $700 million. The latter figure is about twice the estimated total budget of *Rings,* including the footage added to the extended editions. In terms of proportion of negative costs to total gross, *Rings* was nearly as profitable as *Titanic.* The cost of Cameron's film was 10.9 percent of its final gross, while that of *Rings* was 11.4 percent. (The difference would have been more than made up for by the larger number of ancillary products *Rings* spawned.) In the long run, New Line got a considerable bargain, and Jackson's team definitely put the money on the screen.[34]

Shaye presumably would have foreseen only some of these financial advantages when he suggested making *Rings* in three parts, and even in his most optimistic estimates he probably didn't anticipate just how successful the film would be. Still, Jackson could not have picked a better time to approach the studio with an expensive project. In mid-1998, New Line had just come off the most successful year in its history. During 1997, it had distributed a pair of prestigious and successful art films, *Boogie Nights* and *The Sweet Hereafter;* a political comedy, *Wag the Dog,* which profited from its coincidence with the Clinton-Lewinsky scandal; and the first *Austin Powers* film. For once there had been no notable failures among its releases, and 1998 was also shaping up well.

Granted, *Rings* could be seen as having great franchise potential. But why would Shaye take on an expensive project with Jackson attached as director? Unlike Ordesky, Shaye was not a big fan of the Kiwi's films. As he told an interviewer in late 2001,

> There's no question that Peter didn't have the experience for a project this big and to be honest, I hadn't liked all his movies. But he's made one movie, "Heavenly Creatures," that I really liked. And I really liked him: He's a decent guy with no arrogance or hubris. So I believed in his good faith and I bet on his ability. It doesn't sound very rational, but sometimes trusting your instincts isn't a very rational thing to do.[35]

Despite Shaye's admiration for *Heavenly Creatures,* New Line had passed on distributing it—wisely, since the film lost money. Miramax had released it, thus linking Jackson to the firm and, two years later, giving him his chance to obtain the *Rings* film rights.

Shaye portrays his decision to go with Jackson as a hunch, driven by instinct. Yet Jackson had one enormous advantage that goes unmentioned in accounts of the project's move from Miramax to New Line. For the three weeks during which that project was in turnaround, Jackson essentially controlled the film rights to *Rings*—on loan from Miramax, as it were—if he could find a buyer. It probably did not seem to him during that worrisome period as if he wielded such power, but we should remember that those rights had never been available on the open market. In 1967 (coincidentally, the year Shaye founded New Line), United Artists had approached Tolkien and eventually obtained the rights. In 1976, Zaentz had acquired them through a direct deal with United Artists. After the disappointment of the 1978 version, Zaentz had sat on those rights. They had not gone on the table for bidding in 1995, when Jackson approached Miramax about the project. Weinstein was able to buy them solely because he had helped Zaentz by rescuing *The English Patient.* When Weinstein put *Rings* into turnaround in 1998, it was the first time that the rights to adapt the novel had ever been openly offered for sale within the film industry. Unlike any other executive in Hollywood, Shaye saw the advantages of seizing that opportunity, and only Jackson could bring those rights with him from Miramax to another producer.

Moreover, Jackson was not selling only the rights but an entire package.

By the time the director pitched the project to Shaye, it had already been in preproduction for eighteen months. Jackson's companies in Wellington had created huge numbers of designs, miniatures, and maquettes. By the conditions of the turnaround, the finished designs, sets, objects, and proprietary computer programs would have to be purchased from Miramax for $12 million above and beyond the adaptation rights. New Line could hardly scrap them all and start over with a new director and production team. So Shaye's decision essentially was not so much a case of, "We will allow you, Peter Jackson, to direct *The Lord of the Rings*" as it was, "You, Peter Jackson, will enable us to produce *The Lord of the Rings*."

New Line's commitment to undertake the three-part film was quickly made, and Shaye and Lynne agreed to all the onerous terms that Miramax had imposed for the turnaround. New Line would pay the $12 million up front, as well as the required first-dollar percentages. Apart from a check to cover the costs of the preproduction, New Line also had to promise 5 percent of the gross box-office take to Miramax and another 5 percent to Zaentz. According to Kamins, "Miramax knew this was for real. They couldn't believe it. I think Miramax was utterly stunned. I think Harvey set these draconian conditions under the theory that there was just no way on God's green earth that Peter was ever going to be able to get someone else to bite off on it."

Harvey Weinstein's disappointment must have been considerably tempered by the financial results. So low was Eisner's faith in *Rings'* success that he split the 5 percent evenly between Disney and the Weinsteins personally. (Five percent of the nearly $3 billion international gross of *Rings* would be close to $150 million.) Both Weinstein brothers would also receive a credit as executive producers on the film, even though they were paid in full for all their expenditures and did not contribute to the project after the deal with New Line was consummated. (A teasing comment on the Weinsteins' participation appears in the final credits, where the sketch under Mark Ordesky's and the brothers' names shows a tiny figure leading two enormous trolls on leashes; see figure 3.) Later, in 2004, during the acrimonious period in which the Weinstein brothers were about to leave the company they had founded, *Variety* pointed out that Disney's 2.5 percent of *Rings'* gross would essentially have covered its entire $80 million purchase of Miramax in 1993; by the time the Weinsteins left, the company was valued at $2 billion.[36]

The legal wrangling over the deal went on for weeks, and Miramax twice extended the turnaround. Finally, on 24 August 1998, a New Line press release announced that the company would be producing *Rings* in three parts at a budget of "more than $130 million." That figure was approximately the

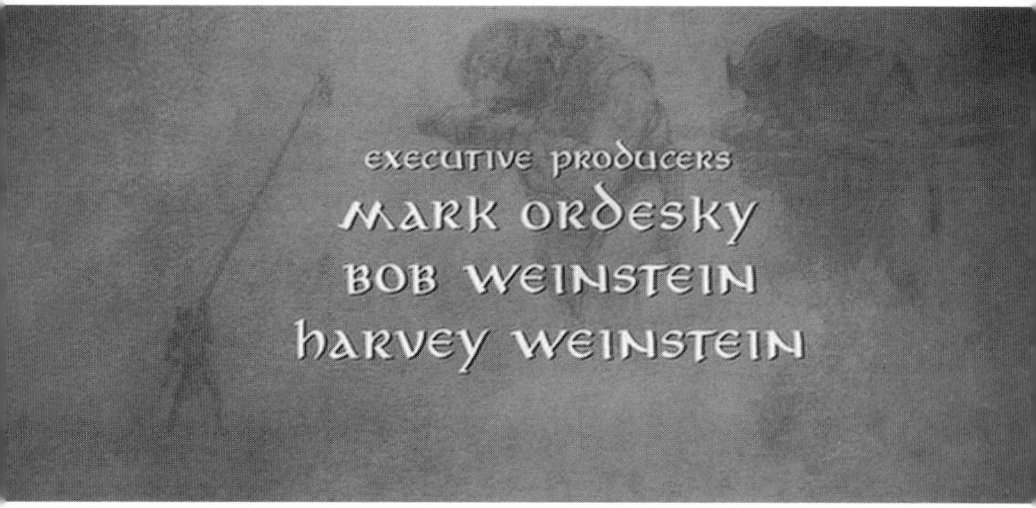

EXECUTIVE PRODUCERS
MARK ORDESKY
BOB WEINSTEIN
HARVEY WEINSTEIN

Figure 3. Harvey and Bob Weinstein's credits in *The Return of the King*.

amount that Eisner had forbidden Weinstein to pay for a two-film version, and it was quoted not because New Line was being naive or disingenuous but simply because a new budget could not be devised until the three-part script was finished.[37] Thereafter the official budget was raised to $270 million. The initial press release announced that principal photography would begin in mid-1999 and last one year, and that the films would be released at six-month intervals, with Christmas-summer-Christmas premieres. It also stated that "Weta Digital, Jackson's innovative special effects firm based in New Zealand, will be responsible for the elaborate computer generated visuals demanded of the epic project."[38]

By the end of 1998, Jackson was already negotiating for a delay, wanting to finish his storyboards and animatics. The contract stipulated that principal photography had to begin by October 1999;[39] ultimately it commenced on 11 October 1999 and lasted until 22 December 2000. The parts appeared in three successive Christmas seasons, from 2001 to 2003.

Despite the emotional roller coaster that Jackson's team went through during the Miramax period and despite the fact that the project ended up much better off with New Line, Kamins points out that Harvey Weinstein made the trilogy possible:

> There's no question that the $12 million that Harvey spent made New Line saying yes possible. Because I don't know, if we'd simply walked into Bob

Shaye's office with the three books, saying, "I want to make these three books into three movies, or two movies," if Bob Shaye would have had any reason to say yes. He had the benefit of looking at that documentary. That documentary that Peter made was the result of the $12 million that had been spent.

CAST AWAY ON A POLYNESIAN ISLAND

Imagine living in a country where the most important
industry is making a film of *The Lord of the Rings*.
Isn't that a sign of a world you want to live in?

IAN MCKELLEN

After New Line committed to the production, the Weta team went back to its preproduction work. Once that was well advanced, the process of casting the major roles went on during 1999. *Variety* published notices that actors had been found: Elijah Wood (8 July), Ian McKellen (26 July), Christopher Lee (23 August), Liv Tyler (27 August), Viggo Mortensen (reported on 15 October as being in negotiations to replace Stuart Townsend), and Cate Blanchett (27 October). The policy was one of seeking actors with distinguished reputations but not wide enough marquee recognition to command large fees. Indeed, the amounts offered to the actors for the entire filming period seem to have been relatively small. Sean Astin revealed in his memoirs that he was shocked to discover that the $250,000 he had been offered was for all three films, not just one. (Later bonuses after the success of *Fellowship* helped make up for the early penny-pinching.) Astin, like others of the cast, whether or not they already were fans of the novel, decided that this was "the opportunity of a lifetime"[40] and agreed to work for what was essentially scale. One or more of the top names got profit participations.

Behind-the-scenes talent came on board. Many of the designers and department heads had worked with Jackson numerous times, for he tends to be loyal to his collaborators and to inspire great loyalty in them. Most of the team were Kiwis, but staff from abroad filled some core positions in areas where the local film industry was weak. These included Australian cinematographer Andrew Lesnie (who had experience in fantasy films from his work on *Babe* and *Babe, Pig in the City*). The huge special-effects effort was headed by an American, Jim Reigel (*Starship Troopers, Star Trek: Insurrection*), and veteran effects specialist Alex Funke (*The Abyss, Starship Troopers*) came in as visual effects director of photography. In 1999, American producer Barrie M. Osborne, after finishing *The Matrix* in Sydney, decided not to produce that film's much-delayed sequels. Instead he took over on *Rings,* replacing Kiwi producer Tim Sanders (whose next project was *Whale Rider,* 2003). Co-producer Rick Porras, an American, was postproduction supervisor on *The Frighteners* and worked with Robert Zemeckis on *Contact* (partially shot in New Zealand). First assistant director Carolynne Cunningham, from Australia, had held that same post on many Australian films and on *Heavenly Creatures.* Hundreds of workers came from abroad for the labor-intensive postproduction tasks of digital animation and sound mixing.

On 11 October, shooting began with the scene of the four Hobbits' first encounter with a Black Rider. The location was a park on the side of Mount Victoria, in the midst of the city and minutes away from the studios in the suburb of Miramar. It was one of about 140 places on both the North and South Islands that would be used during filming. Others were extremely remote. For views of the Fellowship on snowy mountainsides, the cast and crew had to be flown up via helicopter. One of the most spectacular locales, the one used for the Rohirrim capital Edoras, was very difficult to reach. Mount Sunday and the surrounding ranges lie tucked away in an area of the South Island, far from any town and accessible only by air or a dirt track. The crew had to build a road in and spend months transporting material and constructing the Golden Hall and surrounding buildings (plate 2).

Even with fifteen months, an unusually long period of principal photography, the whole film could not be directed by one person. At times as many as six units were shooting at once, some supervised by second-unit directors far from Wellington. Veteran Kiwi director Geoff Murphy (*Utu,* 1983) returned to New Zealand for *Rings* and shot the Rohan scenes of the Uruk-hai and the Rohirrim riders among Central Otago's bleakly beautiful rolling hills and shale outcroppings.[41] John Mahaffie directed the second unit for a time and moved on to Unit 1B, doing key work on Film 1's chase to the Fords of Bruinen and the Helm's Deep battle. Walsh directed many of the scenes involving Gollum and those with Arwen. Boyens and Porras pitched in by directing additional units, and Osborne filmed part of the fight with the Uruk-hai near the end of *Fellowship.* Satellite feeds were set up, allowing Jackson to track all the active units in real time on rows of TV monitors. At the same time, more work went on in studios and warehouses in Miramar, where sets were built and miniatures filmed. The studios bore letters, and at its height the production was occupying buildings from A to around P or Q.

Early on the decision had been made to create all the props, costumes, and furniture from scratch and from the actual materials appropriate to them. Artisans were tracked down all over the country. Coopers were hired to build barrels, master leather crafters to fashion horse harnesses, and jewelers to create the various crowns and brooches. At the same time, Weta Digital acquired far greater computing power, and its digital experts developed software programs that could generate huge, realistic-looking armies and render Gollum's appearance convincingly.

In the meantime, New Line was raising money to pay for all this. The firm, although a wholly owned subsidiary of Time Warner, operates independently and had to come up with the financing. The company supported the production in three major ways. Most important, New Line financed the film in traditional independent fashion by preselling foreign distribution rights to companies around the globe. Not surprisingly, though, New Line often faced an uphill battle in doing so, since those companies would have to commit to all three films at once, sight unseen. Rolf Mittweg, New Line's president and chief operating officer of worldwide distribution and marketing, spent more than two years putting together an international ensemble of twenty-five distributors, many of them small, independent firms that already had multiyear output deals with New Line. *Variety* reported that these advance deals secured around 65 percent of the film's negative costs.[42]

A big franchise like *Rings* also offered another way of making presales: licensing agreements for a wide range of games, action figures, T-shirts, and the like. In November 2002, Lynne revealed that the risks to the firm were not as great as they might appear: "There was a leap of faith. But what Bob and I attempted to do was build in as much protection as we could to a commitment that was unprecedented. We had substantial investment from our international partners on every film and actual cash advances for a variety of licenses before we started one frame of shooting."[43] Moreover, Shaye has pointed out that *Rings* was made over three years, and New Line's production budget was big enough to cover its share of the costs.[44] That would not be surprising, since *Time* reported that "New Line's initial investment in the franchise was just about $25 million per movie."[45]

A few months after *Fellowship*'s premiere, *Variety* summed up how effectively New Line had diluted its risk: "Foreign presales guarantees and merchandising-rights deals allowed New Line to commit $270 million to the production of three *Lord of the Rings* films, with only 20% of that production expense at risk. New Line is also on the hook for U.S. marketing costs, thought to be about $50 million for the first installment of *Rings,* though not in international, where foreign territorial buyers shoulder marketing expenses."[46] Ironically, if New Line's contribution to the cost of the three lengthy parts of *Rings* was indeed in the neighborhood of $75 million, it approximated what Michael Eisner had in 1998 wanted Miramax to spend on a single two-hour version.

It was very exciting, a kind of buzz in the air. It really
seemed like everyone was there just to see *Lord of the Rings*.

JUDY ALLEY
Merchandising Coordinator, *The Lord of the Rings*

In late 2000, principal photography was winding down. The entire production had been conducted with such secrecy that few people—including New Line officials—had any idea what the film would look like. A bit earlier in the process Osborne had had an idea about how to reassure them. He described to Jackson something that had worked for him when he was producing *The Matrix*. That film had also been shot far away from its home base, Warner Bros., in the Fox Studios Australia complex in Sydney. Joel Silver had asked Osborne's team to put together a single sequence of ten to fifteen minutes to galvanize the Warners marketing department by convincing it that *The Matrix* could make a lot of money. The filmmakers quickly edited Trinity's opening escape across the rooftops. That effort had succeeded, and the same thing could presumably be done for *Rings* with New Line. Jackson's team had not had time to do anything with the idea, but on 3 January 2001, Mittweg wrote to Jackson asking for a twenty- to thirty-minute preview that New Line could show in May at the Cannes Film Festival, seven months before *Fellowship* was to be released.[47]

The three-day Cannes event, which followed the preview with publicity interviews and a lavish party, was in its way as dramatic a moment in the trilogy's history as was the little meeting where Jackson pitched his project to Bob Shaye. This time, however, the drama played out on the world stage, as distributors, exhibitors, the press, and influential fan webmasters realized that Shaye's gamble had not been so risky after all and excitedly spread the word that Jackson had fashioned an extraordinary movie.

For New Line, the Cannes event had two main goals. The firm wanted to reassure the foreign distributors, many of whom had waited anxiously for years to see some footage and find out if their leap of faith in committing to all three parts of *Rings* was justified. In a few territories, primarily Germany and Eastern Europe, the second two parts remained unsold, and New Line hoped to obtain the final commitments at Cannes. Second, Cannes would provide an occasion to present *Rings* to the international press. "Just getting a buzz out there," Osborne explains, "because there was a lot of negative buzz about *Lord of the Rings.* A crazy, speculative thing to make three films at once. A crazy, speculative thing to give Peter Jackson such a big production and do it in New Zealand."

The international distributors weren't the only ones who needed reassuring. Jamie Selkirk suggests, "I think New Line was starting to get concerned. They hadn't seen anything up to that point." As far as finished footage was concerned, this was literally the case, since essentially none of the special-effects shots was in finished form by early 2001. New Line executives had had little but facilities tours and demo reels to quiet their doubts about Weta Digital being capable of doing the film's complex CGI.

The idea of doing a single extended sequence was brought up again, and the question became, what to show? Osborne describes how Jackson used the preview to the advantage of the production as well.

> Peter just kind of out of the blue thought—he's a very clever guy—he thought, I'm going to use this not only to accomplish what New Line wants to accomplish, but I want to do something that's going to actually kick-start Weta from being in R and D, thinking that they have all this time to research and develop stuff to actually producing finished shots. So he picked the most visual-effects-intense sequence, which was the Mines of Moria, from Film 1.

Jackson also pointed out at the time that a big action sequence, including the Fellowship's battle with a cave troll and flight from thousands of Orcs, would best satisfy New Line's international distribution partners.[48]

The effects team were convinced that they could never make their deadline. Much of the Mines of Moria sequence involves elaborate miniature sets combined with live action, as when the Fellowship leaps a gap in a stairway, a large portion of which collapses. The actors moving through these miniature sets are often digital doubles, and the cave troll is one of Film 1's most elaborate digital creatures. Weta's Matt Aitken, who was supervising the creation of the cave troll and the actors' digital doubles, recalls:

> Cannes, that was a huge deadline for us, really where we had a change of management here, and the people who came in were faced with, like, two or three months where we had to get, really, what is the heart of Film 1 and a lot of visual effects work up to scratch and pretty well finaled. A lot of that was the way it went into the final film. We did revisit some of it. In some ways that was the

toughest deadline we've had to work to in the whole trilogy, was getting that Cannes footage ready. And, yeah, people loved it, so it all worked out fine.

As Aitken says, the deadline was only met because the Mines sequence was cut together lacking some of the footage that the filmmakers knew would be in the finished film and with some of the shots also still at the "CBB" (could be better) stage. The preview included a few shots that did not make the final edit, and many that did looked distinctly different because they had not yet been digitally graded. For example, the memorable extreme long shot of the Fellowship surrounded by thousands of Orcs shows Gandalf's staff casting a bright light that washes out our view of some of the actors. In the Cannes footage, the glare—later added digitally—is not present, and the Fellowship is perfectly visible.[49] The preview also jump-started Howard Shore's work on the score, and he finished the music for the Mines of Moria scene in time for inclusion.

During this rush, Peter Skarratt, the first assistant editor, pointed out to Osborne that the sequence would not work on its own because many viewers would not know the characters. The decision was made to include a montage before the Mines sequence, introducing the main characters, the Ring, and the quest. Another montage afterward would hint at action to come in Films 2 and 3. In the midst of the postproduction rush on *Fellowship* itself, a young cutter named Jabez Olssen was assigned the job of editing the opening and closing montages. Temporary music not by Shore was used during these segments.

The result was a twenty-five-minute preview reel. The opening showed Gandalf's arrival at Bag End to visit Bilbo and shots of the main characters in key scenes like the Council of Elrond. The closing montage was faster, more like a theatrical trailer, with a flurry of shots from *Towers* and *Return* that included two high points in Mordor: Sam's declaration, "I can't carry it, but I can carry you!" and Frodo's "The Ring is mine!" So important was the preview to New Line that Shaye flew to New Zealand to see how it was shaping up.

In early January 2001, work on the Cannes party began as well. *Rings* supervising art director Dan Hennah and his wife, art department manager Chris Hennah, were asked to decorate the venue for the party. It was to be held in Le Château de Castellaras, a hilltop castle built in 1927 incorporating elements from actual medieval and Renaissance ruins. The Hennahs visited France for three days to sketch plans and meet the New Line international marketing team. Deciding on an elaborate Middle-earth environment, they went back to Wellington and packed five shipping containers with actual set elements and props.

Returning to Cannes in April, the Hennahs had six weeks to construct the portions of the party settings that could not be shipped. The budget did not allow for many of the Kiwi art department staff to travel to Cannes, but some paid their own way to help with the actual assemblage of the sets and props on the site. Judy Alley, who had handled cloth props and other set decoration, was one of these, and some of the film's staff members who happened to be traveling in Europe cut short their vacations to pitch in. Some ended up sleeping on the floor in other staff members' rooms. They had five days to transform the château and its grounds into something resembling Middle-earth.

New Line flew in print and media journalists from all over the world, as well as several of its nervous foreign distribution partners. As an acknowledgment of the new importance of the Internet to publicizing films, the company also invited a few webmasters: Harry Knowles of the influential general movie site Ain't It Cool News; Calisuri, one of the founders of TheOneRing.net; and representatives of major Dutch and German sites. Around three hundred journalists participated in the junket, though no doubt many of those were already in town to cover the Cannes Film Festival.

New Line rented an auditorium in one of the main festival venues, the Olympia, a nine-screen multiplex in the center of town. Coproducer Rick Porras supervised the installation of special equipment needed to project the print, the sound track and images of which were still on separate strips of film. Backup prints and equipment were brought, to ensure that these crucial screenings were not botched. Secret design and technical elements absolutely had to be kept from spies and thieves, and a guard remained in the projection booth at all times when the print was there.

The first screening was for the film's cast and crew, as well as New Line VIPs and guests. Kamins recalls the atmosphere:

> Right before the first screening at the Olympia theater Peter and Bob Shaye and Fran and Mark Ordesky and I, we were all kind of huddled in this little stairwell. There was a look on Peter's face and on Bob's face that I'll never forget, because it was this bizarre combination of the most exciting kind of hope combined with the most unbelievable, gut-wrenching terror. The answer to that question as to which one they should ultimately feel was going to be realized in a matter of moments.

One of Jackson's Wellington facilities, The Film Unit, which combined editing, sound mixing, and processing, was responsible for putting together the preview and projecting it. CEO Sue Thompson describes how nervous she was before the screening, knowing how much was hanging on it: "It does make for interesting tension when your chairman and your biggest client is sitting there watching the preview of *Lord of the Rings,* and they're all in one and the same person. That sort of means that failure is not, as they say, an option. I also knew that at that stage Pete and Fran had a lot to risk on the success of the films." By that point, Jackson and Walsh were deep in debt after building up the filmmaking infrastructure in Wellington—including loans they had taken out to buy The Film Unit—so they had an enormous personal stake in the preview.

Jackson gave a brief introduction, and the twenty-five-minute film was screened without mishap. Thompson recalls watching it not as a technician but as an audience member: "I just burst into tears. It was a sort of relief and pride, all at the same time. And I looked over, and there was Mark Ordesky going like this [presses hands together in a prayerlike gesture], with his hands in front of him like that. I think that was probably a shared moment. We both sort of looked at each other and . . . [heaves big sigh of relief]."

Many of the actors were present, and according to Orlando Bloom, "Afterwards there was a stunned silence, and then it was like, 'Can we see it again, please?'"[50] That reaction seems to have been typical for the cast and crew. Judy Alley recalls, "I can remember at the end of it there was just this moment of absolute silence. I think some people started clapping. There was a bit of a standing ovation, and no one quite knew what to do. We were just a bit starstruck, having seen this amazing thing." Even the ordinarily phlegmatic press were overwhelmed. Chris Hennah says, "The press are usually pretty reserved. They clapped and cheered." Dan Hennah adds, "Suddenly this thing that we'd put so much into had got this really positive reception from people you didn't expect to respond at all. You'd expect a few murmurs and a lot of walking out of the theater."

The auditorium held only a few hundred people, and interest quickly became so great that extra screenings were held. Memories vary, but it seems that three were planned and ultimately five presented. Sitting behind two reporters at one of the screenings, Osborne heard one of them remark to his companion when the lights came up, "I thought Tolkien was going to be boring." The preview had achieved its goal with the press.

News of the screenings spread quickly. Kamins recalls, "It was viral. It was incredible. I was walking around not only wearing my Cannes badge but then

New Line had given me this sort of all-access badge that had *Lord of the Rings* on it, and literally everybody would stop me, wherever I went: 'God, is it true, is it true that the footage is great?'" Invitations to the Sunday night party became the hottest item at Cannes.

As for New Line, Osborne describes the change after the preview: "I don't think anybody at New Line was really convinced that it was going to happen until we were in Cannes in 2001, that they really, really knew that they had something. Maybe Mark Ordesky might have believed that we had something earlier than that, but I think that they were probably skeptical all the way up to that time." Harvey Weinstein, who must have been torn between regret at losing the project and glee at the prospect of his and his brother's 2 ½ percent of the gross, was gracious, calling the footage "spectacular" and predicting, "They have another 'Star Wars' on their hands."[51]

New Line and the distributors could also have taken heart from a Canal+ interview with Jackson that ran on 11 May. Sound bites from people exiting the preview screening were interspersed with the interview. Apart from the "It's wonderful!" and "I can't wait to see the rest!" sorts of remarks, one comment was prophetic: "There's in my opinion one of the biggest babes I ever saw, Viggo Mortensen."[52] New Line's initial fear that the film would not attract women or be a good date movie would be put to rest as the film's male-babe factor set in.

After screenings, reporters were bused out to the château, where tents had been set up on the grounds, and cast and crew were waiting for interviews. One day was given over to print reporters, arranged in groups of around fifteen each. The interviewees would appear in succession for brief question sessions, and the same ones cycled through the process for each group of journalists, all day long. To speed things up, the interviewees were also grouped: the Elf actors who were at Cannes (Liv Tyler and Orlando Bloom), the older, distinguished British actors (Christopher Lee, Ian McKellen, and Ian Holm), the three writers, and so on. Broadcast journalists had their turn on another day, with each crew getting one-on-one access to each interviewee for five minutes. Jackson claimed that on one day he was interviewed seventy-five times.

On Sunday evening, 13 May, the event culminated in a party planned for 1,500, though people who were there estimate the crowd at somewhere between 2,000 and 3,000. The weather was hot and clear, perfect for an outdoor evening affair. New Line had remembered to invite all the Kiwi crew members who had come to Cannes. At party time, they were still racing to put fresh fruit, bread, flowers, and other perishables into the Hobbit market, and as the first guests arrived, they dashed off to change their clothes.

The party decor had been arranged to give guests a sensation of entering into the world glimpsed in the preview, with areas given over to the Elves, the Hobbits, the Rohirrim, and other cultures. The process began as guests alighted from their cars and walked up a red-carpet-covered path toward the château. An Elvish chamber group played music off to the side. Dan and Chris Hennah describe the scene just inside the entrance:

> DAN: We got about ten children there—wonderful little French children— who we costumed up as Hobbits, and we gave them baskets full of rose petals—
>
> CHRIS: Real rose petals—
>
> DAN: The idea was that they gently threw them up in the air and they'd sort of flutter down on the red carpet—
>
> CHRIS: in front of people as they arrived—
>
> DAN: but of course the children got far too excited and started throwing them at people. It was great!

The guests also encountered sinister Black Riders circling on their horses in the gloom beyond the lighted path.

As Osborne put it, the setting gave "a flavor for the quality of the production. Not only would you see this film, but the people that came through this party would see the quality of the props and the set dressings and the wardrobe." Inside the château, for example, Théoden's throne, gleaming and intricately carved of solid oak, stood in a room simulating the hall at Edoras. To reach the refreshments and dancing area, guests strolled through a re-created Hobbit village, with a market square and pub. A "party field" with bunting and lights strung in the trees suggested Bilbo's birthday party (glimpsed in the preview). It had picnic tables in the center and was lined with tents where food and drink were available, with "Hobbits" serving refreshments (plate 3). Tucked away to the left of the main entrance, the facade of the Green Dragon Inn served to hide the portable toilets.

The decorations were intended to keep guests talking about the preview. The Hennahs describe how people could get drawn into the Middle-earth environment:

> DAN: What we'd done was taken the small Bag End over there, deliberately so that people could walk right through inside Bag End.
>
> CHRIS: But they'd have to bend over—

Figure 4. Galadriel's boat on the swimming pool at New Line's Cannes party, Le Château de Castellaras. (Courtesy Judy Alley.)

DAN: from a Gandalf point of view—

CHRIS: and then we built the oversized Prancing Pony so that they'd go into the bar and have to sit on the high stool—

DAN: from a Hobbit point of view—all of their drinks at the bar, which was way up there.

The château's long, slender swimming pool, located on a terrace overlooking a mountain view, had Elvish arches placed around it, and Galadriel's boat floated on the water (figure 4). As guests departed, they were handed a swag bag, a collection of *Rings*-related gifts, including a Hobbit-size pipe and pack of tobacco and a small model of Frodo's sword, Sting.[53]

The Cannes preview reel went through many later screenings in various international cities for press, distributors, and exhibitors. Since Jackson would not be attending to present the footage, that spring, during the pick-ups for *Fellowship,* he shot a brief introduction. A single tracking shot shows Gandalf's cart moving along a country road, just as when Frodo and the Wizard meet early in *Fellowship.* McKellen, in costume as Gandalf, drives the cart, and Jackson, in his ordinary clothes, sits in the false-perspective seat, so that he appears the size of a Hobbit. Gandalf begins: "I'd like to introduce you to my friend and passenger, Peter Jackson." Jackson responds, "Thank you, Gandalf," and gives a little background to the production: "New Line Cinema have given us an amazing opportunity to live and breathe Middle-earth for the last fourteen or fifteen months. We actually started shooting on October the eleventh, 1999, and we're actually still shooting today, which explains why I can't be with you for this screening." When he finishes, Gandalf murmurs, "Very good, Peter," and they rush off, supposedly to Bilbo's party.

Shortly after Cannes, Shaye and Lynne returned to New York and showed the preview to the AOL Time Warner board, which was impressed, and to a group of U.S. distributors. There were subsequent screenings to distributors, exhibitors, and press. A witness's account of one of the more routine later screenings suggests that the enthusiasm generated at Cannes was generated again in less high-profile circumstances. At the end of August, Cliff (Quickbeam) Broadway, a regular columnist for TheOneRing.net, was invited to a showing at New Line's Los Angeles office. He was eager to see the famous footage, but the rest of the two dozen or so attendees apparently were not. Broadway describes them:

> The audience, all jaded Hollywood types, seemed mainly talent management and reps from different exhibitors. I heard bitchy gossip about how "difficult" some stars were and some hushed bits behind me concerning the "desperate financial gamble" of the three films. Catty and restless people. Typical L.A. . . . When all was done, I led the applause. It didn't take much. A noticeable change had come over the jaded audience that was so unconcerned 24 minutes earlier.[54]

By this point trailers in theaters and on the Internet were showing briefer glimpses of similar footage, and, despite some lingering trepidation, fan enthusiasm was growing.

NEW LINE'S GAMBLE REDUX

Despite the triumph at Cannes, New Line had some reasons to be nervous in the months leading up to the December release of *Fellowship*. For one thing, the company's fortunes had declined dramatically since the successes of the late 1990s. The firm's 1998 output had included the Adam Sandler hit *The Wedding Singer*, as well as the debut films of two future franchises, *Rush Hour* and *Blade*. In 1999, the second *Austin Powers* film far outgrossed the original. But in 2000, Adam Sandler's popularity was not enough to carry *Little Nicky*, which became one of the most prominent of New Line's failures of the period. It was eclipsed in late April 2001 when, less than three weeks before the *Rings* Cannes event, the notorious *Town & Country*, a much-delayed Warren Beatty romantic comedy, opened. With a $90 million budget and $15 million more in publicity costs, it grossed $3 million domestically on its opening weekend and went on to an international total of a bit over $10 million.

The *Town & Country* disaster came in the wake of a major shake-up at New Line. AOL and Time Warner's merger had become final on 15 January 2001, and mass layoffs in various subsidiary companies quickly began. In what seemed a harbinger of things to come, Warner Bros. was entirely spared, while New Line lost more than 100 employees, or roughly 20 percent of its staff. By the end of January, AOL Time Warner had fired 2400 people overall.[55] New Line was also ordered to keep its budgets for individual films down in future.

No doubt the positive buzz from the Cannes preview provided a needed boost, but as the December release of *Fellowship* approached, the trade press began to play up New Line's high-stakes risk again—especially when the November release of Warner Bros.' *Harry Potter and the Sorcerer's Stone* proved an enormous success that might eclipse that of the conglomerate's other wizard film.

At the end of November, *Variety* ran a front-page story suggesting that AOL Time Warner was throwing its support to the *Harry Potter* franchise and giving short shrift to *Rings:*

> These must be strange times if a $270 million, star-laden project based on an all-time bestseller with a rabid global following can be considered an underdog. But that's the perception of New Line's "The Lord of the Rings" trilogy in the wake of the extraordinary promotional hoopla and record-breaking B.O. for "Harry Potter and the Sorcerer's Stone" from sister company Warner Bros.
>
> The worldwide launch Dec. 19 of the trilogy's first installment, "The Fellowship of the Ring," will be an acid test of New Line's ability to pull its weight within the AOL Time Warner empire, and to justify its continued existence as a quasi-independent unit.
>
> NL has released more than its share of flops in recent years, and AOL is not likely to be impressed by anything less than a blockbuster.
>
> But tongues wagged when the New Yorker's interview with AOL TW chief Gerald Levin hit newsstands Oct 16: "Harry Potter" was held up as the acme of corporate synergy, while "Rings" rated no mention.
>
> And in London's Financial Times Nov. 16, AOL TW chief operating officer

Richard Parsons said, "The biggest thing on the marketing council's agenda this year was 'Harry Potter,' because we all appreciated what this means to AOL Time Warner in terms of the magnitude of the franchise."[56]

About a week later, the *Los Angeles Times* reiterated that New Line might be at risk of being folded into Warner Bros.: "The early reviews [of *Fellowship*] have been raves. But with AOL Time Warner making cutbacks everywhere, the movie's box-office performance could play a major role in whether New Line survives as a stand-alone studio or is absorbed into big-sister company Warner Bros. Films. In short, 'Rings' could be Shaye's last hurrah, the final dice roll in his 34-year tenure at New Line." The author pointed out that Parsons had recently said he had "'looked real hard' at merging the two film companies" and had imposed a "voluntary" cap of $50 million on the budgets of future New Line projects.[57]

The press is always concerned to dramatize its stories, and articles about the potential demise of New Line made for good copy. As we have seen, however, New Line had effectively underwritten large chunks of the film's costs with its distribution and licensing agreements. Under Shaye's leadership, it had weathered lean years in the past. A number of people within the production or experienced in the workings of the independent film market have claimed that New Line was unlikely to have lost its identity through absorption into AOL Time Warner even if *Fellowship* had been a box-office disappointment.

IN THE DARKNESS SPELLBIND THEM

Accurate or not, all such speculation vanished as *Fellowship* grossed $47 million domestically on its opening weekend.[58] Although that was only the tenth-highest opening weekend for the year, with *Harry Potter and the Sorcerer's Stone* first at $90 million, *Fellowship* proved to have stronger legs. Whereas *Sorcerer's Stone*'s opening was 28.3 percent of its final $317.5 million, only 15.1 percent of *Fellowship*'s total $313 million domestic gross was earned during that first weekend. *Fellowship* did not completely disappear from theaters until 22 August 2002, more than two weeks after the theatrical-version DVD was released.[59] By February 2002, another front-page story in *Variety* showed a cartoon of Gandalf and Harry surveying a map of the world, cooperatively conjuring up "World Wizardry" for AOL Time Warner.[60] *Fellowship*'s international gross was $860.5 million, comparing favorably with *Sorcerer's Stone*'s $976.5 million.

The first film's immense popularity had a major impact on the remainder of Jackson's project. Across Films 2 and 3 the growing budget is apparent, especially in the number and complexity of the CGI shots. Jackson's hope to release both theatrical and extended-version DVDs became a reality. The constrictions of budget that had forced designers into compromises for the first film eased. Principal photography had long since finished, but a large portion of the film's cost was absorbed by special effects. Over the next two years, as the second and third parts went through postproduction, the overall budget crept to somewhere around $330 million. The filmmaking team was able to bring the cast and key crew members like Andrew Lesnie back to New Zealand for months of pickups during both 2002 for *Towers* and 2003 for *Return*. Ambitious upgrading of the technical facilities in Wellington was undertaken, with a view toward making these two parts more polished and more epic in scale.

Fellowship drew mostly favorable reviews. It received many awards and a remarkable thirteen Oscar nominations, given that there was only one for a cast member (McKellen as supporting actor). It won in four of those categories. Speculation immediately began that *Return* would take Best Picture two years later. New Line and the filmmakers continually tried to downplay such talk in the press, but within the company and among the filmmakers there grew to be a definite focus on Oscars.

Towers came out as planned on 18 December 2002, and, like the first part, showed remarkable staying power. It did not go out of distribution until the end of July 2003, a few weeks before the theatrical-version DVD appeared in stores. The film's reviews were even more favorable. *Towers'* international gross was $926 million. It received six Oscar nods, including Best Picture, and won two statuettes. The smaller number of nominations plus the failure to nominate Jackson for best director led some commentators to speculate that the trilogy had peaked early and missed its chance at anything but technical and design awards. Clearly, though, the decline in nominations simply signaled that the Academy members were waiting for the trilogy to be complete before showering it with honors. As *Variety* pointed out, "While most audiences concede it's superior to the first one, many media stories clucked that 'Towers' got 'only' six nominations. Compare that with one for the 'Star Wars' sequel and none for the second 'Harry Potter,' and it's clear the franchise has widespread industry support."[61]

Anticipation for the third part was even keener, fueled by Jackson's and the cast's and crew's frequent claims in interviews that it was the best and most spectacular of the three. New Line agreed to set the world premiere not in one of the American or European cities where such events usually take place but in Wellington—even though its population was only around 300,000. Jackson had backed New Line into that agreement a year earlier, when at the New Zealand premiere of *Towers,* held in Wellington, he had claimed that Mark Ordesky had an announcement to make about where the world premiere of *Return* would take place. Trapped, Ordesky said Wellington—a moment captured on film and included in the supplements to the *Return* extended-version DVD.[62]

Return outgrossed its predecessors, bringing in $1.1 billion internationally, putting it second only to *Titanic* (in figures unadjusted for inflation).[63] The film was withdrawn from distribution earlier than the other two parts, its last day in theaters being 3 June 2004, a little more than a week after the theatrical-version DVD appeared. Presumably the timing resulted from the fact that New Line did not need to sustain interest over the summer leading up to the marketing campaign for another part.

Return was nominated for eleven Academy Awards. The filmmakers were confident about the technical and design Oscars but less certain that the picture, director, and scriptwriting prizes were in the bag. Philippa Boyens confessed to me that she had expected the latter award, along with the male acting statuettes, to go as a consolation prize to *Mystic River*—a plausible worry, given that in recent years the Academy voters had tended to share the wealth and not give any single film a large number of Oscars.[64] Bookies in Britain had no doubts about the top prize, however. The odds at betting chain Ladbrokes saw the film go from a solid 1–2 favorite when the nominees were announced to an unprecedented 1–12. Five days before the ceremony, a Ladbrokes spokesperson announced, "We have been forced to close the books on the Oscars. Everybody thinks that this is one film to rule them all."[65]

Science-fiction/fantasy buffs were less sanguine, being used to seeing their favorite genres passed over for industry awards, and perhaps simply not wanting to get their hopes up too much. They need not have worried, for as Steven Spielberg said upon opening the envelope to present the final award of the evening, Best Picture, "It's a clean sweep!" The total number of Oscars won by the trilogy was seventeen, though in a less publicized ceremony, the Academy also gave two technical awards to programs and applications developed for the trilogy.[66]

Bob Shaye's supposed gamble was vindicated, and six months later he and Michael Lynne found themselves on the cover of a thick supplement to *Variety,* named as the trade paper's "Showmen of the Year."[67] Shaye's prudent aggression had led to an instant classic and one of the most successful franchises in film history.

CHAPTER 2

———

Not Your Father's Tolkien

Now, our main villain is an eyeball, which you know,
you wouldn't do that if you were making
a James Bond film.

PETER JACKSON

DIRECTOR AND CRITIC PETER BOGDANOVICH has succinctly described what
a lot of people have sensed about recent Hollywood cinema: "You look at
the average, well-made movie of the '30s . . . well, not average, but the good
movies of the '30s: *Trouble in Paradise* or *The Lady Eve* or *The Awful Truth.*
If you look at it today, you'll see that those films were made for adults, but
kids could see them. Whereas today, films are made for kids, and adults are
expected to tolerate them."[1] This is not strictly true, in that there are still
many films made largely for adults, and some outgross many a franchise
blockbuster. *The Sixth Sense* spent years on the top-ten list of the highest-
earning films in markets outside the United States. *A Beautiful Mind*'s domestic gross of $170,742,341 was more than twice that of New Line's next
franchise release after *Fellowship: Blade II,* at $81,676,888. Such films are some-
times less attractive to studios, however, for they are difficult to gauge in terms
of box-office potential. They may be surprise successes, such as *The Full Monty*
and *My Big Fat Greek Wedding,* or they may depend on Academy Award
recognition to boost their earnings, as happened with *Shakespeare in Love* and
A Beautiful Mind. They might also look like sure things but fail to lure audiences. *Cinderella Man* reunited director Ron Howard and star Russell Crowe
and was expected to repeat the success of *A Beautiful Mind*—and yet it did
a fraction of the business. The fact that *Rings* attracted many adults and won
many Oscars, however, should not obscure that it was of necessity aimed pri-

marily at teenage and young-adult audiences. Baby boomers who had kept rereading Tolkien's book were not a substantial audience compared with the numbers of moviegoers needed, and they could probably be assumed to be automatically interested in the film.

Louis Menand's review of *Fellowship* for the *New York Review of Books* suggests as much. Menand read *Rings* at age eleven, in 1963. His memory of the book, he says, "is a residual sense of the lore of Middle Earth, the stories upon stories that the characters and the narrator tell, an elaborate, unfinished saga of another world—erased, by now, of almost all detail. I do not remember *The Lord of the Rings* as a violent book. I remember it as an eleven-year-old's Proust." Menand saw the film with a fourteen-year-old. "I said to him, 'They really made a lot of stuff up for the movie.' He patiently explained to me that everything in the movie is an almost literal recreation of the book." Menand makes a good stab at explaining the generational difference in perception:

> What I had read as a kind of historical novel, he had read as a fantasy adventure. His visual imagination was shaped by a completely different stock of stylistic referents, from *Xena, Warrior Princess* to *Crouching Tiger, Hidden Dragon,* and most of all from the virtual reality of computerized games. Hundreds of orcs swarming up huge pillars in underground caverns, enormous armies flattened by a burst of supernatural light, people being swept up hundreds of feet into the air—these are all the ordinary images of PlayStation, Game Boy, and computer games like Ages of Empires or Diablo II. . . .
>
> Peter Jackson's first cinematic love is horror movies, and *The Fellowship of the Ring* is nearly a horror movie in its intensity. Young kids will be scared. And for kids pushing fifty, there is a lesson about the evolution of the mind's eye over the last thirty-five years that may be a little painful. It's not Proust anymore.[2]

Proust seems an odd comparison. Tolkien, it seems to me, wrote the sort of book Dickens or Scott might have, if he had lived into the late Victorian/early Edwardian period, when fantasy had become more fashionable and created classics like H. G. Wells's *Time Machine* (1895), Bram Stoker's *Dracula* (1897), and Arthur Conan Doyle's *Lost World* (1912). Tolkien has traits in common with Dickens, from the superb descriptions and dialogue to the occasional lapses into cliché and sentimentality. Still, Menand's general point is well-taken. A book about imaginatively conceived characters on a lengthy journey interspersed with skirmishes has been turned into what some might see as a gallery of battles and monsters.

Tolkien was writing his novel in the 1930s and 1940s, the era of films like

The Awful Truth and *The Lady Eve,* a period when, as Bogdanovich says, adult tastes in literature and films largely ruled the mainstream popular-culture market. Jackson's film was made in an age of adolescent tastes, and he has given us a film for the current generation. We shouldn't forget, however, that that generation includes many adults who do not simply "tolerate" such films as *Raiders of the Lost Ark* or *Alien* or *Terminator 2* or *Back to the Future.* They love them.

At first glance, an adaptation of *Rings* would not hold an obvious appeal to either young people or action-film-loving adults. There were two major obstacles to the success of a potential franchise. First, fantasy films were notoriously box-office poison, and there was no way of disguising the fact that *Rings* was a fantasy. (Almost everyone involved in doing publicity for the film downplayed its fantasy elements and emphasized its realism and sense of history, but the press seldom took the hint.) Second, despite Bob Shaye's enthusiasm, Tolkien's fans were not like those of *Superman* and *Batman.* Those superhero comics had originally been aimed at a broad general audience, and many knew them only through television series. The fans of Tolkien's novel were on average better educated and, since many of them had been reading the novel repeatedly since the 1960s, probably on average older. They were also extremely protective of the book, in part through having been burned once by the 1978 Ralph Bakshi version. A significant number of them also had websites and were ready to pounce.

From the beginning, both the filmmakers and the New Line publicity machine adopted a careful policy: start by wooing existing fans and then broaden the campaign to lure those who had never read the books. To a considerable extent, New Line succeeded by launching its official website early and catering initially to lovers of the book. Jackson's team had the harder job. They had to win over the many skeptical fans long before they actually had any footage to demonstrate that they were being true to Tolkien. Then they had to come up with a film that would live up to the hype. There was no option, by the way, of simply writing off the fans as mere cranks and focusing on the general public. New Line's early estimate was that those fans would buy about 25 percent of the tickets.[3] In hindsight that seems like a considerable exaggeration, but the film was made and marketed under that assumption.

In his foreword to *Rings,* Tolkien warned readers against interpreting his novel allegorically: "I much prefer history, true or feigned, with its varied applicability to the thought and experience of readers."[4] The filmmakers seized upon this notion of "feigned history." They set out to re-create what would nowadays be called the "richly realized world" of Middle-earth by treating it realistically and conveying a sense of history. In the richly realized world of modern fiction, especially fantasy, the author depicts the milieu in extensive detail, going far beyond the needs of the plot. If the filmmakers could craft a dense onscreen world that seemed true to Tolkien's novel, they could perhaps win over the fan base. The result would give the fantasy genre its first prestige film, doing for it what *2001* had done for science fiction and *The Godfather* had done for gangster pictures.

A richly realized world was not, however, sufficiently appealing to the much larger audience of non-Tolkien-readers. For them, the narrative was altered and simplified. It took advantage of the novel's many major settings, fantastical creatures, and huge battles, all of which lent themselves to special effects and epic scenes of a sort familiar from blockbusters in various genres.

PRESTIGE AND POPULARITY

Biopics, big-budget historical epics, and film adaptations of literary classics often do not wear well. They tend to be self-consciously respectful and thereby rather cautious—and often stodgy. Hollywood has a long history of prestigious literary adaptations. In the earliest decades of the cinema, Shakespeare plays or Dickens novels would be crammed into a fifteen-minute reel. During the golden age of Hollywood, the wealthier studios delighted in lavish adaptations of the classics. Yet most of these are films that we do not return to watch again with relish. MGM's big, brightly lit films like *Romeo and Juliet* (1936), starring forty-two-year-old Leslie Howard and thirty-five-year-old Norma Shearer as elegant versions of the teenage lovers, or *Pride and Prejudice* (1940), with Laurence Olivier and Greer Garson, today seem stiff and by the numbers.[5]

In contrast, many of the great American films are the unpretentious genre pictures, often adaptations of popular literature: John Ford's canonical Western, *Stagecoach* (1939), which was taken from an obscure short story, "Stage to Lordsburg," or Howard Hawks's hilarious *His Girl Friday* (1940), which was born out of a casual notion that changing one of the two male protagonists of Ben Hecht's and Charles MacArthur's hit play *The Front Page* into a woman might prove amusing. Similarly, Paul Muni made his reputation in biopics of the 1930s and won his Oscar for *The Story of Louis Pasteur* (1936), but he is likely to be remembered primarily for his starring role in Hawks's gangster film *Scarface* (1932).

Genre films are still made, and the divide between them and the prestige product persists. In the years after World War II, foreign-language imports, shown in little, specialized cinemas, convinced many doubters that the movies could be an art form after all. More people went to college after the war, and many came to feel that an educated person should favor artistically important films. Knowing little about the cinema, they have tended to gravitate toward epics, biopics, and adaptations of literature: *Doctor Zhivago, Sense and Sensibility, Patton, Gandhi, Out of Africa,* and *Gladiator.* These *seem* like the sort of thing that one should admire.

Tolkien may still be looked down upon by some for having written mere fantasy, but by the mid-1990s, he was gradually gaining acceptance within the academy as a major novelist—probably because some of those in college at the time of the first really high wave of Tolkien fandom in the 1960s were now tenured and teaching what they liked. The project to film *Rings* seemed to promise a standard-issue big-budget adaptation of a major novel. Casting classical actors and former Oscar nominees like Ian McKellen, Cate Blanchett, and Ian Holm bolstered that impression.

When I walked into a theater to see *Fellowship* for the first time, I went dreading that it would be a drastic departure from the novel and/or turn out to be the very sort of middlebrow film that I usually dislike. To my relief, it was neither. Despite inevitable reservations about some of the changes made in the adaptation, I enjoyed the film. Its adapters had not drained the life out of the book. The first *Harry Potter* film had premiered in the previous month, and reviewers routinely accused it of stiff, bland adherence to J. K. Rowling's novel. In comparison, the popular press found *Fellowship* livelier, more spontaneous, and generally more fun than the competing wizard film.[6]

At first I wondered why I enjoyed watching *Fellowship* even though it was the sort of thing I did not care for: Oscar bait with a literary pedigree. Was it simply because I was a Tolkien fan and, like so many, wanted it to be good? It took me a few more viewings and a bit of pondering on this paradox to realize that Jackson's *Rings is* a popular genre film. Or, rather, it mixes conventions of several popular genres into its overarching fantasy structure: martial arts action, horror, swashbucklers, war, and even hints of Westerns. (The casting of Christopher Lee should have given me a clue.) True, it moves into the elegant, respectful mode at times, primarily in the scenes dealing largely with Elves. Overall, however, it conveys the sense of excitement that the filmmakers felt in making it, the love of the material that Tolkien fans share.

Surely the popular-genre conventions used in *Rings* helped make it into such a broad success, whether or not the filmmakers had planned it that way. Older audiences could watch Legolas swinging heroically on the side of a giant elephant and be reminded of the similar antics of Douglas Fairbanks Sr. or Errol Flynn. (Bob Anderson, who was perhaps Hollywood's leading sword master and had worked with Flynn in the early 1950s, taught Orlando Bloom and the others how to execute movie swordplay.) For younger audiences, the same scene might recall passages of other big action films, like *Spider-Man,* or video games. Perhaps most crucially, like several other directors of his generation, Jackson was inspired by the animated sequences in mythological fantasies by Ray Harryhausen. Using computer-generated imagery in the service of a strong narrative, Jackson could avoid the sorts of risible stories in which Harryhausen's work tended to be embedded. *Rings* has the feel of a film that people who love fantasy, horror, sci-fi, war, and thriller films might make if given $300 million—and apart from sci-fi, elements of all those genres lurk within Tolkien's novel in an understated way.

In interviewing the filmmakers, I hoped to elicit information about influences and how the conventions from these genres got into *Rings*. Unfortunately, the moment I mentioned "popular genre conventions," they seemingly took that as a pejorative term—which was far from how I intended it—and insisted that they had not set out to make a blockbuster and were not deliberately incorporating such conventions into *Rings* to make it appeal to a younger, broader audience. Rather, they had tried to create Tolkien's detailed, historically plausible world on the screen.

My point was, and is, that they had done both. My main disappointment (and perhaps failure) as an interviewer was that in most cases I did not have time to pursue this point and persuade the filmmakers that I admired the energy they infused into the trilogy by drawing on unpretentious genre cinema. Fortunately, in my talks with them, in published or broadcast interviews, and in the DVD commentaries, occasional specific comments make these filmmakers' love for popular cinema spill forth. For example, I talked with Sue Thompson, CEO of The Film Unit, about how *Rings* might be different from the film as it would have been made at Miramax:

KT: [The films] are not obviously prestigious and lofty. They have a popular sense to them as well.

ST: Very much so! They need to. That's what they were made for.

KT: They are popular genre films. They're not *Shakespeare in Love.*

ST: Thank goodness! [Laughs]

After the third part came out, Jackson told an interviewer, "I do think it was the same sensibility that made *Bad Taste* and *Meet the Feebles* and *Braindead* that made *Lord of the Rings*. I'm exactly the same guy as I was 10 or 12 years ago. . . . I could just as easily tomorrow go back and shoot a zombie film, and I'd love to."[7]

Perhaps not all the echoes of popular genre cinema in *Rings* were put there deliberately, but most of these people are fans, and the trilogy reflects their enthusiasm.

KUNG FU ELF, SAMURAI WIZARD

In broadening the appeal of *Rings,* Jackson and company did not willfully and cynically exploit Tolkien's novel. All indications are that this was a labor of love for most of the cast and artisans involved. Those who had never read the book—like actors Viggo Mortensen and Ian McKellen and editor Jamie Selkirk—rapidly became as devoted to the project as those who were fans. The amount of effort, expense, and ingenuity behind the film's design and technical aspects reflects a dedication beyond what could conceivably go into most fantasy franchises. But in striving to realize their vision of the film, its makers could hardly expect to receive backing, let alone the considerable re-sources and creative freedom they wound up with, without recognizing the realities of the current market. They managed to convey something of the complexity of Tolkien's created world while simplifying the narrative and in-corporating modern genre conventions that would appeal to a broad inter-national audience.

Some lovers of the novel, especially within the world of academic liter-ary criticism, have charged the adaptation with betraying the spirit of Tolkien's work. Even those most disappointed by the narrative, however, al-most invariably praise the design. David Bratman's elaborate and erudite cri-tique sums up this attitude: "Each year as I sat in the theatre, I felt as if I were seeing two films at once: one in the visuals, which was faithful and true to Tolkien, and another in the script and the general tone and style, which was so unfaithful as to be a travesty." Bratman and others seem not to real-ize that only a mammoth audience, most of them unfamiliar with the books, would suffice to pay for the epic, detailed design that they so admire.[8] The filmmakers knew that obtaining an adequate budget to bring Middle-earth to the screen with its cultures, landscapes, monsters, and battles portrayed richly and believably would involve making changes that would result in comprehensible, appealing films.

How did they go about that? Most obviously, the films introduce more and longer action scenes. Although Tolkien's *Towers* and *Return* have war scenes that lend themselves to big set pieces, *Fellowship* is limited in such possibilities: the Nazgûls' attack at Weathertop, a brief battle in the Mines of Moria, and Gandalf's fatal confrontation with the Balrog. The Watcher in the Water (the creature in the lake outside the Moria West-gate) and the cave troll appear for two brief paragraphs each; the Watcher grabs Frodo with one tentacle, which Sam chops off before the Fellowship flees into the Mines. The cave troll never actually enters the Chamber of Mazarbul but retreats after Frodo stabs its foot.

These scenes have been considerably expanded, incorporating imagery of horror, action, and fantasy films. Jackson has described this aspect of the film adaptation: "One of the real motivations for me to want to make *The Lord of the Rings* was the monsters. It seems like a strange thing to admit, because obviously the film has a lot more going for it than just monsters. But I've always thought it would be great to do, you know, a fantasy film in that Harryhausen style, but with computer-generated creatures."

Jackson has also remarked on some of the specific creatures. Of the Watcher in the Water he says, "In the book it's not really much more than a tentacle that sort of squirms out of the water and then gets chopped off, and I just wanted this creature to be a little bit more monstery than that." He also refers to drawing upon popular action conventions: "The introduction of the Balrog didn't happen quite in this way, but we just wanted to make a sort of rollicking Indiana Jones–type sequence out of it, really, to have some fun with it."[9] Jackson wanted to set the Shelob sequence off with distinctive music. Because Howard Shore had scored many of David Cronenberg's horror films, Jackson recalls saying to him, "Listen, let's have some of that stuff. This should be like *The Fly*."[10]

The two other films maintain the occasional atmosphere of horror conventions. One clear case comes in the sequence of Théoden's healing. In the book, Théoden remains lucid, but Gríma's treacherous counsel causes him to drift into despair and to waste away. Gandalf "heals" the king through sheer eloquence and force of personality. The film posits more simply that Saruman has possessed Théoden, and Gandalf performs a sort of exorcism. Similarly, in the novel Frodo pauses amid the Dead Marshes and stares, briefly mesmerized by the dead faces beneath the water. In the film he falls forward, and the corpses actively menace him. The Black Riders, Shelob, the Wargriders, and the many types of Orcs and trolls—and even the Jekyll-and-Hyde figure Gollum—also borrow from tropes of horror films. Saruman, here a sort of Dr. Frankenstein figure, is not breeding the Uruk-hai, as in the book, but creating them in a vast workshop, with the treacherous Gríma as his evil assistant. On the *Return* DVD commentary, Richard Taylor comments on the

Army of the Dead, "I thought they had certain overtones toward some of the Italian zombie movies of the 1970s, and that's a good thing in my book."[11]

All this does not imply that *Rings* at times lapses into being an ordinary horror film. A comment in the *Hollywood Reporter* suggests how placing such elements in the context of Tolkien's narrative transformed them: "The exultant creepiness of horror films is Mr. Jackson's instinctive filmmaking style. He exaggerates it here in epic terms, and the grandeur is astonishing."[12]

The filmmakers have linked other recognizable genre conventions to some characters. Barrie Osborne has discussed drawing on a variety of war and martial arts sequences for inspiration: "We had a research assistant compile all the battle sequences you could imagine, from various films, like *Ben-Hur*, *Braveheart*, even kung fu movies, like Woo-ping Yuen's *Once upon a Time in China* (Yuen was the kung fu fight choreographer on *The Matrix*). We used that research to develop different battle styles for the different cultures of Middle-earth." Based on such background material, Tony Woolf, in charge of "cultural fighting styles," devised moves for the stunt performers and for the motion-capture team to use in creating the panoply of gestures given to the digitally generated Massive extras.[13]

The widespread impact of martial arts choreography derived from Japanese and Hong Kong films is reflected in *Rings*' fights and battles, and that fact was emphasized in publicity. Bloom described in a magazine interview how Legolas changed between Films 1 and 2:

> I become Action Elf on this movie. The bow was my signature weapon, but there's also some close combat stuff where I've got these two white knives and I get them wet, you know. Stunt coordinator Bob Anderson honed my fighting skills and I had a great stunt double called Morgan. He taught me most of my routines—showed me some really flashy moves. Most of those stunt people were amazing; black belts in everything.[14]

Many of the stunt performers came from a group that was assembled by Kirk Maxwell, himself a martial arts expert. The Asian influence comes through at Edoras when, deprived of his bow and knives, Legolas proves adept at manual combat, striking a soldier behind him with a kung fu backward punch, one of Bruce Lee's signature tactics (figures 5 and 6).

Perhaps more surprisingly, in *Towers* Gandalf gains traits of both martial artists and superheroes. In the book, there is little change in the Wizard's appearance between his incarnations as the Grey and the White—apart from the admittedly distinctive characteristic of shining from within after his return,

Figure 5. Bruce Lee's double backward punch in *Fist of Fury*.

Figure 6. In *The Two Towers*, Legolas uses the same tactic during a skirmish in the Golden Hall.

a fact that he disguises, as in the film, with a gray cloak. He does not grow younger-looking, and his hair is white from the start. His power is enhanced, but the book gives only sketchy indications as to how or why. The filmmakers clearly wanted to create an obvious physical contrast between the character's Grey and White identities so that audiences would grasp that a profound change had occurred.

In interviews leading up to the release of *Towers,* McKellen almost invariably used the term "samurai" in relation to his transformed character:

> "The turn of the battle of Helm's Deep sees Gandalf commit himself samurai-like to the fray." (*SFX*)
>
> "He's wearing white samurai clothes. He's a commander, not a bumbling one. He is a different character." (*Total Film*)
>
> "He is reborn literally. He is now Gandalf the White, more energetic; he's a commander, a samurai. He's got a job to do and he's not going to be distracted this time." (*Empire*)[15]

A number of commonly used publicity images show Gandalf wielding his staff as if it were a sword or club (as he does during the battles of Films 2 and 3).[16]

In fact Gandalf the White's film image has virtually nothing of the samurai about it. (Samurai attached themselves with unswerving, unquestioning loyalty to a single master, whereas Gandalf strives to unite the peoples and races of Middle-earth.) If Gandalf draws upon any martial arts figure, the white-bearded *sifu* (master) of Chinese martial arts narratives would seem more likely. These characters, often monks, dress all in white, carry carved white staffs, and are mysterious sources of wisdom and great power—though they can be the hero's ally, teaching him or her martial arts, or the ultimate villain to be defeated (figure 7). (Pai Mei in *Kill Bill 2* is a white-bearded *sifu.*) The white-bearded *sifu* is one rare case within action genres where an elderly man is seen as more powerful than his younger opponents, because of his long practice and devotion to his particular brand of martial arts. By contrast, the elderly samurai tends to be a weakened and pathetic figure.

I pointed this resemblance out to Ngila Dickson during our interview. Her response was, "Yeah, in fact, I'm very aware of some of those movies, in the sense that years and years ago when I did *Xena,* we used to look at a lot of these movies. Certainly if it existed anywhere, it would be in a very subliminal corner of my mind, though, because what I was trying to do was, as Ian said, make a younger and more vital version of Gandalf." The White costume, she says, essentially follows the design of the Grey one, but with a re-

Figure 7. A white-bearded master in *Executioners from Shaolin.*

duction in the size of each element to make it more suitable for action. Though such a reference was not intended, filmgoers steeped in martial arts films might well make this connection upon seeing Gandalf the White.

Apart from being a martial arts figure, new imagery also makes Gandalf a sort of geriatric superhero. With Legolas as a kung fu fighter, the Hobbits as humble everyman figures, Gimli as the comic warrior, and Aragorn as the heroic warrior, Gandalf, with his supernatural powers, remains as the most obvious candidate for this role. The opening sequence of *Towers,* showing Gandalf fighting the Balrog as the pair plunge down the abyss below the Bridge of Khazad-dûm, is filmed with rapid movements toward and away from the camera, as well as several horizontal compositions and rapid pans as the two flash past the lens, all suggesting that they are flying as much as falling. Only a few shots are composed with the pair hurtling downward (as in John Howe's vertical painting *Gandalf Falls with the Balrog* [1997] that inspired the sequence). In *Fellowship,* Gandalf is last seen floating downward into darkness on his back, but after his plunge off the bridge in *Towers,* he whizzes down headfirst, catching up first to his sword and then to the Balrog— implying some sort of propulsion beyond gravity (figure 8). In one of the interviews quoted earlier, where McKellen uses the samurai comparison, the author's text invokes another action film of 2002: "'Unlike some action heroes,' [McKellen] chuckles, tickled by the notion of being classified in the same bracket as Vin Diesel [in *XXX*], 'we do see Gandalf off duty. He's still very humane.'"[17] In an early interview, Dickson suggested something of the new Wizard of *Towers:* "[McKellen] wanted a costume that conveyed Gandalf's regained physical prowess and fighting ability. The resulting gown is superhero meets Sporty Spice—a sensible ankle-length gown and robe in heavy-weave ivory cotton embroidered with gold thread."[18]

Perhaps less obviously, *Rings* owes debts to the Western. In speaking of the locations near Poolburn in Central Otago, whose rolling hills and dramatic shale outcroppings depicted Rohan, Jackson has said, "Whenever you can put a camera down, and literally see 50 km in one direction, and have no power poles, no houses, no roads, it's just expanse, it suddenly gives the film that kind of epic John Ford western quality of tiny figures in this big landscape."[19] In the supplements on the *Return* DVD, Jackson remarks on the shot where Shelob is wrapping Frodo in her web, and Sam's hand, holding Sting, comes into the foreground of the shot: "It's like a gunslinger shot, a sort of Clint Eastwood hand slides into the side of frame" (figure 9). Gandalf's sudden appearance during the Rohirrim's apparent suicide charge at Helm's Deep, seen astride his rearing horse on the crest of a ridge and then thundering down at the head of Éomer's band of warriors, irresistibly recalls the cavalry riding to the rescue in a Western.

Certainly the cast and crew did not calculatingly think about incorporating such genre conventions in order to broaden the film's appeal. Indeed, Weta weapons designer Daniel Falconer insists that although he and his colleagues studied Asian martial arts traditions, "It wasn't a design phase that was directed either by a target audience, in a sense, too, in that I personally was certainly never thinking, 'We have to make this appeal to this demographic' or anything like that. It was always very much a design process that was driven by doing something realistic to the subject matter." But clearly these people love popular cinema, including Asian martial arts movies, and are steeped in its conventions. Rather than striving to make *Rings* an "important" film, they made it to appeal to themselves—and thus to the vast numbers of people who share their tastes.

SIMPLIFIED COMPLEXITY

Jackson, Walsh, and Boyens were confronted with the task of telling a single, continuous story across three lengthy parts released at one-year intervals and also shaping each individual part to create a sense of satisfaction in itself. They had to simplify without losing the epic quality and density of the

Figure 8. Gandalf "flying" during the fall with the Balrog in *The Two Towers*.

Figure 9. The "gunslinger" shot as Sam confronts Shelob in *The Return of the King*.

original. They had to make tens, even perhaps hundreds, of millions of spectators who walked out of Film 1 be willing a year later to walk into Film 2, and then to walk out of Film 2 willing to do the same for Film 3. (As it turned out, many of them proved willing to walk in to see each part multiple times.)

Initially, though, in the Miramax period (1997–98), the story would be told across two two-hour features. Those features were not simply a compressed version of the trilogy that eventually got made under New Line. Galadriel and the Elves of Lothlórien, for example, were entirely eliminated. Assuming that a conventional romance was necessary, the scriptwriters wrote scenes between Aragorn and Arwen that spell out their dilemma straightforwardly. Early on they meet by a stream in the woods:

ARWEN: Then share your life with me.

ARAGORN: And have you watch me age and wither and die before your eyes?

ARWEN: You know I would give away my immortality to be with you, to grow old with you.

ARAGORN: Your people raised me as one of their own. I cannot repay them by taking their brightest jewel, their Evenstar!

ARWEN: Did you come here to fill me with despair?

ARAGORN: I came here to try to make you understand! Arwen, you must cross the Sea and dwell with your people in Valinor. It is the way it must be!

ARWEN: My life is with you or I have no life!

ARAGORN: No!

ARWEN: Oh, you stubborn . . . man!

Boyens made it clear to me that the writers hoped they would only have to use this version to find backing for the film:

When we sold these scripts, we sold them on the basis of the classic Hollywood love story [laughs], and we were doing all of those things quite deliberately and quite against our better instincts, because we didn't particularly want to do that. But it was the only way that we saw that we could make these [films]. We definitely had in mind this hope that we would then be able to rework the script back toward the world that Professor Tolkien had created.

Once the project moved to New Line, the writers essentially scrapped the two-part version and started over. They took another eighteen months to create a three-feature script. Now that they were safely into production again, they moved away from the salable Hollywood romance.

Fans who have objected to each and every departure from Tolkien seldom acknowledge that the original novel is convoluted and intermittently difficult to follow. The most devoted readers occasionally need to consult the author's appendixes for clarification, and many also own thick reference volumes. As the films came out, numerous fan magazines tried to help the uninitiated get up to speed on Tolkien's world.[20] To a nonreader, the film was potentially confusing. As Boyens explained, "It involved very careful handling of the language and the endless string of weird names. I was afraid it could become a geek movie, solely and exclusively for people who read it 20 times!"[21] Jackson suggests how the writers strove to balance fans and novices: "We sort of had this rule of thumb that we were writing it for the people who had read it ten years ago, not ten months ago."[22] Thus fans would recognize the book's overall shape, with the most memorable scenes, but they would not be catered to to the point of mystifying others.

Inevitably there were changes. Boyens remarked,

> I would hope the fans would understand what we were trying to do. You can't not make a decision that you thought was right for the film because you were terrified of what the fans would say. You just hoped that they would understand. We really didn't try to change things for the sake of it. It was always driven by the necessity of telling this story on film and shaping it for film.[23]

Some fans did accept that. Others were not so forgiving. Rumors of moments in the film that differed from the book circulated for years on the Internet. One fan, Ancalagon the Black (named after Middle-earth's most powerful dragon), undertook the acerbically entertaining "A Complete List of Film Changes." Ancalagon gleaned these from a wide variety of sources, described them, suggested the possible pros of the change, and concluded with a con, occasionally a specific comment but usually the generic: "This change is an invention of the filmmakers and does not represent Tolkien's work or characters" (figure 10).[24]

Even fans of the books who largely took the film to their hearts were vociferous in their complaints about certain changes. In the book, Faramir is completely admirable, telling Frodo of the Ring, "I would not take this thing, if it lay by the highway." In the film he becomes threatening and tries to take the Ring, though ultimately he relents. Elves come to fight side by side with the Rohirrim at Helm's Deep, when no such thing happens in the novel. Ar-

Figure 10. *Fox Trot,* 8 February 2001. (*Fox Trot* © 2001 Bill Amend. Reprinted with permission of Universal Press Syndicate.)

wen plays a major role in the film, while she barely appears in the body of the novel (though there is extensive material about her in Appendix A, which the filmmakers used). During the entry into Mordor, Frodo sends Sam home, but in the book they remain together until separated by accident in Shelob's dark lair. Two new characters are added or expanded: Lurtz, the leader of the Uruk-hai band that attacks the Fellowship in Film 1, and Gothmog, the deformed leader of Sauron's forces in Film 3.

To many these seemed like willful changes. In some cases the writers explained specific decisions in interviews, although often in publications where fans would not see them. Such explanations show that, whether or not one agrees with the changes, they resulted from deliberate, reasoned decisions. Responding to a question concerning Faramir, Jackson said of the character's declaration that he would not take the Ring:

> For us, as filmmakers, that sort of thing creates a bit of a problem because we've spent a lot of time in the last film and in this one [*Towers*] to establish this ring as incredibly powerful. Then to suddenly come to a character that says, "Oh, I'm not interested in that," to suddenly go against everything that we've established ourselves is sort of going against our own rules. We certainly acknowledge that Faramir should not do what Boromir did and that he ultimately has the strength to say, "No, you go on your way and I understand." We wanted to make it slightly harder, to have a little more tension than there was in the book. But that's where that sort of decision comes from.[25]

Jackson and Boyens have given similar explanations for the other changes that I have mentioned.[26]

I asked Boyens about some other changes that I had not seen discussed in previous interviews. She cheerfully proffered explanations in each case.

KT: Why have Elrond show up bringing Anduril to Aragorn in Rohan rather than him taking it with him from the beginning and Elrond staying home?

PB: Sure. Aragorn has the shards of Narsil right from the beginning [i.e., in the novel], and the sword is reforged very early on. The problem with that is, it doesn't get *used*, really, symbolically for ages. It gets buried. You can't, in good storytelling, forge a sword in the first film and then bring it back into play. Always if you can embed an event in character and make it, as we did—hopefully—a decision Elrond must make, to reforge that sword, it carries more dramatic tension. It gives more psychological depth to this symbol. So we decided that the forging of the sword and the giving of the sword to Aragorn would go into the moment when it would be most symbolic for him to use it, which would be the Paths of the Dead. And also what it would mean for him to receive [it].

The reason we chose Elrond was because he does send his sons to Aragorn [in the novel], and we couldn't do that, just could *not* introduce the two characters that we really hadn't had time to establish and the audience really wouldn't give a toss about. So we decided to honor the intention of Tolkien there and have Elrond confront him with the prospect—as he does, really [in the book], by sending word, "Remember the Paths of the Dead, if you need haste, remember the Paths of the Dead." He is the one who prompts Aragorn in the book, so we just took it further and made it a much more interesting, I think, conflict and choice for Aragorn. We also wanted to add someone to bring news that Arwen was failing, that her fate is tied to that of the Ring.

At the end of the Warg-rider skirmish in *Towers,* Aragorn falls over a cliff and is presumed by the others to be dead. The episode is not in the book at all, but according to Boyens,

> We needed to separate him from his peers, because we wanted him to be the one to deliver the news [of the approaching Orc army], because we needed a conflict to drive Helm's Deep. We chose the conflict to be the two most interesting characters at Helm's Deep, which we decided were Aragorn and Théoden, the two who could come head-to-head.
>
> We also thought there would be a huge payoff in the third film, when Théoden rides to the aid of Gondor. So we needed to set up this defeat, in a way, for Théoden: that it is Aragorn who saves them at Helm's Deep.
>
> We also needed a moment of connection with Arwen, which we wanted to

be alone. We wanted her to almost call him back. We wanted to do all of these things, but it had to be done in a filmic way.

I also asked why, when in the book the Army of the Dead only help Aragorn seize the Corsair ships, in the film they travel to participate in the Battle of the Pelennor. To Boyens, the crucial function of the Paths of the Dead sequence is for Aragorn to wield the reforged sword, proving himself to be the rightful heir to Gondor's throne. Beyond that, however, "Now, yes, take over the pirate ships, but that would have been kind of limp and lame. OK, he's taken out the pirate ships, so that's fine, Minas Tirith is safe. It's not dynamic storytelling. So it's all to do with dynamic storytelling. Also, you bring out your big storytelling guns, and driving from a big, huge climax like Pelennor Fields, all elements of the storytelling have to be engaged at that point."

I suspect that we could have gone on all day, and Boyens would be able clearly to explain every single alteration made in the narratives. Probably no fan will ever accept all such justifications and become completely reconciled to every difference. Still, with all the complaining over the changes that fans disliked, far less has been said about other changes that arguably improve upon the book. My own opinion is that the elimination of Tom Bombadil was all to the good, since his character seems not to fit into Middle-earth (and indeed he originated in some early poems of Tolkien's). Beyond that, Boromir's character is more touching and complex than in the book, where he has little to do between the Council of Elrond and the moment when he tries to take the Ring. Certainly his death scene is distinctly more dramatic and moving than in the novel.

The film's realization of the Paths of the Dead episode improves upon the comparable material in the book—where, in order to preserve the surprise of Aragorn's appearance in the Corsair ships, Tolkien has much of the episode told in flashback after the battle's end. Even little touches, like Gandalf blowing smoke in the shape of a boat, can improve on the book. In the novel the Wizard's smoke manifests its magic by flying about, chasing other smoke rings, changing colors, and so on, but such effects would take a long time to play out. When we see Gandalf blow the smoke shape, we immediately sense for the first time his magical nature, and the moment creates a motif linking to the Grey Havens scene at the end. (The smoke-boat derives from the novel's description of one of Gandalf's fireworks at Bilbo's party.) Perhaps most strikingly, the extraordinary beacons sequence develops a minor moment from the novel into one of the film's highlights, with swooping helicopter shots over the White Mountains and equally soaring music.

Despite the changes, the writers left untouched some of the aspects of the book that most Hollywood studios would object to. The result is a mildly unconventional film by classical standards. For example, Boyens comments on how in dealing with the romance, they wanted to adhere more to the Norse legends that had inspired Tolkien: "We wanted to keep [Aragorn] and Arwen apart, as Tolkien did, because that was actually much truer to that sensibility of saga storytelling, and we thought it would be very interesting to see if we could actually break that genre and actually tell a love story with two people who must endure a separation, that it could be a more mature love story."

The narrative has other unconventional qualities. "Nine characters on a quest? If you were starting from scratch, you wouldn't do it," Boyens remarked to an interviewer.[27] Screenplay manuals say that a film should have three to five main characters or, in an ensemble film like *The Big Chill,* seven or eight significant characters.[28] The Fellowship members alone exceed that number. In interviews, the screenwriters sometimes point out that they had to introduce and help the audience remember a remarkable number of significant characters—twenty-two, by their count. I think they underestimated. There are twenty-three central or quite significant characters in the film: Frodo, Sam, Merry, Pippin, Bilbo, Gandalf, Saruman, Legolas, Elrond, Arwen, Galadriel, Aragorn, Théoden, Éowyn, Éomer, Gríma, Boromir, Faramir, Denethor, Gimli, Treebeard, Gollum, and Sauron. If we include smaller roles that require recognition from one scene to another, such characters as Gamling, Haldir, Gothmog, and the Witch King deserve mention. Apart from Bombadil, few characters of any note have been eliminated altogether. The number of characters is roughly the same as in Robert Altman's *Nashville* (1975), which is widely considered innovative in its juggling of such a large ensemble. Although *Nashville* creates fewer links among the characters than does *Rings,* it has a single overall setting as a unifying factor. In *Rings,* cutting among the events pertaining to each major character or group gradually becomes more of a juggling act as the Fellowship breaks up and pursues separate paths.[29]

Most traditional Hollywood films use considerable redundancy to make sure that as many of the audience members as possible will be able to grasp names, temporal relations, and plot points. Usually any important information will be given more than once, and often three times. With *Rings,* as a result of the condensation of an extremely long book, there is little time for redundancy—a redundancy that the large number of characters and the quickly shifting locales seem to call for. There is some, of course. We are told many times that Frodo must throw the Ring in the fire, that Sauron is evil, that Orcs will attack Helm's Deep, that Sauron's armies will attack Minas Tirith, and so forth.

In contrast, though, there are important plot points that are given only once, and sometimes briefly at that. In Fangorn Forest there are only fleeting indications that Treebeard has taken Pippin and Merry to see Gandalf the White and at the Wizard's bidding has agreed to harbor them. Similarly, at the Prancing Pony inn, there is barely a clue that Aragorn is a friend of Gandalf's. He says quietly at one point, "You can no longer wait for the Wizard, Frodo," but there is no indication, as there is in the book, that Gandalf has specifically told Aragorn to meet him and the Hobbits at the Pony. Once out of Bree, Merry asks Frodo how they can be sure that Aragorn is Gandalf's friend, so at some point in between he must have told them he is. Knowing the novel is some help, of course, but since incidents like Treebeard taking Merry and Pippin to see Gandalf the White in Fangorn Forest are not included in the book, the veteran fan is sometimes no better off than any other viewer.

The alternative, taking the time to introduce plot information and then repeat it redundantly, would have meant cutting even more of the novel's action. Jackson's team opted to depend on the film's spectators to make the effort to follow along. The same impulse is evident in the decision not to include summary scenes or a crawl title at the beginnings of Films 2 and 3. New Line was in favor of such introductions, but Jackson was not, and as so often happened with this project, he got his way.[30]

Many of these changes upset some fans of the books—though my impression is that the majority of the others accepted the film as entertaining and the changes as simply creating another version of the same basic story. Indeed, over and over in explaining why he made decisions to include something, Jackson says it was because he thought it would be "fun." In the director's commentary track for *Return,* he tells why he ended up not using footage that he had shot of what happened later to the other characters—Legolas, Faramir, and so on:

> I thought the film played fine. The scenes that have gone in are the scenes that I just thought would be fun to have in, and fun is actually the word. Not because they need to be in to make the film better, because sometimes putting them in can make the film worse. But those are not the reasons why. The reasons why is that they're just fun to have in, and the scenes that I don't think are particularly fun to put in, I don't put in. Actually fun is the best way to describe it. I don't make any decisions any deeper than that, really.[31]

It's hard to imagine John Ford using that justification for what he put into "a job of work." Howard Hawks or Steven Spielberg might occasionally talk about wanting to make a scene fun, but they would not be so insistent on it. And whatever one might think of fun as a principle guiding aesthetic decisions, Jackson clearly is in tune with the popular audience. Take the scene of Legolas killing the *mûmak*, which Jackson added because in the first two parts audiences had responded so well to the "action Elf" bits. On the postproduction commentary track, associate editor Annie Collins remarks, "That scene—kind of cheesy. I mean, people just love it in the theaters," and Selkirk responds, "One of their favorite sequences."[32]

The immense enthusiasm evidenced by millions unfamiliar with the book proves that the filmmakers managed to balance pleasing fans and winning a vast new audience for Tolkien's story. Moreover, the fact that so many members of that new audience reacted to the film much as readers did upon discovering the novel in the 1960s suggests that however much the filmmakers may have altered the plot and characters, they have retained much of the spirit and ideas of the original.

So, is Peter Bogdanovich right in saying that movies are made for kids these days, with adults tolerating them because they have nothing else to watch? Not exactly. In modern Hollywood, some films are marketed to niche audiences. In the 1930s and 1940s there was much less targeting of specific segments of the audience. Boys and men might go to double features of B Westerns and other genre films, but most A films were aimed at a family audience.

Today a film aimed primarily at young people can be profitable largely because slasher films, teen comedies, and parodies like *Scream 4* tend to be inexpensive to make. A gross of $40 million looks good on a $10 million investment, but teenagers alone cannot provide a hit when a film costs $150 million. Most of the highest-grossing films of recent decades are aimed at both adults and children, that same family audience that has been around since nearly the beginning of movies.[33] "Children's" films like *The Incredibles* and *Shrek* take care to include humor that adults will appreciate. Franchise films have to aim at the broadest possible audience, and they can't do that by appealing primarily to children. As of April 2006, the fifty films with the highest domestic grosses include only four rated R (*The Passion of the Christ, The Matrix Reloaded, Beverly Hills Cop,* and *The Exorcist*). The target rating in most cases is PG-13, implying a general audience that includes all but small children. Is *Raiders of the Lost Ark* really pitched at a different level than the Errol Flynn vehicle *The Adventures of Robin Hood* (1939)? The people who went to *Rings* were corporate Hollywood's ideal audience: just about everybody.

CHAPTER 3

Handcrafting a Blockbuster

> I guess the way that we tried to hint at the depth,
> which is all that the film could really do,
> was partly the design process.
>
> PETER JACKSON

THE TRILOGY EVOKED POPULAR GENRE conventions to make a broadly appealing film, and it simplified the narrative to aid those unfamiliar with Tolkien's novel. In compensation, cinematic technique offered ways of preserving a sense of the complexity of the original. In particular, the film's dense visual and aural design—some might say "overdesign"—portrays a richly realized world. Fans who might object to some of the liberties taken with the story could be consoled by the fact that the physical world described so extensively in the novel was created in rich detail up on the screen.

CONTROL GEEKS

The methods Jackson's team used to create Middle-earth on film were unconventional by Hollywood standards. The quality of the materials was unusually high, and specialist artisan labor was used, driving up costs. Jackson's habit of frequently changing the script on short notice and making decisions during shooting meant that sets and props could not be planned for in an economical way.

Basically Jackson and his team were working much as they had on previous films, all of which, except *The Frighteners,* were low-budget independent movies. Now they applied those methods, some of them very casual, to an expensive event film. *Rings* is in fact an independent film, but it is one made by one of the largest independent producing firms, New Line. It seems very likely that if the company had supervised the making of the trilogy closely, it would have pressured the filmmakers to cut costs.

No doubt realizing this, Jackson was determined to have the production entirely under his control in New Zealand. In Wellington, Jackson and his partners Richard Taylor and Jamie Selkirk owned companies that would handle every filmmaking task from pre- to postproduction: Weta Workshop for the design elements, Weta Digital for the computer-generated imagery, the Stone Street Studios for the actual filming, and The Film Unit for processing, sound mixing, and editing. The vast majority of the production staff were Kiwis, and most of the heads of departments had worked for Jackson before, in some cases from his first features on, and they were (and are) deeply loyal to him. They also knew his working methods.

Agent Ken Kamins recalls one telling aspect of the original negotiations to make the film at Miramax. Jackson made it clear that he did not want to have Saul Zaentz as a producer on the film. According to Kamins:

> It's not Peter's way. He didn't want a producer sitting over his shoulder. In fact, I remember quite vividly Peter's concern when we were in these discussions with Harvey, because there was a story about *The English Patient* in *The New York Times*. There was a photograph, and it was a photograph of [Anthony] Minghella looking into a playback monitor on set, with Saul leaning over his shoulder and looking at the same image. Now, producers do that all the time, and actors do that all the time. Everyone looks at the playback monitor. But there was something about that particular image that Peter found a little scary. He just was concerned that if Saul were in fact a producer on the movie, that he'd be living with Saul leaning over his shoulder the whole time.

Jackson was assured that that would not happen, and the deal went forward.

The supervisory link between New Line and Jackson's team was Mark Ordesky, one of the executive producers. Ordesky was very different from Zaentz. At the time of the turnaround deal, Zaentz was seventy-seven and one of Hollywood's elder statesmen. Ordesky was thirty-five. He was a former Dungeons and Dragons addict, a longtime Tolkien fan, and an admirer of Jackson since *Bad Taste* (1988); he had worked with Jackson in trying to develop the *Nightmare on Elm Street* script. By acquiring such films as *Shine*, *Once Were Warriors,* and *Rumble in the Bronx* for New Line, he had picked up considerable experience in the Pacific Rim area, and so he went into this project knowing the working methods in Australia and New Zealand. Ordesky has described his work on *Rings* as acting as a "translator" between New Line executives and Jackson: "Most of it for me, personally, was simply making sure that everyone, from New Line to our overseas partners, to our licensees, etc., understood what we were doing and to keep everyone's fears in check."[1] There's no mention here of trying to explain to Jackson what New Line would have liked him to do, and the "we" consists of Ordesky and the filmmakers. Osborne confirms this role as "translator": "We had a great supporter in Mark Ordesky, who was very much an advocate for the film, and he was in many ways the point person, who would explain what our intentions were to New Line and win Bob Shaye and Michael Lynne over to what our plans were."[2] Whatever bothered Jackson about that photo of Zaentz hovering over Minghella, he clearly didn't see it in Ordesky.

BY FANS, FOR FANS

In the scene in *Return* where Pippin steals the *palantír* from Gandalf during the night, a brief bit of business involves him slipping a round jug of roughly the same size under the Wizard's arm (figure 11). In the actors' commentary on the extended DVD of *Return,* Billy Boyd talks about his suggesting that substitution during the filming. He calls it "the Harrison Ford thing," referring to the opening of *Raiders of the Lost Ark,* where Indiana Jones tries to avoid tripping a booby trap by replacing an ancient idol with a bag of sand:

> I said to Pete, "You know what I'd love to do? I'd love to do, what do you call it, 'the Harrison Ford thing.'" So I said, "Why don't I get the jug and put the jug there?" And he said, "Oh, you can't, because it's the wrong scale. It's not Hobbit-scale." And then this guy from the back went, "Uh, actually we have it made in Hobbit-scale as well." There was never anything in the script or us talking to anyone that we were going to use that or that anyone was going to lift it up, but they had made it in two scales, just in case.[3]

I'm sure props get made "just in case" on many productions, but for *Rings* it must have happened a lot more often than usual.

Jackson's working methods make it very difficult to carefully plan ahead in the way that one might expect on a major production of this sort. I have said that the film was essentially overdesigned. Indeed, several aspects were overdone. Philippa Boyens has said that the script was far too long because she and Jackson and Fran Walsh had no real idea of how much material was

Figure 11. One of two jugs made for the *palantír* scene from *The Return of the King*.

needed. This excess length means that it was difficult to prepare the sets, props, and costumes with the sort of efficiency that Hollywood loves. Some objects were never used or were used in scenes that ended up on the cutting-room floor. Actors were encouraged to make suggestions on set, as Boyd did for the scene with the jug, thus encouraging the design departments to make extra props. Since Jackson treats the storyboards rather cavalierly, designers could not predict which of the objects that did get used would be close enough to the camera to be clearly visible onscreen.[4]

From early on Jackson used a very fluid approach to filmmaking. The scriptwriters were notorious for making frequent changes in the dialogue and handing the new material to the actors ten minutes before filming. The production staff on-set was organized in such a way as to allow for these changes. Production designer Grant Major has described how the approach differed from that used in Hollywood. Each of the filming units had its own standby art department crew with a standby art director, checking the set dressing and props. That is not unusual, but Major adds,

> Our structure is a little bit different from the way that they do things in America. We have a standby art director who answers to Peter Jackson. So whenever Peter wants some alteration or whenever an actor wants to have something specifically done on the day, that goes through the art director, who then

wrangles the on-set set dressers or the standby props or the standby greens people, and so on and so forth. . . . That's part of Peter's style of doing things, where he'd be kind of inventive on the day.[5]

The same was true of the costume department. Asked during a Los Angeles press junket just before the premiere of *Return* how many of the costumes which she had designed had remained unseen by the camera, costume designer Ngila Dickson responded:

> I think the reality is that both Richard [Taylor] and I are aware that you don't know what the hell Peter's going to do next. So the answer to that is be prepared for everything. And part of that is to be prepared for someone to say all of a sudden—Peter will say, "Well, no, take that armor off" or "Take that top off and we'll do something where you look a lot more relaxed." If you haven't made that whole under-part of the costume work, then you're standing there going, "Um . . . " One thing that none of us ever wanted to do was say no to Peter.[6]

The improvisatory, let's-try-it-this-way approach smacks more of small, independent filmmaking, but in the end it worked just as well on one of Hollywood's most ambitious projects. The filmmakers were vindicated, for the design helped win over skeptical fans and impressed many more who had never read about Middle-earth.

For much of the production, New Line would have known relatively little about all this. Jackson was not forthcoming about what he was doing. Selkirk recalls: "We didn't show anything to New Line for a long time, and I know they were getting concerned. We sent the dailies over. They saw the dailies—that's all they saw." Dailies—each day's shots just as they come out of the camera—consisted primarily of multiple takes of actors in New Zealand landscapes or in front of blue screens. No special effects, no music, and no backgrounds in many cases. For the most part, information beyond that had to depend on Ordesky and a few visits by New Line's copresident, Bob Shaye (figure 12). Amazingly enough, the first view that Shaye and others had of a significant amount of finished footage—particularly special-effects footage—was the Cannes preview reel put together in early 2001.

Inevitably the filmmakers' eccentric approach and the studio's concerns led to tension and conflict. Jackson has been frank about this period. New Line, in his opinion, was "used to making much smaller-budget films, and very American-type films, I would say, and then here we are, these fairly oddball

Figure 12. Bob Shaye (right) with Ian Holm and Ian McKellen at a birthday party held for Shaye on 3 March 2000, during one of his visits to Wellington. (Photograph © Keith Stern, courtesy McKellen.com.)

New Zealand filmmakers making the biggest film they had ever done, and trying to give it an English sensibility." He recalls the period of the filmmaking as tense, with "some quite nasty sparring between lawyers. New Line were slowly becoming aware of what was at stake. The budget of the film was going up as the special effects got more and more complicated and the scope of the films kind of expanded beyond what they thought it was going to be." Jackson adds that after the success of *Fellowship,* "It has sort of settled over the last two years, into a period of grudging respect between us, and I certainly respect the freedom that they have given me and am appreciative of that."[7]

The great geographic distance between the filmmakers and New Line cushioned the workings of the production from such tensions. Ian McKellen recalls, "Actually, the day-to-day working of the film was not interrupted for most of us by any division that there might have been in temperament or style or policy between the artists and the financial interests—because after all, we were divided by thousands and thousands of miles."

New Line's awareness of growing costs echoes what happened in early 1998, when Miramax got concerned about the expanding budget. Unlike Miramax, however, New Line stayed the course. Osborne comments, "The bottom line for them is whatever else might be said, they continued to support the film throughout the whole journey, and it was not an easy journey. They never really pulled any curve balls in making the films. When we needed more support financially, they were always there. We could always get their support. Not always happily, but they were always there." Coproducer Rick Porras confirms:

> They were definitely worried, and there was friction off and on throughout the making of the films, no doubt about it. But compared to other studios, they definitely had a tradition of giving more room to the filmmaker. They would respond to stuff, but Peter always had a lot of leeway to approach the way he wanted to. Sure, they would argue and butt heads at times, but I feel like in the end, Peter was able to persevere and get there on issues.

An incident that occurred near the end of principal photography demonstrates how the loyalty of Jackson's team also gave him considerable control. On 16 December 2000, New Line's president of domestic theatrical marketing, Joe Nimziki, met with the director concerning the *Rings* publicity campaign. One of his purposes in visiting Wellington was to meet the cast, who would be involved in the upcoming press junkets, parties, and premieres. The occasion soured when the filmmakers and actors saw the proposed poster design. Based on its audience research, New Line had concluded that *Rings* would appeal primarily to teenage boys, and the design was busy and garish. The actors backed Jackson up, threatening not to participate in the marketing campaign if it proceeded along those lines. Jackson had a mock-up poster made, featuring muted tones and a simple design centered on an image of the One Ring. The design was not used, but it gave New Line a sense of what the filmmakers considered appropriate.

The poster problem reflects the learning curve that New Line went through concerning *Rings*. Clearly at this stage the studio still saw the trilogy as a conventional franchise blockbuster and was conceiving the marketing as if *Rings* were parallel, as Shaye had thought, to *Batman* or *Superman*. Such incidents as the publicity disagreement seem to have led the studio to realize that this was a more prestigious franchise. Nimziki left New Line the following May and was replaced by Russell Schwartz, president of USA Films. The previous experience of the two men seems to reflect New Line's change of approach. Nimziki had been hired in 1999 and handled campaigns for *Rush Hour 2, The Cell, Final Destination,* and *Next Friday,* the standard genre fare that was New Line's specialty. Schwartz, in contrast, had helped launch films such as *Four Weddings and a Funeral, Fargo, My Left Foot,* and *Cinema Paradiso*. In announcing the change, president of worldwide distribution and marketing Rolf Mittweg described Schwartz as "an industry innovator and leader who is equally savvy juggling mainstream blockbusters and sophisticated arthouse projects. Moving forward, New Line has one of the most prestigious slates in its history."[8] The filmmakers were pleased with the publicity campaign that Schwartz ran, and the cast willingly participated in junkets and other special events.

In general, Jackson's perseverance was noted within the industry. In 2004, special-effects legend Stan Winston was asked about the fact that studios were increasingly making artistic decisions about films and imposing them on directors. Winston replied,

> Part of being a director is knowing how to deal with all of those people, knowing the right battles to fight. . . . Studio execs are always breathing down your neck, wanting to watch the budget, wanting to put in stuff. You fight the battles. It doesn't kill a good movie to have a really big effect—so the studio wants the effect in there? Fine. It doesn't mean that you have to surround it with a stupid scene, bad writing and bad acting. No, I don't blame the sorry state of movies on producers or on the studios. I blame it on directors who aren't tough enough to do what Peter Jackson did, what Jim Cameron did.[9]

One area of agreement between filmmakers and studio was that no test screenings would be held for any of the three films. Most significant Hollywood films are tested on audiences before the final cut. Considerable reworking, especially of endings, may follow such tests. Early on, it had been assumed that *Rings* would be tested as usual. Eventually decision makers worried that such screenings might result in images from the film appearing on the Internet. According to a managing director of Online Testing Exchange, a major Hollywood market research firm, too much is at stake for blockbusters like *Rings* and *Star Wars* from the potential for piracy and negative buzz created by fan website reviewers infiltrating the audience.[10] Instead, in June 2001, the month after the Cannes preview, Shaye flew to Wellington to view a rough cut of *Fellowship* and pronounced himself satisfied. As Jackson later put it, Shaye was the only test audience the film ever had.

I've discussed how Jackson and company got a great deal of control over the project, as well as some of what they did with that control. The question remains, Why did they want to make the film in this way? Obviously they poured an enormous amount of energy, time, and enthusiasm into their work on the film, distinctly beyond what would have been necessary. Here we must confront the geek factor.

A large percentage of the people working on the film were great fans of the book. Art director Dan Hennah had read it regularly since childhood. Fran Walsh suggested that her friend Philippa Boyens be brought in as a cowriter because she was a longtime Tolkien devotee. Viggo Mortensen had never read the book, but when he was preparing to turn down the role of Aragorn, his son, a Tolkien fan, insisted that he take it. As I was conducting the interviews for this book, it was relatively rare to find someone who had not read the novel well before starting work on the film.

Jackson and his fellow writers frequently emphasized in interviews or on the Internet that they were movie fans making movies for other fans. Jackson went on Ain't It Cool News and New Line's official site to connect with fans and make them feel part of the filmmaking process. In some ways, the writers didn't have to consciously aim these films at the typical teenage or young adult fan—they were those fans, or their kids were. When I asked Boyens about elements of popular genre filmmaking in *Rings,* she replied, "I think that there were certain conventions that began to slip in there, certainly in the latter two films, because the story could encompass them, and there were certain points at which I think we were playing to our children and what we knew our children would love to see. And they're certainly children brought up on a lot of those exciting, edge-of-your-seat action films." I also asked whether the martial-arts aspect of Legolas's character had been in the script. Boyens said it had not been intended, but "having said that, [Jackson] does love John Woo and things like that, but it wasn't a conscious thing. I think it got more conscious, like Legolas with the *oliphant,* killing the *mûmakil.* That was definitely one for the kids. One for Billy Jackson, I suspect." (That scene was not added to the film until the pickups during 2003.)

Jackson and Taylor are not just fans but downright movie geeks. They and many of the employees of Weta Workshop are avid model makers, and they collect action toys and movie memorabilia. If you walk into the offices of Wingnut Films, the first thing that confronts you is a pair of mannequins wearing original space suits from the first *Planet of the Apes,* reflecting Jackson's avid love of film collectibles. The first time I visited Weta Workshop to interview Taylor, he delightedly showed me a beautifully preserved, very impressive statue of a film superhero from the 1940s or 1950s (I have no idea which) that he had mail-ordered and just received. The second time I interviewed him, more than a year later, the New Zealand dollar had strengthened. Although this was bad for luring potential business in from the United States, Taylor commented, "It's great for all of our hobbies. Everyone in the Workshop has gone mad buying off Amazon! I can buy my resin-model kits and things now, because they're affordable." In a sense, these people made *Rings* by playing around with hundreds of millions of someone else's dollars, doing on a grand scale what they loved doing for fun. Of course they intended, as Jackson frequently emphasized, to make money for New Line—but they did it the way they wanted to.

Film historian David Bordwell has suggested that modern cinema has developed an approach called "worldbuilding," where filmmakers aim to create "a rich, fully furnished ambience for the action." He traces the trend back to *2001: A Space Odyssey* (1968), with its futuristic real brand-name props and its depiction of the mundane logistics of jogging or losing a pen in a weightless environment. *Alien* (1979) took the idea further by depicting meals and equipment malfunctions in an aging, grungy spaceship. *Blade Runner* (1982), *All the President's Men* (1976), and *Gladiator* (2000) all share a propensity to jam settings with detail, all to create authenticity, fantastical or historical.[11]

The *Star Wars* and *Star Trek* sagas, however, pushed the concept of building complex worlds from scratch even further. The *Star Trek* universe spanned multiple television series, films, and books, and George Lucas published a comic book and a novelization of *Star Wars* before the first film was released. Franchises lend themselves to worldmaking, since the length of the storytelling and the breadth of the ancillaries offer the possibility of exploring the created world in a more leisurely fashion than is ordinarily possible.

The Middle-earth created in Tolkien's novel is perhaps the epitome of a richly realized world. Across a book of about a thousand pages, Tolkien could be remarkably precise in laying out the various races, cultures, and locales of the continent. As a signal officer in World War I, Tolkien had training in mapmaking, and he designed a map of Middle-earth for inclusion as a foldout in the novel. He wrote a volume of appendixes providing historical background for the main races and cultures in the novel. Allen & Unwin insisted that he reduce these considerably to fit at the back of the third volume. Even in truncated form, the appendixes include chronologies; family trees for the main Hobbits; brief histories of Gondor, Rohan, and the Dwarves; and an obsessively complex explication of calendars. One of the appendixes fills in the backstory and future of Aragorn and Arwen's relationship; that tale was used in the film to expand her role.

In the main text, Tolkien drops in names of fictional trees and plants, and his descriptions of landscapes are among his greatest strengths as a writer. He famously created languages for the various peoples, Sindarin being what is spoken by the Elves in the film. As a historian of real languages, Tolkien could not let it go at that, and he also invented Quenya, the Elvish equivalent of Latin, from which Sindarin derived. There are scraps of Khuzdul (Dwarvish), Orcish, Entish, and the Black Speech of Mordor in the book.

The novel is presented as an ancient document written by the Hobbits, and Tolkien purports to be merely its translator. After the novel was published in the mid-1950s, Tolkien treated his invented world as a topic for historical study, writing extensive drafts explaining more about the Wizards, the characters' names, the background of Galadriel and Celeborn, and so on, all presented as if they were further translations or his own scholarly research concerning a real place. And there was a demand for it. Fans often mailed him questions. Tolkien's reply to one of them explained why an adequate supplementary volume would be impossible:

> But the problems . . . which the extra volume will set, will seem clear if I tell you that while many like you demand *maps,* others wish for geological indications rather than places; many want Elvish grammars, phonologies, and specimens; some want metrics and prosodies—not only of the brief Elvish specimens, but of the "translated" verses in less familiar modes, such as those written in the strictest form of Anglo-Saxon alliterative verse. . . . Musicians want tunes, and musical notation; archaeologists want ceramics and metallurgy. Botanists want a more accurate description of the *mallorn,* of *elanor, niphraedil, alfirin, mallos,* and *symbelmynë;* and historians want more details about the social and political structure of Gondor; general enquirers want more information about the Wainriders, the Harad, Dwarvish origins, the Dead Men, the Beornings, and the missing two wizards (out of five). It will be a big volume, even if I attend only to the things revealed to my limited understanding![12]

Apart from his unfinished essays on his created world, Tolkien drew Middle-earthian plants, textiles, and heraldic designs.[13] He left multiple versions of drafts (published posthumously) recounting the entire history of his mythological world, Arda, the planet on which Middle-earth is a continent. Numerous reference volumes appeared to help readers sort out the saga. Many fans take this sort of thing *very* seriously and study Tolkien's richly realized world with nearly as much devotion as he did.

The filmmakers essentially determined to approach the film in the same way. One of the commonest statements in interviews about *Rings* is that they considered the story to be history rather than fantasy. Taylor puts it this way: "A good point is, if you start from the fantastical, the actor is always demanded to wink at the audience—'Just buy into this, just go along with it'—where if you start off at the *total* reality, the audience can begin to accept the fantastical as it builds around them."

Tolkien was stymied in his attempts to provide enthusiastic fans with the multifarious "research" they wanted him to do about his invented world. He had to continue teaching at Oxford and supporting his family. The filmmakers had the advantage that such research was their job. They could divide the labor among many departments and experts who pursued individual lines of inquiry into weapons, fortress architecture, and the anatomy of imaginary creatures.

The design of *Rings* is detailed to a degree that goes beyond most, if not all, Hollywood films. The opening sequences of *Blade Runner* perhaps reach the same level of detail, but that film doesn't maintain such density thereafter or create the extensive portrayal of multiple cultures that gives *Rings* its distinctive look. Probably the film's careful, imaginative design, more than anything else, won over fans and made them more willing to excuse the changes in the plot. The process began long before the films appeared, with trailers, magazines, and making-of documentaries revealing glimpses of characters and settings that looked surprisingly familiar.

But how to pull all this material together?

THE DETAILS OF A RICHLY REALIZED WORLD

Alan Lee and John Howe, who were the concept artists, brought a lot of the style with them. They were spreading themselves interdepartmentally as well. It would never have worked if we'd all beavered away on our own, because we would have come up with quite different solutions.

GRANT MAJOR
Production designer

In the summer of 1997, René van Rossenberg, owner of the Tolkien Shop in Leiden, the Netherlands, was startled to receive a phone call from New Zealand placing a large order for posters, calendars, books—anything that contained illustrations. Van Rossenberg remembers the experience clearly: "It is not daily I get an order for thousands of dollars. When the payment arrived in my bank account it was from Wingnut Films. The name meant nothing to me. . . . Later on I learned that Wingnut Films is Peter Jackson's company. He used the material I sent him to see how Middle-earth was depicted in the past. From it he picked Alan Lee and John Howe to do the art design."[14]

Alan Lee, John Howe, and Ted Nasmith were the most famous Tolkien illustrators, having for years provided paintings for Houghton Mifflin's calendars and various editions of Tolkien's books. Their illustrations have given countless readers concrete notions of what Middle-earth looked like. Lee and Howe agreed to come to New Zealand, and they were ultimately credited as conceptual artists. They supplied thousands of sketches and paintings to guide the designers and help create a unified look for all the research and projects going on in the various filmmaking departments. Selections from these, along with drawings and paintings by other designers involved in the film, have been published as a series of licensed coffee-table books.[15]

In some cases the filmmakers went back to Lee's and Howe's earlier illustrations. Several scenes contain specific compositions and designs of settings or costumes or objects that were taken from paintings. The Helm's Deep sets closely echo an illustration that Lee had prepared for an edition of *Towers*. The arched, recessed gate at the top of the causeway, the slanted section of wall rising to join the keep, the crenellated wall, and the attackers' ladders are all reproduced. The only significant difference is that Lee's wall curves slightly outward and the film's curves slightly inward—which is actually more practical for portraying an attack by a densely packed army.[16] For Saruman's tower, the film's designers closely followed Lee's version of Orthanc from an earlier illustration of Gríma arriving after the Ents have flooded the area. Here the image was used quite directly, according to Lee: "There were a couple of things that Peter really liked in the books that I'd done. He really liked Orthanc. I had done a big picture of Orthanc, but it was only the bottom third of it. So I designed the rest of it to match up."[17] *Gandalf Returns to Bag End,* a 1994 painting by Howe, shows Gandalf arriving at the Hobbit hole not for Bilbo's party but on a later occasion when he comes to visit Frodo (plate 4). Note the two round windows on either side of the door, the large tree leaning forward and looming over the facade, the curving steps, the pointed wooden gate, the wickerwork fence, and the yellowish cast to the grass. These elements recur in the scene of Gandalf arriving at Bag End early in *Fellowship* (plate 5). The large tree above Bag End was built by the set department. (*Gandalf Returns to Bag End* is shown twice in the pitch tape that Jackson used to sell the project to New Line.)

Howe tended to be the source for the monsters, and his versions of Fell Beasts in *The Dark Tower* (1989) and *Éowyn and the Nazgûl* (1990) closely resemble the final design, with spikes on the creature's helmet, chin, and neck. Lee's 1991 scene of Shelob stalking Frodo as he looks up at Cirith Ungol includes all three in the same image and is notable in part for its view of the tower through a steep V-shaped gap in the cliffs. The film breaks this moment into a series of shots, but the deep gap and glimpse of the tower beyond are very similar. An extremely clear example is Howe's *The End of the Third Age* (1999), a dramatic image of a huge eagle emerging through the smoke to rescue Frodo and Sam after the eruption of Mount Doom. Virtually every element of the painting reappears in the comparable shot: the diagonal composition with the flow of lava, the smoke trails of falling molten debris, Gwaihir appearing from the distance at the right of the shot. The shot had to have been derived from the painting, since in the book the entire rescue is shown from Gandalf's point of view, so there is no mention of the eagles appearing in the distance. These and other echoes of the paintings are far from continual, of course, and there are settings that the artists had never depicted in published images. Still, the look of numerous scenes would be reassuringly familiar to many fans.

TheOneRing.net cofounder Chris (Calisuri) Pirrotta was invited to view the *Rings* preview at Cannes in 2001. Pirrotta described to me the impact the preview had on him:

> It was funny, because it did change everything, really, at that time. Up to that point, there was a cautionary enthusiasm about what was going on: "Who's this Peter Jackson guy? Look at the movies he's made. Who are some of the actors?" It was up till that point, and then I saw that, and I was just like, "You've got to be kidding me," and I literally was in tears. I just couldn't believe it because it was something that you envision in your head, and someone actually taking it from your head and putting it onscreen—which is scary, which is *very* scary. So I knew right then that it would be really good. If Peter could have his way and continue to do what he was doing, we're going to have an amazing movie.

Pirrotta's abrupt change of heart indicates the impact of the Cannes event on the attitude of many fans, but he also expresses what became a fairly common reaction among readers, who often claimed that the film had captured their own mental images of Middle-earth.

A few days after his initial ecstatic report on the Cannes preview, Pirrotta posted a more detailed description that evidences how much respect die-hard Tolkien fans had for Lee and Howe:

Yes, Bag End is Bag End. It is EXACTLY the Bag End that we have seen from John Howe and Alan Lee. I think this is one of the greatest aspects of the footage and the entire project. Through my discussion with Peter Jackson and Richard Taylor, you really get a sense that both Lee and Howe were the visionaries behind the creation of Middle-earth. And since these two artists, I think, exemplify what Middle-earth should look like, we as fans should be beaming with excitement.[18]

Apart from helping to win the hearts and minds of fans, Lee and Howe had earlier featured very prominently in Jackson's pitch video, helping to convince Bob Shaye to take on the project.

Lee and Howe helped to unify the conceptions of the various designers, but that unity was also in large part the contribution of Weta Workshop, one half of Weta Ltd. The Workshop handled the design and execution of most of the physical objects that were used for the film, apart from the sets. Weta Digital, the other half, handled nearly all of the CGI work. Ultimately the unity of style came from Jackson, who approved virtually every detail. Production designer Grant Major has said, "Peter actually had this stamp with PJ on it that he definitely used."[19]

Jackson's control extended into areas usually ignored by directors. Alberto G. Cañizares, the general manager of *Rings*' Spanish distribution company, was surprised when he had to get the director's approval for voice actors who would be doing the dubbing: "Audition tapes, for every single major voice that was going to be used in our version of the movie. I thought that was incredible. Jesus, does he have enough time to do all that stuff?" Multiply that time by the number of languages into which *Rings* was dubbed, and it becomes apparent that Jackson took great pains to make sure that all aspects of the film fit together seamlessly.

For most Hollywood productions, props and set elements are made by specialist companies. Creature puppets and prosthetics, for instance, might be commissioned from Jim Henson's company. In Miramar, however, virtually all the physical objects for the trilogy were made by companies that were minutes apart, with the designers meeting and working in close coordination. Weta Workshop gathers several of these specialties under one roof. For *Rings,* the Workshop's departments were responsible for prosthetics, armor, weapons, creatures, and many large miniatures. The Three Foot Six art department was responsible for the design and execution of all props, furniture, some of the jewelry, and all the sets besides the miniatures. Ngila Dickson's department dealt with the costumes and part of the jewelry.

At Weta Workshop, personnel easily hopped among departments. For example, Daniel Falconer was the person largely responsible for the Elvish armor and weaponry, but he also was the main designer for Treebeard, who definitely falls in the creatures department.

Two major decisions were made early on that guided the designers' approach. First, the film would follow Tolkien in treating the story as history rather than fantasy. Not only did the designers differentiate the various cultures and races of Middle-earth from each other, but they also tried to reflect their historical backgrounds. Most obviously, the characters pass various ruins, especially near Gondor, notably the Argonath, giant guardian statues on the Anduin River carved in the glory days of the kingdom. The Weta designers studied the changes in historical armors of various real cultures and tried to make the style of Elvish armor evolve in a similar fashion. The helmets in the prologue have been altered noticeably in the three thousand years between that era and the Helm's Deep battle.

Similarly, there was an attempt to keep all the invented creatures plausible by real-world principles of anatomy and physics. Early on, for example, a computer program was developed that allowed for musculature to be added to the skeletons of imaginary beings like the cave troll and to stretch or compress realistically during movements.[20] Weta made the Nazgûl's huge Fell Beasts' wings big enough that they would suffice to lift a body of that size off the ground. When I interviewed Taylor along with designers Falconer and Ben Wootten, they started comparing the creatures in *Rings* to those of other films. In Taylor's view,

> The cave troll is a fantasy creature, but its anatomy complements our real world exactly. It's a sumo wrestler, a bull, a huge creature. The Balrog is the same.
>
> You go to *Dragonheart.* How can a creature of thirty-five feet long get lifted off the ground by wings that only have a twenty-foot wingspread? Because it is a world of fantasy. In the world of Middle-earth, our wings have to be the size of a 747 to lift a creature off the ground.

Taylor credits much of this precision to Wootten, whose combined training in zoology and design had been influential and inspired the group "as we pursued an authentic realism." Wootten admits, "I am the wet blanket when it comes to creature design. [Weta colleague] Jamie Beswarick is the same. We will always fight to make the anatomy as real as possible." The filmmakers imposed sets of constraints upon themselves—cheerfully accepting the fact that such constraints inevitably made their jobs much more complicated, difficult, and time-consuming.

Another problem of realism arose from the fact that the Hobbits had to be convincingly short. When they interacted with other races, the sets, props, and costumes had to be built at two different scales. So thoroughly was the contrast carried through that fabric for the costumes was woven with different widths of the same thread. For the Hobbits, costumes for the main Hobbit actors were made of thread thicker than that used for the clothes of the small actors who stood in for the Hobbits in some scenes. Similarly, the thread for Ian McKellen's Gandalf costumes was narrower than that used for the tall actor who doubled for him in scenes with the Hobbits. Such requirements had to be explained to the weavers who were hired to create the cloth. Dickson describes the complications of dealing with such contrasts in scale:

> the most difficult element, which meant that your palette of fabrics became radically reduced, that you could begin to design with. Because you had to bear in mind what it was going to translate to when it went down in scale and when it went up in scale. And sometimes you had costumes going in both directions, so you then had to contemplate fabrics that had no texture, fabrics that you could apply a texture to and thereby control its scale appearance so that you could replicate it in the different scales. And the weaving!—we had to try and work with weavers, which was one of the true nightmares of *Lord of the Rings*—getting that across to somebody and then actually achieving the result that was up to the standard that was required.

The contrast of scales confronted everyone involved in designing the film.

The second major design decision was that everything would be made from scratch. Kiwi artisans were hired for virtually every task. (The only objects used in the film that were created outside New Zealand were the contact lenses, which were made to order by firms in Los Angeles and Sydney.) Coopers who used traditional methods were hired to make barrels, and glassblowers created goblets. Jonathan Campbell, a bronze-caster and sculptor hired to work on the weapons and armor in the films, commented, "They had a specialist swordsmith from England come in to make the swords in exactly the way they would have been made in ancient times, and they reverted back to crafting methods that hadn't been used for centuries just to create that authenticity."[21] In short, almost all of the 48,000 objects made for the film were manufactured as if they were to be used in the real world, not simply to create illusions in a film. The few exceptions were crafted from lighter materials. These included some pieces of armor and many of the weapons, which were too heavy and dangerous to be made of steel. Much of the chain mail was assembled from slices of plastic tubes.

There are materials for simulating wood convincingly in films, but Théoden's throne, a remarkably beautiful piece of furniture, is made of solid oak, intricately hand-carved and finished. Admittedly, this throne is seen in close views, but less important pieces of furniture were also made of real wood with great care. "In a normal film you wouldn't do this," art director Dan Hennah explains, "but for us it was important because Peter Jackson is such an organic director. He is going to go in for a close up and a piece of chair is going to be in focus. It has to be as good as everything else in the film."[22] Smaller pieces were treated with similar attention. The leather-working department alone employed thirty-five people. Its head was a third-generation leather master whose father had helped build the state coach for Elizabeth II's coronation.[23] A forge was set up in Weta Workshop to make the armor and weapons.

In sum, items that in the real world would be considered custom-made luxury goods were lovingly crafted for a movie. Hollywood productions typically do not operate that way. True, publicity for some films touts the fact that the floors of a certain set were made of marble actually imported from Italy or that the dresses worn by the heroine were made by a famous fashion designer using expensive materials. But in most cases this is done only for selected, major items that will be obvious to the spectator. It's not done for barrels or the calligraphy on paper scattered around sets.

The principles of a richly realized world demand that these expensively created objects register without being explicitly noticed. Alan Lee says of the room shared by Gandalf and Pippin in Minas Tirith, "We put a huge amount of detail into these sets, really, and if the camera just kind of glances across it very, very quickly, you barely see it, but the fact that it's there and it's just part of the texture in the background only helps make the place feel more lived-in and more real."[24]

Some things are not noticed because they are part of clutter in the backgrounds of scenes. Saruman's study is crammed with books, specimens, and heaps of scrolls. A close view of the character provides an intriguing glimpse of bones and a glass jar with something in it, but the rest of the array is too indistinct to make out (figure 13), and the same is true in the reverse shot of Gandalf. A selection of these particular objects was included in the touring museum exhibition. Upon seeing them one might ask, "Were these in the movie?" Of course they are there, and they do contribute to a sense of clutter, but every individual object looks as if it were made to be handled in close-up.

Figure 13. Intriguing clutter in Saruman's study in *The Fellowship of the Ring.*

Other elements are clearly visible and not part of a cluttered scene, but they are small and unobtrusive. Karl Urban spoke of how easy it was to get into character with the settings and costumes that were provided: "There are engravings on my helmet that say in Rohirric, 'This helmet belongs to Éomer, son of Éomund—may he ride forth with valor.' It was just incredible. Individually handcrafted rivets in my armor—instead of just doing a generic dome—no two rivets were the same. They are like museum pieces."[25]

Some items "hide" in plain sight, requiring special knowledge for even keen-eyed fans. Consider the spiral-flighted arrows of Lothlórien. In the April 2003 issue of the *"Lord of the Rings" Fan Club Official Movie Magazine* (which was available only to club members), Taylor described them:

> The flights are goose-feather and are spiraled around the shaft of the arrow. When an arrow is fired with a spiraling flight, it makes the arrow go much more accurately, and the elves have discovered this. We suggested that [the rest] of Middle-earth hadn't yet discovered this technology. It's a tiny little detail that no one will ever see, but it's all there for the taking for people who are interested![26]

When I read that, I assumed that one would not be able to see these spiral flights on the screen. During my tour of Weta Workshop that October, Falconer showed me a display of weapons from the film, including one of these Lothlórien arrows. Two months later, seeing all three films on Trilogy Tues-

Figure 14. Just before the Last Battle we see one of several views of Legolas's arrows in *The Return of the King* (*lower right*).

day, the day before *Return*'s release, I found that they are clearly visible in many shots. The Lothlórien archers carry them, and Galadriel gives Legolas a quiver of such arrows (figure 14). That gift-giving scene appears only in the extended edition, but in both versions he carries the quiver throughout the rest of the film—and the rest of the film does not lack close views of Legolas.

In late 2003, a tie-in book, *"The Lord of the Rings": Weapons and Warfare,* was published, bringing the information on spiral-flighted arrows to a larger audience: "The flights were long white goose or swan feathers, and these were skillfully tied to the shaft in a spiral pattern with a single cork-screwing loop of gold wire. Lórien arrows were the only ones at that time to employ a spiral fletching, so it can be assumed that the Elves were unique in discovering that an arrow fired with a spiraling flight is much more accurate than a normal one."[27] In true Tolkien style, the text of *Weapons and Warfare* treats its subject not as a designed element of a film but as a feature of an actual historical culture.

A few elements of design in the film are intelligible only to die-hard Tolkien fans. Grant Major decided to use Dwarvish runes in the Chamber of Mazarbul. As he explains:

Balin's Tomb was a hall of records for the Dwarvish culture that lived underneath the ground there, and the hall of records being written by stone craftsmen and all that sort of stuff, was largely chiseled into the walls. Of course it was all in Dwarvish, so 99 out of a hundred people wouldn't be able to read Dwarvish—or probably even 999 out of a thousand. But for those people who could, I wrote specific parts of the Dwarvish history, which I learned from the book, that was then translated into Dwarvish.

That task fell to David Salo (credited as "Tolkien linguist"), who prepared the passages of runes to be used in the set. Predictably, websites sprang up to record and translate these passages into English, with participants in the project using the pause buttons on their DVDs and also production photos such as the ones reproduced on pages 50 and 52 of *Weapons and Warfare.* There are at least two such websites. Salo brought the whole thing full circle by contacting one of the sites and providing the original English text. It's likely that some of the participants in the project were disappointed when he did.[28]

In effect, Salo's contributions to the film constitute another instance of "overdesign." The entire film could have been done in English, but early on the decision was made to include passages of Elvish and others of Tolkien's invented languages. Salo had started learning Sindarin at age eight when *The Silmarillion* was published, and he began collecting all the Elvish words he could.[29] When he ran across a mention of the film project on an Internet site, he managed through mutual friends to contact Philippa Boyens and send his résumé. Once hired, Salo did all his work via fax and later e-mail, although he sent audiotapes and videotapes (and later, as the technology progressed, MP3 files) of himself reading the texts for the use of the language coaches in New Zealand. "Judging by what actually appears in the movie," says Salo, "I would say that they did their job very well." He was on call day and night. As shooting progressed and more passages in other languages were composed, one of the writers would call to discuss what was needed. Salo translated dialogue and poems written in English by Walsh and Boyens. He also composed some of the texts himself: inscriptions engraved on the main characters' swords,[30] Saruman's invocation of the storm (in Quenya, the archaic form of Elvish), and Éowyn's lament at Théodred's funeral in *Towers'* extended edition (in Old English and inspired by the laments in *Beowulf*).

Expert consultants on both fiction films and documentaries often complain that their advice is largely ignored. Not so in this case. Salo's first task was the set of translations for the sword inscriptions. In March 1999, he received a message from Howe (himself an expert on medieval armor and weaponry) asking him to jot down his sources in the margins in future translations and adding, "References are very important to us." Salo sent back two pages of precise and detailed information on each element of the words he had used in the inscription on Frodo's sword, Sting, referencing where in Tolkien's writings they occurred. Howe responded by apologizing for having put Salo through this little test, "but I am sure you agree that we have to be sure we are doing our best to get things right." Praising Salo's scholarship, Howe assured him that he need not provide such references in the future.[31]

Though virtually no film viewer would be able to interpret (or even see clearly) the swords' inscriptions or understand the Khuzdul chanting on the musical track during the Moria battle, the filmmakers went to extraordinary lengths to retain something of the linguistic underpinnings that Tolkien considered so central to his created world.

The level of detail and the quality of the craftsmanship raised the budget. Not surprisingly, designers and crew members don't mention this fact in interviews. Taylor did touch on it when I talked with him: "People have commented since we finished the film, 'My gosh, you guys were insane! Why go to that trouble to put in all that detail? It's never seen. It's obsessive. It lost you money, whatever.' We put it in because it *is* seen, because it *is* important, because without visual *clutter*, you can't create historical reference. Our world is all about clutter." There is something weirdly admirable, I think, about how much trouble these people were willing to go to in order to make what in many scenes was very high-quality, very expensive clutter.

DIGITAL DESIGN

In early 2002, *Fellowship* was pulling in hundreds of millions of dollars worldwide. The unexpected scale of the success of Film 1 led to a loosening of the budget for Films 2 and 3. The total cost of the three parts went from $270 million to around $330 million. On the whole, the additional money did not extensively affect the settings, props, and costumes. By the release of *Fellowship*, principal photography on all three parts was completed. There were lengthy pickups for Films 2 and 3, however, and Grant Major referred in my interview with him to a "no-budget" approach to sets and other physical elements during that period. Jackson had considerable leeway in upgrading the design elements in the pickup shots.

The main impact of the extra funding came in the area of special effects. Almost all the digital work on the visuals of the other two parts remained to be done. The number of CGI shots grew with each new part of *Rings,* from 540 in *Fellowship* to 799 in *Towers* to 1,488 in *Return.*

Jackson had chosen *Rings* when he was looking for a project to show off

Weta's proficiency with digital special effects. In interviews, he frequently pointed out that only with such technology could Tolkien's world be realized with the proper scope, detail, and believability. Standard programs were used, most centrally Maya for modeling and animation, RenderMan for the addition of surface textures and colors, and Shake for compositing.[32] Even so, the technology as it existed in 1997, when research and development began, was not adequate to realize the film as Jackson envisioned it. In particular, how could he present Gollum convincingly? And how could digital technology create crowds of extras that didn't look like animated figures?

The holy grail of computer animation had long been the realistic depiction of human skin. *Toy Story* and other early CGI features stuck largely to non-human characters with smooth surfaces. *Monsters, Inc.* solved the problem of adding fur to a computer figure, but the main characters were fantastic creatures interacting with a stylized little girl. *Star Wars: Episode I—The Phantom Menace* introduced a vaguely humanoid computer-generated character, Jar Jar Binks, into a live-action movie, but although the animation was impressive, the character so annoyed many viewers that the achievement was undercut.

Human skin is translucent, and light passing through it scatters in a way that had been impossible to emulate with early CGI. Based on principles already known within the industry, Weta found ways of creating Gollum's skin by simulating subsurface scattering. Industrial Light & Magic did the same in its work on Jar Jar Binks. In 2004, the Academy of Motion Picture Arts and Sciences gave a technical award to Weta animators specifically for "their implementation of practical methods for rendering skin and other translucent materials" and a parallel award to ILM technicians.[33]

A second Weta accomplishment won a technical award that day: the Massive program, developed by Stephen Regelous specifically for *Rings*. The program allows for the mass duplication of human and animal figures that can be programmed to move independently, giving for the first time the sorts of realistically diverse crowds so crucial to *Rings'* marching and battle scenes. Regelous gives the basic figure a very simple artificial intelligence, along with an ability to sense its surroundings and a repertoire of motion-captured movements. The multiplied figures then interact and behave independently of each other. Ten thousand Uruk-hai could attack Helm's Deep, and the individual soldiers would not move in lockstep with each other. Part of the scope of Middle-earth could be conveyed.

Weta Digital grew in size and sophistication, especially between Films 1 and 2. The technical improvement can be seen in a pair of high-angle extreme long shots of figures on bridges (figures 15 and 16). In *Fellowship*, the camera glides spectacularly over the characters as they run across the Bridge of Khazad-dûm, but the digital nature of the figures is still fairly obvious. By the Helm's Deep battle in *Towers*, a similar high view of Aragorn and Gimli fighting a crowd of Orcs is made up entirely of digitally generated figures and looks far more convincing.

Much of the live action was filmed in front of blue and green screens, and one of the most pervasive uses of CGI was to match actors and real setting elements into backgrounds created with miniatures and digital imagery. Whole landscapes could be rearranged. The first view of Orthanc as Gandalf gallops toward it places the miniature of Saruman's tower into a real vista in the Glenorchy area on the South Island, but with additional mountains photographed elsewhere and jigsawed into the shot.

The surge in the number of effects shots was not the only reason that the films got progressively more difficult. One of the animators at Weta Digital explained to me that no significant technical breakthroughs in CGI occurred between *Towers* and *Return*. Once the methods for creating Gollum had come together in Film 2, Film 3 could be made with much the same software. The real difference for the last part was the growing density of the effects shots. The complexity and hence the time spent on CGI for a shot depend on factors like the number of different elements, planes of action, different directions of movement, and the crossing of moving figures in front of or behind each other. Add in the fact that some of the aerial views of, say, the Nazgûl swooping over Minas Tirith during the battle combined miniatures and live-action footage with complex CGI, and some of these shots became fiendishly difficult. The animation of the horses running in all directions under the legs of the charging *mûmakil* must be among the most complex pieces of CGI work accomplished to that time.

CGI shots can also be altered right up to the last minute, which fits Jackson's just-in-time working method. He kept requesting more and more moving elements in shots that technicians thought were nearly finished. A brief passage ("The End of All Things") in the DVD supplements to *Return* demonstrates how this happened: the heads of the various special-effects areas recall with horrified amusement the challenges thrown at them late in post-production, including the addition of trolls glimpsed in the backgrounds of shots during the street fighting in Minas Tirith. These additions put enormous time pressure on the staff, but they also were very expensive, demanding more equipment and personnel. Such changes hadn't been planned or

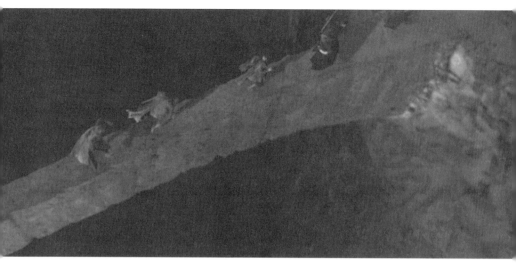

Figure 15. Digital doubles running across the bridge in Moria in *The Fellowship of the Ring*.

Figure 16. Digital doubles fighting on the causeway at Helm's Deep in *The Two Towers*.

budgeted for. As with the sets, costumes, and props, the CGI for these films cost more than it would have needed to.

On the other hand, the outcome justified the methods. One or more of the film's three parts won Oscars in every major design and technical category, and *Rings* won the special-effects award three years running. Just as Tolkien's names and languages sound real because he was an expert philologist, the weapons, costumes, sets, props, and special effects in the film create an impression of a continent's different cultures because the designers and artisans put an enormous amount of research and expertise into them.

Once the fans were able to see this rich realization of Middle-earth, most were thoroughly won over. They also recognized that this was not blockbuster filmmaking as usual. The fans had grown to see Jackson as a maverick up against the Hollywood machine. The physical distance of New Zealand from Hollywood became a symbolic one as well. In 2003, one fan writing to the letters column of the Fan Club magazine addressed the director (reflecting as she did the widespread cynicism in the fan community about the Academy ever awarding major Oscars to a fantasy film):

> To Peter Jackson: Don't get sweet-talked by the movie big shots in Hollywood into moving away from New Zealand to go to New York or California. Stay in New Zealand and only do the pictures you want to. You may end up losing the Oscars for best picture and director, but you've already won the hearts of all your fans around the world. When we feel depressed from our daily work routine, we will watch the movies and be transported to a magical place that no Hollywood director can take us.[34]

This passage may at first seem a little naive, but it captures one essential component of Jackson's strategy for independence and control—distance.

Other powerful directors have realized the same thing. Producer Branko Lustig has worked with Steven Spielberg (*Schindler's List*) and regularly with Ridley Scott (*Gladiator, Kingdom of Heaven,* and others). He likes to work in Morocco, where three of Scott's films have been shot. According to Lustig, Scott makes frequent last-minute changes in the script. The filmmakers never consulted on these with Twentieth Century Fox, the producer of *Kingdom of Heaven:* "They are just the people who give the money. They are interested in what is happening, but a director like Ridley doesn't give them the chance to be interested."[35] In the age of globalization and coproduction, more and more Hollywood or Hollywood-funded films are being shot offshore, away from their producers' watchful eyes. This may actually be a good thing for both the studios and moviegoers. A major study of Hollywood's workings argues that neither studio supervision nor market research nor tweaking after test screenings betters a film's chances of success: "None of our results is more surprising than the finding that hard-headed science puts the creative process at the very center of the motion picture universe. There is no formula. Outcomes cannot be predicted. There is no reason for management to get in the way of the creative process. Character, creativity and good story-telling trump everything else."[36]

A handful of directors with name recognition among the public, like Ridley Scott, can demand to work with minimal studio oversight. Jackson's difference is that he managed it without a hit to his name. There is an element of truth when Jackson remarks in a DVD supplement, "If I was going to sum it up, I'd say it was the biggest home movie in the world."[37]

PART TWO

Building the Franchise

CHAPTER 4

Flying Billboards and FAQs

I think the key turning point was the mutual love affair
between television and publicists.

ROGER EBERT
film critic

IN TRYING TO GIVE A film a strong opening weekend, marketers have swelled
ad budgets enormously. In 2002 the major studios spent $3.1 billion on print
and media ads, up an astonishing half a billion dollars from the year before.
And that year a trailer for a big Hollywood release cost an average of
$500,000 to $1.2 million. Because of the fierce competition, these expenses
cannot effectively be cut, so the problem is to find ways to offset them. The
next chapter will consider how fans can be recruited at little or no cost to
publicize a release. But, as we will see, those fans may become unruly. The
studios have other options that are easier to control. Through the 1990s, a
new system for orchestrating publicity and offsetting marketing costs grew
to maturity. *The Lord of the Rings* arrived at a moment when its makers could
take full advantage of new opportunities.

In selling a film to the public, studios have long relied on the three legs of
marketing: theatrical preview trailers, television advertising, and the graphic
design that will appear in newspapers and on posters outside theaters. During 2002, the year of the big uptick, New Line spent $31.4 million to publicize *Towers* in broadcast and print media, with the bulk, $18.9 million, going for spots on network television; newspapers trailed at $5.9 million and
cable TV at $4.5 million. The overall ad-buy constituted a respectably low
12 percent of *Towers'* domestic box office by year's end.[1]

But New Line did not pay for nearly all the advertising that featured the *Rings* franchise. It drew heavily on a trend toward "brands partnering," in which a film company strikes a deal with firms that sell brand-name products. Usually the partner agrees to spend a certain amount, often in the tens of millions of dollars, on ads for its own merchandise that include characters from the film. Stores often set up large cardboard "standees" of characters juxtaposed with their product, sweepstakes are run, and publicity materials for the film are packaged with partners' products. (For *Fellowship*, JVC created a tie-in DVD player with images from the film on the box and a DVD with a brief making-of promo, "A Glimpse of Middle Earth," in it.)

Brand partnering has had a fairly long history, most often tied to actors' endorsements of consumer goods. In the 1950s a magazine advertisement might feature a star with a cigarette or a beer, along with mention of the star's upcoming film. The practice became far more systematic in the 1980s, when makers of children's films began partnering with fast-food chains. An industry milestone was reached in 1996 when Disney signed a ten-year contract whereby McDonald's agreed to promote no other company's movies. Nowadays almost any major brand can associate itself with a film. Cingular linked with *Spider-Man* and saw its sales spike, particularly in downloads of graphics, ringtones, and games based on the film.[2] If possible, the brand is also featured within the film itself. With a fantasy like *Rings*, product placement was not an option, but in other respects it could maximally exploit partnerships. Here, as on other dimensions, the timing of *Rings*' arrival allowed it to reap the benefits of a trend that was consolidating in the late 1990s.

Some of *Rings*' partnerships changed from film to film. Gateway, General Mills, and Sharp came and went, to be replaced by Duracell, 7-Up, Chrysler, and Parker Brothers. Tourism New Zealand was a partner throughout. Verizon Wireless signed as a partner shortly before the release of *Towers* and stayed on. Newman's South Pacific, a company specializing in tours to New Zealand, was a long-term partner, as was MTV. The film featured unusual promotions, as when a card included in the *Towers* DVD led to a website offering $500 toward the purchase of a Chrysler minivan—the logic being that the model contained a DVD player.[3] This sort of association, with a high-end product or a more dignified service, proved crucial to *Rings*' brand partnering, reinforcing the film's image as a prestigious effort, not a popcorn adventure. Comparable partnerships were formed with local brands in other countries.

The risk of going down-market was dramatically illustrated in the run-up to the first installment. On 1 June 2001, New Line and Burger King announced a partnership. The cast and crew weren't terribly happy with this, but it was sprung on them too late for protest. The fast-food chain committed to a $30 million ad campaign. Its ten thousand restaurants had *Rings*-themed food containers on which the official website's URL was printed. There were two levels of products: for kids, small plastic giveaway figures, and for older fans, four "collectible" glass goblets with carved likenesses of the main characters and light-up bases for sale.[4] Burger King ran a sweepstakes for a trip to New Zealand and put a link to *Fellowship*'s trailer on its website. All this did not placate the online fans, who complained loudly that the deal violated New Line's promise not to sully the trilogy with cheap tie-ins. A headline in the *Hollywood Reporter,* "The Lord of the Onion Rings," aggravated the image problem and caught on as a slogan of ridicule on the Internet. In November, Tehanu posted a brief excerpt from Burger King's press release under the title "How Many 'Lord of the Onion Rings' Jokes Have You Heard?" The excerpt included a passage that ran, "To add to the excitement of this blockbuster promotion, BURGER KING® customers can experience new and improved onion rings at the only fast food restaurant that offers this choice. The enhanced onion rings will be offered with a creamy, zesty dipping sauce and are available in three sizes: medium (15 rings), large (20 rings), and king (24 rings)." Tehanu commented, "I guess if they don't agree with you, you can experience 'the return of the king.'"[5] Significantly, New Line did not partner with Burger King for Films 2 and 3. It is possible that Burger King found the terms too expensive, or maybe the studio was tired of onion ring jokes.

Fans were far more favorable to a higher-toned partnership that was also quite imaginative. Air New Zealand had the advantage of being one of the few marketing partners strongly associated with the country where the films were being made.

Air NZ met with New Line only shortly before *Fellowship*'s release in late 2001. The initial goal was to associate Air NZ with the film and to build up a database of potential customers from people who clicked onto the website. In the autumn of 2002, New Line and Air New Zealand entered into a promotional partnership, covering both the theatrical releases and the DVDs, which lasted for two years. The highest-profile initiative involved decorating the outsides of two planes with giant decal images of main characters. Those two would be replaced by two differently decorated planes for *Return,* but when it was announced that the world premiere would be held in Wellington, New Line gave permission for all four planes to fly until the partnership ended (plate 6). These planes, used only for international flights, generated enormous publicity for both brands. Despite a rainy day, the media turned up at Los Angeles Airport to see Mark Ordesky, Barrie Osborne, Elijah Wood, and a few of the other actors present the "Frodo" 747 on 18 December 2002, as they were about to depart on it to attend the New Zealand premiere of *Towers*. Fans who spotted the planes sitting on tarmacs photographed them and posted the images on websites.

The partnership also gave Air NZ the right to call itself the "Airline to Middle-earth." Images used for tourist agency posters and outdoor billboards showed pristine New Zealand landscapes with captions like, "The movie is fictional, the location isn't" and "Visit Middle-earth. They haven't taken the set down." Publicity material for Air NZ was handed out in theaters, and reporters coming to the world premiere of *Return* received the company's electronic press kits (EPKs) on CD-ROMs. Air NZ travelers watched trailers and making-of documentaries for the film. The seats on the four decorated planes had *Rings*-themed headrest covers, the staff wore *Rings* badges, a lengthy audio program on the trilogy was available, and a postcard with an image of the appropriate plane was given to each passenger. In December 2003, one of the decorated planes carried the actors back to the United States after *Return*'s world premiere. The 2004 Academy Awards presented yet another opportunity for promotion. The airline put tickets for New Zealand trips into the gift baskets given to the presenters, performers, and other VIPs running the ceremony. When Air NZ's success led it to add a nonstop San Francisco route in June 2004, the "Frodo" was used a final time at the mayor's request to help publicize the city's new airport. Air NZ removed the decals one by one. The last flight, on 23 October 2004, carried a group of fifty-four Japanese tourists in *Rings* costumes.[6]

The cross-promotional effects of such partnerships are evidenced by the fact that New Line temporarily added a "travel" category to its online *Rings* shop, giving Air NZ a place to offer its vacation packages to a ready-made audience. The airline in turn provided tickets to allow New Line to run another sweepstakes in August 2003, just before the release of the *Towers* theatrical DVD. New Line also provided licensed merchandise and tickets to premieres so that Air NZ could run contests. Fans loved the Air NZ campaign, and many of them traveled on the airline as they went to tour movie locations.

Rebecca Weaver, manager of partnership marketing for Air NZ's American office, stresses the degree of coordination among partners that New Line provided, helping them maximize these cross-promotional benefits. Each year before the DVD release, New Line had a "partner summit," where new partners could learn about existing ones and explain their own plans. Weaver says,

"I would present some background information about Air New Zealand plus some of the past *Lord of the Rings* initiatives that we'd undertaken in this market. It was just a great networking opportunity, then, to be able to sit there and watch the other companies and identify which ones would make good connections." Arrangements were made in the United Kingdom for partnerships with brands like Virgin Megastore, Royal Mail, and Warner Village Cinemas to promote the "Airline to Middle-earth."

Lucy Powell, communications manager for Air NZ's Los Angeles branch, sums up how *Rings* helped draw attention to the company.

> We're a part of popular culture that previously we wouldn't have been able to be on our own. We show up in the entertainment sections of a newspaper or a magazine. It's the Tolkien fans, it's the movie industry, it's this whole other audience that we could never reach otherwise. I think it's probably put the country and the airline on the map in a way that we just never had been before.

Even with the end of the partnership and the right to call itself the "Airline to Middle-earth," Air NZ's publicity staff still tries to use images that are "Middle-earthy" or "Lord-of-the-Rings-ish." The offices receive inquiries from travel magazines planning stories that will mention the *Rings* connection. And the effect will probably live on with the franchise. As Powell laughingly notes, there may be an "über-geek" boxed set of the film, reminding fans yet again of the New Zealand connection. Such possibilities could lead to further ad hoc arrangements with New Line, especially now that the production of *The Hobbit* has been announced.

Brand partnerships are easy to control, with studio approval of products and publicity and contractual stipulations about timing and funds spent on advertising. To fans, however, they can sometimes smack of crass commercialism. Another way of partnering for inexpensive publicity, however, is considerably less obvious to the public.

THE RISE OF INFOTAINMENT

We are so used to learning the weekend's box-office results on Monday-morning TV that we may forget that it was not always so. For most of the twentieth century, the U.S. public ignored the inner workings of the film industry. True, stars showed up to promote a film on a handful of talk shows, either network (*The Tonight Show*) or syndicated (hosted by Merv Griffin, Dinah Shore, and the like). But celebrity gossip was the province of tabloids and fan magazines, and the audience was unaware of which film won the weekend or the intricacies of power struggles within studio boardrooms.

Now, however, we have infotainment—soft show-business news that permeates serious news outlets, the mainstream general press, the Internet, and a host of entertainment-centered TV programs. Why the shift? During the 1970s, cable television began to be widely available, leading to keener competition to fill swaths of airtime. Like "reality" programming, infotainment was cheap to put on the air, and it tended to be attractive and uncontroversial. Studios were eager to supply clips, canned interviews, and stars to promote upcoming movies. As *Variety* said, "The explosion of channels and celeb-driven publications . . . has fostered a veritable celeb circus."[7]

This was also the period when morning talk shows began adding brief review segments. Gene Shalit joined the *Today* show in 1973. In September 1975, Gene Siskel and Roger Ebert's film-review series *Opening Soon at a Theater Near You* debuted on a Chicago commercial station. In 1978, renamed *Sneak Previews,* it moved to PBS. Commentary on current films was thus certified as educational—both information and entertainment. As channels proliferated, more infotainment programs appeared, the most notable being *Entertainment Tonight,* launched in 1981. Cable's success pressured the networks to compete. By 1998, cable channels surpassed the broadcast networks in prime-time viewership for the first time; by 2002, the networks' overall share of the audience dropped to 48 percent.[8] They began to include more soft news, as when ABC's *Good Morning America* devoted enormous coverage to the 2005 Oscars.

The demand for movie-related content intensified with the spread of the Internet. Pundits had long complained that television was discouraging people from reading. Now video games and surfing the Net were luring audiences away from TV. Networks, channels, and websites fought for attention. Soft news—not just show business reportage but coverage of crime (abductions, car chases), real-life melodramas (runaway brides), and faux celebrities (the blonde teenage-girl idol du jour)—could plug the gaps between hard-news stories or even crowd them out.

Changes in the film industry encouraged this trend. During the 1980s and 1990s, the television networks were bought by conglomerates that also owned movie studios. When *Rings* was being released, such conglomerates controlled all six networks: Viacom (CBS and UPN), Time Warner (the Warner Bros. Network, aka The WB), NBC Universal (NBC), News Corp. (Fox), and Disney (ABC). In mid-September 2006, CBS and Warner Bros. merged UPN and The WB into a jointly owned network, The CW.

These networks own *The Tonight Show with Jay Leno, Late Show with David Letterman,* and other programs that feature celebrities introducing tempting clips from their newest movies. They also control more than sixty major cable channels—including ones that habitually publicize movies, such as E!, VH1, and MTV. They own other media assets, including entertainment and celebrity-oriented magazines like *People, InStyle,* and *Entertainment Weekly.*[9] Not surprisingly, they use a synergistic blend of their media outlets to publicize the films that their studio wings produce and distribute. *Entertainment Weekly* was started in 1990 by Time Warner, which later acquired New Line. The magazine brought out a special edition devoted to *Rings* just as the theatrical DVD of *Return* was about to hit stores.[10]

One forerunner was Walt Disney. Ever on the leading edge of film franchises, he started the *Mickey Mouse Club* series in 1955, and ABC paid for it as it would for any ordinary program. Yet the series promoted Disney's characters and products. Beyond the popularity of the show, ABC had another reason for supporting Disney. In 1954 ABC helped finance the building of Disneyland, of which it owned a one-third stake, and late that year it started running a television series of the same name, which advertised the theme park as well as the characters and products.[11]

Another early example was the Academy Awards, which were broadcast on network TV from 1952 on, and this glamorous event became an early prototype of infotainment. Cable fed the appetite for awards shows, from the Independent Spirit Awards covered on the Independent Film Channel to the British Academy of Film and Television Arts awards (BAFTAs) on BBC 2 and BBC America. In 1996, the Golden Globe Awards moved from cable to NBC and steadily gained viewership. The January time slot and international flavor of the Globes, given by the Hollywood Foreign Press Association (HFPA), can boost the crucial overseas market for Christmas-season releases. As *Variety* put it, "Studios know the promotional value of awards shows: They're essentially splashy infomercials for new pics." Studios attract viewers' interest by sending celebrities to such ceremonies. At the Oscars, they provide part of the entertainment by laughing at jokes, applauding during tributes, and reacting emotionally to the presentations. Lorenzo Soria, president of the HFPA, which holds the Globes ceremonies during banquets, says of the stars, "If they're not presenting or winning, you see them eating and drinking and hugging friends, and crying and laughing. And I guess in our culture people are fascinated by this sight."[12] Such occasions create further chances for red-carpet or backstage press interviews and sound bites that are stitched into news coverage.

The surest sign of the growth of infotainment is what Hollywood people call the horse race: weekend box-office coverage. In 1976, the Nielsen ratings company founded Nielsen EDI, a centralized service that telephoned theaters across America, gathered box-office receipt totals, and passed them on to the studios. Industry journals like *Variety* subscribed to EDI and published a weekly top-fifty box-office chart, but that didn't appear in print until days after the fact. The mainstream news did not take much notice. But the 1990s saw weekend totals creep into *USA Today* and other newspapers. In 1997 and 1998, several websites like Box Office Guru and Box Office Mojo began to supply overnight box-office figures for free. Now networks and cable channels like CNN could report the weekend numbers as a routine part of Monday morning's news.

Similarly, the seemingly mundane announcements of deals between stars and their producers, agents, and directors used to be confined to specialized journals like *Variety* and the *Hollywood Reporter.* Now, as a writer for *Screen International,* a British film-business magazine, put it,

> If a story appears in a trade paper about a new project featuring (say) Leonardo DiCaprio or Harvey Weinstein, it will instantly show up in the consumer press. There is a huge public appetite for information that [a generation ago] would have seemed relevant only to the industry. Newspapers, magazines, and TV shows have specialized departments and reporters devoted to entertainment news. Radio DJs, talk-show hosts, and especially box-office charts often influence the public's movie-going decisions more than film critics' reviews do.[13]

As Alex Fogelson said, coverage of entertainment news had become an industry unto itself.

This change was both a blessing and a curse for the studios. With more attention focused on films and their stars than ever before, studio publicists face a greater task to keep certain information from leaking out. News of plot twists or endings (spoilers) can make the film seem less exciting when it is ultimately released, and actors are routinely required to sign "nondisclosure agreements," vowing not to reveal a film's plot beyond what is okayed by publicists. Even worse, damaging news about stars might make filmgoers stay home. In the summer of 2005 alone, three such incidents occurred. The disappointing performance of *Cinderella Man* was at first blamed on an altercation between Russell Crowe and a hotel employee. Rumors of Brad Pitt leaving his wife, Jennifer Aniston, for his *Mr. and Mrs. Smith* costar Angelina Jolie had studio officials nervous about public reaction. Polls predicted that

Tom Cruise's eccentric, sometimes aggressive behavior on talk shows would adversely affect the box-office take for *War of the Worlds*. It seems unlikely that the stars' offscreen antics harmed these films. (*Cinderella Man* fell victim to a poor release slot, *Mr. and Mrs. Smith* earned nearly $440 million worldwide, and *War of the Worlds* provided Cruise's career-best opening.) The real point is that show business commentators treated speculations about the box-office effects of celebrity behavior as news.

Infotainment poses another risk: broad coverage of too many aspects of a movie might confuse the public. The studio wants to highlight a film's genre, the stars and the characters they play, the plot's main premises (but not its outcome), and so on. Trying to steer the juggernaut of infotainment to stick to such basic information presents new problems, but marketers have overcome them in some clever ways.

THE MAKING OF THE MAKING-OF

Historians looking back at *The Blair Witch Project* (1999) attribute its surprise success to its ingenious website. The film had additional help, however, from two making-of documentaries on cable. In 1998, even before *Blair Witch* had shown at the Sundance Film Festival and been bought for distribution, the Independent Film Channel coproduced a short documentary about it. After Artisan acquired *Blair Witch,* the Sci Fi Channel ran an hour-long program a few days before its release.

Making-ofs have become routine, but behind-the-scenes footage was shot for many older movies. In the 1950s and 1960s, there seems often to have been someone with an amateur film camera on the set. Such material was usually handled casually, as mementos for cast and crew, without an eye to its being cut together into a comprehensible documentary. But studios sometimes created making-ofs to screen at exhibitors' trade shows, hoping to entice theater chains to book the films. Until recently the public seldom saw such footage. Since the late 1990s, however, making-ofs are routinely arranged in advance of a film's production.

Such documentaries form one of the main components of a DVD's supplements. In the age of infotainment, a making-of for a major film is also likely to be broadcast in advance of the release, usually on a cable channel aimed at an appropriate audience.

Who makes the making-of documentaries, and how do they get on television? Since they are in effect advertisements, we might expect that the studio pays the cable station to run them, and sometimes this happens, especially if the studio is mounting an Oscar campaign. Yet during the 1990s, Hollywood came to recognize that people would buy promotional items that had once been free. Fans, they discovered, would buy posters, character standees, and other items that companies previously had supplied just to theaters. Likewise, in the infotainment era, a cable channel considers a documentary about a major upcoming film to be a highly desirable program. Initially cable firms would buy the rights to air such making-ofs as if they were standard television fare, but as such documentaries have proliferated, channels often run the program only if the studio buys a certain amount of advertising time. In either case, the studio might enhance the documentary's appeal to the channel by including an exclusive peek at a scene from the film. The *Quest for the Ring* program on Fox in 2001, for example, contained a portion of the Moria sequence that before then had been seen only in the Cannes preview. It also had a short ad for *Fellowship* at every commercial break—small promos wedged inside a large one.

Peter Jackson began making features in the mid-1980s. The Criterion company had released the first laser discs with supplements in 1984, with its *Citizen Kane* and *King Kong* releases. Given that Jackson was a laser disc collector, it seems highly likely that he was aware of these, especially the latter. He has arranged for extensive behind-the-scenes documentary footage for all his films. (He speaks of someday going back and assembling a making-of for each.) He directed a four-and-a-half-hour film, *The Making of "The Frighteners,"* for the 1996 special edition laser disc of *The Frighteners*. (In 2005 this making-of was rereleased on the Director's Cut DVD of *The Frighteners*.) Jackson was also well aware of the historical importance of *Rings* and knew that he should not treat its making-of shorts casually. He arranged for particularly detailed video documentation of every stage and ordered that virtually everything from the production be kept. Each version of every shot or sound that was saved to hard disk was preserved, so that a filmmaker could trace the entire evolution of special effects or the mixing of sound.

Although a few one-off films about one or another installment were made, three filmmakers recorded throughout the production process. Costa Botes shot candid footage for one feature-length, unnarrated documentary for each part. Dan Arden combined interviews and on-set footage to create making-ofs for cable and for the theatrical DVD supplements. Michael Pellerin shot additional material and put together more extensive documentation for the extended-edition DVD supplements.

Botes's friendship with Jackson went back to the 1980s, and they had codirected *Forgotten Silver* (1995). When Botes heard about the *Rings* project, he told Jackson that he was interested in covering it, and New Line agreed to pay to have it done. According to Botes, "Peter's only instruction to me was to try and document it warts and all." New Line seems not to have realized what a mammoth task documenting *Rings* would be. As of 1999, before principal photography began, the plan was for Botes to direct three forty-five-minute making-of programs (one-hour TV shows with room for commercial breaks), to make a feature-length documentary about the whole trilogy, and to assemble eight hours of documentary material on each film for the DVD supplements. (At this point there was no distinction between the theatrical and extended-edition DVDs.) Botes suggested that six hours per part might be more feasible, and he set out to create this mass of multipurpose footage.

Botes and Hayley French, a second camera operator, spent nearly every day of principal photography recording behind-the-scenes footage on digital video. It was all candid material, with the subjects in some cases not realizing they were on camera. About halfway through filming, New Line began to realize the scope of *Rings* and decided to bring in separate directors for the publicity making-ofs and the DVD supplements. Botes carried on, trying to condense his mass of footage (all of which is the property of New Line) into three feature-length documentaries. His hope was for a theatrical or at least a DVD release. In late 2004, Jackson spoke of an eventual reissue of *Rings* on high-definition video: "I am really determined to make sure that those are a main feature on this box set that will be coming out in a year or two. They are really great."[14] Instead, however, New Line chose to release a third round of film-plus-supplements DVD sets on 29 August 2005. Each of the three sets included both the theatrical and extended versions of one part of the trilogy, accompanied by the appropriate Botes candid making-of. Reviews and fan comments expressed annoyance that New Line would try to sell the trilogy yet again and wondered why Botes's documentaries were not simply released separately on DVD. In fact, the actors and filmmakers had agreed to have documentary camera operators constantly observing them only if the resulting making-ofs were used to promote the trilogy and not to make money separately. Oddly, the advertisements for these DVD sets simply mentioned "all-new documentaries" in small print, minimizing the one appeal these new releases would hold for most fans.

As soon as Arden and Pellerin began their work, both were given access to all of Botes's footage. He sent copies of what he had shot to New Line to form a library for other filmmakers to use. Arden credits Botes with making *Rings* "the most documented movie project ever." Botes's footage is, however, as Arden points out, very different from what one sees on the typical DVD supplement: "I think that what he was able to do gives you a closeness to the production, almost like home movies, that you never see on big movies." Arden and Pellerin both drew upon it extensively. As Pellerin says, "It would be ridiculous not to. His stuff is through everything." Throughout the documentaries that New Line sponsored or sanctioned, most of the candid, behind-the-scenes shots come from Botes's footage.

Botes has expressed disappointment that so much of his material reached the public eye before he could finish his own films. Still, much unseen footage remained, and his three features are very different in tone and style from what fans had seen up to their release. Until the belated 2006 release, the sole public screening had been, by permission of New Line, at the Wellington Film Festival in July 2004. Botes's program note said, "It was never designed to be part of a marketing effort. It wasn't even meant to be seen for another couple of years, when it and its two companion pieces are provisionally earmarked for release as part of a DVD box set. It is presented here, exclusively to this Festival, as a work in progress, and a taste of things to come."[15] The major fan website TheOneRing.net reviewed it, noting how the cast and crew got so used to Botes and his partner that the pair could "candidly observe what went on around them. The result is that you see people laughing, swearing, and working through disasters and triumphs. The whole thing leaves you in awe at the achievement of every last one of them."[16] Ultimately these three making-ofs, as New Line marketing executive Matt Lasorsa said, gave the studio "the chance to refresh the franchise."[17]

Once the impossibility of one filmmaker handling all the documentary projects became apparent, Dan Arden was brought aboard to produce and direct three shorter, more infotainment-oriented making-ofs. He had made TV shows on various subjects, often for the Discovery Channel. He was a longtime Tolkien fan and a Jackson fan as well. During the making of *The Frighteners*, Arden visited Wellington to interview Jackson and some crew members for *Movie Magic*, a TV series on special effects. That contact proved crucial when Arden heard about the *Rings* project and wrote Jackson about possibly making the related documentaries. Jackson sent him to Mike Mulvihill at New Line Home Entertainment, but Mulvihill told Arden that Botes was already making them.

At that point Sandy Murray, with whom Arden had worked previously, was hired by New Line. Among her duties was the supervision of the *Rings* promotional programs. Arden, still eager to participate in the project, floated the notion of a documentary series that would intertwine the making of the films and an exploration of the book's themes and Tolkien himself. Murray agreed to partially fund the project with travel and expense money during his early visits to England and New Zealand. Material Arden gathered by interviewing Tolkien experts ended up not only in the TV documentaries but also in a tape Arden made, *Welcome to Middle-earth,* which ran in bookstores to promote Houghton Mifflin's tie-in guides and visual companions to the film. (It was recycled in the *Fellowship* theatrical DVD supplements.) The Tolkien material also went into a separate documentary on *Fellowship* that Arden produced in 2001 for National Geographic Television, *Beyond the Movie: "The Lord of the Rings."*

It wasn't long before Arden was working consistently on the film's documentation and marketing. Starting later than Botes did, in July 2000, he visited New Zealand half a dozen times during principal photography and pickups. He interviewed Jackson three times and most of the main cast members about four times, so that they appear in different clothing and settings in the course of the documentaries. The exception was Cate Blanchett, who was in Wellington only for a single two-week stretch. Arden was told he could have one hour with her, but every day the word was, maybe tomorrow. On Blanchett's last day, when she was finishing many hours of work and faced a 6:00 A.M. flight the next day, Arden was told that the interview was impossible. After much pleading, he got producer Barrie Osborne to concede that he could have ten minutes with Blanchett—but that if he went a second over, he couldn't come back on set. Osborne would stand behind Arden during the interview to enforce that dictum. Arden told his cameraman to tap him on the shoulder to signal time running out. The interview came in at nine minutes and forty-five seconds. Arden recalls, "She was so remarkable that there literally wasn't a second of that interview that didn't end up getting used a zillion times." It was the only on-set filmed interview with Blanchett.

Between interviews, Arden shot behind the scenes. Out of this footage, supplemented by Botes's material, he made a documentary for each part of the trilogy. *Quest for the Ring* appeared on Fox (and again on FX) in the autumn of 2001, preparing the way for *Fellowship*'s release. *Return to Middle-earth* (2002) ran on The WB to promote *Towers.* Arden's final film, *The Quest Fulfilled: A Director's Vision* (2003), was used to promote *Rings* to Academy members and as a DVD supplement. After Arden's first National Geographic Society special, *Beyond the Movie: "The Lord of the Rings,"* was aired, it was released as a separate DVD and later also included in the gift-box edition of *Fellowship*'s extended version.[18]

Like Botes's behind-the-scenes footage, Arden's material was shared among people making a variety of documentaries. He sent his master tapes to New Line, which copied a set for his use. Another set was given to editor Karina Buck, hired by New Line to assemble footage for the electronic press kits and the brief clips that were at intervals put onto New Line's official *Rings* website. The Botes and Arden material was also available for other TV-promo films like *A Passage to Middle-earth: The Making of "The Lord of the Rings,"* made in-house at New Line for the Sci Fi channel (shown in 2001 before and after the release of *Fellowship* and included on its theatrical DVD); Starz Encore's *On the Set: "The Lord of the Rings: The Two Towers"* (2002; also on the theatrical DVD); and MTV's *Making the Movie: "The Lord of the Rings"* (2002; not included on the DVDs). Certain striking quotations tended to show up over and over in these documentaries and clips.

With Films 2 and 3 New Line stopped depending so much on making-ofs that it had commissioned. Perhaps there was by this time not enough of the Arden interview material to stretch to yet another round of documentaries. New Line permitted certain TV venues to make their own programs. It was another way for other firms to pay for *Rings* promotional materials. With New Line's cooperation, Bravo produced a making-of documentary. *Page to Screen: The Lord of the Rings* premiered on 17 November 2002 and ran several times during the season of *Towers'* release. Although New Line provided publicity photos and clips from *Rings,* as well as some behind-the-scenes footage, Bravo's production team did an informative new round of interviews, including some with Bob Shaye, noted Tolkien authority Tom Shippey, and the editor of the *Hollywood Reporter.* The National Geographic Society made a second film, *Beyond the Movie: "The Lord of the Rings: The Return of the King"* (2003), which included excerpts from another round of interviews with cast and crew members done by Arden during *Return* pickups. *Beyond the Movie* used interviews with historians, stock images, and reenactments to draw parallels between the *Rings* story and actual historical events. It appears as a supplement on the *Return* theatrical DVD.

E! also produced its own special, *Behind the Scenes: The Lord of the Rings: The Return of the King,* the Biography Channel carried *Bio Extra: The Lord of the Rings Trilogy,* and A & E ran perhaps the most original and effective of the late making-ofs, *Journey to Middle-earth.* Produced by ABC News and shot during the pickups for *Return,* it traces a single day in the filming and includes interviews with Jackson between takes and a scene being shot in the Edoras interior set.[19] In February 2004, a Canadian production firm filmed a live concert of Howard Shore's "The Lord of the Rings Symphony" in Montreal. Some comments by Shore were added, and the program, *Creating The Lord of the Rings Symphony: A Composer's Journey through Middle Earth*, aired on Canada's Bravo! Channel on 4 September. Adding "Howard Shore" to the beginning of the title and correcting the final name to "Middle-earth," New Line Home Entertainment created a DVD that was made available exclusively in the gift-box edition of *Return*.

In all, combinations and recombinations of the footage shot by the three main documentary filmmakers showed up in many contexts. Some of these publicized the film and its ancillaries, some generated additional revenue *as* ancillaries, and some did both. Arden's *Welcome to Middle-earth* was shown in bookstores, some of his making-ofs were shown as in-flight movies by Air New Zealand, and some of his interviews were excerpted on the EPKs. When New Zealand's national museum, Te Papa, mounted its touring *Rings* exhibition, it wanted some explanatory clips available at the push of a button on monitors next to the displays. Director Roxane Gajadhar, employed by Story! Inc., drew upon a dizzying variety of sources, primarily Botes's footage, some interviews with Richard Taylor, Barrie Osborne, and Alan Lee that she shot herself, other interviews by Arden and Pellerin, and Weta Digital archive footage.[20] The official website, lordoftherings.net, at intervals posted behind-the-scenes clips edited by Buck from Botes's and Arden's footage. These were also recycled as theatrical-version DVD supplements. And Pellerin shot and edited a fifteen-minute preview each for *Towers* and *Return* for inclusion on the *Fellowship* and *Towers* theatrical discs, respectively. These were also shown to distributors—sort of a less dramatic version of the Cannes preview of 2001.

Rings squeezed more publicity out of its making-of footage than any franchise had ever done before. Once again, the historical timing of the trilogy proved perfect. The films were released just as behind-the-scenes documentaries were becoming a major promotional tool, and New Line realized that such ancillaries could be used and marketed in multiple ways, just as *Rings* itself could. The huge amount of background footage remaining unused promises that still more documentaries will be made. Jackson has spoken of assembling a diary of the making of *Rings,* which would further extend the franchise.

By now making-ofs are routinely done for virtually any film, since even without an airing on television in advance of the release, they can provide supplements for the DVD. Even TV series have begun this practice. In 2004 the producers of *Lost* sent a crew to Hawaii to film the making of the two-hour pilot.[21]

You're a reporter for a small fan magazine or a local morning-news program assigned to write a brief article or a three-minute TV segment about *Towers*. You've seen the film at an advance press screening, but you need to know more about it. You also need some photos for your article, or clips to spice up your TV spot. As with most of the entertainment press, your knowledge of the franchise consists of having seen *Fellowship* a year ago and read some stories in popular magazines. Where can you turn to make yourself seem reasonably expert? The electronic press kit that your editorial office or station received from New Line Cinema's marketing department would be your starting point.

Since the silent era, distributors have supplied the media with a press kit for every major release. In the old days, the kit consisted of packets of eight-by-ten publicity photographs along with a booklet of background information, including feature stories for lazy journalists to replicate. Today, EPKs make texts and stills available in compact, downloadable form, along with interview clips, trailers, and musical passages. New Line was among the first studios to add an interactive marketing department, and in 1994 its head, Gordon Paddison, experimented with digital means of replacing press kits, mainly to save the costs of shipping. Websites did not exist at that time, but he tried delivering materials to journalists by file transfer protocols and on floppy disk.[22]

The producers grant permission for all this material to be used in a media context publicizing the film. As we have seen, the contents were assembled by Karina Buck, who made use of Arden's interviews and of the still images taken in New Zealand by the official *Rings* stills photographer, Pierre Vinet. Publicists Claire Raskind and Melissa Booth gathered information from the various heads of departments and sent it in, mostly for use in press releases but also for the EPK. Each of the actors sat down for a lengthy on-camera interview from which brief clips were extracted.

The press kit for *Towers* consists of two CD-ROMs packaged in a modest cardboard slipcase. The cover shows a key image already seen in posters and other advertising visuals: Sauron's Dark Tower in the left foreground and Saruman's Orthanc in the distance at the right, with a vertical grouping of the main characters. Disc 1 contains "Photography" and disc 2, "Special Materials." Disc 1 starts with a brief trailer for the film, similar to ones shown on TV and included on the DVD, with Cate Blanchett's voice intoning over a collage of shots: "There is a union now between the Two Towers, Barad-dûr, fortress of the Dark Lord Sauron, and Orthanc, stronghold of the wizard Saruman." This statement succinctly explains the film's dramatic premise and the title. The trailer goes on to emphasize Gollum, the most important new character in Film 2, and we glimpse him and hear his muttering as he creeps up on the Ring-bearer in the clip's ending. If you're a TV presenter, it's likely you'll cut to this trailer as you are describing the film.

As the trailer fades, the menu appears, accompanied by Howard Shore's music. Navigating through an EPK is similar to looking at DVD supplements that consist mostly of galleries of images. The user has a choice of thirty photos of various characters, displayed in sets of six thumbnails. These lead to small selections of the photos of the main characters that became so familiar in fan magazines: a view past Saruman's and Gríma's shoulders of the immense ranks of Uruk-hai assembled outside Orthanc, Théoden surrounded by his soldiers on the steps of Helm's Deep. Since Orlando Bloom has become popular, you glance over the images of Legolas on offer. There are two, one with the Elf just standing and looking beautiful, another with him brandishing knives. You choose on the basis of whether you assume that your audience slants more toward females or males. The last batches of photos on offer emphasize Rohan, which is a major new element in the second film, and Saruman, the Uruk-hai, and Helm's Deep, all connected with the great battle scene that was a big draw for action lovers. The final images show Jackson, who became a star in his own right after Film 1, directing on the plains of Rohan in one, simply looking thoughtful in another, and in the Osgiliath set talking with cast and crew.

You don't need to write your own captions for your article if you don't want to, since each photograph has an accompanying line. One of the Saruman images, for example, is labeled "Saruman (Christopher Lee) commands his legions of Uruk-hai to attack Helm's Deep in the central film of New Line's epic-adventure trilogy, *The Lord of the Rings: The Two Towers.*" But Jackson's team wanted to keep secret the designs of the two most eagerly anticipated characters of the second film: Gollum and Treebeard. The EPK provides only tantalizing glimpses of them.

If you're a television journalist, you'll find the contents of the second *Towers* EPK disc more useful. A tiny segment of four shots leads to the general menu: Characters, Gollum, Helm's Deep, and Special Materials, each with its own submenu. Under "Characters," we can choose "The Fellowship" (figure 17), "Rohan Culture," "Gondor Culture," "Creatures," and "Evil Forces." Choosing that intriguing "Creatures" section, you are not surprised to find it again hurrying past the two main attractions. The Treebeard section is quite brief, with text focusing on Merry and Pippin's encounter with the Ent. There are two pictures of Treebeard himself: a fairly close one and a rather

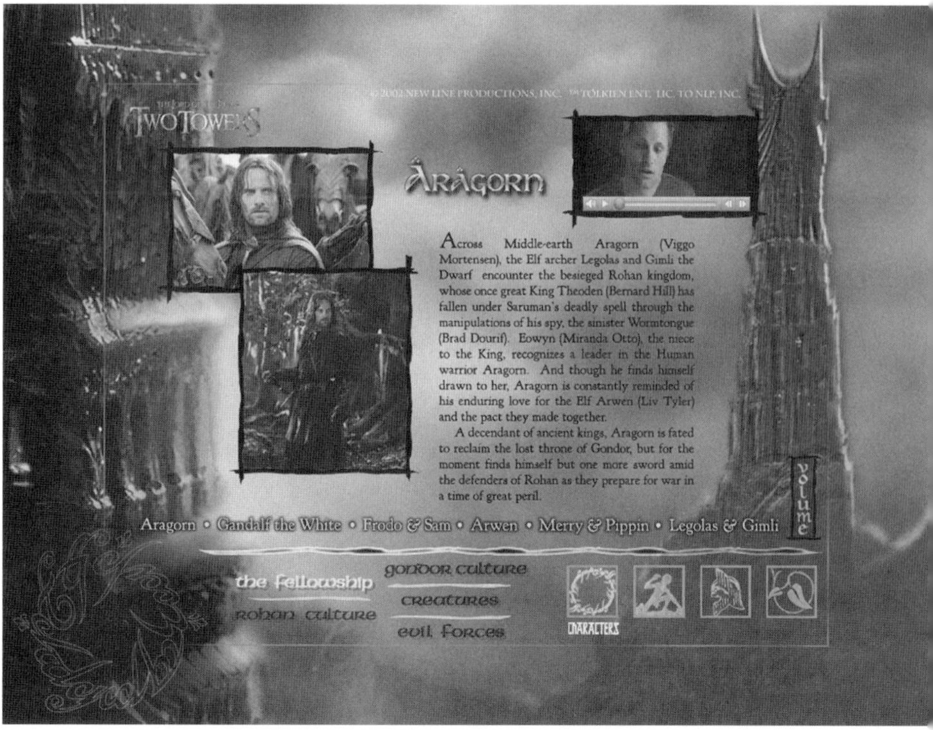
TWO TOWERS
Aragorn
Across Middle-earth Aragorn (Viggo Mortensen), the Elf archer Legolas and Gimli the Dwarf encounter the besieged Rohan kingdom, whose once great King Theoden (Bernard Hill) has fallen under Saruman's deadly spell through the manipulations of his spy, the sinister Wormtongue (Brad Dourif). Eowyn (Miranda Otto), the niece to the King, recognizes a leader in the Human warrior Aragorn. And though he finds himself drawn to her, Aragorn is constantly reminded of his enduring love for the Elf Arwen (Liv Tyler) and the pact they made together.
A decendant of ancient kings, Aragorn is fated to reclaim the lost throne of Gondor, but for the moment finds himself but one more sword amid the defenders of Rohan as they prepare for war in a time of great peril.
volume
Aragorn • Gandalf the White • Frodo & Sam • Arwen • Merry & Pippin • Legolas & Gimli
the fellowship
rohan culture
gondor culture
creatures
evil forces
CHARACTERS

Figure 17. The electronic press kit: Under the "Characters" category, there is the Fellowship, including images of and text about Aragorn.

unclear little one of him holding the two Hobbits. These two particular images are not downloadable, so you could describe Treebeard if you want, but you couldn't illustrate his appearance.

Thwarted, you move to the "Gollum" section, which masterfully provides considerable information without allowing any of its photos or clips to show more than flashes of the new character. (*Fellowship*'s brief, darkly lit glimpses of Gollum essentially revealed only that there was such a character. He was extensively redesigned for the following installments.) One computer-generated image presents an unrendered Gollum as a shape made up of shiny bands. A text explains how the animation was based on Andy Serkis's performance, and a clip of nearly two minutes shows Jackson watching Serkis performing for motion capture. Another clip offers part of Gollum's first appearance in *Towers* and his fight with the Hobbits, but it is cut so quickly that the viewer can catch only an impression of the creature.

The "Evil Forces" section is fairly detailed. A twenty-second clip shows

Saruman and his battle preparations. Gríma appears in a flurry of images lasting twelve seconds—and, interestingly, containing two shots atop Orthanc in the scene where he finally stabs Saruman. This scene was originally planned to come late in *Towers,* but instead it was put off until *Return* and ultimately seen only in the extended DVD version. The inclusion of these shots illustrates a persistent problem. Marketing staff had to work on the publicity and merchandising while Jackson's team was still shaping the film. The EPK "Evil Forces" chapter ends with brief synopses, and photos (mostly without clips) are provided for some of the more prominent Orcs and the Wildmen (the Easterling troops seen by Frodo, Sam, and Gollum marching through the Black Gate into Morder).

The final section, "Special Materials," offers the original theatrical trailer, from which most of the clips on the EPK are derived, as well as logos of the film's title, two maps of Middle-earth, the two standard posters, a text on Howard Shore's sound track with photographs, and production notes, all downloadable. When you have taken what you need and exited the EPK, you come to a page of contact information for the heads of New Line's various marketing offices.

Reporters were not limited to the thirty illustrations on this pair of discs. New Line also had an Internet press site where production photographs could be downloaded. For *Towers,* a separate disc 3 was circulated, containing information on special effects. Similarly, the main two-disc EPK for *Return* was supplemented by an extra single disc of additional photographs, and as the Oscar race geared up, a series of EPKs of photos were issued for Sean Astin and other possible nominees.

For a journalist working in the world of infotainment, the EPK is a godsend. You know only what the publicists want you to know, but you know enough to appear well-informed. You can cover the film as if it were news, illustrating your piece with images and footage, all the while hitting the notes that the marketers want hit. Like brand partnerships and making-of documentaries, the EPK demonstrates the full range of control that a modern film enterprise can exercise over the image of its product. And like other publicity artifacts, the EPK itself has value. Wait a few years, and sell your *Towers* kit to an avid collector prowling eBay.

FREQUENTLY ASKED QUESTIONS

EPKs go out far and wide, and reporters for small media outlets must rely mostly on them and the Internet. Writers working for national media outlets, as well as for major-market newspapers and television stations, get a more select introduction to the film. They are invited on press junkets.

A junket brings the reporter to a central site—the studio, a location, a rented hotel meeting room in a city where a premiere is occurring—for intense but orchestrated exposure to the film and its stars. The company provides transportation, lodging, and a per diem (in the $150 to $200 range). Junketers receive goodie bags, known cynically as swag bags, full of licensed products, some promotional items for the film, and perhaps a costly gift or two.[23] The reporters get brief access to the stars and key behind-the-camera talent, and in some cases they visit the set. Such junkets have been widely criticized as pressuring reporters and reviewers to create favorable stories so that they will be invited on future junkets.

Such press events have been going on for decades. *Chicago Sun-Times* film critic Roger Ebert recalls one lavish junket when Warner Bros./Seven Arts flew a large number of reporters to the Bahamas for a week, showing off five of its main 1969 releases, including *The Wild Bunch.* Ebert was also among a group of journalists who visited the set of Blake Edwards's *Star!* (1968). Yet in the 1960s, junkets were rare. It was cheaper for studios to fly stars and directors to the main cities for interviews with local reporters. In Chicago, Ebert was able to have fairly lengthy interviews with such figures as Francis Ford Coppola, Martin Scorsese, and Otto Preminger. Usually when journalists did the traveling, they were not in groups but did one-on-one interviews with stars or visited sets on their own, as Ebert did for films like *Camelot* (1967) and *Ryan's Daughter* (1970).

The situation changed in the 1980s with the burgeoning of infotainment coverage on television. As Ebert points out, local news is often among the highest-rated programming for a station: "Local TV stations, especially in mid-sized markets, love to be able to say, 'Our Joe Blow or Jane Doe was in L.A. last week and talked to Tom Cruise about his new movie.'" Brief access with the reporter and star facing each other in director's chairs and with a poster behind the star could yield a three-minute segment or, as Ebert says, "Maybe it would be a series, you know, 'Our chat with Tom Cruise continues tomorrow.'" With so much publicity available outside the biggest cities, studios started bringing the press to the stars.

Junkets are costly, but the advantages are considerable. The event attracts reporters who write for influential publications all over the world. (Distributors in some countries pay the expenses for a journalist or two to attend.) Apart from content, the agreement with the studio typically controls how the result can be published or broadcast. As Ebert describes it, "When can it run, where can it run, how can it run, how long can it run."

Above all, the junket situation allows the studio's publicists to guide the interview process. Reporters may agree in advance to avoid certain topics. Hints that an actor may be gay or references to arrests or marital discord can get an interviewer ejected and banned from future junkets. In June 2005, Brad Pitt and Angelina Jolie appeared at two thirty-minute press conferences for *Mr. and Mrs. Smith*. Rumors of a romance between the two that had damaged Pitt's marriage led lawyers to warn the roughly one hundred international journalists present that if they asked any personal questions, the event would terminate immediately. When publicists demanded that the published stories "not be used in a manner that is disparaging, demeaning and derogatory,"[24] reporters complained. Still, information about new films and their stars is the coin of infotainment, and news media have a vested interest in remaining in the favor of movie companies.

The mechanics of most junket interviews are standardized. A star or a small number of stars will sit in a hotel room, a film location, or a set throughout one day, perhaps joined by the director or other key crew members. Batches of print and radio journalists come in and spend perhaps fifteen minutes asking questions in the manner of a news conference. As soon as one group leaves, another takes its place. A second day is devoted to TV reporters, who receive one-on-one face time. This privilege is balanced by the brief exposure— around five minutes, ordinarily—that the reporter has. The cameras filming these interviews are run by the studio, which may request retakes or edit the results. Tapes or discs are then given to the reporter.[25]

Anyone who followed media coverage of the *Rings* saw the same photos and clips over and over and heard familiar answers to familiar questions. We might think that a studio publicity department would want more variety, to keep spectators interested while following such coverage. The studio's goal, however, is to link each main character, each major plot line, and other important components of the film to one or two simple concepts that will "brand" the film and help it float above the clutter of competing publicity. Diversity of coverage matters less than keeping journalists on topic.

Such repetition happens in most press junkets, since the reporters have so little time with the stars and have probably not done much research concerning the film. The bane of most interviewees is the most frequently asked question. In 2005, Leonardo DiCaprio, asked about such questions, responded, "The one that comes to my mind is: 'What do you have in common with Howard Hughes?' I just got off this huge press junket for 'The Aviator,' so I got asked that 50 times a day."[26] Publicist Ernie Malik recalls how he triggered a question while working on *The Alamo:*

> When they had the junket at San Antonio, I had put in my production notes that Jason Patric, who played Jim Bowie, had drunk a shot of Tabasco sauce every time he had to hack—because Bowie was dying of consumption or whatever it was, and so he felt the way to get that hacking to an extent that looked really painful to the character was to drink straight Tabasco sauce. Well, I put that in the notes, and *every* journalist that came into that interview room with him asked him about that!

During the shooting of the first *Rings* installment, there had been press conferences in Wellington, and individual reporters were allowed to visit the set. The press junket to Cannes in May 2001 was the first time that the actors sat down for small-group interviews. New Line gave over the usual one day to print journalists and one to broadcasters. Art director Dan Hennah did not participate himself, but he was nearby, supervising the ongoing preparations for the party on the last night, and he describes the cycle of interviews as "relentless." Costume designer Ngila Dickson was helping set up the party and provides a vivid description of the scene: "I watched those actors talk to people *all day long.* They sat at these tables, and the interviewers just revolved through the seats opposite them, and the same questions were being asked, and on it went, and I just thought, 'You people are remarkable!'" Philippa Boyens, who had never taken part in a junket before, commented: "I didn't realize what I was letting myself in for. I did 50 interviews a day, one after the other, each about five minutes long, where the journalists asked me almost exactly the same questions each time. I realized then that the film industry isn't as glamorous as you think it's going to be."[27]

The *Rings* cast soldiered through many other junkets and interviews. During the pickups for *Towers,* journalists from New Zealand, England, France, Sweden, Italy, Germany, Japan, the United States, and Australia spent five days on the set, interviewing the actors and talking with Jackson between takes.[28] Groups of stars flew from city to city for the main premieres, with a press junket at each stop. For *Fellowship* these included the world premiere in London on 10 December 2001; the North American premiere in New York, with the proceeds benefiting World Trade Center causes; Los Angeles for another benefit screening; and on to the New Zealand premiere in Wellington on 19 December. The success of the first film ramped up the attention paid to the other two. On 30 November 2003, the members of the cast and crew of *Return* faced hundreds of reporters in Wellington on the eve of the world premiere (see plate 1). The day after the premiere they flew to Los Angeles and immediately faced another set of interviewers at a two-day junket at the Four Seasons Hotel in Beverly Hills. One Internet reporter remarked, "The [interview] rooms were as small as they were for *Texas Chainsaw Massacre* (my room was only five people—a delight for L.A. and even more so for a movie this large)." Groups of three exhausted people, including actors and other talent like Howard Shore, cycled through brief question sessions. Asked whether he was relieved or sad that *Rings* was over, a jetlagged Elijah Wood replied jokingly: "It doesn't feel over because we have so much to go in terms of releasing the film and the promotion of it. In terms of relief, next year when we don't have another junket to do and we don't have to plaster on a fake smile and plow through this shit again . . . (laughs)."[29]

Facing a new round of interviews each time one of the film's three parts was released, the large cast and crew heard the most popular questions very frequently indeed. Ngila Dickson told me that hers was, "How many times did you have to design Gandalf's hat?"—and warned me that she ups the number each time she is asked. Sure enough, months later when I opened the *Rings* special number of *Entertainment Weekly*, the article on Dickson quoted her as saying that she did twenty designs for the hat. Assuming the questioners meant start-over, from-the-ground-up designs, one has to believe that a costume designer who had to do that would not have a job for long, but clearly it was the sort of thing that reporters thought fans wanted to hear. Indeed, reporters seem to be aware of this repetition. McKellen notes that during a junket, "Someone will come forward and say, 'I know you get asked all sorts of questions. I'm not going to ask you the questions everybody else asks you, so I'm going to say, "What is the question that you're most asked?"'"

Filmgoers almost never see the regimen of junket interviews. A rare exception comes in Jackson's filmed "Production Diaries" for *King Kong*, where the entry for 26 November 2004 shows unit publicist Melissa Booth talking to the camera as she ushers a small group of journalists onto an exterior set and improvises some brief question sessions with the stars between takes.[30] In the postproduction diaries on the film's two-disc DVD, Jackson remarks on the *Kong* junkets, "I think the question I ended up talking about the most with the journalists was how I saw the original *King Kong* on TV when I was 9 years old. I told that story . . . *often.*" Another revealing scene is included in the *South Bank Show*, a British television documentary about McKellen that was being shot during *Return*'s pickups and premiere. One segment cuts together shots of reporters questioning the actor during the 30 November 2003 junket in Wellington.

FIRST INTERVIEWER: What's the most frequently asked question?

MCKELLEN, with no hesitation: "How does it feel coming to the end of this long journey of making the films?"

SECOND INTERVIEWER: What's it like, coming to the end of this long journey?

THIRD INTERVIEWER: Is there a real sense of achievement for you?[31]

This, of course, was a generic question that worked for any member of the cast or crew.

Reporters are quite aware of this convention. One who was able to talk with McKellen and Andy Serkis directly after the Los Angeles junket described earlier wrote: "Sir Ian, 64, and Mr. Serkis, 39, who portrays the creature Gollum in the film, had flown in from New Zealand just two days before. They were suffering from jet lag and from answering the question 'Is it bittersweet to be at the end of the trilogy?' 65 times in a row during publicity interviews."[32] That particular question, however, worked only for *Return*. There were plenty of others. The Hobbit actors were repeatedly solicited to tell their tale of woe about getting up at 5:00 A.M. to have their false feet applied. McKellen was asked over and over whether it bothered him that he would be remembered more for playing Magneto and Gandalf than Richard III and other classical roles. In discussing Shelob in *Return,* Jackson repeatedly obliged reporters who inquired about his fear of spiders. The actors who played the Fellowship (apart from John Rhys-Davies) all got tattoos with the Elvish numeral nine. Once this secret slipped out, interviewers battened onto it.

The publicity campaign comes to resemble a game of "Jeopardy," with the EPKs (along with the film's website and periodic press releases) supplying the answers to the journalists, who are supposed to come up with the right questions, which will then elicit the correct answers from the actors. The reporter knows what the actor will say, but he or she can play the insider, with access to the stars, and elicit the same information worded differently. As one studio head of marketing remarked, "EPKs provide stars with their templates for the interview shows."[33] Indeed, the texts in the *Towers* EPK sections on the characters sometimes quote the actor, who gives the same sort of brief description of the character that he or she might later repeatedly provide to any number of journalists—if those journalists are savvy enough to ask the right questions.

Ebert points out that repetitiousness is almost inevitable in questioning stars

> because the sessions are so short and because the nature of television is that you have to get *them* to say it. They get pretty stupid questions. For example, I may well know who Hilary Swank plays in *Million Dollar Baby,* but it doesn't work on television unless *she* says, "I play a woman who wants to be a boxer." You have to have *her* saying it. So you say, "Well, tell me about this character you play."

Similarly, when the actors repeat a small repertoire of responses, they're not just being lazy or unimaginative. Their task is to ensure that consistent information and ideas about the film come across in the vast numbers of articles and interviews that will be published, broadcast, or posted. That was especially true for *Rings,* with its numerous characters and complex plot. During the junket and talk-show interviews, stars have to concentrate on maintaining their enthusiasm and giving the impression that they are hearing these repetitive questions for the first time. It might be more exhausting for them to field unexpected questions and conjure up fresh answers. Viggo Mortensen occasionally dragged interviewers into less familiar territory. One fan-magazine reporter who failed to steer him back on track determinedly provided the answer that she had failed to elicit from the star—the by-then-famous anecdote about the "Fellowship" actors getting souvenir tattoos. Wrapping up the article, she wrote, "It's clear that he holds [his *Rings* experience] in high esteem, as something unique in the rubber-stamp machinery of Hollywood filmmaking (he even famously got a tattoo, along with his nine [*sic*] Fellowship castmates, to commemorate the event)."[34]

Normally the performers and filmmakers who participate in junkets don't receive extra pay for them. Keith Stern, webmaster of McKellen.com, describes the stress of it. "They're very well cared for generally, as movie stars are, but that doesn't make up for the grind and gruel of traveling, packing, unpacking, hotel, driving, everything else that's involved. And then sitting there and answering the same questions over and over and over again. But it's part of their job." Most contracts stipulate that the actor will participate in the publicizing of a film—doing any number of junket interviews, traveling from one national premiere to another, and appearing on talk shows—unless he or she is actively working on another project at the time. There are ways of dodging the junket, but actors understand the long-term benefits. If the film succeeds partly because of their support, they can command a higher salary in the future. As junkets expand in size and length, however, there are occasional rumblings from actors that some pressure should be brought to have studios pay them for all this additional time and effort.

Despite the grinding routine and the hundreds of thousands of dollars they cost, junkets remain an efficient marketing tool. They lead to widespread, largely enthusiastic coverage in most of the significant media outlets worldwide. They allow the local reporter to give the sense of having direct access to the star and thus speaking authoritatively. The public will usually get no sense of how short and orchestrated that access was or how many other reporters might have been present. This is partly because journalists have refined a writing approach that disguises the nature of their reporting. All of them clearly have a stake in giving the impression that they have exclusive news. Writers have become adept at implying that during a set tour they were alone or had only a photographer in tow. The typical article starts with an anecdote about an actor's or director's behavior during or between shots, revealing something characteristic about the production and ideally emphasizing some visual detail to make it clear that the reporter was really there. Then the writer fills in the backstory, explaining the origins of the project and how key personnel overcame difficulties in script preparation, casting, or location shooting. In an article on *Superman Returns* for *Newsweek,* the reporter begins by describing a scene in which the villains beat up Superman and push him over a cliff:

> Playing this scene just once would be rough. [Brandon] Routh will be beaten and tormented for hours. "He's very heroic normally," says director Bryan Singer, sipping an iced vanilla latte. "You just happened to catch him on a bad day."
>
> By the time "Superman Returns" lands in theaters next summer, it will have taken Warner Bros. 11 torturous years to get the movie off the ground. At one point in the mid-1990s, Tim Burton was going to direct Nicolas Cage as the man in tights.[35]

This article, published more than eight months before the film's release, ends with another anecdote from the filming, a chat with the costume designer about the controversy over the tightness of Superman's trunks. If an article is to be published shortly before the film's release, however, the writer may mention having "caught up" with the filmmakers during postproduction. The fact that many other journalists have been granted access, usually at the same time, is artfully omitted, as is the possibility that the catching up was done via a phone call.

Once in a while, a reporter will be charmingly straightforward about the limited access. Melissa J. Perenson, of *Sci Fi,* wrote, "It's early Friday evening, usually a key social hour for a Hollywood 20-something. But [Elijah] Wood isn't enjoying an evening out—at least not just yet. For now, he's on the phone with this journalist, evangelizing about *Return of the King.*" A representative of the *Rings* fan club magazine attended a junket for *Fellowship* at the Waldorf Astoria in December 2001 and began his report, "What fan wouldn't want to attend a Hollywood press junket? Imagine a whole day of major stars and filmmakers being trotted out one by one to answer whatever questions you can throw at them." The author explains how junkets work and describes the stars and other talent entering and leaving the room for twenty-minute sessions of questions.[36] The result is a livelier piece than more discreet infotainment reportage.

Junkets aim at getting as many articles and reviews and clips into the popular media as possible. Their opposite is the exclusive article, granted to a major outlet like *USA Today.* In such cases the reporter is allowed on the set during filmmaking under carefully controlled circumstances. Claire Raskind and Melissa Booth escorted and supervised reporters and photographers during their on-set visits. In such cases, a clear arrangement is made, with the studio agreeing not to allow other reporters the same kind of access and the publication agreeing to run the story at the time designated by the studio. For *Fellowship,* New Line wanted early images that reached the public to show the Hobbits and Gandalf in the bucolic Shire. So in January 2000, *Vanity Fair* came onto the Matamata set of Hobbiton, when those scenes were being shot. "The Hobbits Are Coming" appeared in the October issue, presumably timed to start a slow build of publicity up to the release of *Fellowship,* still fourteen months off. The *Vanity Fair* coverage happened before the Cannes preview of 2001, though, when few journalists had any idea of just how important this film would be. The four-page article was buried in the back of the magazine and wasn't mentioned on the cover.

Today's wealth of publicity options holds out the possibility that a tiny film like *The Blair Witch Project* can become as widely known as *Titanic,* the current benchmark for a must-see movie. Brand swapping, infotainment, and other new means allow a studio to construct a strong image of the experience that the film will provide. A franchise amplifies the effect, since once the first film becomes successful, infotainment providers will be all the more eager to cover the subsequent entries in the series. The studio can also promise to extend that experience through merchandising, making-ofs, and other supplementary promotion. *Rings* took advantage of all the promotional resources that had been developing throughout the 1990s.

While publicity was being arranged in the real world, New Line's interactive department was designing an Internet campaign. Huge numbers of Tolkien fans were on the Web already, and they were eager to help spread the word. But not all of them were going to stick to studio press releases or stay on message. They had their own ideas of what was interesting about this movie, and some of those ideas lay well outside the realm of infotainment.

CHAPTER 5

Click to View Trailer

When you buy a commercial on television, you lease
the consumer for 30 seconds. But if you can get a
consumer engaged online, you can own that
viewer for 30 minutes.

JIM MOLOSHOK
Yahoo!

STUDIO MARKETING RELIES ON CONTROL over publicity, but control is
hard to maintain. With the rise of infotainment, the more people know about
the inner workings of show business and the private lives of its celebrities,
the more they want to know. The introduction of the Internet provided a
new forum for the circulation of fact, rumor, and opinion. For many spectators
shopping for a movie to see, a casual glance over some general film sites might
provide enough information. For the devoted fan of a specific star or director or series, there is no such thing as enough. Harry Knowles, founder of the
most successful fan-originated movie site, Ain't It Cool News (AICN), has said,
"When I consulted with Lucasfilm on StarWars.com, they asked me, 'What is
it that fans really want?' And I said, 'Fans want to know if you're using Phillips
head or flat-head screws on your sets, don't you understand!? Fandom wants
to know *everything*. There *isn't* enough information you can give them.'"

Studios might be willing to reveal what sorts of screws they use in their
sets, but they're not about to tell fans everything. Inevitably their need to
keep many things confidential clashes with the fans' desire to know every last
detail, and the Internet has become the main arena for this struggle.

Online information can come from official and sanctioned websites supervised by the studios or from the unofficial sites run by fans. Fan webmasters

and their collaborators are willing to pour astonishing amounts of their own time and money into sites that publicize the products of big Hollywood studios—even in the face of secrecy or downright opposition from the studios themselves. For years Hollywood had ignored the tremendous value of this free publicity, but during the period of *Rings'* production and release, it began to understand the potential of online fandom. Such enthusiasm and labor are, however, difficult to control. Fans may provide extensive publicity, but they can also ferret out secrets and post them in cyberspace. Letting the fans find out enough to keep them intrigued without allowing them to divulge too much is a balancing act that Hollywood has still not fully mastered. Peter Jackson's clever handling of the problem provides a model that will surely be taken up by others.

HOLLYWOOD DISCOVERS THE INTERNET

There's just an amazing timing issue, that the 'net came
into general, everyday use for most people in the western
world at the same time as this film was announced.

ERICA CHALLIS
"Tehanu," TheOneRing.net

Internet movie marketing is sometimes assumed to have begun with the official website for *The Blair Witch Project* (1999), but many movies had sites before that. New Line's senior vice president of worldwide interactive marketing, Gordon Paddison, was a pioneer in this regard. In 1995, Paddison built an official site for *Mortal Kombat,* generating 100,000 hits in an era when few fans were on the Internet.[1] In March 1998, about three months before the *Blair Witch* site appeared, Paddison's team launched The Lost in Space Galaxy. Apart from information on the film *Lost in Space* and the original television series, the site offered games, downloadable wallpapers, an online shop, and other interactive components.[2]

Still, the *Blair Witch* site did differ from the typical official movie site in important ways. It went online extremely early (June 1998), promoting a film that did not even have a distributor until more than half a year later, when it screened at the Sundance Film Festival on 24 January 1999. The site proved that a microbudget independent film could be publicized online to spectacular effect, and far more cheaply than on television. It also demonstrated the power of initially targeting a niche market, in this case young horror-film fans who were likely to use the Internet. The filmmakers cleverly presented the site's content as factual documents concerning a case of witchcraft and murder. Many Web surfers took the film to be a documentary. One person who caught on to the ruse helped perpetuate it by starting the first *Blair Witch* fan site in December 1998. Responding to fan interest, the filmmakers added new information to the official site weekly.[3] The *Blair Witch* campaign was too oddball for all its tactics to be completely replicated, but it demonstrated to Hollywood how original thinking could make websites more effective. The film, with an estimated budget of $35,000, grossed $204 million worldwide.

At the same time, New Line was also proving the power of the Internet. In June 1999, a month before *Blair Witch* was released, *Austin Powers: The Spy Who Shagged Me* reached the theaters. By the week before the film's opening, its modest site was receiving more than a million page views a day. In 2000, New Line's poorly reviewed *Final Destination* was a hit largely based on Paddison's website.[4] Meanwhile, New Line was initiating its campaign for *Rings*. In this case, however, there were many Tolkien fans who already had websites and thousands more who were willing to work for those sites or build their own once they became fans of the film. A huge unofficial campaign grew up in parallel with the official one.

SPY VS. SPY

Blair Witch emerged from nowhere and had to create attention with an online gimmick. *Rings* did not. Publicist Melissa Booth says with a laugh, "Unlike some productions, where you're trying to encourage people to come to the set and have a look and cover it, our main job was to *not* be in the press every day. Because otherwise, with the Internet, as soon as you've got something in a local newspaper, you've got it all over the world."

The key to whetting fans' appetites was limiting access, but fans proved hard to manage. They were prepared to spend time and money to get even a glimpse of inaccessible material. On 30 September 2002, for example, the first full-length trailer for *Towers* was made available for twenty-four hours exclusively on AOL, before being placed on the official site, lordoftherings.net, on 1 October. Several show business and Tolkien-fan websites with access to AOL quickly uploaded the trailer themselves, so non-AOL users had access to copies during most of that twenty-four-hour period. Because these copies could take an hour to download on a dial-up connection, fans had to go to some trouble to view those fuzzy, jerky images. Nonetheless, as remarks on those web-sites clearly indicate, fans reveled in getting something highly desirable ahead of its official date of availability. The same trailer premiered theatrically on 4 October, an event of considerably less note to site managers and fans, since trailers are viewed far more often online than in movie theaters—and, be-sides, anyone can go to a movie theater.

Sites were also keen to get graphics of unreleased publicity materials and licensed products. On 13 September 2002, for example, Lights Out Enter-tainment posted two new "screen shots" from the menu of the extended DVD version of *Fellowship* well before its November release.[5] Around 17 September 2002, TheOneRing.net displayed four hitherto unseen *Towers* graphics for popcorn bags (figure 18).[6] In January 2003, warofthering.net posted im-ages from the tie-in calendar for *Return,* several months before the calendar itself became available.[7] Descriptions of trailers and DVD footage were posted as well. Knowles apparently was given a copy of the *Towers* trailer about a week before it appeared in theaters, for he described it shot by shot, com-plete with dialogue, on Ain't It Cool News.[8] On 12 September 2002, Tolkien Online summarized the additions to the extended-edition *Fellowship* DVD from a script. The same site ran a sketchy account of the first full *Towers* trailer on 24 September 2002, a week before its Internet release.

Authors of such articles are coy about their sources. Knowles attributes his access to the preview footage to Gandalf, while the Tolkien Online folks write: "We sent a flock of Crebain from Pasadena to see what news they could find of the upcoming trailer, and they reported back, 'The trailer is AWESOME, the fans have much to look forward to next week.'" (Crebain are the bird-spies that fly over the Fellowship.) Fans who had not seen the trailer itself but only read this description of it reacted with comments that must have been gratifying to those publicizing the film: "Oh GOD! I can hardly wait!!!! * jumps up and down * // OMG!!!! // Can't Wait!!!!!!!!!!!!!! // What a Teeeeaserrrr!!! // wooo!!!!"[9]

Initially the filmmakers sought to conceal as much as they could from snoopy fans. On 30 August 1998, Jackson went on Ain't It Cool News to an-swer fans' questions. He said good-naturedly in his introduction, "After this brief warm shower together, Harry and I return to our different sides of the line—us trying to maintain secrecy . . . and he using his low-life methods to publish it all on the net." On 31 December, he returned for a second round of questions. One fan asked him to reveal where some of the location shoot-ing would take place. Jackson responded, "We have a few key locations nailed down. I'm not going to be specific because I don't want to see photographs

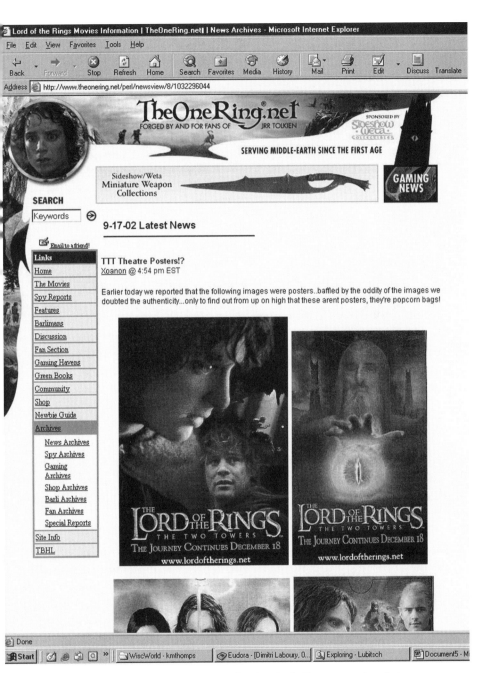

Figure 18. Anything might count as news on fan sites, including popcorn-bag designs. (Courtesy TheOneRing.net.)

appearing on the net!"[10] Jackson told me that his main use of the Internet was to monitor spy material:

> The only real, serious reason, I guess, that we were reading it, beyond just being curious and having amusement from what people were perceiving we were doing, was in case there were any leaks or security issues that we needed to know about, so suddenly if something showed up on the Internet that shouldn't have done, then we had to know about it, because for all we know, we may have had an employee that was stealing stuff. I mean, we actually didn't have that at all. We had one person that stole some tapes at one stage, with some footage. But you're sort of monitoring it just to make sure that there's nothing going on out there that you need to know about in terms of material leaking out.

Jackson refers here to an incident that occurred in 2000 during principal photography, when a stuntman pleaded guilty to stealing the tapes and trying to sell copies over the Internet.[11]

Rumors and hints fed fans' appetites, but the ultimate dream was to leave the cyberworld and hit the set. From the start of the production, fan sites competed to feed that desire by posting scoops or "spy reports" that helped their readers vicariously experience the filmmaking process. These sites recruited spies living in New Zealand, and a long-running tussle between webmasters and New Line began. The studio was happy to provide news to a limited number of popular, trusted sites, but it wanted to be the origin of all information about the filmmaking. Throughout the shoot, security guards and fences surrounded areas where filming occurred. Scenes for *Rings* were shot on roughly 145 different locations, so savvy spies could track down a unit filming in local parks and valleys. Security was a particular problem in the quarry in Lower Hutt where the filmmakers built full-size sections of the Helm's Deep and Minas Tirith sets. Fans trained cameras with long lenses across the valley to capture images probably made more intriguing because of their fuzziness. The cliffs and tangled fields above the quarry became hiding grounds for spies trying to photograph a corner of a set or costumed extras smoking between takes.[12]

Jackson and his team—most of them Internet users themselves—would come to be slightly less worried about curious fans as the project progressed, and they began cooperating in a limited way with two of the most powerful of the "spy" sites. They would drag New Line with them. Ultimately, the unofficial Internet campaign for *Rings* taught Hollywood much about how fans could promote a blockbuster.

At one point when the trilogy was still being released, a search on the string "Lord of the Rings" resulted in about eleven million hits. A significant proportion of those pages represented companies selling *Rings*-related merchandise and others focused on the novel, but there were also many sites consistently devoting much or all of their content to the film itself. Although some of these sites were doing things of which New Line disapproved, all of them were publicizing *Rings*.

Imagine this vast campaign, official and unofficial, as an archery target. The few sites that had New Line's complete or nearly complete approval would be in the bull's-eye. The first ring—a very narrow one indeed—we can call the "quasi-sanctioned" sites. These obtained limited access to the production through the filmmakers' cooperation but without any initial agreement from New Line. Moving to the next ring, we encounter sites that gathered news from a variety of sources but had no direct access to the filmmakers. The more important ones did have the privilege of being on New Line's list to receive press releases and other publicity material. Such sites are sometimes called "multipliers," because other sites link to them or repost the news items, thus carrying New Line's information to an ever-expanding audience. Such sites also usually depend on volunteers around the globe to send in news, gossip, scans of magazine articles, and so on. Farther out on the target, we find the fan sites that center not on news but on the webmaster's personal interests. Often they concentrate on photographs, typically of one or more actors. Finally, in the margins outside the target's rings lie fan-generated parodies, fiction, and art.

New Line created or endorsed only four websites to publicize *Rings*.[13] Most centrally, of course, there was (and is) the company's own *Rings* site. Its home page included a link to the website of the licensed Lord of the Rings Fan Club.[14] New Line bolstered its official site by arranging for a general entertainment website, E! Online, to run a series of on-set reports. The studio did not plan to exploit personal cast or crew websites—such sites were in their infancy at the time. Nonetheless, Ian McKellen's site quickly became one of the main sources for fans wanting behind-the-scenes *Rings* news.

New Line's Official Site

New Line's publicity department began with one signal advantage: many fans desperately wanted to love the films. (The same phenomenon can be observed in other fandoms, such as those for the *Star Wars* and *Star Trek* series.) One such fan, Scott Edelman, the editor of fan magazine *Sci Fi,* articulated this desire clearly and succinctly in an editorial. Edelman identifies himself as an ex-hippie who loves Tolkien's novel. He recalls:

> So when I first heard that director Peter Jackson was going to tackle filming the trilogy, I grew fearful. I had long since given up the dream. Perhaps, I told myself, turning those particular words into cinematic reality was unfeasible. Not every story is filmable. Maybe we should just be glad that the books had been written in the first place, and forget about trying to do the impossible.
>
> Even though I had enjoyed Jackson's earlier films, I was confident that when *The Fellowship of the Ring* appeared on the screen, it would cause me to weep. I can't remember when I was so nervous attending a screening. I guess that was because my lifelong love of Tolkien had left me feeling invested in the critical success of the film in a way that just wasn't present for the average genre film.
>
> As it turned out, the film indeed brought me to tears, though not for the reasons I feared. At my first glimpse of The Shire, I was able to relax. And with each passing instant, I nodded and thought, "Yes, yes, that's it, he's nailed it." Jackson's obvious love for Tolkien filled the screen, and I was transported to many places—not only back to Hobbiton, but back to my childhood dreams as well.[15]

As this passage suggests, however, many fans were also extremely skeptical about the movie. The studio and filmmakers tried to reassure these people via the Internet. Like the film itself, the Internet campaign had to both appeal to the built-in fan base and create a new, larger audience. Given that more than three years passed between New Line's acquisition of the project and the premiere of *Fellowship,* the wooing of these two publics was lengthy and convoluted. The studio started by concentrating on the existing fans.

New Line established the Lord of the Rings website (www.lordoftherings .net) quite early, in May 1999.[16] Here the producers and others with financial ties to the films released news tidbits at brief intervals, with the occasional large revelation. Such a tactic aimed to maintain fan interest during the long gaps between the interlarded releases of the films and DVDs and to whip up enthusiasm before each release. Many webmasters cooperated enthusiastically, and their sites linked to lordoftherings.net. *Variety* wrote of it, "There are global armies of devotees who view the Tolkien epic not as a corporate asset but as holy writ, and Paddison straddles the line between their needs and the demands of AOL Time Warner's global marketing machine."[17]

Among other things, the Internet made it possible for digital publicity items to be given away on a mass scale at minimal expense. As Paddison said, "We go where the fans are and give them stuff."[18] The film's website featured downloadable screen savers, wallpapers, interviews, brief behind-the-scenes clips, and trailers. On 7 April 2001, the first theatrical trailer for *Rings* was made available exclusively on the site. It set a record, with about 1.7 million downloads in the first twenty-four hours and 6.6 million in the first week. (For a comparison, the trailer for *Star Wars: Episode I—The Phantom Menace* was downloaded a million times on its first day.)[19] The website was covered widely in print, broadcast, and online media, generating additional free publicity.[20]

Since New Line is owned by Time Warner, Paddison could easily place advertisements, links, short informational texts, and the like on AOL itself (including a link to AOL's online ticket agency, Moviefone), Netscape, and AOL's instant-messaging service, ICQ. New Line could run travel sweepstakes on these sites, with trips to New Zealand as the top prizes, as well as smaller contests giving away licensed merchandise. The AOL keyword "Lord of the Rings" was included in much print advertising, drawing more people onto the Internet. In many cases, the much-vaunted synergy that was supposed to develop among the components of large media conglomerates in the 1990s didn't meet expectations, but Paddison managed to make alliances within AOL Time Warner work for *Rings*.

The official site proved inexpensive, too. Although New Line spent only 2 percent of its marketing budget on its web campaign, exit polls after *Fellowship*'s release revealed that more than half of the spectators had gained some information about the film from the Internet. As Paddison pointed out, the Internet's efficiency as a marketing tool comes from the fact that it is the cyberworld equivalent of word of mouth (word of keystroke, perhaps). Like Jim Moloshok of Yahoo!, Paddison knew that the Internet can give potential moviegoers a longer exposure to publicity, at a fraction of the cost of TV ads. New Line's *Rings* site has been highly influential, and it literally became a textbook example when Paddison contributed a 54-page case study of the trilogy's marketing campaign to the second edition of *Internet Marketing*.[21]

Later in the official campaign, lordoftherings.net sought to lure in those who had not read Tolkien's novel. As Paddison said, "People click down into the site, and before they know it, they turn geek."[22]

E! Online and the Force of Hobbit

While lordoftherings.net concentrated on wooing existing fans, New Line sought a partner to help make the film appeal to newcomers. During the summer of 1999, as the start of principal photography approached, Paddison arranged a deal with E! Online, which had an editorial partnership with AOL. (This deal was consummated before AOL merged with Time Warner.) Apart from the connection with AOL, E! Online's audience offered what the studio considered desirable demographics. On the basis of New Line's early market research, female filmgoers would constitute, as Paddison put it, "a secondary but key audience." The research had indicated, misleadingly as it turned out, that nearly 75 percent of Tolkien fans were males in their early teens to early thirties, went to comic-book conventions, participated in role-playing games, and liked *Star Wars, Star Trek,* and *Buffy the Vampire Slayer.* *Rings* was not, New Line feared, a date movie.[23] E! Online's audience was 61 percent female, 63 percent of whom were between the ages of eighteen and thirty-four and went to the movies monthly.[24]

E! Online was commissioned to create a series, "Force of Hobbit: On Location," that would appeal to people who had never read Tolkien. Scott Robson, executive editor for the website, contrasted the series with what the official site was posting: "It's a different kind of content, for people who might not know the difference between Frodo and Sam Gamgee."[25] An agency in Auckland hired John Forde, a 1999 graduate in film and media studies from the University of Otago.[26] According to Melissa Booth, Forde was given monthly access to some aspect of the filmmaking. The reports were approved by New Line and Jackson before being uploaded.

Forde got along well with the cast and crew, which shows through in the enthusiastic tone of the reports. Like many visitors, he was invited to be an extra, as a Gondorean soldier, an experience that he described to envious fans. Forde's series began appearing on 12 January 2000, a few months after the beginning of principal photography, and it ended on 1 December 2001, with *Fellowship*'s London premiere.[27] Traffic on E! Online spiked for a few days after each posting. Overall, there were on average 700,000 page views per month. During the period immediately preceding the release of Film 1, *Rings* was generating 34 percent of all traffic on E! Online.[28]

The Lord of the Rings Fan Club

We may think of a fan club as expressing the spontaneous upsurge of devotees' idolatry, but more often than not the film industry creates fan clubs. On 17 October 2001, two months before the release of *Fellowship,* Decipher Games announced the formation of the Lord of the Rings Fan Club. Decipher was licensed by New Line to run this club and to publish *The Lord of the Rings Fan Club Official Movie Magazine.* (A prominent games firm founded in 1983, Decipher also produced the licensed trading-card game and role-playing game based on *Rings*.) Dan Madsen, who had started a fan club for *Star Trek* in 1979 and subsequently founded a business to run the official *Star Wars* fan club, was Decipher's partner in obtaining the license. He subsequently managed the club and conducted many of the interviews for the magazine.

The Fan Club offered some commonplace benefits, including a "collector" lithograph, the bimonthly magazine, and a 10 percent discount on merchandise.[29] In addition, it hit upon a brilliant gimmick. Charter members would have their names listed after the credits on the DVD versions. (The extended-version DVDs had not then been announced, but ultimately the names appeared there rather than on the theatrical versions.) The densely packed list runs for twenty minutes. Elijah Wood was the first member to sign up, and other actors' and crew members' names appear as well. This unprecedented acknowledgment of the fans, absorbing them into the most authoritative version of the film they adored, represents the sort of strategic inclusion that its makers—many of them possessed by the fan spirit themselves—offered to *Rings'* admirers.

The same sort of inclusion was offered online. As a licensee of New Line, the Fan Club was able to run a sanctioned website, which set up a community area in which fans could interact. Through it, individuals or small groups spontaneously began forming local branches of the Fan Club that could meet in person. In Düsseldorf, Kathryn Buchhorn (Skybly) organized such a branch, creating another website, www.of-the-shire.net, with a chat room, reports on local Fan Club get-togethers, and a "Middle-earth Scrapbook" that introduced members to each other through photographs and biographical sketches. By early 2002, the Düsseldorf group included 230 members, big enough to warrant an article in the Fan Club magazine, which also launched a regular column called "Fan Focus." Buchhorn voiced a common view among fans, online and off: "This is what I still love most about this place—we are a really diverse group, with people from all walks of life, and yet there is a real family feeling about the Fan Club."[30] The "family" notion crops up again and again in this club and in some of the unofficial fan sites. In the case of the Fan Club, the metaphor was literalized more than once. Madsen corresponded with a woman on the website, met her in person at one of the Oscar parties put on by TheOneRing.net, and eventually married her.

The magazine was built around interviews, notably an update with Peter Jackson in nearly every issue. The editors captured some of the sense of participation associated with the Internet by inviting readers to submit questions and by including some of those questions in every major interview. Club member Mary Kiesling wrote to praise an interview with Howard Shore:

"Also, he answered the question I submitted! I'm over the moon!"[31] The magazine contained numerous regular features, including letters to the editor (MailBaggins), announcements of new merchandise, and a section of minor news items. Most issues also included one surprisingly detailed article profiling a manufacturer of licensed merchandise, from the huge video game company Electronic Arts to Star Toys, a small German company creating resin and vinyl model kits. The series "Unsung Heroes" profiled lesser-known members of the crew, such as the greensmaster and a helicopter pilot. The "Artifacts" series dealt with the craftspeople responsible for the props and costumes. Despite its cumbersome title, *The Lord of the Rings Fan Club Official Movie Magazine* offered a serious and thorough survey of the entire franchise. In 2004, it won an award for excellence in layout and design.[32]

McKellen.com

If the official film site was aimed at existing fans and E! Online's series attracted neophytes, the site that drew people from both groups came from one of the most respected British stage actors of the day and the third oldest of the major cast members. Christopher Lee remarked, "In the film we were both several thousand years old, but in the real world he is some twenty years younger than me, which is young enough to have the habit of keeping a diary in a laptop."[33] (McKellen was sixty when he began work on *Rings;* Lee was seventy-eight.) The diary was added to McKellen.com, which had gone online on 1 September 1997—nearly two years before its owner was chosen to play Gandalf.

The site grew out of McKellen's resistance to the idea of writing his memoirs. The introductory note calls it "my online autobiography." The impetus to start it came in early 1997, when the actor was in Los Angeles to star in *Apt Pupil* (1998). During filming, he had enough spare time to act in *Gods and Monsters* (1998) and to perform his one-man stage show, *A Knight Out.* Not having a laptop to revise the latter, he contacted a computer-adept acquaintance, Keith Stern. Stern recalls, "He found out that I was doing these newfangled things called websites. I'd done one for myself and done one for Spinal Tap, the group and the movie." Given that the proceeds from *A Knight Out* were going to charity, Stern donated his services to create a website for the show. "People came in from all over the country after seeing it on the Internet. Those were early days, early 1997, and anything you put on the Internet that was of any interest or quality at all would tend to get more than its fair share of attention." Impressed, McKellen asked Stern to create a personal website for him.

Many of the features of the site have become fairly standard, but at the time there were no models. "Even the idea of separate photo galleries and the terminology of labeling them 'galleries' was original," says Stern. "Maybe somebody else did it before, but not to my knowledge." Even today, few sites devoted to an individual are so elaborate. From crates stored in McKellen's basement, Stern rescued photographs, programs, and other memorabilia, creating an online archive of modern British theater history. By June 2005 the site contained more than a thousand pages, and many boxes of documents remain to be uploaded.

To keep the site fresh, Stern encouraged McKellen to keep a behind-the-scenes *Rings* diary and suggested he call it "The Grey Book" and later "The White Book." The names derived from Tolkien's original "Red Book of Westmarch" (the book containing *The Hobbit* and *The Lord of the Rings* that Frodo gives Sam), adapted to Gandalf's colors. The first entry in "The Grey Book" was posted on 20 August 1999, shortly after McKellen was cast in *Rings*. Stern couldn't take a camera on set, but his posted snapshots showing McKellen and the other actors amid stunning New Zealand scenery impressed fans. The last entry of "The Grey Book," on 14 December 2001, covered the London premiere of *Fellowship*. On 25 June 2002, "The White Book" began. It dealt with the pickup footage for Films 2 and 3 and ended on 12 November 2003, after McKellen had done his last dialogue dubbing.

When McKellen arrived in New Zealand in January 2000, he was the only one of the major cast members posting on a personal website.[34] The reaction of the other stars to Stern's initial visit to Wellington suggests the novelty of actors' sites at the time. "It all started about the day I arrived on set in May of 2000. I mean, every one of the actors wanted a website, and as soon as they found out that I was there—and they'd all seen Ian's website—it was just a series of meeting after meeting with all the actors in their hotel rooms to do what I could to get their feet wet on the Internet." Hectic shooting schedules prevented them from creating sites right away, but eventually Stern built websites for Andy Serkis and Sean Astin.

McKellen wrote the first on-set Grey-Book report (25 January 2000) in Matamata, where he had begun with the scenes in Hobbiton. His diary created an unintended rivalry with Forde's "Force of Hobbit," which contractually had exclusive rights to on-set coverage. By this point Forde had posted only one "Force of Hobbit" entry, which appeared on 12 January 2000 but covered a day of shooting in the Queenstown area one month earlier. Forde had the advantage of using official publicity photos, and he also talked with stars and key behind-the-camera people like Jackson and Richard Taylor. In

Forde's second report (1 February), Elijah Wood remarked excitedly, "This is the first interview I've had. I haven't been able, really, to talk about it, so this is cool now that I'm right into the project. I've been looking forward to this!"[35]

McKellen, however, was already known to millions of fans as Gandalf (and as Magneto in *X-Men*). His website was well established and had been successful from the start. During the release of *Rings*, it fluctuated between 4 and 8 million hits a month, peaking at more than 25 million in December 2003.[36] Fans loved the site because McKellen made interaction with them an integral part of it. When the site was launched, it linked to McKellen's personal e-mail address, and on most days he would answer fifty to sixty messages. When he was cast as Magneto and Gandalf, the flow of inquiries soared. This mail was a revelation for the actor, who had not read the novel before he was cast and knew little of its immense fan base. Later he told an interviewer, "I learned very early on, because I've got a website, and people communicated with me, and they said, 'Look, get Gandalf right, or there'll be trouble!'"[37] By the end of 1999, the number of e-mails flowing in had risen to about two hundred (in a pre-spam era). According to Stern, "With some regret he asked me to take the link off. It seemed to me that I might somehow screen the e-mail coming in so I could pass the most interesting ones on to him. Geek that I am, I naturally thought a forum would be the best way to do it, and the idea of the 'E-Post' was born—'e-mail' being too American for my anglophile taste."

On 22 February 2000 (the month after McKellen arrived for principal photography), the "E-Post" section went online. Each major project had a separate E-Post, with the ones for *X-Men* and *Rings* commencing simultaneously.[38] The contact address given on the website leads, of course, to Stern, who winnows the fans' messages, but McKellen does personally answer each one that appears on the E-Post.[39] His replies occasionally shed light on such matters as changes from the book, as when one fan asked why Gandalf looks so messy and haggard in *Fellowship*. McKellen replied: "Gandalf the Grey is a wanderer and survives a number of long journeys by foot and horseback— he is rarely sitting out of harm's way in his pony-trap. So of course he gets dusty and dirty, without benefit of wayside washrooms."[40] Even now that the trilogy and DVDs have long since been released, the *Rings* E-Post is updated occasionally. McKellen has remarked, "With an autobiography, you finish it, stop writing, go on with your life, but this is always there. I imagine one day I'll be dying and say to the doctor: 'I just need to post this e-mail, to let the fans know I'm dying!'"[41]

The chatty, heavily illustrated diaries and the *Rings* E-Post elated fans even more than the official and the E! Online series. Now they were getting access to the production, "talking" to one of the primary players. The news sections of many fan sites have immediately posted links to each new *Rings*-related addition to McKellen.com. After *Fellowship*'s success, the media promoted the website to a wider audience. *Entertainment Weekly* recommended that new fans eager for information about Tolkien turn to McKellen: "You've got to hand it to Gandalf for delivering the most *fun* site about the films this side of the Misty Mountains."[42]

Although New Line was not entirely happy with having a second on-set series appearing on the Internet, it did not discourage McKellen from posting *Rings* material. The studio tended, however, to take a conservative view of what information should be released, and McKellen was eager to give fans more than they were receiving on the other official sites. As Stern put it, "Our objective was to give people enough information so that they would have an understanding and a confidence that the material was being treated properly and that Ian had a proper respect and understanding of the material and fans." The result was a constant process of negotiation, with Stern as the cautious member of the team. McKellen told me that Stern "found it *extremely* difficult to be taken seriously by New Line, in terms of having meetings or in terms of leeway with what he could or couldn't do without their say-so. It was me who kept saying, 'Oh, publish! Put it on and be damned!'"

Stern agrees that he was more cautious. "My approach was to basically make an agreement with New Line that we would let them see anything and comment on anything that we were getting ready to post. And in exchange for that courtesy, we would hope that they would only squelch what really needed to be squelched." The system worked well. In practice, New Line did not always have time to check the proposed postings. Stern estimates that he sent about 75 percent of stories to the publicity department. In those cases he might say, "I'm getting ready to post something, and if I don't hear from you by tomorrow or the day after, away it goes." Occasionally New Line asked that the piece not be posted; usually, however, the studio approved or did not respond. The rest of the time Stern would simply post and tell the studio to check it online.

Confidentiality remained an issue, since McKellen tended to conform to Jackson's view of what constituted spoilers—not New Line's: "I kept a diary, 'The Grey Book,' and we showed that to New Line, and they took forever approving it. One of the major problems that they were concerned with was revealing the plot. We had to explain to them that the plot was well known [laughs]—particularly to people who would be accessing the website." As Stern says, "The thing about a confidentiality agreement, of course, is, how do you enforce it? What are you going to do, in the end? Big star, little star, what are they going to do, cut him out of the film?" With millions of fans on his side, McKellen could afford to be, as Booth affectionately terms him, "cheeky."

On the few occasions when New Line requested that something be removed from McKellen.com, Stern complied. Deleted items are difficult to track down, of course, since they usually vanish quickly. I happened to check the site on 30 December 2003, and witnessed the beginning of what might be called "The Case of the Missing ADR Pages." ADR, or automatic dialogue replacement, is the recording and postdubbing of vocal material. It was two weeks after *Return's* release, and ten pages of McKellen's ADR scripts had just been posted. These listed snippets of dialogue, breathing, and laughter that he had recorded in a Soho studio, including the scenes in Edoras where Pippin looks in the *palantír* and where Aragorn and Gandalf discuss whether Frodo is alive. New Line urgently demanded that the pages be taken down. Within twenty-four hours they were gone.

Stern and McKellen were never given a rationale, but both were disappointed. For Stern, "It was at a time where we wanted to kind of remind people a little bit about the great dialogue in the film, and particularly Gandalf's great dialogue. I thought these ADR scripts were something that most people hadn't seen before and would find quite interesting." He hopes to repost the pages: "I think they're wonderful and historic, so I think it's perfectly appropriate for us to post them again."

Despite occasional problems like these, New Line learned from experience and changed its strategy. Stern saw an evolution in the firm's attitude toward fans on the Internet: "It worked out just the way I hoped it would: that they would include the fan sites, support the fan sites, and be clever about the way they used the Internet. I realized the Internet would be very, very important to *Lord of the Rings*. I realized that the fans were on the Internet. I was glad that as time went on and things developed, that they at least seemed to understand that and pay attention to it." As McKellen points out, the result was to "feed the *amazing* appetite that there was out there, for millions of people who were awaiting the films with a sort of concerned desperation that Peter Jackson and I thought was a wonderful thing. There were all these fans of the books who were nervous about the film being made but who were on the side of the film. In advance, why put those people off by not feeding them?"

Together, the officially created and the sanctioned sites soon fostered a sense that fans were glimpsing the making of the film through a virtual keyhole. The production process came across as small in relation to big Hollywood shoots, as taking place in a relaxed and friendly atmosphere, and as happening in a beautiful and remote locale uniquely suited to representing Middle-earth.

Still, as Knowles says, there is never enough information to satisfy fans. Webmasters set out to find out far more and give it to the world. Thus began a lengthy struggle between fans and studio, with concessions made and lessons gradually learned in how to deal with each other. In the wake of *Rings,* a slow shift in the attitude of Hollywood companies has become apparent as they realize the enormous value of the free publicity offered by responsible fan sites. The question is, how does one find the responsible sites and avoid having confidential information leak out into cyberspace?

THE RED BAND: QUASI-SANCTIONED SITES

At the end of the 1990s, fan sites devoted to films were just coming into their own. New Line's August 1998 announcement that it would produce *Rings* was timed perfectly to benefit from this vast new potential for free publicity—yet at that time, like other Hollywood studios, New Line was more suspicious of the motives of the fans than eager to exploit their enthusiasm. Jackson and his team, however, gave two websites privileged cooperation, even allowing their founders to breach—albeit briefly—the taboo against on-set visits by "spies." New Line slowly worked out relationships with both sites and received a flood of publicity. Like McKellen.com, Ain't It Cool News and TheOneRing.net made readers feel they had direct access to the production. Here, though, it was through the eyes not of a star but of fans like themselves.

Ain't It Cool News

The Internet made webmaster Harry Knowles the most influential film devotee in the world. Knowles's parents were dealers in popular-culture collectibles, based in Austin, Texas. He built up his appreciation of film history by exploring their huge stores of accumulated material. At the age of twenty-four, Knowles was bedridden by an accident that severely injured his back, not knowing whether he would ever walk again. His link to the world became his Packard Bell Pentium 66, on which he began surfing the Internet. Rather than adopting a nom de net, as virtually all fans did, he contributed to chat rooms as Harry Knowles. He aspired to provide real show business news à la *Variety* or the *Hollywood Reporter.* His first scoop came when George Lucas previewed footage from *Star Wars: The Special Edition* at Texas A&M. After Knowles's online description was immediately reposted uncredited by various sites, he started his own.[43] "I had a collectibles section, which was a big part of my life at the time, the discussion about film, and then just stories from my life."

About two months after Ain't It Cool News (AICN) went online in February 1996, Jackson saw a photo of Knowles there, holding one of eight known surviving *King Kong* one-sheet posters from 1933. Knowles recalls, "Peter, being a *Kong*-phile of the 'moderate' level [laughs], contacted me, thinking, 'Stupid Internet kid, I'll be able to get this poster cheap.' I told him I'd rather see my father dead. Then we just began the mutual *King Kong* and Forrest J. Ackerman appreciation society and started exchanging e-mails back and forth." The two discussed Jackson's current project, his first attempt to remake *King Kong*. Once it fell through, "Peter kind of disappeared for a while."

In the meantime, AICN was gaining prominence. Ambulatory again, Knowles covered the first Quentin Tarantino Film Fest, held in Austin in September 1996. He discovered that Tarantino was faxing AICN's coverage to people like Steven Spielberg. "That was the first clue I had that I was really making any headway beyond my own borders. I was so technically naïve at this point that I knew nothing about counters." Spy-generated reviews from a test screening of *Titanic,* combined with Knowles's prediction that it would become the highest-grossing film of all time (something few people then believed) brought him attention. "For better or worse, I earned my own weird species of celebrity in the process."[44] Knowles says his Talk Back feature was the first of its type, though lists of reader feedback are now common on websites. To him, "It was one of the closest things you could find to pure democracy on the Internet."[45]

On 30 October 1997, AICN carried a brief story entitled "To Kong or to Hobbit, That Is the Question." At that point *Rings* was well into preproduction at Miramax, but the trade press wasn't covering the project. The next month, Knowles carried a brief, excited announcement that Jackson would make *Rings.*[46] The site pledged itself to support the project. In February 1998, thinking that Miramax was about to terminate the production (and, indeed, Bob Weinstein was by now worried about rising costs), Knowles ran a scathing editorial, "Lord of the Rings!!! Does Miramax Lack Nerve?"[47] He recalls, "I talked about how each of the films could bring in a billion dollars worldwide. I'm sitting there like some sort of Nostra-Harry, basically stating what wound up happening. The reason is that I just believed it was true." When Miramax put *Rings* into turnaround that summer, AICN lambasted the firm. "It's a project [for which] you could create frothing lines of hungry fans panting to be let in. . . . I bet I have a few bazillion fans of the books on my side with this one. Oh, well, I guess Miramax always has *Total Recall 2.*"[48]

AICN deals with popular film culture as a whole rather than specifically with *Rings*. Still, it played a crucial role in blurring the borders between the officially sanctioned sites and those generated by fan enthusiasm. After New Line's 24 August announcement that it had acquired the *Rings* project, Jackson decided to contact fans using AICN. There was, after all, no official *Rings* website yet. He describes it as

> something I did on my own, without New Line's input at all. I don't think I even asked permission to do it. What's interesting about Harry's site obviously is that you get all that feedback stuff where people put all their comments on. The feedback just went crazy, and it was mostly of a slightly hysterical nature. It was mostly fans of Tolkien, of the books, who were dubious about the films, who didn't know me. They didn't have a clue about what I was going to do. I hadn't done interviews about it, so nobody had heard from me about my thoughts about it. There was all this hysterical stuff going on where people were saying things like, "Oh, I bet a Hollywood film, there's no way they can have four Hobbits and no female Hobbits. I bet that Sam will become a girl Hobbit."

Jackson wrote to Knowles, proposing that they solicit inquiries from fans, from which Knowles would pick the twenty most interesting or common ones for the director's responses.

On 26 August AICN invited fans to send questions. Knowles boiled the results down, passed them to Jackson, and posted the answers on 30 August. Knowles thinks one reply especially connected with fans. Asked what moment in the novel he was most eager to capture, Jackson poetically described the Helm's Deep battle as if it would be a historical re-creation based on archaeological evidence. For Knowles, "You read and you just get cold chills over it."

The questions and answers were enormously popular: "It was the very first real press on *Lord of the Rings* where it was the director actually stating what he was going to do." Jackson did another session of twenty questions on AICN on 31 December.[49] This time the questions and answers were edited to form a conversational flow among Knowles, Jackson, and the fans. Questioners were delighted to have such access. Underdog prefaced his question by saying, "Peter, first I want to thank you for being human enough to get down in the mud and play with us." Some fans seemed already to feel themselves as allied with the director against the Hollywood system. One participant asked, "Do you have it in black and white on a contract that the editors aren't going to have a heyday with your film and make some butchered Bakshi-like piece of shit that has a total running time of a little under 3 hours?"

New Line had not been consulted about Jackson's cooperation with AICN and wanted it stopped. The director intended to do more question sessions over the following years and ended the second set with, "Let's do it again!" It was not to be. According to Osborne, doing the sessions "was strictly a Peter decision. Initially New Line was very much against that and squashed it, asked Peter not to do that, and so Peter said, 'Fine,' but over time, Peter won New Line over to the idea that we'd have Harry down here." Nearly two years after the second twenty questions, Knowles reported directly from the set during the last week of principal photography.

Despite the question sessions, considerable fan opposition to Jackson's project lingered. Knowles recalls an incident shortly after the first one. He was participating on a panel at the annual science fiction/fantasy event, Dragon Con (3–6 September 1998), and when he asked the audience of two thousand what they thought of Peter Jackson directing *Rings,* most of them booed. AICN would help to gradually convince the doubters.

The twenty-questions sessions gave AICN a higher profile and an aura of reliability. Several months later, it received an even bigger boost. Following the death of film critic Gene Siskel, of *Siskel & Ebert & the Movies,* Roger Ebert sought a replacement. For several months guest reviewers joined him on the program. Most were traditional media reviewers, such as Kenneth Turan of the *Los Angeles Times.* Knowles, who appeared on the 24 April and 31 October 1999 episodes, was the only Internet reviewer among the guests. Thus he was anointed "an official critic," as he puts it. To the public, he was not a mere fanboy anymore. Many fellow fans would claim that AICN gradually ceased to be a fan site at all, given the money Knowles eventually made with it and the many Hollywood connections he forged. Looked at another way, however, Knowles and some other webmasters invented the category of professional fan.

Knowles's relationship with New Line also improved. Paddison happened to be from Austin, and the two met during his visits to his parents. By late 2000 dealings were friendly enough that New Line gave Knowles permission for the on-set visit as *Rings'* shooting ended. He paid for his own flight, though Jackson insisted on covering his hotel. As far as New Line was concerned, he was there strictly as a guest, not a reporter.

Jackson was not naive enough to think that Knowles would post nothing during his visit, but he describes how even he was taken aback at the result:

> I didn't get into it, because I didn't want to be overly protective. He was coming to visit, and he was sitting on the set, and he had his laptop, and he was

[taps fingertips on table as if typing] on set. I didn't really have a clue what he was actually, really doing, other than I thought he'd obviously write *something* about it. And then the first day he's here, I click onto his site that night, and there's this hugely long report on everything that we'd done that day. And so it was like, "Holy shit! He's doing everything," and the second day I was kind of aware now that everything I was saying and doing was now getting typed in, which was a little more intense than what I'd imagined. But we were in a pretty relaxed state, because it was the end of a long shoot.

New Line seems to have been less philosophical about the series of lengthy reports, which appeared from 22 to 27 December 2000. According to Knowles, "New Line was freaking that I was on-set writing the reports, but once I started, they couldn't stop me." Influential print publications complained about Knowles's preferential treatment, which may have driven home to studio officials how powerful AICN was. The series was allowed to continue.

Quint, a young film-buff friend of Knowles who contributed to AICN, was not so lucky. New Line gave him, too, permission to visit the set, this time in the spring of 2003 during the pickups for *Return.* He wrote nothing then, but when he returned in July, Paddison and New Line's unit publicist for *Rings,* Claire Raskind, agreed to Quint's doing some reports comparable to Knowles's earlier ones. He wrote up a description of Christopher Lee during the filming, which was posted on AICN.[50] According to Quint, "I got an e-mail from Mark Ordesky the next day, saying that I needed to stop writing and that I was invited as a guest, not as press." Paddison had received messages from magazines and newspapers like *USA Today,* which had held off publishing material on *Rings* at his request. They threatened to publish their stories immediately if Quint's series continued. Although Quint hadn't signed a nondisclosure agreement, he ended his series to avoid causing Jackson trouble. The other reports he wrote during that visit have never been posted. The incident illustrates how exclusive agreements with traditional news outlets can lead to a conflict with fan sites. But as such sites grow and drift into the mainstream, they can compete on a more even footing for scoops that they formerly had to get from spies.

As a sign of how things have changed between studios and fan sites, when Quint returned to visit the *King Kong* set in October 2004, Universal agreed to his posting reports on AICN, providing that studio publicists could vet them first. Knowles attributes this increased access partly to Jackson's new power as a director and partly to the fact that AICN is unusual among fan sites in sending a key staff member to spend a significant stretch of time on the scene. And as Quint summed it up when describing Knowles's on-set reports, "[The fans] could tell he was being honest about it. That's what really showed through in those reports. It didn't sound like somebody who was bought and paid to go out there."

Like most fan sites, AICN was initially a money-losing endeavor, dependent on the unpaid labor of its owner and contributors. Despite receiving some early donations amounting to slightly over $10,000, Knowles says, "I sunk ninety thousand of my own money into it, which was my book deal. I used my book deal to get me through the bottom falling out of the Internet. When you have a sinkhole like that that you're sinking money into, you realize, geez, I could've paid off my house." Quint started with AICN as a volunteer. Initially he received funds from Knowles to replace a computer and for travel to events like Comic-Con. After the collapse of the Internet bubble in 2000 and the decline of advertising income, he went back to covering his own expenses.

At that time, Knowles was working through an advertising agency that paid him 30 percent of revenues from ads on AICN. He decided to try selling ads directly, approaching Sony and New Line. Paddison accepted a four-year deal for a banner ad on the site's main page at considerably below standard rates. (Knowles is quick to specify that the deal had no effect on how his writers discuss New Line films—as evidenced by an adverse review of *Blade III* in late 2004.) In 2005, New Line renewed its deal, and several other long-term advertisers came on board. As Quint points out, New Line advertises on several major film-fan sites. "Gordon just knows that their demographic, especially for what they were doing during *Lord of the Rings* days, were sites like Ain't It Cool, CHUD, Coming Soon, those kinds of places."

Quint moved from writer to editor in the summer of 2004, still on a volunteer basis, but the site's finances had improved enough that by the end of that summer he was on the payroll. By then Knowles had also arranged a deal with Amazon.com to receive 15 percent on sales generated by traffic from a link on his site. With AICN's links generating nearly half a million dollars in purchases each quarter, AICN's share would be around $300,000. Together with advertising revenue, the site's finances were finally healthy.

Asked about the overall impact of *Rings* on his website, Knowles replies, "Oh, God! Huge!" For one thing, feeling that he had an actual influence on the production encouraged him to keep the site going. For another, it "created a certain level of trust between me and my audience." Moreover, he credits his close relationship with Jackson as leading to New Line's long-term advertising contract with AICN. Finally, he thinks that the success of the film after Jackson's team cooperated with Knowles "has helped the film industry to recognize the Internet not as a negative place and not as something that's there to destroy you, but as something that can be a support system."

AICN is not a *Rings*-centric site, and it has moved on. Like many touched by the film, however, Knowles sees it as a high point in his life. "I don't know if I'll ever love somebody else's project as much as I love *Lord of the Rings,* simply because it was such a leap of faith to say it was going to be right. When it got eleven Academy Awards, like many *Lord of the Rings* fans, I was crying, but *unlike* many *Lord of the Rings* fans, it was such a complete cry because I had gotten on board *so* early."

TheOneRing.net

What would become far and away the most successful fan site wholly devoted to *Rings*—both books and films—originated in an unprepossessing little page with no name and a lengthy URL housed on the Geocities domain. Erica Challis (nom de net, Tehanu), a professional French-horn player in Auckland, had recently met Michael Regina (Xoanon), a student in Network Technology at CDI College in Montreal, via the Internet, as a result of their mutual interest in fantasy and science-fiction films. Both were excited at the prospect of *Rings* being made, but the site really grew from Challis's love of her country's natural beauty, over which she had hiked extensively.

> I put photos of New Zealand up because I wanted to show people why it was a good place to shoot the movie. I think we might have had one or two reports from TV One. We hardly had anything. So I started writing a series of articles on what is fantasy, why do people need it, why did Tolkien write what he wrote and what influence he had, and Mike started writing a whole series of essays on how you could turn *Lord of the Rings* into a film and what kinds of thing you would have to think about. We were really just speculating a lot.[51]

Challis's site was admired by Tolkien fan Chris Pirrotta (Calisuri), a student in digital media at Pennsylvania State University, who brought in Bill Thomas (Corvar), a computer expert in Kenosha, Wisconsin. The two Americans offered to design a more enticing-looking site. The four cofounders' talents meshed: Challis reported from New Zealand, Regina edited the content, Pirrotta designed the look and navigation of the site, and Thomas handled the technical and financial aspects of installing and maintaining the site in its new home (figure 19). The group wanted the domain name TheOneRing.com, but because that had already been taken, the new site became TheOneRing.net (TORN). The owners of the TheOneRing.com domain name had not yet

Figure 19. The four founders of TheOneRing.net on a panel at the One Ring Celebration in early 2005: *from left:* Chris "Calisuri" Pirrotta, still wearing Elf ears from an earlier skit; Michael "Xoanon" Regina; Bill "Corvar" Thomas; and Erica "Tehanu" Challis. (Photograph by the author.)

put their site online, and they grudgingly changed its name to Tolkien Online. (Perhaps due to a copyright or trademark problem, in 2005 the owners reverted to the original name, The One Ring, www.theonering.com.)

Challis and Regina's "green site," so called because of its dark green background, posted its first news on 10 April 1999. It became TheOneRing.net on 9 May.[52] The new design, still in use, became instantly recognizable to fans seeking *Rings* news. TORN burgeoned. On 27 June, the cofounders issued a plea: "With all the additions that we are making to the site, we find that the 4 of us are needing another person to lighten the load. So we come right out and ask: 'wanna work for us?'" On July 3, an announcement named new volunteer staff, including Quickbeam, nom de net of Cliff Broadway, an actor, playwright, and serious Tolkien buff. Xoanon instituted the site's "Green Books" section, for essays and articles, and Broadway became one of its regular contributors; it has remained a core feature. The Chatroom and the Gaming Havens were also added.

The central focus for many users, however, remained the news items, posted daily on TORN's home page. Challis hiked doggedly over hills and fields near Matamata (soon to be Hobbiton) and around the Queenstown area. Her photos initially showed nothing but New Zealand landscapes perhaps destined to be filming locations. These vistas not only hinted at what might appear in the film but also introduced international fans to the beauties of this remote country. Challis also monitored news leaks and sought glimpses of the preparations for filming. (An early post contained information on the Hobbit holes being built.)[53] Activity intensified when principal photography commenced on 11 October.[54]

Fan and reporter espionage was routine in the early months of filming. Then an event now famous in the annals of online *Rings* fandom occurred. On 16 January 2000, Challis, who had done her share of photographing through fences, was served with a trespassing notice. Challis recalls what led up to that moment:

> One of the reports described the quarry site where they built Minas Tirith and Helm's Deep. Basically I was describing how you could get to watch them filming. I said, it'd be really difficult because there's a lot of gorse and blackberry. You would probably lose your way, but you could probably steer if you kept track of the power pylons which go overhead at that point. And I did this knowing perfectly well that *I* wasn't going to—I mean, I'm in my late thirties. I'm not going to be crawling around there at night.

The security staff tracked Challis from place to place through her reports, and upon returning home, she was served a notice banning her for two years from the quarry site. E! Online had exclusive on-set coverage, and Forde noted in his January "Force of Hobbit" entry: "Spies from TheOneRing.net have been spotted trying to gain access to the set. But security has been tightened even further in an effort to ensure that no more news or photos leak out."[55] The reference was to a fashion magazine that had printed photos of Liv Tyler in costume—which perhaps made New Line particularly nervous about spies at that time.

Challis mentioned the notice to some reporters who themselves were being chased away from filming locations. She recalls, "Probably out of boredom and frustration, they decided to turn that into a story, and they sort of blew it up into this big thing: 'This poor little fan is being oppressed by this big film company.'" After the story appeared in the papers, she was interviewed on national television. Challis may have intrigued the media because she was not a typical teenage male fan (many of whom actually did crawl through the gorse above that quarry), but a slight, intelligent, polite thirty-six-year-old woman.

The publicity drew the attention of the filmmakers. Jackson's account of the incident reflects how the studios and filmmakers were confronting this new phenomenon of fan-site spies:

> The One Ring was initially seen as quite a threat in the sense that they were clearly out to spy on us—which was a novelty for us. Never in my life have I ever had an Internet site trying to find out everything that we're doing. It wasn't anything to do with us, but New Line got incensed, and they put a legal trespass notice on her personally. The paranoia about what The One Ring was finding out was growing, and it was making them more determined, and I just felt it was all getting a bit out of control.

A truce was reached about a week after the notice was served. Challis was again in Matamata to show the Hobbiton area to a tourist. She ran into a security guard whom she knew, and he suggested that she talk to Barrie Osborne. Challis left her card at the production office, and Osborne phoned her. He recalls, "I brought her out to Hobbiton, and she got to meet Ian McKellen, and she was overall thrilled with that. Again, [it was] mostly driven by Peter, who said the best tactic is to welcome her instead of driving her away." Jackson confirms this: "I said to Barrie, 'If you like her, if she's actually a decent sort of person, why don't you just give her a surprise and tell her to jump in your car and you'll drive her onto the set?' Barrie went off, and we kept shooting a scene with Ian McKellen on the cart arriving into the village." Challis recalls that during the drive to Matamata, Osborne was on his cell phone with New Line's publicist, reassuring her about allowing a spy onto the set. Jackson says that once he met Challis, "We invite her just to sit down right beside me, and I chat to her, and she meets Ian McKellen, and all this sort of stuff, and we just say, 'Hey, we're sorry about this trespass thing. It was stupid, and let's just all behave in a better way.'" All parties agreed that the filmmakers would try to accommodate TORN without New Line having any editorial control over postings.

Challis naturally wanted to post a description of her one day on set, and she was given permission. She recalls the online reaction: "A lot of the major people following *The Lord of the Rings* just wouldn't believe it, they wouldn't post it. They were just either spitting with jealousy or they wouldn't believe it." Once it became clear that TORN had gotten "the scoop of all scoops," many fans labored under the impression that Challis had regular on-set access from then on. In fact she went back to the position of peering in with her nose to the fence. When she later visited Wellington, she was invited on-set again, provided that she would not report on what she saw.

The single report gave TORN a powerful reputation as a reliable news source. Challis's day in Hobbiton was the beginning of a special relationship between the filmmakers and TORN that has not ended even now. Most of the cast and crew read the site regularly. Booth says she sometimes used TORN to keep track of actors' birthdays so that she could arrange for presents.

Cliff Broadway had worked for McKellen.com for several years, and though he had to keep confidential much of what he learned in that job, occasionally McKellen and Keith Stern would provide special news items for TORN. In November 2000, as a result of his work on both sites, Broadway was allowed to visit the set for a week and wrote five reports—though, unlike Knowles, Broadway delayed posting them for a year until shortly before *Fellowship* appeared, to maximize interest.[56] Although the reports contained information about *Towers* and *Return* as well, New Line did not protest.

TORN also hosts the quasi-official Jackson fan site, The Bastards Have Landed (http://tbhl.theonering.net/index.shtml).

As with AICN, the early period of TORN was rocky financially. With no guarantee of reimbursement, Bill Thomas, the most gainfully employed of the group, paid several thousand dollars for expenses. Eventually TORN began to make money. Where AICN depends on advertising, TORN built up income through merchandising. In December 2001, Sideshow Weta, producer of collectible statues and busts, arranged for a link on the site. Fees on sales provided TORN's main source of income (and a career opportunity for Chris Pirrotta, who was hired as Sideshow's webmaster). It also earned income through its links to Amazon.com and other retailers of *Rings* merchandise. Thomas was repaid, and profits go to various charities. The staff still receive no income and usually forgo reimbursement for small expenses.

The site's relationship with New Line slowly improved. Gordon Paddison provided press releases and other material, as he was doing with a few dozen other sites. On the other hand, he monitored TORN and occasionally asked for items to be removed. In one major incident, an unrendered image of Gollum surfaced and was briefly posted. Pirrotta recalls, "Then we're like, 'Wait a second! Didn't we tell Weta that we weren't going to put it up? Aw, crap!' Because this is how One Ring operates. It was just 'Mike? Take it down! Take it down!' But by the time *we* had taken it down, it spread out through the Internet." TORN also posted April Fool's news items. When, on 1 April 2002, the site reported that Andrew Lesnie's Best Cinematography Oscar had been rescinded, neither New Line nor Jackson appreciated the humor, and the item was deleted.

TORN played a crucial role in maintaining the *Rings* franchise, through the series and beyond. From that and other sites New Line discovered the virtues of cooperating and negotiating with fans. Says Alyson McRae, the film's first marketing coordinator: "I think [Gordon Paddison] had to develop relationships with them because [New Line] really wanted to control the release of information, and a lot of these fan sites were very effective in cutting across that. It was very important to him to build a relationship so that he could say, 'All right, you've got that, but we'd like you to hold off,' or 'I can give you this, but—'." If point people like Knowles and Challis could be brought into the inner circle and would pledge to keep some secrets, the fans' experience could be enhanced and their loyalty solidified.

THE BLUE RING: MULTIPLIER NEWS SITES

New Line's first effort at Internet publicity simply gathered material for its own site. The idea was to control all the information, without recourse to fan outlets. Soon, however, Paddison saw that a degree of cooperation with those sites was advantageous. As he put it, "New Line chose to embrace the existing Tolkien 'eco-system.'"[57] The practice Paddison drew upon was viral marketing, which depends on people who receive news about products passing it along to others, who then pass it along. "The best way to advertise your product," he notes, "is to have your best friend advertise it by sending it to you. That way the message doesn't come from New Line, it comes from someone you trust."[58] Obviously such a tactic assumes that the first people who receive the news want to share it. *Rings* fans were ideal for viral dissemination of information.

Paddison not only ran lordoftherings.net but also cooperated with a group of sites that grew from about 25 early on to 50 by the end. Press releases and images were provided to those, and then other sites either linked to them or reposted the items, spreading the material like ripples on a pond. Paddison has described how he found the "QEIB," or "quantifiable early Internet buzz" in his search for *Rings* multipliers: "It's nice simple science. . . . I look for which Websites index highest for frequent moviegoers in this target demographic: 17 to 24 males who are 220% more likely to attend this movie based on genre."[59] The point, again, is not to convince them to go—they presumably would anyway—but to convince them to communicate their enthusiasm to others.

One such site was Tolkien Online (now The One Ring, www.theone ring.com). Founded in April 1999 by two friends, later joined by a third, who were fans of the books, the site was slanted toward the novel but covered the film as well. Like so many webmasters, they contributed a significant part of the salary from their regular jobs to support the site. "Monthly, it costs us the mortgage of a mid-size house to keep it running," one of them explained, adding, "At night when I check my dozens of emails, there's usually one that says, 'I really love the site! I check it every day. Thanks so much for giving me such a great place to share my love of The Lord of the Rings.' And that's what keeps us wanting to work on the site every night and weekend."[60]

Shortly after *Fellowship* opened, longtime Tolkien fans Fatty and Iluvatar set out to create their own *Rings*-based website. After months of layout, design, and gathering of content, on 21 June 2002, War of the Ring (www. warofthering.net) went online and grew rapidly. Initially it had fewer than a thousand daily unique hits, but a year later it was averaging more than 1.6 million hits a day, 35,000 to 40,000 of them first-time visitors.

WOTR's popularity did not go unnoticed. Although representatives of this site did not visit Wellington to view filmmaking, New Line and its licensees cooperated with them to a considerable extent. Like TORN, WOTR's in-dex page carries news stories relating to the novel, the film, the video games and other products, the actors' and crew members' activities, and anything else remotely related to Tolkien. There is an extensive art gallery, with im-ages by famous Tolkien illustrators and by fans, an archive of interviews, and a separate department for information about the film. As is typical, the web-masters spend an enormous amount of time keeping the site going. Although advertising and commissions on products sold through links bring in some income, they were forced to solicit voluntary subscriptions, which has been a common tactic for some of the large sites.

Paddison's multiplier effect worked very well. Consider a brief series of post-ings on another prominent site, the Council of Elrond (www.council-of-elrond .com), on 29 September 2002 (underlining indicates links).

Tolkien Online has gotten hold of four new Two Towers advertising posters. Pretty nice! Check them out! Thanks Mormegil!

Over at The War of the Ring you can find some nice pictures and infor-mation about the Universal/Black Label FOTR game. Looks like fun! Thanks Fatty!

The New Zealand Herald interviewed Marton Csokas (Celeborn) about his role as Yorgi, a Russian villain in XXX. (Thanks peta)

Fatty from <u>War of the Ring</u> has some *downloads* available of the new LotR games. They also have some <u>nice pics</u> from the extended DVD and some pics from *The Two Towers*. Check them out! (Thanks Fatty!)

The large number of *Rings*-oriented websites creates an enormous amount of overlap and repetition. Fans are not likely to miss any significant news.

Grudging though New Line's cooperation with fan sites might occasionally have seemed, it went distinctly beyond what most Hollywood studios and directors did for major sites devoted to other films. Neither George Lucas nor Twentieth Century Fox gave TheForce.net the sort of input that Jackson and New Line did for TheOneRing.net, AICN, and the multipliers. Because the studio and the filmmakers cooperated with so many fan sites, webmasters were willing to police themselves and to remove spoilers or other items if asked to do so. Coproducer Rick Porras points out how remarkably few spoilers got out, considering the size of the production, the number of outdoor locations, and the sending of filmic elements around the globe. "I can only take from that that it wasn't just *our* diligence, but it was also the helpful diligence of those gatekeepers out there on the web."

Much of Hollywood has been slow to learn how valuable a resource fan websites can be. In June 2004, when *The Chronicles of Narnia: The Lion, the Witch and the Wardrobe* was about to start principal photography in Auckland, I interviewed its producer, Mark Johnson, and unit publicist, Ernie Malik. Erica Challis had been making tentative inquiries about receiving cooperation to start a *Narnia*-related website or Web page hosted on TORN. I told Johnson and Malick something about TORN and its founders and how they were providing free publicity for *Rings*. They knew about TORN but were surprised to learn that the people running it poured a great deal of their time and money into the site without payment from New Line. After talking with Challis herself, Johnson and Malick agreed to cooperate in a smaller *Narnia* site hosted by TORN, TheOneLion.net (www.theonelion.net). Initially Challis was allowed four set visits, resulting in five articles, but the Buena Vista Pictures marketing department okayed their posting only at increasingly long intervals, with the last one not coming out for more than a year. Challis also posted the usual sorts of spy reports, and marketing requested that some items be removed. Deciding that Disney was treating her as an unpaid employee, Challis stopped working on TheOneLion.net, which became essentially a multiplier site posting studio press releases and other news.

As this incident suggests, Hollywood's acceptance of fan-generated publicity is uneven. Not all studios are willing to cede even a modicum of control in exchange for free coverage by fans. In 2004, *Variety* queried fan webmasters and found that they considered Sony, New Line, and Warner Bros. to be the most receptive to their sites, while DreamWorks and Universal were the least.[61] As Hollywood discovers the value of such publicity, however, more studios will undoubtedly figure out how to ensure security without quashing fan enthusiasm.

Jackson himself has understood the potential of fan sites better than perhaps any other director. For *King Kong,* he cooperated with TORN to form another hosted site, KongIsKing.net. On the first day of principal photography, Michael Pellerin, producer-director of the *Rings* extended-version DVD supplements, began filming behind-the-scenes footage. Without any involvement from Universal aside from financial support, Jackson and Pellerin sent in a series of eighty-nine short videos to form a production diary, posted frequently on KongIsKing.net.[62] In effect, Jackson became his own spy. (The contact address on the site, spymaster@kongisking.net, acknowledged that role.) In several episodes, Jackson reads out questions sent in by fans, addressing them by name. This approach gave him not only a closer connection with grateful fans but also more control over what information became public. With access up close and personal, who needed to stand pressed against the chain-link fence? Jackson even staged a comic scene of the crew chasing after a fictional spy (day 36), as if to flaunt the lack of real ones. *Entertainment Weekly* remarked, "Jackson's determination to turn himself into a kind of reality TV character is in some ways a heroic gesture, more an expression of his love for moviemaking than a commercial stratagem."[63]

No doubt, but the diaries could be both. Since fans will pay for promotional material—even material that has previously been available for free—Jackson released fifty-four of the entries on two DVDs, *"King Kong"—Peter Jackson's Production Diaries,* on 13 December 2005, the day before the feature's theatrical release. In October the production diaries had been removed from KongIsKing.net. (The postproduction diaries, thirty-five of them, appeared on the two-disk release of *Kong;* as of mid-April 2006 they remained on KongIsKing.net.) One fan-magazine writer commented: "As a past contributor to Frederick S. Clarke's *Cinefantastique,* where in-depth on-set reportage of fantasy film production originated, for better or worse, I find it fascinating that such reportage—the stuff of small circulation fanzines 20–30 years ago—has now vaulted into the upper strata of the DVD mainstream."[64] Thus Jackson took a logical step forward in turning fan-friendly publicity material into a revenue-producing stream.

Jackson's *Kong* diaries may have started a trend. Bryan Singer (who visited the set of *Kong* and appears in the production diaries) started a video blog on the production of *Superman Returns*. Like Jackson, he chose a fan site, BlueTights.net, rather than the film's official website (which contains a link to BlueTights.net). Having a director like Jackson or Singer pressing the flesh or signing autographs along a red carpet during a premiere offers a few on-lookers a brief brush with fame. The Internet allows fans to read the film-maker's detailed accounts addressed to them or replies to people like them-selves, and this may give them an even greater sense of contact with filmmakers than personal appearances do.

CHAPTER 6

Fans on the Margins, Pervy Hobbit Fanciers, and Partygoers

What would the film industry be without
the obsessed?

AL LIEBERMAN AND PATRICIA ESGATE
The Entertainment Marketing Revolution

LEAVING THE OFFICIAL AND QUASI-OFFICIAL sites and moving to the more
peripheral areas of the target, we reach the realm of fan sites that receive no
input at all from the studio or filmmakers, directly or through linking to multipliers. These sites arise spontaneously and display the enormous range of interests and imagination of their founders and contributors. The marketers cannot control what these sites do. It may be hard for executives in New York or
Los Angeles to understand why fans treat comments signed by Iluvatar or Fatty
or Ancalagon seriously. In a few past cases, not liking how some fans have ap-
propriated their work, Hollywood filmmakers and producers have tried to
squelch sites devoted to their franchises. Ultimately they seem to have realized that such coercion simply calls more attention to the sites and makes the
studios look like ogres. New Line has adopted the general attitude of the industry: toleration, acceptance, or even in some cases cautious encouragement.
After all, these fans are, in their own way, promoting the films they love. As
Lieberman and Esgate say above, the industry depends on obsessive fans.

Once fans socialize in cyberspace, they often want to meet each other. Many
Rings sites have provided the means for organizing parties, and in a few cases
New Line has accepted them as well.

Lilith of Sherwood's first *Rings*-related page was created on 28 January 2002, shortly after the release of *Fellowship*, but she was no newbie. She had read the novel at the age of ten in the late 1960s and had been a devotee ever since. Like many fans, however, she chose to ignore most of the prerelease *Rings* coverage, trying not to get her hopes up that the film would live up to the novel.

Also like many fans, Lilith became an immediate convert upon seeing *Fellowship*. She recalls, "I went on opening weekend and loved it desperately. And then spent the next couple of months catching up on the Internet on everything that I hadn't read." A longtime Ian McKellen fan (she had traveled regularly from Chicago to London to see him on the stage in the 1980s), she also became fascinated with Elijah Wood. A veteran of a number of fandoms from the late 1970s on, Lilith already had a website devoted to her other main interest, figure skating, that hosted a sci-fi/fantasy site started, as she recalls, in 1999. On 28 January 2002, she added a *Rings* section to the latter with a layout of fourteen photographs of Wood headed, "Happy Birthday, Elijah."[1] The *Rings* portion soon took up so much time that by the end of the year Lilith handed the running of the skating site over to a friend and removed the sci-fi/fantasy pages.

Lilith's Lord of the Rings Site (http://lilithlotr.com/) is an excellent example of a small site that does not try to stay current by posting news items each day. Rather, it reflects its owner's personal tastes. The primary content is photographs, grouped by actor. The links on the home page lead to sections on Wood, McKellen, Orlando Bloom, Sean Bean, Viggo Mortensen, and Liv Tyler—though Lilith admits to neglecting the Bloom section, given how many websites on him sprang up. A keen amateur photographer herself, Lilith sets her site apart by attending events and posting exclusive images of them. She estimates that during the time that the films were being produced and released, she made significant trips to events five or six times a year.

Like many owners of individual fan sites, Lilith works in a completely unrelated job as an administrative assistant in a real estate appraisal company. After twenty-five years with the same firm, she has a flexible vacation schedule that allows her to travel to places where the actors appear. For years she devoted most of her free time to the site and has spent a considerable amount of money on it—not so much for hosting and bandwidth as for travel and purchases of items to scan and post. "My highest cost is when I was maintaining my articles section, which is now way behind. My articles section I saw as sort of what defined my site, because it was so much more complete than anyone else's. I was quite often spending two hundred dollars a month on magazines until February of this year [2004], when everything pretty much started tapering off for *Lord of the Rings*."

We have seen that a big site like Ain't It Cool News or The OneRing.net can fund itself and even make a profit. Lilith has almost no income from her site. She has had five separate hosts, mostly paid for, though when I interviewed her, she was temporarily being hosted for free on a larger site. Her commercial links, including to Amazon.com, bring in barely twenty dollars a year. She has a small income from selling duplicate collectibles and copies of her own celebrity photographs on eBay, which has helped underwrite her purchases of items for scanning.

Lilith's home, a one-bedroom apartment in a pleasant older brownstone on the north side of Chicago, resembles a self-storage unit stuffed with *Rings* collectibles, magazines, videotapes, DVDs, photographs, posters, and, of course, books. In between, as if added as an afterthought, are a few modest chairs, a mattress, and a desk. The main furniture consists of shelves to hold her collection, which occupies most of the floor space as well.

Lilith is, she would unashamedly admit, totally obsessed, but she is no antisocial depressive hiding from the world. She is articulate, intelligent, confident, witty, and generous. She was pressing *Rings* paper plates and bookmarks on me as soon as I arrived and by the end of my visit was lending me rare videotapes to copy. She knows many like-minded fans and gets together with them at film festivals, fan conventions, and other events where the *Rings* actors appear.

Gatherings of fans and public appearances of cast or crew members at conventions and parties have been an important facet of Lilith's site. For example, she went to New Zealand in 2003 to take a special tour of *Rings* locations offered by Red Carpet Tours in celebration of the world premiere of *Return* on 1 December. A photographic diary of that trip can be found on her website (figure 20), as can collections of photographs from Comic-Con 2004, the Lincoln Center screenings of the trilogy with several stars in attendance in January 2004, and various appearances by cast and crew for book signings.

There is a distinctly altruistic side to the contents of her site, which she views as an archive preserving ephemeral material. Just as her own first birthday greeting to Wood is still on the site, she has hundreds of texts and images available for others to enjoy. Lilith talks about the fact that she is one of the few to cite the sources of the articles she posts. (I first encountered Lilith when using her website to read articles I had not been able to track down.) Now that the film is over, Lilith foresees no fundamental change in her site.

Figure 20. Lilith of Sherwood in Wellington, following in the footsteps of the *Fellowship* actors by getting a tattoo. (Photograph © Lilith of Sherwood, used by permission.)

For one thing, she has a huge backlog of *Rings*-related material to scan and upload: "It's going to take me another three years just to catch up. Because mine is just driven by me and not what anybody else wants to see, I may concentrate more on, say, Ian and Elijah than other things."

For Lilith, fandom has been personally fulfilling. She loves photography, and the site allows her a forum to present images that many people want to see. She gets to travel to interesting events and occasionally interact with the celebrities she admires. Like most fans, she loves being in the presence of the celebrities and being able to talk with them, but she quite clearly does not want to be a pest. She speaks of standing in lines at book signings, trying to think of something to say that might interest the star. She also disapproves of some of the antics fans indulge in to draw attention to themselves: "I can understand the compulsion to be noticed at all costs. I guess I can theoretically understand it because I want to be noticed myself. If I can't be noticed for something that is at least interesting, if not wonderful, I would rather not."

Is Lilith noticed? When I interviewed Keith Stern, I asked whether he recognized the name. He recalled having received e-mail messages from her and said that he and McKellen have come to recognize a group of fans who show up at the actor's theatrical performances, book signings, and premieres: "You look around and say, 'Where are they?' so, yes, there's that core, which on *Lord of the Rings* could have been fifty or sixty people." Far from being dismissive of such enthusiasts, Stern adds, "If you're going to be an obsessive fan, I think Ian McKellen is as good an actor as you can find to be obsessive about."

ON THE MARGINS: FANFICTION AND FANART

At the beginning of 1970, Tolkien was struggling to complete *The Silmarillion,* which he would leave unfinished at his death three years later. He wrote to one of his sons, "When you pray for me, pray for 'time'! I should like to put some of this stuff into readable form, and some sketched for others to make use of."[2] Seemingly he realized that the world he had created was so vast as to invite other writers to contribute to chronicling it. He could not have conceived, however, just how vast and varied a body of Middle-earth writings and artworks would eventually arise from the ranks of his novel's fans and later from those of the film.

Fans have been creating their own artworks based on films, TV shows, and books for many years, but the Internet has allowed the broad dissemination of works that used to be strictly personal or shared with a few like-minded people. Henry Jenkins, one of the first scholars to study fan creativity, has termed this activity "textual poaching." Fans around the globe are using the characters and images of *Rings* in a way that may appear to violate copyright or trademark laws—though such activity has been credibly defended as fair use.[3] Whatever the legal status of these creations, their sheer quantity would make enforcement extremely cumbersome. Moreover, some companies are perhaps reluctant to harass fans who are, after all, providing free publicity of a sort. The companies may also not want to draw attention to unapproved sites.

Humor and Parodies

Whole websites and pages exist to collect or link Tolkien-related humor, whether inspired by the novel or the film. Among the more prominent are Tolkien Sarcasm (http://flyingmoose.org/tolksarc/tolksarc.htm) and Ring-bearer.org's humor section (http://www.ringbearer.org/modules.php?op = modload&name = Sections&file = index&req = listarticles&secid = 3). Links to a number of items can be found at directory.google.com/Top/Arts/Movies/Titles/L/Lord_of_the_Rings_Series/Humor. These include the pair of "Engrish Captions" pages, featuring frame captures with risible English subtitles from the Asian bootleg DVDs. These include Galadriel's comment during the mirror scene in *Fellowship,* "You are a wing baron Frodo" and Merry's assurance to Treebeard in *Towers,* "We are not oaks we are hobiks."[4]

One of the most famous humorous websites resulted from a typical fan tendency to seize upon seemingly trivial aspects of films and run with them. Two students, Iris Hadad from Israel and Sherry de Andres from England, became fascinated with one of the Elves present at the Council of Elrond, although he does not speak and occupies all of three seconds onscreen. After meeting on TheOneRing.net and discovering their shared devotion, the two decided to celebrate the Elf's beauty by naming him and creating a website for him. The reaction "Frodo is great—who is that!!?" gave rise to the acronym Figwit, and this highly un-Tolkienesque name stuck. Figwit Lives! went online in March 2002 (www.figwitlives.net; figure 21).

Hadad and de Andres were amazed when their site quickly became a sensation. A link posted on TORN led to a flood of hits, so many that the site, then hosted on a small, free Geocities account, went down within five minutes. Even upgrading to a larger paid site later in the day was not enough, and only after a friend agreed to host some of the files could Figwit Lives! cope with its sudden popularity. Now having a name to connect with the face, other Figwit fanciers created additional sites devoted to the Elf, universally described as "pouty." The phenomenon was big enough to attract major media attention, with *USA Today* running a story on Figwit Lives! and Bret McKenzie, the extra who played Figwit. The story quotes de Andres on the secret of the Elf's appeal for fans: "His enigmatic broodiness worked its magic on them."[5] In August 2002, the pair got the chance to meet the object of all the fuss when McKenzie and his partner Jermaine Clement brought their musical group, Flight of the Conchords, to a comedy festival in Scotland. The Scottish Tolkien Association threw a garden party for McKenzie and his admirers.

Unlike most fan sites, Figwit Lives! actually influenced the filmmakers. Some members of the cast and crew were well aware of the Figwit phenomenon, and the producers decided to bring McKenzie back for a walk-on role in *Towers,* but he was out of town. Later, the filmmakers needed an Elf to say a single line in the *Return* forest scene where Arwen decides to stay in Middle-earth. This time McKenzie was available, and the scene allowed "Figwit" to return and finally to speak—though he appears in the credits simply as an "Elf Escort."

The three writers' discussion of this scene in their commentary on the

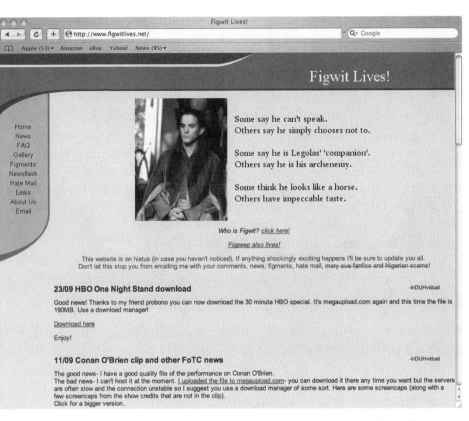

Figure 21. The home page of Figwit Lives! with Bret McKenzie as the pouty, silent Elf. (Courtesy Figwit Lives!)

extended-version DVD tends to confirm that Jackson was not as au courant on fan sites as some of those fans might have imagined:

JACKSON: That was Fidwit, isn't it? What's his name, Fid-, Fij-, What's his—?

WALSH: No. *Fig*wit.

JACKSON: Figwit. That was actually put in just for fun, for the fans, because we didn't even know about this character. I can't even pronounce his name, yet this guy was created by the fans, really. He was an extra in the Council of Elrond scene, and so much fuss had been made about him over the last couple of years that we had this moment where we wanted to have just this brief moment with an anonymous Elf, but we thought, well, rather than making him anonymous, let's make him Fig-, Figwid.

WALSH: Fig*wit*.

JACKSON: What?

WALSH: "Frodo is great . . . who is that?"[6]

Even the official licensed products associated with *Rings* were affected when in July 2004, Decipher Games included a trading card depicting the Elf as he appears in *Return* in one of its game packs. Although the card names him (with an apparent pun) as "Aegnor, Elven Escort," a note below declares, "Affectionately referred to as 'Figwit' by his contemporaries at Rivendell."[7]

The links section of Figwit Lives! lists eleven other sites devoted to McKenzie's character. That number remained constant from January to October 2005, so it appears that the phenomenon had leveled off. Figwit Lives! is seldom updated. McKenzie has moved on. The Flight of the Conchords has become more prominent, featuring on Rolling Stone's "Hot List" in 2005, a BBC 2 radio series, and late-night American talk shows. In September 2006, HBO announced that it had ordered a pilot and 11 episodes of a half-hour comedy starring the Flight of the Conchords.[8]

One of the cleverest and most elaborate parodies of the film occupies the site Lord of the Peeps (www.lordofthepeeps.com) based on candy Peeps, the little marshmallow chicks and bunnies typically sold in the United States around Easter. A whole genre of Peeps websites has evolved on the Internet (a list of which can be found in the links section of Peeps). The creators may simply place the Peeps in real locales and take a series of photographs of them, but the animal shapes and the blandness of the candies encourage costuming and elaborate staging in miniature sets.

The Lord of the Peeps (Peeps) uses this approach. Its creator, Genevieve Baillie, has been building the site with the help of her parents since 29 May 2002, when she was a chemistry major about to graduate from college. She and her mother were devotees of the novel and were at first skeptical about the films, but *Fellowship* converted them into fans. The Peeps site centers on an elaborate re-creation of the film's mise-en-scène in miniature, with costumed bunny Peeps playing the characters and chicks doing duty as horses. (As Baillie says, "At the end of the day I've often sat there and said to myself, 'I just spent the whole day dressing marshmallows.'")[9] Computer-generated imagery provides eyes, landscapes, weather effects, and the like (figure 22).

The density of the site comes only partly from the "movie," however. Peeps parodies the fan culture around the franchise. Its home page has numerous links of the type that one might find on a large fan site: News, Previews,

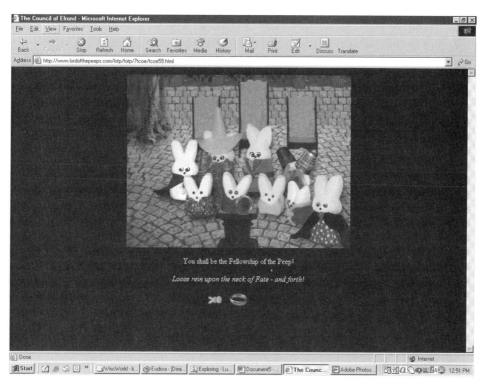

The Council of Elrond - Microsoft Internet Explorer

File Edit View Favorites Tools Help

Back   Forward   Stop   Refresh   Home   Search   Favorites   Media   History   Mail   Print   Edit   Discuss   Translate

Address http://www.lordofthepeeps.com/lotp/lotp/7tcoe/tcoe59.html   Go

You shall be the Fellowship of the Peep!

Loose rein upon the neck of Fate - and forth!

Done   Internet

Start   WiscWorld - k...   Eudora - [Dimi...   Exploring - Lu...   Document5 - ...   The Counc...   Adobe Photos...   12:51 PM

Figure 22. The Fellowship is formed in The Lord of the Peeps. (Courtesy The Lord of the Peeps.)

Movie, Images, Interviews, Extras, Reviews, Comments, Links, and Shop. According to Baillie, "That's really been the most fun—not just writing the book chapters, but writing all the interviews, news stories, and other extras, and being dead serious about the whole thing. I've even written horrible 'Peeps' fanfiction!" The shop contains tiny clay "action figures" of Gandalf ("With hat-wearing action") and Frodo ("With staring action") in packages that replicate the color and graphic design for the licensed *Fellowship* merchandise. The remarks in the reviews section vary a theme: "'Someone has too much time on their hands. Very cute, though,' meig; 'Could I *PLEASE* have a little of the free time these people obviously have in such abundance?' Tracy." The interviews section includes conversations with Bunny Boyd, Sean Peepstin, and Orlando Peep ("Well, I'm into the whole extreme sports thing. Which doesn't really make the producers happy, but hey, you're only fresh once. But I get in big trouble with the makeup crew if I stay out at the beach long enough to get carmelized.").[10] The Extras section offers a screen saver of Frodo that juxtaposes a large image of the Peep/Hobbit on the left with three smaller images in boxes arranged vertically at the right—the same layout used in lordofthering.net's many *Fellowship* screen savers.

Such features, along with the links section, take the Peeps site beyond the level of movie parody. Some links take the visitor to real websites "that cover Tolkien's work and a movie version that stars human actors." The most notable, however, connects to another Baillie creation: The One Peep, with home page graphics, layout, and typeface that closely match those of TheOneRing.net. The One Peep contains departments paralleling some of TORN's. A "Spy Photos" site uses Peeps to re-create actual spy photos posted on TORN during the film's production (such as actors in Black Rider costumes smoking between takes). The "Fan Section" offers a few parodies of fanfiction and fanart. Another link on The One Peep's home page leads to a Forum section, where the threads, postings, and noms de net have a nuttiness that is almost indistinguishable from what sometimes appears on real LiveJournals and Yahoo! lists.

Baillie "thought Figwit was such a delicious fandom phenomenon that I couldn't resist including him." Hadad and de Andres noticed this and immediately started a Figpeep Lives! site (figure 23), an homage to an homage to an homage. As with The One Peep, Figpeep Lives! replicates the layout and style of its original, Figwit Lives!

Although the traffic on Lord of the Peeps fell off during 2005, Baillie thinks this may be due partly to the lack of updates. Having started graduate school, she no longer has "too much free time on her hands," but she and her parents hope to continue building the site.

Fanfiction: Gen, Het, FPS, and RPS

Those who use the Internet primarily for news or shopping can have little sense of just how many fans are creating stories ("fics") and artworks based on characters and situations from books, films, comics, video games, cartoons, and TV shows. In the pre-Internet days, far fewer fics or artworks were created, and they were either shared only among family and friends or published in small photocopied magazines, universally referred to as "zines," which typically were sold through the mail or at fan conventions. The Internet caused an explosion in the number of fandoms and the number of fics and artworks being created. Zines still exist, but they are now marketed over the Internet as well as at conventions.[11]

Rings seems to have generated a moderate level of fan creativity before the

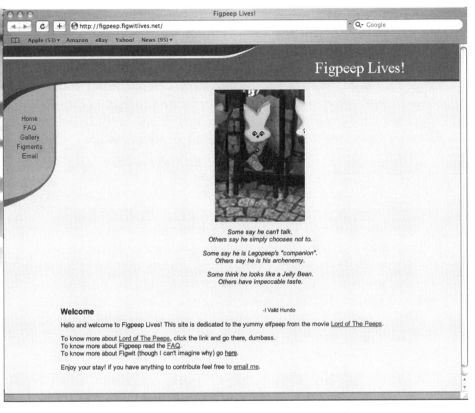

Figure 23. The home page of Figpeep Lives! (Courtesy Figpeep Lives!)

release of the films, but within weeks of the December 2001 release of *Fellowship,* Yahoo! groups and archives of fics and fanart were being created by the hundreds. More recently LiveJournals have become a popular way of posting stories and images. Authors write scenes that could fit plausibly into the worlds of the novel or the film, adhering to "book-canon" or "film-canon" (also termed "book-verse" and "film-verse"). Many authors, however, simply adopt the settings and characters' names to spin narratives that have virtually nothing to do with the plot of either.

There are many genres of fanfiction, all of which fall into the broad categories of gen (general), het (heterosexual), FPS (fictional-person slash, usually just referred to as slash), and RPS (real-person slash).

Gen fics typically take situations from the books and flesh them out, as when some of the minor Hobbits who have only a few lines in the book become the protagonists of new tales. Het stories are pretty much what one might expect: male/female romances, with or without erotic content. "Slash" fics center around same-sex romance, also with or without erotic scenes. Far and away the majority of *Rings* slash stories are male/male, though there are occasional female/female pairings as well, known as "femmeslash." "Slash" refers to the punctuation mark used to indicate the pairing, as in one of the most common *Rings* couples, Aragorn/Legolas. Fanfiction groups and archives have widely adopted the Motion Picture Producers Association ratings, from G to NC-17—though most NC-17 fics contain scenes far more explicit than anything in mainstream American films with that rating.

One clearinghouse for fics is fanfiction.net, which compiles writing based on all sorts of mass-media sources, from books and cartoons to movies and television programs. This is the place to find romantic tales written by girls frittering away their time in chemistry lab and boasting about it. As of 9 January 2006, the site listed 38,806 *Rings*-related works; it lumps book-verse and movie-verse together. (An additional 1,775 pieces were based on Tolkien's unfinished epic, *The Silmarillion*.) This body of material comes in a distant second to the 227,046 based on the Harry Potter books and films, but Tolkien material is developed on other sites too (especially given that fanfiction.net bans explicit erotica). Hard numbers are impossible to obtain, and any estimate is a guess, but it seems likely that the number of *Rings*-based stories could approach a hundred thousand. If one includes role-playing games, which are essentially group-authored stories, the total rises considerably.

Gen

Most gen fics based on *Rings* are book-canon, since the vast history of Middle-earth sketched out by Tolkien in *Rings*' appendixes and unfinished manuscripts provides endless narrative possibilities. The doings of minor Hobbits, Aragorn and Arwen's lives after the novel's end, and major events stretching back through the First, Second, and Third Ages all form the launching point for "fillers" that extend the author's mythology.

Fans have, however, filled in the film's action as well. For example, Pipfan's "Seek and Find" details Pippin's role in the Battle of the Pelennor, including his search for Merry and the two Hobbits' experiences in the Houses of Healing afterward. Anso the Hobbit's "A Light in Dark Places" similarly has Pippin and Merry in Minas Tirith telling each other about their experiences while apart—using the events and dialogue from the film rather than from the novel. Slightly Tookish's "On the Shores of the Sea" expands the Grey Havens scene to focus on Pippin's farewell to Gandalf after the friendship that unexpect-edly developed between them.[12]

There are variants of canon fanfiction as well. "AU" indicates an "alterna-tive universe," where major premises of the plot are changed and the story written to fit the new chain of cause and effect. "Crossovers" involve differ-ent fictional universes interacting, as when characters from the Harry Potter series appear alongside those from *Rings*. Such genres appear in erotic as well as gen fics.[13]

Romantic and Erotic Fanfiction: Het and Slash

Inevitably, fans have involved the *Rings* characters in romantic situations, often with considerable erotic content. These are usually posted on specialist archives and lists and are labeled with warnings and ratings. The paucity of female characters in *Rings* makes het fics relatively rare. The ones that do exist often carry the taint of the widely despised "Mary Sue" plot, where a thinly disguised figure representing the author, usually an idealized young lady sport-ing a vaguely Elvish name, finds herself in Middle-earth and has a romantic adventure with one of the characters—usually Legolas. (The equivalent fan-tasy written with a male character representing the author is a "Marty Stu.") Many fanfiction lists have rules against posting Mary Sues, but they flourish on fanfiction.net.

The obvious romantic heterosexual couples are Aragorn-Arwen, Éowyn-Faramir, and Sam-Rosie. The small Estelio Ammen archive (www.phoenix-fyre.net/forherlove/fanfiction.html), for example, features more than two dozen movie-verse Aragorn-Arwen romances, mostly in the PG to PG-13 range. These include Bellemaine Chercoeur's "Taking Leave from Rivendell," a movie-canon filling-in story showing Aragorn and Arwen together the night before the Fellowship departs on the Quest.

One fic centering on Sam, Rosie, and Frodo in a ménage à trois, "Pretty Good Year" by Mary Borsellino (March–May 2002) created a little subuni-verse unto itself. Other fans started writing fics based on the same premises, filling out the original narrative or creating stories loosely inspired by it. These have been gathered in the "Storytellers" archive (www.phoenixfyre.net/forherlove/fanfiction.html).[14]

The vast majority of romantic fanfiction created around *Rings,* however, has been slash. Most researchers trace the slash phenomenon back to around 1967, when fans of the original *Star Trek* began creating and writing for zines.[15] Captain Kirk and Mr. Spock, like so many partners and buddies in male-centric TV series, proved easy for some fans to reimagine as a romantic couple. Other fandoms—*The Man from U.N.C.L.E., Starsky and Hutch*—inspired slash stories as well. A traditional statistic claims that around 90 percent of slash is written by women, with the rest of the authors being bisexual and gay men. Figures that precise are impossible to determine, given the anonymity offered by the Internet. Many members of Yahoo! groups do not fill out the profile that asks for age, gender, and home country. I ran through the memberships of several lists, and among those who did provide this information, my unscientific impression was that men were in the distinct minority, plausibly under 10 percent.

Rings, with its large, mostly male cast of characters, lends itself to slash and is considered one of the main fandoms for slash fiction.[16] The novel had generated a body of fan writings of this sort, but the appearance of Film 1 led to an outburst of slash writing, much of it by people who had never read Tolkien. A small number of femmeslash stories are written with such pairings as Arwen/Éowyn, but they are very few in comparison with regular slash. (Éowyn features in 30 fics on the Library of Moria site, including all pairings, while Legolas had 361 stories linking him with Aragorn alone.)

Rings slash fiction gained its own online archives. On 10 September 1999, Amy Fortuna founded the Tolkien_Slash group on Yahoo! and a week later the earliest Tolkien-slash archive, Least Expected. For a long time Least Expected was one of the two largest Tolkien-slash archives, but it crashed and disappeared in 2003. In early 2005, Fortuna announced that she and her husband would be rebuilding Least Expected.[17] Least Expected's demise left the Library of Moria, established on 1 January 2002, as the largest and best-known Tolkien-slash archive. Stories are searchable by character and pairing, and the range of characters is vast. Even Figwit appears in several fics (though often under the purported Elvish version of his name, Melpomaen). The library is one of the few sources for femmeslash, which can be located by clicking on any of the female characters' names. (Femmeslash is very much a minority taste among slashers, and its authors risk getting "flamed" with adverse feedback.) The Library of Moria also contains a links section that can direct the reader to additional sites, many dedicated to specific pairings or characters. Increasingly fans are posting fics on LiveJournals, as with Cassandra Claire, the "original pervy hobbit fancier" and author of the well-known "Very Secret Diaries" series (http://www.livejournal.com/users/cassieclaire/).

Fans on the Internet are fond of abbreviating phrases, and slash writers have devised acronyms to indicate various types of stories. "OTP" refers to authors who devote themselves entirely to "one true pairing." The Yahoo! site Axe & Bow (groups.yahoo.com/group/Axe_Bow), for example, posts primarily fics involving the friendship or romance between Legolas and Gimli. Other common OTPs are Frodo/Sam and Aragorn/Legolas. The label "PWP" means "Plot? What Plot?" and refers to fics that are essentially sex scenes with minimal narrative context.

The same genres have inspired fanart as well. A large gallery of both professional and amateur images, none of them adult-oriented, is offered on War of the Ring. Slash photomanipulations (based on film images) ranging from romantic to soft-core appear on the Theban Band website. The Library of Moria also contains a fanart section.[18]

RPS

FPS may seem about as far away from the official areas of the *Rings* Internet campaign as you can get. The fics are pure expressions of the fans' imaginations, lying well outside the marketers' control. There is, however, one related area of fan activity that lies even further away, at the very margins of our cybertarget. Rather than elaborating on the film's characters and story, some fans write or read about fictional relationships among the actors. These stories belong to the subgenre of RPS, or real-person slash.

As of 6 December 2005, the two largest RPS groups on Yahoo! were LOTR_RPS, with 2,756 members (founded 28 December 2001, or ten days after the release of *Fellowship*), and Closer_than_Brothers (founded 28 April 2002), with 1,497 members. Only the former currently has an associated archive, Mirrormere.[19]

RPS came to prominence in fics written about members of boy bands, though it had had a small and controversial presence in slash fandom from the start. *Rings,* with its predominantly male cast, was one of the films that helped expand the genre to actors (even though, as Ian McKellen pointed out to me, it was the straightest cast and crew he had ever worked with). Initially RPS was looked down upon by many FPS writers as being intrusive and exploitative—and as drawing unwelcome attention to slash from the filmmakers, especially the cast. An early article on *Slate,* otherwise sympathetic to slash fiction, declared that "actorfic" violated fanfic's basic principle of being fantasy: "Writers risk enraging straight actors. Slash infuriates actors even when it focuses only on fictional characters."[20] This attitude toward RPS slowly changed across the period during which the three parts of *Rings* were being released. McKellen perhaps inadvertently contributed to this change in December 2002 when his E-Post answered a fan's inquiry about what he thought of RPS fics: "Do you consider them slanderous to your good character and/or to the good character of any actor/movie/etc?" McKellen (who had by that point read at least one NC-17 fic about himself) replied fairly cautiously, "I am not well acquainted with slash but find nothing harmful in sharing fantasies about favourite characters or their interpreters. Within the context of such sites even Real Person stories seem unobjectionable as they are clearly fictional."[21] This response was widely debated on fan groups. By the time Film 3 appeared, RPS was somewhat more tolerated. As an indication of the change, on 1 January 2004, the Library of Moria added an RPS section.

After the trilogy's release, the actors departed to their separate projects, and *Rings*-devoted sites became diluted with pairings involving one of the actors with his costar in a subsequent film. Some among them appeared in public with female companions. RP het fics have resulted. These are often, however, Mary Sues or jealous fantasies in which the star and his girlfriend or wife break up.

THE FILMMAKERS AND THE INTERNET

Pete probably more so, I think.
Fran and I would tend to be on eBay shopping.

PHILIPPA BOYENS
on the scriptwriters' Internet monitoring

Fans were aware that members of the cast and crew were looking at *Rings*-related websites. McKellen's E-Post contains the following exchange:

Q: Do you and Peter Jackson ever visit Tolkien sites on the Internet?

A: I don't know where Peter gets the time but he seems to be au fait with the Tolkien sites and often refers to them in detail. I make occasional anonymous visits and am sometimes tempted to correct the wilder speculations in the correspondence columns. Having this outlet, I keep quiet. And so, it seems, does Peter.[22]

Those running such sites could imagine that the filmmakers were occasionally hovering near them in cyberspace.

Many fans probably thought that the polls run by some of the main *Rings* sites were a means of gathering information that would guide decisions during the lengthy production process. Such a belief would give a sense of fan access to and involvement in the making of the films—and hence perhaps a tolerance toward changes made in the adaptation. Certainly some of the questions asked on TORN appeared to solicit opinions with this thought in mind: "If you had to remove a character from the movies to save time or streamline the story, who would it be?" and "Who is your ideal composer for the LOTR movies?" The cofounders of TORN have assured me, however, that none of the questions used was suggested by the filmmakers or New Line.[23]

Jackson has repeatedly declared that fan writings on the Internet had little if any effect on decisions regarding the making of the film. He told me:

> A lot of interviewers have asked me, "Did the Internet ever make you change the way that you did the movies?" and the answer is, no. I can't think of an example of something we read or saw on the Internet that made us go, "Oh, we have to change the film, or we have to change the script," because we were making a movie, and the people out there were speculating, and so we just felt we knew what we were doing. But the speculation is what's interesting. You basically know what you're doing, because you're the ones who have a script— they don't. You're dealing with the actors every day, you're shooting a movie, you know the designs of everything, they don't. So you know what you're doing. What the Internet is, is it provides an interesting piece of entertainment as to what all the speculation is [about] what you're doing. So you read it out of curiosity.[24]

Similarly, producer Barrie Osborne has made it clear that the Internet's role lay primarily in stimulating and maintaining fan interest and enthusiasm, despite the risk of spoilers. "It's always a fight about how much imagery gets let out. And a lot of stuff went out on the net that you wish had been held back. But I think it was great. Peter's a real internet fan and he's on it all the time. I'd go by his house early in the morning and you'd see his lights on and know he's on the net or he's doing emails at 4:30 in the morning. And I think that informed some of what we did."[25]

Jackson says that he was not on the Internet as frequently as his colleagues have suggested. I mentioned Osborne's remark about seeing his light on in the wee hours, and Jackson replied, "Probably doing e-mail, or doing script revisions is more likely at four o'clock in the morning." When I asked whether he had looked at some of the fringe sites, the fanfiction and so on, he said, "I've never really looked at many sites. Was there fanfiction? No, I never read any of that stuff." He did monitor a relatively small number of sites, such as AICN and TORN, regularly.

Although some RPS writers seem fondly to believe that they fly under the radar of the studios and escape the notice of cast and crew, many of the people involved in the film have been well aware of them. Casting director Liz Mullane remarks on the differing reactions among the actors: "Some of them just dealt with it brilliantly. Others got a bit spooked by it. But it was sort of the Kiwi way. We just thought it was hilarious." Among those who coped were Elijah Wood and Dominic Monaghan, who were often paired in fics. Both actors have taken the whole thing in good humor. During the same month in the autumn of 2005 *Newsweek* happened to speak with both of them. Monaghan's interview included this exchange:

> NEWSWEEK: Do you read what they say online?
>
> MONAGHAN: I check out all these scandalous rumors about me and Elijah Wood having beautiful sex with each other.
>
> NEWSWEEK: Are they true?
>
> MONAGHAN: About Elijah and me being boyfriend and boyfriend? Absolutely true. We've been together for about nine years. I wooed him.

Wood's interviewer pursued the theme:

> NEWSWEEK: A couple of weeks ago Dominic Monaghan told *Newsweek* that you two were having an affair.
>
> WOOD: Dom's actually going to have my child. We're very excited, very proud. We're going to name it Frodo.[26]

There is a small contingent of writers who truly believe that Wood and Monaghan are an item, but the vast majority of writers and readers are aware that fics are just fics. Kristina, the co-moderator of LOTR_RPS, when she heard that I would be dealing with RPS in this book, wrote, "I just hope you point out that it's not like we're deluded stalkers believing our stories to be real!"[27]

New Line did not issue any directives to the actors on how to respond or not respond to RPS. However distasteful many associated with the film might have found such material, it served as one more way of publicizing the film, and slash authors, both FPS and RPS, were among the repeat viewers of the films, combing the scenes for "plot bunnies" (inspiration). Kristina sums up the value of fanfiction to the studios: "These are the FANS' contribution, their hard, unpaid work. I mean you can buy PR all you like, but the FF writers (and I mean FF in general) do a heck of a job keeping the interest alive. Free of charge for The Powers That Be. Merchandise doesn't buy that kind of devotion."[28]

In his memoirs Harry Knowles recalls being a film geek discovering the Internet: "I realized that, like generations before me—through the late-night radio signal of some midwestern station, through tattered Xerox copies of out-of-print poets or long-lost manuscripts—I was not alone. There were others out there like me."[29] There had always been people with all sorts of obsessions, but the Web gave them a way of finding each other with remarkable speed and all over the world.

For film studios and filmmakers, that ease of communication proved a double-edged sword. Obsessions meant that fans were eager for material fed to them and willing to pass it along to others. But again, as Knowles says, for fans there is never enough information. To probe the filmmaking process, they will resort to spying and gossip. Inspired by the film and the actors, they will create new scenes and story lines and relationships. The variety of websites demonstrates that the studio-generated and studio-controlled campaign constitutes a relatively small portion of a large-scale, popular film's presence on the Internet. The studio may control the distribution of the film through copyright and the production of ancillary merchandise through licenses, but the control of publicity campaigns through "exclusive" media access is dwindling.

Any faint hope the studios might have had of using copyright or other legal means to quash fan websites has most likely disappeared as publicity departments and licensees and filmmakers become more intertwined with the whole fan phenomenon. Fans are now being actively encouraged to write fiction using the characters from films. In mid-July 2005, in anticipation of the upcoming release of *Harry Potter and the Goblet of Fire, Entertainment Weekly*'s print version ran a small notice: "Write your own Harry Potter–style tale at ew.com/potter." The film franchise's producer-distributor, Warner Bros., is part of Time Warner, which owns *Entertainment Weekly*.[30] In February 2006, Electronic Arts and TheOneRing.net announced a fanfiction contest linked to a forthcoming video game: "Create your own short story about the Dunedain and the struggles of the northern kingdom to win great prizes." So many fics were entered that the announcement of the winners had to be delayed. For the second One Ring Celebration (licensed by New Line) in 2006, a *Rings*-related fanfilm contest was held, and on 6 March, TORN added a new section to showcase the entries online.[31]

In 2006, New Line found itself in the midst of a fan-generated phenomenon as its upcoming low-budget genre release, *Snakes on a Plane,* became an object of obsession on many unofficial websites. Some of these included dialogue made up by the fans, and New Line went so far as to use a slightly modified line from one of these websites in the film. Once studios begin doing such things, they can hardly object to fans borrowing characters and plot-lines for their own creations. New Line invited David Finkelstein, owner of "Snakes on a Blog," to the film's premiere, echoing the studio's treatment of the founders of its former nemesis, TORN, asking them to the Cannes pre-view of *Rings* and the trilogy's premieres.[32]

Rings provided an early demonstration of how a filmmaker could, against his producer's wishes, connect directly with the fans. The explosion of fan sites created an unofficial wing of a franchise, and Jackson's response pro-vided a model that the industry is gradually imitating.

FANS IN RL

On fan websites and lists, "RL" stands for "real life." Just as the Internet had proven a remarkably quick way to bring like-minded people together in cy-berspace, it provides a new and efficient way for them to organize social events in RL. One of the simplest and more widespread has been the line party. Groups of fans assemble to entertain each other during a long wait outside a theater. Such parties predate the Internet, but the online fan community has systematized them to a new degree.

Chat rooms and bulletin boards can spawn parties. TORN provided a reg-istration system for parties, which then attracted people who signed up as members. For *Towers,* 771 parties were organized, with more than ten thou-sand people pledging to attend. The largest such party, in Salt Lake City, at-tracted nearly a thousand. Local stores sometimes donated *Rings*-related prizes, and at the larger parties, manufacturers of licensed goods might show up to demonstrate games and give away products. Charity raffles, trivia contests, and other activities filled the waiting time. As with websites, fans were will-ing to donate their time and money to organize these events. The official Fan Club magazine wrote approvingly: "These leaders—who volunteer weeks and sometimes even months of personal time and often their own financial re-sources in exchange for 'thank you's' as payment—are the real movers and shakers of the line-party movement."[33]

Diane Greenlee, of Madison, Wisconsin, knew about small, informal par-ties but discovered the possibility of organizing one at TORN. Trilogy Tues-day, marathon screenings of the extended editions of the first two parts and the premiere of *Return* in about a hundred cities nationwide, was approach-ing. After someone else dropped out of running a line party for the December 2003 event, Greenlee decided to arrange one herself. Twenty-seven fans signed up. Greenlee made badges for the group, came up with prizes for trivia contests, and brought an Aragorn standee to mark the party's place in the line. The group began gathering at 7:00 A.M. (the earliest the theater would allow people on the grounds, for security reasons). The first film did not start until 2:00 P.M., but given the very cold weather, the theater opened its doors at 10:00 A.M. Once the group got settled in the theater, they passed the time with the trivia contest and other diversions. Greenlee commented on how vital the Internet is in such activities: "I can't imagine any other way that a diverse group of people from so many places could come together and do such a thing as a line party. I also think the Internet makes it easier for fans of movies like LOTR or Star Wars to easily find other fans. Until I got on the Internet, I pretty much felt isolated regarding my fandom activities, but it's incredibly easy to find other like-minded fans."[34]

More traditional parties—indoors, in normal facilities—brought fans into proximity with their idols. Once more, the studio and filmmakers realized that they should cooperate with the fans to strengthen the franchise, and the webmasters were ideally positioned to serve as point people. The most famous *Rings* parties were thrown by TheOneRing.net each year on the night of the Academy Awards. The first came about at the suggestion of Carlene Cordova, a contributor to the site and later the director of the documentary on fan culture *Ringers: Lord of the Fans*. Having had some experience organizing parties, she directed the planning. Sideshow Weta's close links to the site led it to sign on as the main sponsor the first year, paying the deposit and lending the event a legitimacy that brought other support on board. "The One Party to Rule Them All" took place on 24 March 2002, on one floor of the Hollywood Athletic Club. The four cofounders of TORN had never met in RL, and Erica Challis recalls, "We all had a moment of 'Is that you?' when we first met, which is weird seeing as how on the screen we're so familiar."

There was entertainment, with Cliff Broadway as emcee and a giant-screen TV for watching the Oscars. The cast and crew had been invited, but, as one of TORN's cofounders, Bill Thomas, says, "The first year we had *no* commitment that anybody from the productions was going to come. The morning of the first party, we heard that Peter Jackson had called Ian McKellen and said, 'Are you planning on going to the OneRing.net party?' Eventually they showed up, and it was just incredibly exciting." Shortly after midnight, Jackson, Walsh, Boyens, McKellen, and Ordesky arrived, along with Oscar winners Howard Shore (best score), Jim Rygiel, Randy Cook, and Richard Taylor (special effects). Around two in the morning they went on to other parties. McKellen says he went simply because Jackson asked him to. Despite all the fan input on his website, "That was the first time I really realized how personally people were relating to these films." Afterward he called the other actors and told them he had had a good time.

The second year TORN ran "Two Towers—One Party" (23 March 2003), which occupied the whole Athletic Club. Not only was it larger, but there was space enough to provide for a VIP room, allowing the cast and crew to escape at intervals from their adoring fans. The sponsors were a who's who of New Line licensees: Sideshow Weta, EA Games, Games Workshop, Houghton Mifflin, and the Noble Collection. The Iraq war had just started, and Jackson and Walsh stayed in New Zealand. McKellen was absent, but on his recommendation Billy Boyd, Dominic Monaghan, and Sean Astin were there, as well as many of the main designers, Barrie Osborne, and others of the cast. Some of the licensees, along with New Line, provided items that were combined into packages for a raffle, and a silent auction to raise funds for TORN included signed posters and Sideshow Weta collectibles. Tickets for the party itself were sold through Sideshow Weta's website starting on 8 January, and by 24 January all eight hundred were gone.

Towers may only have won two Oscars, but TORN presented Osborne with a "Golden Gandalf"—an Oscar-like gilded statuette with Gandalf's head and hat, made by Sideshow Weta. It was in the awards case in the Three Foot Six lobby, along with the BAFTAs and other honors, when I visited seven months later. Broadway again emceed and says that of all the celebrity guests he introduced that night, Alan Lee, Tolkien illustrator and production designer for the film, got the most thunderous applause. "They loved him, and I almost felt that I had brought J. R. R. Tolkien onto the stage himself." Bibliophile Cordova recalls, "I felt this swell of pride, that these people were the coolest people in the world because they gave the loudest ovation for the *illustrator.*"

TORN had made money off the first two parties, and the "Return of the One Ring" party, on 29 February 2004, proved a shock. The new venue, the American Legion's VFW building, was much bigger, and new antiterrorism regulations resulted in unexpectedly high costs for fire marshals, armed security guards, and metal detectors. Bill Thomas, who runs the financial side of TORN, points out that the building was just a big, bare room, and they had to rent lights and audio equipment. A VIP tent for the celebrities had to be set up in back. "To say 'tent' doesn't quite convey it. You can have a very, very *nice* tent with a floor and heating and bathrooms and such and a full bar." Not all the usual sponsors wanted to continue to lay out money now that the trilogy was over, and none of the extra costs had been factored into the ticket price. TORN owed approximately $70,000 to Premiere Events, the company that had organized the party. Pirrotta considers that the evening was worth it. (TORN managed to pay off the debt in a little under a year.)

The third party provided an ironic reflection of how powerful the biggest fan site had become. Because the venue was close to the Kodak Theater, while New Line's own party was a long drive away, Jackson took the entire *Rings* group to TORN's party after leaving the Governor's Ball. To add injury to insult, the TVs at the New Line party could not receive ABC's signal for the first hour of the broadcast, leaving the filmmakers who had not been invited to the live ceremony unable to watch their colleagues receive their awards. The Film Unit's Sue Thompson recalls being so frustrated at missing the film's mounting triumph that she was one of several people tempted to push the technicians aside and tackle the repairs. *Entertainment Weekly* reported that the champagne also ran out, though Thompson assures me that the martinis did not.[35]

At TORN's party, the winners stood on the stage and displayed all twenty-seven Oscars to the cheering guests. Some of the cast stayed on at the TORN party, and Osborne recalls:

> By the time we got back to the New Line party, I think New Line had given up on us, and the New Line party was starting to break up. In fact, most of the parties were breaking up, because nobody with an Oscar was showing up at any of these other parties. So we were left to go back to Peter's room until the Four Seasons decided they'd had enough complaints and asked us to go to sleep at about 5:30 in the morning.

Variety noted of the New Line party, "Guest of honor Peter Jackson didn't arrive until 1:30 A.M., having stopped by a fans party nearby."[36]

There were other fan parties. TORN held one in Wellington the night before *Return*'s world premiere. The official Fan Club ran an "Into the West" party in 2004, for those who were unable to get tickets to the TORN party. Tickets sold out in about ten minutes. And of course there were numerous smaller, more informal fan parties across the country, both for the Oscar nights and on many other occasions.

FILMS ABOUT FANS

When I attended Trilogy Tuesday in December 2003, the packed house of five hundred included perhaps half a dozen people dressed in vaguely Middle-earth-style costumes. Naturally, during the intermissions the local TV reporters singled them out to interview. There is no doubt an impression that

Rings fans all run around in costume reciting Elvish, though this is far from the case. In costume or not, these fans are an enthusiastic, witty, and articulate lot. Several of the actors have remarked on how intelligent and educated *Rings* enthusiasts are in comparison to many members of other fandoms. It was inevitable that documentaries would be made about them.

In early 1999, a young man named Stan Alley applied for a job working on *Rings* in the art department, and he was a "standby props" person throughout the production. During the period of the pickups for *Fellowship,* in early 2001, he was sharing a flat with Bret McKenzie, the actor who played a nonspeaking role as an Elf at the Council of Elrond. When McKenzie was suddenly made famous in fan circles by the creation of the Figwit Lives! website, Alley conceived the idea of a documentary about the phenomenon. Work on *Rings* delayed the project, but eventually Alley followed McKenzie to Edinburgh, where the Flight of the Conchords was performing in a comedy festival. There he met the two founders of Figwit Lives! at the Scottish Tolkien Society's party, an event filmed by Alley. Since that point, Alley says, "It's really just got a lot bigger than I ever thought it would be. Partly because the events there unfolded and the story was so good." He was also able to interview Jackson, Ordesky, Osborne, and various cast members about "Figwit." The narrative of Alley's film fortuitously developed to a dramatic conclusion when McKenzie was cast for the small role in *Return.* Alley was on-set and recorded the actor as he ran through his one line over and over before the scene was shot.

The result is a charming one-hour documentary, *Frodo Is Great . . . Who Is That?!!* (coproduced and codirected by Hannah Clarke and Nick Booth). It contains *Rings* footage, however, and negotiations with New Line over rights and what might ultimately be done with the film dragged on. Along with Costa Botes's making-of documentary, New Line agreed to have it shown at the Wellington Film Festival in 2004. As of early 2006, there remains the possibility that it will receive a DVD release or perhaps be broadcast on TV or shown at a *Rings* convention.[37]

At the time *Fellowship* came out in late 2001, Carlene Cordova was working at Sony Pictures Entertainment, running the company's websites and producing red-carpet interviews with celebrities to put on them. She met Cliff Broadway, one of TORN's writers, at a book signing. In January 2002, Cordova was laid off from Sony when its Internet department was dissolved. Since her husband was earning a good living, she started volunteering for TORN. Using Cordova's show business contacts, she and Broadway began shooting brief interviews which Cordova edited on her computer and which were then posted on the site. They came to know the actors, as well as filmmakers like Jackson and Walsh who visited Los Angeles.

That summer, while covering a book signing by Viggo Mortensen, Cordova and Broadway found themselves increasingly talking to the fans. The same thing happened at the 2002 Dragon Con (a major fan event held in Atlanta each Labor Day weekend). According to Cordova, "We shot a bunch of stuff there, and I was like, 'You know, this is a movie. There's a movie here.' That was really what cemented it." They decided to make a film on *Rings* fandom, ultimately titled *Ringers: Lord of the Fans.* With no funding, they were confined to the local area, shooting interviews at places like the *Towers* line party at the Vista Theater. At Comic-Con in July 2003, they set up a "confessional booth" in the *Rings* display area, flanked by licensees' exhibits—EA, Sideshow Weta, New Line, Houghton Mifflin, and the Noble Collection—where fans could sit in private and answer questions.

Cordova and Broadway attended the 2003 Dragon Con as invited guests, drawing standing-room crowds for their presentations on the *Ringers* project. Soon they had some investors and were able to travel to England and interview Tolkien scholars and fans. Barrie Osborne invited TORN (which was hosting the *Ringers* website) to cover *Return*'s world premiere in Wellington, and while covering it for the website, the pair also interviewed fans who were taking Red Carpet's special tour planned around that event. The filming, intended to last for a few months, extended to sixteen. A friend of Cordova's provided an editing suite, and the filmmakers began to assemble a feature from around 150 hours of shots. Some of the footage that made it in included a brief interview with Genevieve Baillie and a comment from Lilith of Sherwood during the "confessional booth" segment. Dominic Monaghan provided *Ringers*' voice-over narration. The film premiered at the Slamdance Film Festival in January 2005. On July 14 the filmmakers announced that *Ringers: Lord of the Fans* had been sold to Sony Pictures Home Entertainment, and it was released direct to DVD on 22 November 2005.

Again and again in fan writings on the Internet and in the pages of the Fan Club magazine, people speak of the "communities" that have been formed through *Rings.* The "Fellowship of 22," a group of Fan Club members from around the world, traveled to Los Angeles for the first TORN Oscar party. Most of them had never met before, and they came early to socialize. They visited the Fashion Design Institute, which had a display of *Rings* costumes, and toured an exhibition of Viggo Mortensen's art.[38]

Out of the online bonding and RL events came lasting friendships and genuine community. In the Fan Club magazine, Jincey, a volunteer on TORN, expressed the sentiment succinctly as she praised its cofounders: "Thanks to these four folks, who met for the very first time in 'real-life' on Oscar Sunday, we have all discovered that we are not alone; that we are part of an immense worldwide community." After the last party, Challis reflected on the fans and how they had traveled from many places to attend it:

> But that is just the least tremor of the earthquake that these films were. For many people, the books and the movies turned their lives around in ways they could never have foreseen. They followed their strong attraction to *The Lord of the Rings* and what it represented for them, and their feelings pointed them toward new friends, new pastimes, new talents, new jobs, new countries, a new life entirely. This is not something that we intended to happen; nor did the film-makers. I don't know if this is something you can plan for.[39]

Challis herself discovered a love of writing while working on the website. After taking a journalism course, in November 2005, she began writing travel articles for a newspaper. She was doing what she wanted to do at the start, hiking around New Zealand and talking about ways people could enjoy it.

PART THREE

Beyond the Movie

CHAPTER 7

Licenses to Print Money

We got our faces scanned for toys to be made, and
that's when I started getting my head around the fact
that this could be something really big.

DOMINIC MONAGHAN
Premiere, November 2004

THE NEGOTIATIONS BETWEEN SAUL ZAENTZ and Harvey Weinstein for the
production and distribution rights to *Rings* were lengthy, but the deal made
perfect sense for Zaentz. He had let those rights lie unused for years. Now
someone else was putting up the money for a franchise. If the film succeeded,
it could generate a huge number of ancillary products.

Zaentz may make more money on *Rings* than anyone else. Apart from his
rumored 5 percent of gross international box office, he retained the hundreds
of Tolkien-related trademarks that he had acquired in the 1970s and simply
licensed New Line to license other companies to manufacture merchandise.
Every item and advertisement for these products carries some variant of this
cumbersome message: "© 2002 New Line Productions, Inc. The Lord of the
Rings, and the characters, names and places therein,™ The Saul Zaentz Company d/b/a Tolkien Enterprises under license to New Line Productions, Inc.
All rights reserved."

Like foreign distribution rights, fees for ancillary licenses were a major factor in New Line's financing of the *Rings* project, and the studio immediately
started to line up merchandisers. And like the distributors, most of the licensees had to commit to all three *Rings* parts well in advance, in many cases
while principal photography was still going on. One of the biggest early deals
came when Toy Biz announced on 12 June 2000 that it had secured the rights

to make action figures for the entire trilogy. By mid-December, New Line had licensees in several core categories, including the video games (Electronic Arts), tie-in books (Houghton Mifflin in the United States and HarperCollins in the United Kingdom), trading cards (Topps), apparel (Giant), and gifts (Applause)—all for the trilogy as a whole. The New Line booth at the mid-2001 Licensing International show displayed action figures, collectible busts, and miniature weapons. Initially New Line held back and limited its licenses to around one hundred, but the plan was to expand that number slowly if *Fellowship* was a hit. By the end of the year, New Line reportedly had earned $55 million per part of the trilogy in licensing fees—and once each item's sales reached a threshold, royalties would be forthcoming as well.[1] After 2001, New Line opened the gate wide, and more than three hundred lines of products were licensed by the time *Return*'s theatrical-version DVD appeared. New Line reported that $750 million in worldwide retail sales had been generated.[2] With each release of a film or DVD, a new wave of products was launched.

From the start, Tolkien's fans feared that New Line would use *Rings* to profit from a lot of cheap or silly tie-in products. New Line repeatedly insisted that only high-quality merchandise would be licensed. In fact, a two-tiered system developed, aimed at different age-groups and tastes. Toy Biz and Giant put action figures and clothes into mass-retail stores, while stationery, tie-in books, collectible toys, and gifts would be sold in bookstores and similarly dignified outlets.

As with the marketing campaign, New Line went through a learning curve with the film's merchandise. When a film company licenses another firm to make ancillary products, the studio puts together a style guide so that the products and packaging can have a uniform look, even though dozens or even hundreds of different firms might be creating those ancillaries. Initially New Line put together a *Rings* style guide in New York. Like the initial poster mock-up shown to Jackson, however, the proposed guide proved unacceptable. Jackson recalls that it "sent us into a really bad tailspin because it was very, very tacky and very cheesy-looking artwork. So at that point we persuaded New Line to involve Richard Taylor's Workshop and his design guys much more in the style guide, and so we were happy that that got onto a slightly better footing." As Alyson McRae, who was merchandising coordinator at the time, points out, why redesign everything in New York when the original designers are available? Daniel Reeve, the mapmaker and calligrapher for the film, contributed scripts, borders, and maps for the packaging. A style guide was created for each of *Rings*' three parts. The designers provided color palettes for each race of characters, as well as a different overall color to be used for each film: muted tones of green for *Fellowship,* reddish-brown for *Towers,* and gray-blue for *Return.* The reconceived style guides are elegant books that themselves might have made very popular ancillary products.

Decipher, the same company that had undertaken to run the trilogy's fan club, with attendant website and magazine, also took out two licenses for products likely to appeal to *Rings* fans: a trading-card game (TCG) and a role-playing game (RPG). Products for both of these games have continued to appear long after the theatrical and DVD releases of the trilogy occurred.

Early Decipher products had included the popular "How to Host a Murder Mystery" series of games, but the company branched into TCGs with *Star Wars* and RPGs with *Star Trek. Rings* was its second RPG, and the firm obtained licenses to use characters, places, and situations from both Tolkien's novel and Jackson's film. RPGs are built around books, in this case a "core book," a "sourcebook" apiece for *Fellowship* and *Towers,* add-on guides (*Fell Beasts and Wondrous Magic Sourcebook* was the first), helpers (a *Narrator's Screen,* designed to assist whoever is controlling the game), and maps. Matt Forbeck, who collaborated on writing the early volumes, recalls the tight security surrounding the scripts for the films. While working on the line, he was permitted to see only the script for *Towers* and only for several hours. It came printed on colored paper to prevent photocopying, and he had to read it, return it immediately upon finishing, and make do with whatever notes he managed to take in that short time. New Line also provided imagery, and the books are heavily illustrated with color photos from the trilogy.

Ideally the volumes would have appeared around the time of the trilogy's theatrical releases. Although the contents of the books were finished on deadline, there were lags until they were actually published, which Forbeck puts down to cash-flow problems at Decipher. The first of the main RPG volumes, the *Core Book,* appeared in late August 2002. (A more elementary stand-alone book, *Through the Mines of Moria Adventure Game,* had been published in late January 2002.) It was followed by a boxed set of maps in November. These were executed by Daniel Reeve, who had done all the calligraphy for the films, and would reassure fans about New Line's promise of quality merchandising.

The delays experienced by the series could be advantageous in some ways. Forbeck went to see *Towers* after having finished its sourcebook but before it was published. Not surprisingly, given Jackson's working methods, the film differed considerably from the script Forbeck had read, and he quickly turned in a set of changes. "So from that point of view it worked out pretty well," he says. "It means the books as an artifact are going to be more useful over the course of time, but from a marketing point of view it was a horrible decision." The *Fellowship* sourcebook appeared in March 2003, with the one for *Towers* following in July.

As Forbeck points out, "The problem with role-playing games in general from a publisher's point of view is, once you sell somebody the first book, they don't really need anything else. They have a system. They can go off and play and do everything else on their own. They only buy the additional books because they are helpful—but they're certainly not necessary." The add-on and helper volumes appeared steadily through 2003, and the series wound up in July 2004.

Decipher's TCG was far more lucrative than the RPG books, and there are apparently plans to issue new packs of cards until at least the middle of 2007. At the end of January 2004, the firm moved into the digital world by offering the option of an online trading-card game. The Internet would seem less suited to RPGs, but in October and November 2005, Decipher began selling expanded versions of two of its out-of-print add-on volumes, *Isengard Sourcebook* and *Paths of the Wise,* as pdf files available only online. Thus two of the *Rings* trilogy's traditional types of ancillary products reflect the increasing impact of the digital revolution on Hollywood franchises.

Proposed products were run past the filmmakers, though they were not always allowed much input on whether a product was sufficiently dignified. Merchandising coordinator Judy Alley recalled that occasionally they raised objections. "The only one I can really think of that was deemed to be inappropriate at the time—although I believe it did eventually go ahead—were bobble-heads. New Zealanders probably never heard the term before, and we were horrified when we found out what they were." The bobble-headed dolls did go ahead (made by the Upper Deck Company), and they proved highly successful. They made their way into Ian McKellen's E-Post when one fan queried, "What is the most ridiculous piece of LotR merchandise you have seen?" McKellen replied, "I was sent a grey Gandalf with a big nodding head and ill-proportioned body, like those dogs who bob about behind the back windows of cars. I kept the silly fellow on the mantlepiece until he fell down one day and I wrung his neck and chucked him away." Bobble-heads are evidently a strictly American tradition.

Fans found some of the high-end collectibles particularly attractive: jewelry, an elaborate chess set, and replica swords from the Noble Collections, more replica swords from United Cutlery, and above all the busts, plaques, weapons, models, and statues put out by Sideshow Weta. Established in 1994, Sideshow was a manufacturer of polystone statues and busts based on popular films and television series, including James Bond, *Star Wars,* and *Buffy the Vampire Slayer.* A representative of Sideshow saw New Line's display at the Licensing International show in 2000 and expressed interest in making a line of collectible objects. Richard Taylor had already told David Imhoff, senior executive vice president of marketing and merchandising, that he would like to design the collectibles in-house at Weta Workshop. The two firms arranged to collaborate. Weta designers and sculptors who had worked on the film created the prototypes, and Sideshow distributed the limited-edition pieces worldwide. These were enormously popular.[3]

In 2005, after the agreement between the two companies ended, Sideshow announced the creation of a new line of larger models of the trilogy's main characters. In February 2006, Gentle Giant revealed that it would make a new line of licensed collectible statues, to be released starting in the autumn. Weta's designers, having moved on to create collectibles based on *King Kong* and *The Lion, the Witch and the Wardrobe,* were not involved in these new products. The continued market for such merchandise more than two years after the release of *Return* reflects the durability of the franchise. (Other licensees continue to release new items, as with Electronic Arts's video games and Topps's "The Lord of the Rings Masterpieces," a trading card game released in October 2006 and featuring drawings and paintings relating to the film.)

Thanks to digital technology, designers in the toy and model business can scan actors' faces in order to make action figures highly realistic. Weta opted not to use this method but instead sculpted pieces entirely by hand. As the statement by Dominic Monaghan in the epigraph to this chapter suggests, however, the action figures were based on facial or even body scans, and the actors had right of approval on them and on other products derived from such scans. Since these scans involved the actors' direct participation, their contracts specified royalties on the sales of such products.[4]

MUSEUMS AND CONS

Action figures, games, clothes, and other objects linked to a film have been common for decades. Other sorts of merchandise are recent developments. These new components in the larger franchise both bring New Line income and maintain interest in the films and the familiar *Rings* brand now that the excitement of the original releases has slipped into the past.

A striking example of combining income and publicity is the museum exhibition. Film franchises had already encouraged a trend toward exhibitions based around a single series. (An earlier example was *Star Wars.*) In 1999 the

Museum of New Zealand, known by its Maori name, Te Papa, approached New Line about mounting *The Lord of the Rings* Motion Picture Trilogy— The Exhibition. According to Az James, touring exhibition manager for Te Papa, the film offered an opportunity to "fulfill our goal, which was to cele-brate achievements of New Zealanders." Te Papa assembled a selection of props, costumes, and the miniature of Hobbiton in ruins made for the Mir-ror of Galadriel scene. Explanatory video clips were scattered among the dis-plays, featuring brief interviews with cast and crew members. The exhibition opened on 19 December 2002, the day after the New Zealand premiere of *Towers,* and later toured to London, Singapore, Boston, Sydney, Houston, and Indianapolis. One report put the profit on the exhibition at a million dollars, though how that amount was divided up is unknown.[5]

Te Papa's connection to *Rings* continued. After the world premiere of *Re-turn* on 1 December 2003, the New Zealand distributor, Roadshow, threw a huge party for cast, crew, and VIP guests that occupied the entire museum. In 2006, The Lord of the Rings Motion Picture Trilogy—The Exhibition returned to Te Papa, its final venue, where material from *Return* was added.

Apart from the publicity value and the income from ticket sales, the ex-hibition gave New Line a fresh merchandising venue. Shops located near the exits of display areas have been common for major museum exhibitions since the early 1970s, in the wake of the touring Tutankhamen collection. The *Rings* exhibition shops carried only licensed merchandise, on which New Line would have received royalties (figure 24).

Two smaller, nontouring exhibitions were held in Toronto around the openings of Films 1 and 2. They were sponsored by the trilogy's Canadian distributor, Alliance Atlantis. The Cannes event of May 2001 was the inspi-ration, and again Dan and Chris Hennah were asked to choose objects and arrange the displays. A Journey to Middle-earth ran briefly, from 31 Octo-ber to 11 November 2001, in a castle, Casa Loma. It consisted mainly of props, including an Elvish boat and Gandalf's cart.[6]

The exhibition was far more successful than Alliance Atlantis had antici-pated, and the firm arranged for a larger one the following year, held in the Royal Ontario Museum's planetarium for four weeks starting 31 October 2002. One display was a small pond dressed to resemble the Dead Marshes in *Tow-ers,* complete with spectral corpses under the water. The Hennahs describe with relish the startled reactions of unsuspecting attendees upon first notic-ing them. Dan says, "I just spent days watching people. It was so funny. They'd come along and they'd go, 'Oh, this is the Dead Marshes. Oh, that's inter-esting,' and they'd walk up and look into the water and go 'Oh!' and they'd

Figure 24. The shop outside *The Lord of the Rings* Motion Picture Trilogy—The Exhibition exit in the Museum of Science, Boston, 2004. (Photograph © Lilith of Sherwood, used by permission.)

leap backward."[7] So much publicity was generated, even among those who did not visit the exhibitions, that Alliance Atlantis credited the shows with boosting attendance for Films 1 and 2.

While museum exhibitions target a broad public, fan conventions aim at the loyalist. The past twenty-five years have seen the slow rise of a new phenomenon, the professionally run convention. Originally fans ran their own "cons" around themes: science-fiction/fantasy, anime, comic books, specific TV series like *Star Trek,* and so on. Guests from television or film tended to be actors who had played small roles. As the cons grew, attendees demanded famous celebrity guests, and expenses rose. Many of the fans could not put in enough time or money to keep the events going.[8]

The big exception to this pattern is Comic-Con, an enormous event with major stars attending. Started in 1970 by comic-book devotees, Comic-Con is still run in part by fans, but its longevity and growth resulted from the fact that it has gone far beyond its original focus. Gradually it has become a venue for media companies to publicize upcoming films, TV series, video games, and tie-in products. Major stars and filmmakers are not paid to appear at Comic-Con, but they help draw fans to the event. At the 2005 Comic-Con, more than fifty films were trumpeted. Director Bryan Singer showed footage from *Superman Returns* (2006), Charlize Theron came to publicize *Aeon Flux* (2005), and Jack Black, Naomi Watts, and Adrien Brody all presented *King Kong* footage. That year about 103,000 fans attended. The event has become so important that in recent years national popular news media have taken to covering it.

The rest of the con scene has split into two wings. Many fan cons have become small again. They are often more specialized and avoid expensive guest stars. The big celebrity-driven cons are now run by professionals.

The *Rings* initiative began in 2002. Two fans, Stefan Servos, webmaster of the most prominent German site devoted to Jackson's trilogy, Der Herr der Ringe (www.herr-der-ringe-film.de), teamed with Marcel Buelles of the Tolkien Society to run a three-day event, Ring*Con, late in the year. The con was so successful in drawing fans that the German media covered it. Even as the event ended there were rumors that New Line was interested in licensing the 2003 Ring*Con. The organizers had encountered problems in booking actors from *Rings* to appear, and New Line's official support in succeeding years helped solve that problem. Fans unexpectedly came from abroad in 2002, and the lack of English translations caused complaints. Sponsorship by *Rings* licensees allowed for a bigger budget to handle such matters. For the second, expanded Ring*Con, Servos and Buelles turned to FedCon GmbH, a large, long-established *Star Trek* con organizer, for help, and FedCon has been its partner ever since. Things ran much more smoothly the second year, and the fifth Ring*Con was put on in late 2006.[9]

Other professionally run cons have been authorized by New Line from their inceptions. Creation Entertainment, founded in 1971 and based in Glendale, California, has specialized in *Xena* and *Star Trek* cons, but it also coordinates other sci-fi/fantasy pop-culture events. In January 2005, Creation ran the first One Ring Celebration (ORC) in Pasadena, and in August, ELF (which doesn't seem to be an acronym for anything) in Orlando. These were licensed by New Line (which added a "conventions" category to its online shop) and organized in conjunction with TheOneRing.net. Thus five years to the month after serving the infamous trespassing notice on Erica Challis, New Line was doing business with the website she helped to found.

The 2005 ORC is probably typical of the genre. As in most sci-fi/fantasy cons, there were art and game rooms, a costume contest, and a program of panel presentations, organized by TORN, which also guided Creation's programming with a "wish list" of what it thought attendees would enjoy. Creation took care of the main arrangements: handling the finances, booking the venue, arranging for vendors to participate, and negotiating the participation of actors and crew members from *Rings*. Guests are the main attractions of these events, and they range from the stars to actors who played small roles with few or no lines. At the 2005 ORC, all four "Hobbits" and John Rhys-Davies appeared, along with actors who played minor Elves, Orcs, and so on. Designer Daniel Falconer, of Weta Workshop, attended both as a speaker and as a representative of Sideshow Weta (figure 25).

Apart from appearing onstage for brief, chatty talks and question sessions, the stars make themselves available for the fans to have a photo taken sitting beside them, at a cost of sixty dollars, and to get an autograph, also sixty dollars (figure 26). The lesser-known actors command twenty or thirty dollars for these sorts of sessions. Buying a package that includes all the fees of the con distinctly reduces the cost and guarantees a seat near the stage. The fees are divided among the actors, New Line, Creation, and TORN. Clearly the income for the actors is attractive, and some of those who had small roles (Bruce Hopkins, who played Gamling, and Craig Parker, Haldir) appear over and over and have become stars within this realm of fandom.

At the 2005 ORC, I would judge that perhaps 95 percent or more of the attendees were female. (Images on Creation's website indicate a somewhat higher proportion of male fans present at the 2006 con, perhaps due to the appearance of Miranda Otto as one of the main guests.) Many of these fans

Figure 25. Sideshow Weta's display area in the vendors' rooms at the One Ring Celebration, 2005. (Photograph by the author.)

have websites and post photos of the event, further promoting it. For most fans, the chance to socialize with people they have met through chat rooms or fanfiction feedback is at least as big a draw as the stars. In the evenings many attendees go out to dinner together and then gather for private parties in their hotel rooms.

Another Tolkien fan, Louise Henry, used her experience in organizing professional conferences to program the first Fellowship Festival in London in 2004, but the overall event was organized by Access All Areas Events Ltd. Its arrangement of various packages of tickets for access to the celebrity stars was similar to the one ORC used. In 2005, however, Creation scheduled its first ELF event in August, directly opposite the second Fellowship Festival, suggesting that the organizers were beginning to tussle over the small stable of actors available. Whether or not there was a connection, Access All Areas soon announced that there was insufficient support for a third festival in 2006.[10]

Creation went on to present the second ORC (again in Pasadena) and ELF (in Secaucus, New Jersey) cons in 2006. Apart from running these and other cons, Creation manufactures collectibles under license to various film studios and maintains a shop on eBay "auctioning off autographed collectibles

Figure 26. Elijah Wood and fan during the photograph sessions at the One Ring Celebration, 2005. (Photograph by the author.)

gained contractually through celebrity appearances at conventions."[11] How long such cons will remain viable remains to be seen, especially because the same actors tend to appear repeatedly in various combinations, but ORC, ELF, and Ring*Con are planned for 2007 and will presumably continue annually as long as the demand holds up.

Exciting though exhibitions and cons can be for fans, the income they generate is small from the studio's vantage point. In contrast, digital technologies have generated two new products so successful that they now help

Hollywood studios make profits in a period of ballooning production budgets: DVDs and video games.

DVDs offer users obvious advantages over VHS tape. They take up less space, they give superior image and sound, their tracks offer quick access to specific scenes without a fast-forward, fast-backward hunt, and they do not need rewinding. The interim technology, laser discs, had some of these advantages, but it was still a bulky, expensive format. DVDs were attractive to the Hollywood studios as well, primarily because they are far more profitable than VHS. For both DVD and VHS, the studios preferred to replace rentals with the far more lucrative "sell-through" model. In the late 1990s, getting consumers to stop renting VHS tapes became a major goal of the industry, and the studios noticed that buyers favored franchise films over single features.

On 26 March 2002, New Line Home Entertainment announced the release schedule for the DVDs and VHS tapes of *Fellowship*. The timing was clearly carefully chosen, coming two days after the Oscar presentations. *Fellowship* had been nominated in thirteen categories, and fans were hoping against hope that it would win heavily. If it did, the excitement would make the announcements about the DVDs more dramatic. If it lost, interest in the DVDs could prove a distraction, drawing the media and fans away from dwelling on the film's failure. The film won four Oscars, enough to provide some prestige for New Line to exploit. The studio did not follow the common strategy so annoying to DVD buyers of announcing an extended edition crammed with special features only after the release of a regular theatrical edition. Rather, the three DVD options were made public simultaneously.

The theatrical-version DVD appeared on 6 August 2002. It had no commentary track, but a supplementary disc included promotional items— making-of documentaries, trailers, and ads. The most popular segments were previews of *Fellowship*'s extended version and the upcoming *Towers* theatrical release. A brief promotional film for EA's "The Two Towers" video game completed the disc.

On 12 November, the "Special Extended DVD Edition" was released. *Fellowship* contained an additional thirty minutes edited into the film as well as elaborate extras, including four audio commentary tracks and two supplementary discs on the film's production. A more expensive gift-box set came out at the same time, featuring the extended edition with supplements and adding Argonath bookends by Sideshow Weta and the DVD of the first National Geographic special. The supplements of the extended edition were extremely ambitious, and they won prizes and set a new standard for collectors' editions of blockbusters. Similar three-tiered releases for the other parts of *Rings* followed over the next two years. The DVDs of *Fellowship* came along only five years after the new format for home video had been introduced in the United States. They were perfectly timed to help make owning DVDs highly attractive.

In the early 1980s, home video had become widespread with the advent of tape cassettes in the rival formats VHS and Beta. VHS won the competition and became standard. Sales costs were high, so people primarily rented movies and owned only the programs they taped off air. Laser discs were introduced in 1978 but never caught on widely. They were big (twelve inches across), they were expensive, they were recorded on both sides and had to be turned over, and they were not recordable. They remained the province of dedicated film fans and high-end video aficionados, and no more than a million players were sold in the United States. DVDs, introduced in 1997, quickly killed laser disc sales and rental. With better-than-broadcast picture and digital sound combined with a relatively low cost, DVDs also eroded the popularity of VHS.

The *Fellowship* DVDs were ambitious and elaborate, but New Line had been on the leading edge of home video for years and had been a pioneer in creating supplementary DVD content. The company had started modestly enough in 1985, contracting with RCA/Columbia Home Video to distribute its releases on cassette. In 1990, it formed New Line Home Video, whose first VHS release, Rob Reiner's *Misery*, appeared the following year. In 1997, New Line was among the first studios to market DVDs. When players went on sale in February, there were no discs available. On 25 March, New Line released *The Mask*, *Mortal Kombat*, and *Se7en*. The *Hollywood Reporter* has noted that Stephen Einhorn, who has headed the company's video wing since the beginning, "realized the importance of DVD bonus material long before anyone else did, not only for its added value but also as a hedge against pay-per-view and other electronic delivery."[12] *The Mask* was the first DVD to include deleted scenes and a commentary track, extras that had already been a staple of special-edition laser discs. In December, *The Lawnmower Man* became the first DVD to contain an Easter Egg.[13] That same year New Line and DreamWorks were the first firms to offer awards screeners on DVD rather than VHS; New Line sent *Magnolia* to members of groups like the Academy of Motion Picture Arts and Sciences.

In July 2001, the company introduced its "Infinifilm" series of DVDs, starting with *Thirteen Days.* These discs include easy-to-use links that can be activated to appear as the film runs, leading to supplemental content pinpointed to specific scenes. New Line's other series were its Standard Edition and Platinum Edition, with no duplication of titles among the three lines. Infinifilm was intended for major releases, and at the time it was expected that *Rings* would be issued in that series.[14] Ultimately, however, New Line opted for an even more elaborate set of self-contained supplements on their own separate discs, and the film appeared in the Platinum series.

Despite all these innovations, New Line Home Entertainment (as the division's name became in 2001) was not a major player in the area of home video until *Rush Hour 2* appeared on 11 December 2001—one week before *Fellowship*'s theatrical release. Quickly *Rush Hour 2* became New Line's biggest seller to date. "Now, we're certainly in the big leagues with this title," vice president of marketing Matt Lasorsa declared, adding that the studio would use the experience gained with *Rush Hour 2* in planning its strategy for upcoming films like *Fellowship, Blade 2,* and *Austin Powers in Goldmember.*[15]

As ever, New Line stuck to its franchise-oriented strategy in releasing VHS tapes and DVDs. An industry commentator claimed, "More so than its competitors, the studio's home entertainment executives have largely viewed their job as helping the studio decide which films should be made based on video performance. That has translated best in the sequel arena." Ice Cube's 1995 comedy *Friday* earned only $28 million at the box office, but its strong video performance led to *Next Friday,* which made $57 million theatrically. Surprisingly high video earnings led to sequels to the original *Austin Powers, Blade,* and *Rush Hour* films.[16]

All this experience, however, could not have prepared New Line for the vast project that the *Rings*' extended-edition DVDs became. The discs' groundbreaking success depended on hiring an extremely experienced producer-director, offering him an unusual degree of creative freedom, involving the top filmmakers to a rare extent, and coordinating all the companies contributing to the final product.

THE EXTENDED-EDITION DVD SUPPLEMENTS

In 1993 the laser disc format was in its brief heyday. Walt Disney Home Entertainment, seeing yet another way to redistribute its classic animated features, decided to offer special boxed editions of its most popular titles. The films would be spread out over two two-sided discs, giving optimum visual quality. To make the packages more attractive, Disney wanted to add extras.

The firm approached Michael Pellerin to help produce the discs. He suggested that the supplements should exploit the new format. He recalls, "They were just going to release the movie with a gift book or something like that, and I said, No, with laser discs—it's somewhere in between a book and video. It's documentary and interactive. You can present all your treasures not just as a bag of stuff but in context." Pellerin, an avid laser disc collector himself, was inspired by the Criterion Collection (1984–98 on laser disc and thereafter on DVD), a high-end series of classic films. Criterion had pioneered the use of the audio commentaries and making-ofs that are common on DVDs today.

The boxed set of *Snow White and the Seven Dwarfs* had a hardcover gift book, along with a packet of lithographs. It also, however, offered a third disc, "The Making of a Masterpiece," which contained deleted scenes, storyboards, test footage, and an account of the digital restoration of the film. In the boxed set of *Pinocchio,* the book had become a pamphlet, the sound track CD was added, and a third laser disc offered documentaries and supplements.

In 1997, Pellerin joined forces with longtime Disney employee Jeff Kurtti, and they continued to produce supplements for laser disc and VHS tapes, including the successful laser disc for *Toy Story.* In 1999, when John Lasseter of Pixar (whose films were distributed by Disney) wanted to do a collector's edition DVD for *A Bug's Life,* Pellerin and Kurtti switched to the new format. In late 2000, they formed Kurtti-Pellerin and produced numerous Disney and Pixar DVDs, gaining a reputation as one of the top independent DVD producers. (As an indication of why DVDs quickly gained favor, the boxed laser disc set of *Snow White* weighs in at five and a half pounds, whereas the triple-DVD set of *Toy Story, Toy Story 2,* and all their supplements weighs only one pound.)

Pellerin was already a devoted Tolkien fan when he heard about Jackson's adaptation. Working on the DVD struck him as the dream job, but he did not think it was something he could achieve. A short time later, though, in early 2001, he was considering buying a car, and the seller happened to be Evan Edelist, from New Line's DVD department. During a test drive, Edelist asked if there were any current projects from the studio that Pellerin might be interested in producing as DVDs. Just one, he replied. Edelist arranged a meeting with Mike Mulvihill, New Line's vice president of content development. Mulvihill assumed that Pellerin was trying to get New Line as a client and wanted to produce all of New Line's DVDs. Pellerin recalls:

> I stopped Mike and said, "Whoa, whoa, whoa. We've gotta back up here. I'm not after the New Line account; don't want the gig. All I want is *Lord of the*

Rings." . . . That's when I said: "You could probably find a DVD producer that's on the caliber that you need to take on this project. You could probably find a Tolkien authority. Are you going to find both in the same person?" By the end of the meeting we were already planning the show.[17]

Pellerin ceased work on Disney films to concentrate solely on *Rings* (and later *King Kong*). Kurtti is credited as executive producer on the supplements for the *Fellowship* extended disc, but he has remained focused on Disney supplements. The divergence of projects led the team to split up in 2003, and Pellerin formed his own company, Pellerin Multimedia.

The Planning

Pellerin was officially hired by New Line in April 2001, and he first traveled to Wellington in August, along with Mulvihill and Kurtti. This was mainly an orientation visit, with Pellerin receiving detailed tours of the facilities. Mulvihill did not accompany Pellerin on his many subsequent visits to Wellington, so he had considerable autonomy.

From the start of his professional filmmaking career, Jackson was inclined to record behind-the-scenes material for each production and directed his own making-of for the laser disc of *The Frighteners*. Pellerin recognized this as an enormous advantage. In an early interview he declared, "He is the only director that we have worked with who has produced his own deluxe edition. He produced the deluxe edition of *The Frighteners*. So he knows exactly where we're coming from."[18]

By May 2001, when New Line screened the *Rings* preview reel at Cannes, the studio had not yet conceived the idea of a separate deluxe DVD set for each part of the trilogy. *Variety* reported that there would be "a boxed-set director's cut on DVD—for a likely 2004 release. This will probably have more extreme footage than the tamer version released in theaters."[19] By that stage, the "director's cut" clearly meant something far more modest than the extended editions, which added a total of 120 minutes to the film's three parts. The plan then was to release the trilogy in one large boxed set only after the third film's theatrical version came out on DVD. Much later that year, the extended versions as we know them were conceived.

By December 2001, shortly before *Fellowship* was released, the technical team that would create the special-edition DVDs was also in place: Laser Pacific to handle the authoring (the transfer of the film to DVD format) and designers Company Wide Shut to create the menus.[20] As Pellerin and his colleagues began work, they were absorbed into the overall endeavor of making *Rings:* "We were in the bloodstream of the production, as well as for security reasons, we were given production offices in the film production offices. We literally became another little department of the movie."[21] At that point they were nearly a year away from the release of the extended-edition *Fellowship* DVD.

The unusually early planning for the DVD supplements yielded enormous advantages. Most DVDs—at least at that time—were planned much later and in a shorter period. When *The Sixth Sense* was released in 1999, the distributor, Disney, had low expectations for its box-office performance. Its huge success caught the studio without a plan for the DVD. "Consequently," says Pellerin, who was assigned to produce it, "they shot nothing. There was a box of about six tapes that were the total of the EPK material, and there were some trailers. That's it!" Studios quickly realized the importance of planning for supplements, but the monumental scale of *Rings'* DVDs broke new ground. The contents of all three special editions were outlined in 2001. This allowed Pellerin to plan the supplements as one long set of continuing documentaries, just as *Rings* itself was conceived as a single film. "When you see the appendices for the extended edition of *The Two Towers,* you'll see that many of the documentaries have their part two in this DVD release and finally reach their conclusion in the third."[22] Like both Jackson and Costa Botes, Pellerin was producing three substantial films, or in his case a linked set of short films, that would appear over the span of two years.

Working Methods and Techniques

Creating a unified style and tone across the entire enterprise required considerable coordination with the filmmakers. Pellerin typically works with the associate producer of a film, someone with authority but not so caught up in the actual filmmaking as to be inaccessible. This pattern held true with *Rings.* As Pellerin recalls, he and coproducer Rick Porras hit it off right away. "We went into a meeting with Peter, and Peter said, 'So, who do you want your point person to be?' Rick was looking at me going [whispers] 'Not me, not me,' and I went, 'Well, Rick Porras. He wants the job really bad.' So, 'Rick, it's you!'" Porras went on to act throughout the project as a conduit between the DVD and filmmaking teams, recalling, "That felt like a full-time job adding onto my other job."

The result was cooperation at the highest levels of the filmmaking. Pellerin describes the organization:

> The structure that we formed with the production was that Rick would be the
> key point person, and then each department was appointed a representative

to the DVD, who was for the most part the head of the department. For example, the point person for the art department was Dan Hennah, sound was Rose Dority [postproduction supervisor] and Mike Hopkins [supervising sound editor], editorial was Jamie Selkirk. It was all the top people in the department, straight through, including Weta Digital's producer, Eileen Moran.

As a result, the supplements could trace the production process step by step in a way that would be thorough but also easy for the viewer to understand. Another advantage was the unusually large number and variety of the interviewees who appear.

From the moment Pellerin began actively to put his supplements together, he had access to the thousands of hours of Costa Botes's behind-the-scenes candid footage. For Pellerin, "That is one of the greatest assets you could ever hope for." Since Botes had been shooting since the beginning, a good deal of his material was used in the supplements to cover the period of the principal photography, while Pellerin concentrated on the postproduction. Botes's footage is usually easy to spot in the supplements, being filmed mainly on-set and without interviews; Pellerin's contains interviews and shots of editing, sound mixing, and other late-stage processes.

Pellerin began work on the *Return* postproduction shooting a few days before the end of my first research visit to Wellington, and he allowed me to trail him around for an afternoon at Weta Digital to see how he worked. At that point he was simply conducting preliminary interviews, looking for animators who would be comfortable speaking on camera and who had interesting anecdotes. Each described his work on the film and pulled up images of various stages of the design and animation of the *mûmakil,* Shelob, and the Army of the Dead. Pellerin had a single cameraman with him in Wellington, and when I mentioned that the blue and green screens at the Stone Street Studios were being torn down that day, Pellerin dispatched him to record the process and to film anything else of interest that he ran across.

With such a large film to cover—especially with as many as six units working simultaneously—Pellerin could not hope to document it adequately with one interviewer and one camera operator. In effect, his own organization mimics the division of labor for *Rings* on a smaller scale:

I do all the research, or most of the research. Sometimes I share it and then I kind of boil together what I want the interview to be, and then we have different people who've also done research under me conduct interviews, so it becomes about fifteen people over here for a period of time, just getting all the

New Zealand interview shots. Then of course there's London, New York, and L.A., and some in San Francisco.

During the actual filming, there would be three teams, with an interviewer, camera operator, and production assistants, as well as an overall production manager. Back in the Los Angeles headquarters, the team would swell to thirty during the editorial stage.

Some of the interviews were conducted in settings with picturesque backgrounds. Jackson is often shown sitting in one of the plush chairs in the small "movie palace" decorated theater in the Weta Ltd. building. Others, however, were interviewed in less interesting places. Pellerin's team filmed them against green screens and then digitally added flat backgrounds of various colors, all carrying vaguely Middle-earthy graphics to create a visual unity when the scenes were edited together.

Neither New Line nor Jackson's team suggested what sorts of questions Pellerin should formulate. Indeed, in October and November 2003, the filmmakers proved remarkably good sports about having the group record what the public and press were largely unaware of: the frantic efforts to finish *Return* as it slipped far behind schedule.

The supplement "The End of All Things," on the extended-edition *Return*'s last disc, has particular resonance for me because it records what was going on during my first research visit. The segment covers the final weeks of postproduction: daily meetings to discuss progress and suggest ways to catch up; instructions to animators to add more and more trolls, Nazgûl, and other beasts to already fiendishly difficult CGI shots; changes in the editing that forced Howard Shore to rewrite and rerecord passages of music.

When I first met him on 1 October, Barrie Osborne told me that there was some danger that *Return* would miss some of its foreign premieres because there would not be time to do the dubbing and subtitling. That same day, during one of the production meetings, the department heads were gathered to discuss how hiring extra temporary workers or renting an additional editing machine that was available in Singapore might help speed the work. A secretary stuck her head in the door and said that the local six o'clock news would carry an indignant story about the fact that filming was still being done on *Return* two months before its world premiere in Wellington. The meeting was suspended briefly so that the assembled group could watch the item.

The coverage included clips from the film's brand-new trailer, interspersed with the reporter interviewing the mayor about the situation and telephoto shots of extras in Orc costumes in the Stone Street Studios lot. Near the end, a bit of the trailer included Gandalf's voice-over, from *Fellowship:* "All you have to decide is what to do with the time that is given to you." The room dissolved into laughter, and as it died down Osborne commented good-naturedly, "Wow, they showed almost the whole trailer." The race to finish the film became more frantic over the next month and a half, and Pellerin's unusual creative freedom allowed him to chronicle these difficulties along with the standard making-of activities.

Each extended-edition DVD has four audio commentaries running throughout the film. In some cases, the speakers were actually conversing together in a room. That happened with the four Hobbit actors for the *Fellowship* discs. Jackson, Walsh, and Boyens recorded their commentary together; for *Return,* they came for three-hour recording sessions in the Weta Ltd. theater and then stayed to watch the day's rushes from *King Kong.* Early on, however, Ian McKellen insisted on doing his commentary separately, and he advised Pellerin not to record the actors together, apart from the Hobbits. Otherwise, he said, some of them would be drowned out and others would dominate the conversation. Pellerin says that was "exactly what I ended up doing. And also in terms of the logistics of where people are like that, it's the only way it could be done." In most cases he was able to sit the commentators down to watch the film, though it took multiple sessions for such a long movie. This could be done in recording studios in New York, Los Angeles, or London. Some of the actors were in such high demand after the first part appeared that they didn't even have time for that. Instead, Pellerin would simply interview them: "I would have them talk about specific scenes. I would trigger them with, OK, this scene dadada, tell me about the day when, and it was specifically designed to trigger it, so that that would end up in the audio commentary."

The galleries of still images on the DVD were not supplied by New Line or the filmmakers. Instead, the material was gathered at the production facilities in Wellington. Susie Lee, part of Pellerin's team, had been an archivist at Disney, and she sorted through the items available for scanning: about 10,000 for the first two films, of which 4,000 ended up in the galleries. Lee also recorded interviews with the artists, and in some cases one can click on a still image and hear a commentary on it.

The original designs for the menus failed to meet with Jackson's approval. J. P. Leonard, of Company Wide Shut, traveled to Wellington to come up with new designs and found himself collaborating with the department heads responsible for *Rings* itself. Pellerin recalls: "The menus were shot on 35mm with the Mitchell cameras on the motion-control unit. Alex Funke was actually the cameraman and director of photography. Alan Lee was the art director of the menu shoot. Dan Hennah was the set decorator. J. P. directed it. And the props were provided all by the film. So the menus literally are part of the production." In keeping with Jackson's desires, the design eschewed the flashy bells and whistles that characterize so many DVD menus. The aim was elegance. The stylistic links between the DVDs and film went even further when Leonard, having come to New Zealand simply to work on the menus, was asked to design the end credits for *Return*.

The vastness of the project had a considerable impact on Laser Pacific. One of the larger multimedia postproduction houses in Hollywood, the firm had already been involved in New Line DVD projects like *Spawn, John Q,* and the first Austin Powers film. Even for a big company, however, the volume of material involved in the *Rings* DVDs was staggering: about 1,000 menu pages and 19,000 buttons on disc 3 of *Fellowship* alone. To cope with all this, Laser Pacific created proprietary database software. Larry Spangler, the company's director of multimedia operations, remarked, "We've developed some tools to speed up these processes to the point where we can actually handle a project like this." Even so, it could take around five hours to import the project onto the firm's faster machines, and the production line was expanded to cut down turnaround time.[23]

Rings displayed remarkable coordination between the filmmakers and the DVD supplements team. The separate companies dealing with the technical aspects of DVD production were also brought into unusual proximity with each other. Ordinarily, Pellerin says, "The menu company is off doing their thing. You're producing the content of the DVD. The packaging people are doing their thing. Nobody talks to everybody." Under Mulvihill, the various companies worked in concert. "Toward the end," Pellerin adds, "when we're doing the packaging and the menus and stuff, there are these phone conferences. We're all on the phone talking. All the packaging gets sent to me, for my review. All the menus get sent to me for my review and approval. Not usually the way things go, but it does on this project. And it all fits together seamlessly." Although a more collaborative approach has since developed within the industry, Pellerin said in early 2006 that "to this day (even with Universal and *King Kong*) I have never experienced more of a synergy created between the filmmakers, the DVD producer, the menu and package designers than I did on *The Lord of the Rings*."[24]

Pellerin has consistently praised New Line and Universal for their hands-off approach while he was planning and making his supplements for *Rings* and *Kong*. With DVDs as such crucial money earners, however, studios are now creating committees of their executives from various departments to decide what will be in the supplements before the DVD producer is even signed up. At Buena Vista, which had been so casual about DVD extras for *The Sixth Sense,* marketing research is now conducted to determine what supplements consumers want. Pellerin worries that quality will suffer. "I just hope that the people they're hiring are filmmakers and know what they're doing. Once this stops being a creative endeavor, the medium we helped to pioneer will be watered down to its lowest common denominator."[25]

The Extended Version of the Film

Apart from its lengthy supplements, the laser disc of *The Frighteners* contained another precedent for the *Rings* DVDs: a director's cut of the film. At the time when the planning for *Rings* was going on, extra footage from films was usually relegated to a separate DVD supplement, just as the 1996 laser disc for *Aliens* had been handled. But Jackson intended to reedit scenes, change the sound track, and make something far more elaborate than the usual director's cut. The extended edition, he repeatedly declared, was for the serious fans, while more casual viewers would stick with the theatrical version.

Jackson conceived the idea of doing extended versions of the *Rings* installments in late 2001, as *Fellowship* was on the verge of being finished. As he explained:

> Until we actually knew how much deleted footage we would end up with and how worthwhile it was, there was no thought about alternate cuts. Having multiple units shooting three movies at once, out of sequence, with continual script revisions, made it difficult to keep track of exactly how long each of the films was going to be. As it happened, we had nearly an extra hour of deleted scenes for each of the three movies. I've always regarded those deleted scenes as being a legitimate part of our "LOTR" adaptation.[26]

It quickly became apparent that the filmmakers could not put the extended version of *Fellowship* together in time to release it simultaneously with the theatrical DVD. Jackson insisted, however, that it had to appear before the second part's release.

The preparation of the extended versions took so long partly because so much work had to be either finished or redone. Some scenes had been excised before their special effects and digital color grading were finished. Howard Shore did not simply move his musical cues around but composed about an hour's worth of additional music for the new and reshuffled scenes.[27]

The DVDs fit neatly into the franchise as a whole. As with the film itself, New Line sought marketing partners to help promote the DVDs. For the *Fellowship* DVD sets, these included Kia Motors America, Nokia, Air New Zealand, Tourism New Zealand, AOL, Gateway, and Intel. When the *Fellowship* theatrical video was released in August 2002, for example, Kia gave certificates for a free DVD or a VHS tape to anyone test-driving one of their vehicles. New Line provided window clings, banners, and standees, as well as the certificates, all with an image of the main characters. Among other tie-ins, New Line also ran an "Escape to Middle Earth" sweepstakes with a Kia Sorrento (a new model at the time) as first prize.[28] New Line again ran a sweepstakes for two free trips to New Zealand. Coupon booklets for licensed *Rings* merchandise came packed in the DVD box. Joe Pagono, an executive with Best Buy, predicted after New Line's March 2001 announcement of the DVD releases that *Rings* would be a huge seller: "They're the signature titles of the decade."[29]

In true franchise fashion, the various DVD versions promoted the theatrical runs of subsequent parts of the film. As Jackson pointed out, "The DVD release of the theatrical movie was very helpful in maintaining a marketing momentum and profile during the twelve months between the cinema releases of each of the films." In turn, the film promoted the DVDs. A print ad for the extended version of *Fellowship* urged magazine readers, "See this version before you see *The Lord of the Rings: The Two Towers!*" As *Fellowship* fought with *Harry Potter and the Sorcerer's Stone* to be 2002's top-selling DVD in the United Kingdom, the *Hollywood Reporter* remarked that the *Rings* distributor "has the advantage of a massive pre-Christmas theatrical promotion for 'The Lord of the Rings: The Two Towers,' the latest installment of the franchise, which is helping drive sales of its four-disc DVD edition of 'Fellowship.'" The DVDs also promoted each other: at the same time that *Towers*' extended edition topped sales charts, the *Fellowship* extended version, released a year earlier, went back up to number seven on the chart. Finally, the DVDs spawned ancillaries beyond those resulting from the films. Tower Records commissioned an exclusive plastic toy from the popular "Mini-mates" series, a figure of Sauron that was given away with the theatrical-version DVD on the first day it was available and sold for $2.99 thereafter—thus helping promote the DVD and the Mini-mates simultaneously.[30]

DVDs could also be incorporated within other ancillaries. In addition to its *Rings*-based "Trivial Pursuit" game, Parker Brothers brought out "Trivial Pursuit DVD: The Lord of the Rings Trilogy Edition," which included two discs with images and questions. (These were simply clips from the films and production photographs rather than documentary footage of the type used in the supplements.) David Imhoff, New Line's senior vice president of licensing and merchandising, declared that DVD games were a valuable new addition to a film franchise: "Having creative new product in the market continues to drive interest in 'Lord of the Rings.' We know [the Trivial Pursuit game] has had an effect on the DVD sales."[31]

Like other components of the *Rings* franchise, the extended-version DVDs won awards. It is confusing to try and track down and list them, since one of the most prominent sets of awards, bestowed by *Video Business* magazine, kept changing the prizes' names, from the cumbersome Video Business Video Premiere Awards to DVD Premiere Awards to the current DVD Exclusive Awards. These honors cover not the film itself but all the new features added on the DVD. These alterations make it hard to compare just how well the *Rings* sets did from year to year. Nevertheless, it was clearly a bad three years to have one's DVD nominated against *Rings*.

Fellowship and *Return* both had three wins, for best "Overall Extra Features, New Release," "New Movie Scenes," and "Audio Commentary" (director/ writers track). *Towers* also won the extra feature and new scenes categories but lost for audio commentary (perhaps because the actors' and director/ writers' tracks' both being nominated split the vote).

The other major prizes, the DVD Awards (aka DVD Entertainment Awards), are more technically oriented. Again the categories changed, but *Rings* tended to take the same ones. All three films won "Best in Show," "Best Audio Presentation," and "Best Authoring Design"; *Towers* and *Return* picked up "Best Blockbuster Theatrical" and "Best Audio Presentation"; *Towers* won "Best Menu Design" and "Best PC Support." Numerous other awards were bestowed by smaller, often fan-based science-fiction/fantasy groups.

Clearly the *Rings* DVDs set the new benchmark for the quantity and quality of supplements. One review of the special edition of *Mulan* credited it with a "*Lord of the Rings*–size treatment." An *Entertainment Weekly* online poll in early 2005 asked, "Which director is taking fullest creative advantage of the DVD format?" Jackson won 64 percent of the votes, with George Lucas second at 19 percent.[32]

All along Jackson insisted that the longer versions were not "director's cuts." The theatrical versions, he said, were the director's cuts. The new ones were "extended editions." The phrase was copied and varied for other films' DVDs. *The Bourne Identity*'s "Explosive Extended Edition," released 21 January 2003, seems to have been the first imitator. Warners soon followed, providing lots of additional Kevin Costner in its *Dances with Wolves* "Special Extended Edition" (May) and *Robin Hood—Prince of Thieves* "Two-Disc Special Extended Edition" (June). Inevitably "Unrated Special Editions" of raunchy comedies like *Club Dread, Harold & Kumar Go to White Castle,* and *American Wedding* ("Extended Unrated Party Edition") appeared. The same happened for anime series ("Robotech"), TV movies (*Kim Possible: So the Drama*), and even space launches (the *Apollo* and *Saturn* "Extended Collector's Edition" series). Thus *Rings* helped popularize the use of longer cuts of movies as their own DVD supplements.

AND THE FUTURE?

Movie companies have already started issuing films on DVD, then reissuing them with new combinations of extras. Reviewers now routinely comb the supplements to inform potential buyers as to whether enough substantive changes have been made to warrant buying the same film again. On the director/writer audio commentary accompanying the *Return* extended-version DVDs, Jackson, Walsh, and Boyens display their awareness of this aspect of a film franchise. They joke a number of times about the "twenty-fifth anniversary" edition of *Rings.* Jackson, an avid collector first of laser discs and then of DVDs, is well aware, however, that platforms for distributing movies to theaters and to the home will change radically in twenty-five years.

In more serious contexts, Jackson has said that after the introduction of high-definition video, a new boxed set of *Rings* would appear. The question uppermost in fans' minds is, what extras would it contain? Asked in an interview whether there will ever be an even longer director's cut, Jackson speculated that he might someday revisit *Rings,* but "more from the point of doing a documentary. I'm keen to do a documentary on my experience in making the film." Given the vast scale of both the film and the documentary recording of its making, there is plenty of material that was not included in any of the DVD supplements. In the same interview, Jackson also tantalizes fans with hints of additional scenes from *Rings* itself: "There's footage that I don't really feel that I'd want to put back into the movies. . . . But I'm happy to show people those scenes in the context of a documentary rather than a third version of the movies. There's a lot of things from all three films that I'm sure we have."[33]

Another set of potential DVD footage exists: the farewell videos made for each major cast member. These consist primarily of blooper segments and montages of behind-the-scenes footage set to songs somehow appropriate to the subject (such as "Big Bad John" for John Rhys-Davies). These carefully crafted little films, around twenty in all, have become the stuff of legend among fans, who assume that Jackson and/or New Line perversely kept them out of the supplements. In fact, the videos are quite problematic as a commercial release, especially as part of the boxed sets. For one thing, suggestive scenes and the actors' expletives when they fluff their lines are hardly compatible with *Rings*' PG-13 rating. Even for a stand-alone DVD, the rights to use all the popular songs (often two to a video) would have to be licensed, at a cost that New Line might not feel would be justified by potential sales. Finally, such a disc would probably require the approval of all the cast members, some of whom might not want their films, which were made to be played on-set to cast and crew and later in the privacy of the actors' homes, shown to the general public.[34] Nevertheless, these and immense files of other footage might someday extend the DVD portion of the franchise even further. (A blooper reel—not these farewell shorts—was shown at the ORC con in 2006, suggesting that footage left out of the DVDs can be used in other ways, such as providing an attraction for fans to attend an event.)

After the success of *Rings* became apparent, Jackson had the clout to branch out beyond the supplements for his own films. At the time that *Return* swept the Oscars in early 2004, Warner Home Video was preparing an elaborate boxed DVD set for its restoration of the original *King Kong* (1933). As a keen fan of the film, Jackson approached Warner and asked if he could help out with the DVD supplements. *Variety* reported that Jackson "was instrumental in the production of much of the bonus material on Warner's release, even spearheading a featurette about a 45-second segment involving a spider pit that was shot but not included because it was deemed too scary." Warner's *Kong* DVD came out on 22 November 2005, just weeks before Jackson's remake appeared. Although there was no cross-promotional publicity for the DVD and the film, the timing, along with Jackson's participation in the supplements (which he produced in conjunction with Pellerin), generated enormous publicity for both.[35]

Jackson also found a new way to use DVDs as ancillary products. He compiled fifty-four of the short behind-the-scenes segments he had been posting on KongIsKing.net (hosted by TORN) as a two-disc stand-alone set, *King Kong—Peter Jackson's Production Diaries,* rather than taking the standard route of saving them for supplements on the film's DVD. Going on sale 13 December 2005, the day before *Kong*'s release, the clips saw triple use: publicizing the film at intervals as it was made, calling attention to it again just before its release, and becoming a separate ancillary product. (The thirty-five remaining "postproduction" diaries remained on the site and were included among the supplements for the two-disc *Kong* DVD.)[36]

Also in the autumn of 2005, New Line, having failed so far to create a post-*Rings* franchise on the big screen, stayed true to its origins by signing a deal to produce up to thirty-nine Danielle Steel novels as direct-to-DVD films. An executive suggested that the studio could create "a global DVD paperback cottage industry."[37]

BUY, DON'T RENT

As in other areas, *Rings* was timed well for the rise of DVDs. Its preproduction began in 1997, just as the new format was commercially introduced in the United States. By the spring of 2001, when New Line hired Michael Pellerin to produce DVD supplements, that format not only was rapidly replacing VHS but also was becoming one of the most important sources of the studios' revenues. *Rings* would both benefit from and help accelerate the rise of DVD sell-through and the demise of VHS.

For the consumer, one obvious consideration was the price. For a long time videotapes had cost in the range of $70 and up, and most people chose instead to rent them. In 1983, Paramount became the first major studio to encourage sell-through in VHS by pricing *Airplane!* at $29.95.[38] The release's success encouraged a general price drop, and to some extent consumers started buying tapes rather than renting them—especially children's films, which kids could watch time after time on the electronic babysitter. DVDs, however, were relatively cheap to start with, and the price went down quickly. In 1999, the average DVD retail price was $25.65; by 2001, it had fallen to $20.74—less than tickets and refreshments would cost a family of four in a theater.[39] Prices have continued to drift downward.

If DVDs are cheaper, why are they more profitable than tapes? For a start, the cost of producing DVDs is less than that of VHS tapes. Tapes have to be recorded in real time, so every copy of a ninety-minute movie would take ninety minutes to record. DVDs are simply stamped out and can be made far more quickly. In 2002, according to one Wall Street analyst, the wholesale price of DVDs averaged around $16. With $1.00 for the finished disc, $.90 for packaging, $.80 for distribution, and $2.75 for marketing, the gross profit per DVD came to $10.55. The CEO of video-rental chain Blockbuster confirmed this, estimating that profits ranged from $10 to $13 per disc. A DVD selling eleven million copies would yield a $121 million profit.[40]

In many cases, the Hollywood firms do not receive royalties on individual rentals of DVDs and tapes. They make their profit per disc sold to the stores, but every rental is a potential lost sale. In 2002, film distributors received on average 75 percent of money spent buying DVDs and VHS tapes but only 25 to 33 percent of rental fees for both formats.[41] Thus DVD sell-through is the studios' preferred way of disseminating a film for home viewing.

The video release of the theatrical version of *Fellowship* spectacularly achieved the industry's hopes for high DVD sales in proportion to VHS sales, as well as for high sales in proportion to rentals. Seventy percent of the copies of *Fellowship* sold were DVDs, a record at the time. As recently as 2000, DVDs had represented 7 and 12 percent, respectively, for the year's two best-selling video titles, *Tarzan* and *Toy Story.* The *Monsters, Inc.* DVD, which appeared about a month after *Fellowship*'s theatrical version, saw a more typical fifty-fifty split between DVD and cassette.[42]

Fellowship did not, however, do as well on VHS. It ranked number 5 in VHS sales, with the proportion of income from this source being only 23.2 percent as high as the theatrical gross. Perhaps not surprisingly, in 2002 many of the highest-selling VHS tapes were of children's movies: number 1, *Monsters, Inc.* (VHS sales 56.7 percent compared with theatrical gross); number 2, *Harry Potter and the Sorcerer's Stone* (41.3 percent); number 4, *Lilo and Stitch* (56.0 percent); and number 6, *Ice Age* (44.3 percent).[43] For children unable or just learning to read, a VHS player, with its simple backward and forward buttons, would be easier to deal with than the elaborate menus and controls of a DVD machine.

The video sales figures for *Fellowship* compared with its rental income are also revealing. *Fellowship*'s gross income from video rentals—little of which, remember, returns to the studio—indicates that the film performed much as New Line would wish. Among the top DVD rental films, it ranked down at number 19, with the percentage of income from that source a mere 6.9 percent in comparison with the theatrical gross. Among VHS rentals, *Fellowship* was number 26, at 9.1 percent.

By any measure, *Rings* was among the films leading the move away from VHS toward DVD and away from rental toward sell-through. In number of units sold (12 million), it was second in 2002 releases to *Spider-Man* (12.2 million), though in revenue *Fellowship* was number one ($257.3 million vs. *Spider-Man*'s $215.3 million). The disparity reflects the fact that the theatrical versions and the pricier boxed sets were counted together.[44]

Moreover, *Fellowship* was far stronger in DVD sell-through than in any other type of video income. The proportion of its total DVD sales income to its domestic theatrical box office was 82.1 percent. (For all three parts the proportion was actually considerably higher, since the extended editions came out late in the year, and only their income to December 31 is included in these totals.) This was higher than any other film in the top ten except *The Fast and the Furious,* number 8 in sales but with a DVD income of 91.3 percent compared with its theatrical gross. In contrast, a number of popular films had distinctly lower earnings when compared with theatrical income: 53.3 percent for *Spider-Man,* 52.5 percent for *Harry Potter and the Sorcerer's Stone,* 47.9 percent for *Star Wars: Episode II—Attack of the Clones,* and 43.5 percent for *Austin Powers in Goldmember.*[45] Given *Fellowship*'s very high income at the box office *and* on DVD, I think we can assume that most of the people buying the *Fellowship* DVD had probably already seen it at least once in a theater. For VHS sell-through, *Fellowship* was only number 7, with $72.8 million. It did not make the top-ten list for rentals of either DVD or VHS.[46]

In sum, *Fellowship* was a film that most people wanted to see with the best sound and image possible, and they did not want to return it to the video store afterward. That was true for other popular video releases of 2002. Their high box office takings were not followed by comparably high video rentals. As with *Fellowship,* people wanted to rewatch certain films. *Spider-Man,* the top DVD seller, was number 22 in DVD rentals, and *Monsters, Inc.* and *Harry Potter* did not even figure in the top twenty-five. Conversely, some of the most successful films of the year at the box office were not nearly as high on the lists of top DVD rentals: number 1, *Ocean's Eleven* (number 11 in DVD sales); number 2, *Training Day* (number 15 in sales); number 3, *Don't Say a Word* (not in the top 25); number 4, *Mr. Deeds* (number 20 in sales); number 5, *The Others* (not in the top 25); number 6, *Spy Game* (not in the top 25); number 7, *Insomnia* (not in the top 25); number 8, *John Q.* (not in the top 25); number 9, *Panic Room* (not in the top 25); and number 10, *The Sum of All Fears* (not in the top 25). Interestingly, at that point none of these was a franchise film.[47]

Clearly video has brought about a phenomenon where many spectators somehow sense something about certain films and decide to skip them in their theatrical runs and wait for the video release. Perhaps they sometimes make such decisions because these are not part of franchises and thus they know little about them. In such cases, we might expect DVD rental income would be relatively high in relation to theatrical box office. Proportional figures for some films in the top ten for 2001 definitely suggest that many people deliberately waited for the video: *Training Day* (39.6 percent of theatrical gross), *Don't Say a Word* (51.9 percent), *Spy Game* (39.9 percent), and *Insomnia* (36.4 percent). Such films do not do their part in the push toward DVD sell-through. In contrast, *Spider-Man*'s DVD rentals were 5.2 percent in proportion to its theatrical gross, and we have seen that *Fellowship*'s were also low, at 6.9 percent.[48]

During the same year as *Fellowship*'s release, ownership of DVD players rose 58 percent, from 25 million households to 39 million at year's end. Seeing the handwriting on the wall, rental chains and big retailers banded with the studios to purge VHS. In June, Circuit City announced that it would stop selling tapes. Barnes & Noble soon did the same. DVDs had gradually taken over the VHS racks at Best Buy until tapes constituted only 20 percent of the video product by the end of 2002. Wal-Mart and Target started moving VHS movies into discount bins.[49] Rental chains felt the effects of big films—like *Fellowship*—that people preferred to own. In early 2003, *Variety* reported that Blockbuster's earnings were down.[50] (The next year Viacom, Blockbuster's parent company, disposed of it.) The year 2002 was also when total spending on home-video sales and rentals surpassed gross theatrical income for the first time.[51]

From 2002 to 2003, the year when *Towers* appeared on DVD, spending on DVD rentals more than quadrupled, up to 53 percent from 12 percent. Thus in 2003, DVDs' rental earnings edged past those of VHS for the first time. Movie studios, impatient to kill off VHS, took to charging video-rental stores around seventy-five dollars per tape, while they offered DVDs for around sixteen dollars.[52] In 2005, analysts predicted that VHS rentals would not exist after 2008.[53]

Towers echoed *Fellowship*'s pattern, failing to make the top ten among DVD rentals for 2003, though it was number two (after *Finding Nemo*) in sales, at $305.4 million, 89.3 percent of its domestic box-office take. Similarly, in 2004, *Return*'s DVD was not among the top ten rental videos (DVD and VHS figures were combined as of that year), but it was number 2 (after *Shrek 2*) in sales at $274 million, 72.7 percent of its theatrical earnings.[54]

By 2005, the rate of video sell-through had slowed slightly, but one industry analyst blamed it on VHS: "DVD sell-through growth has actually been fairly strong all year, but VHS really pulled the growth rate down. Now that we've pretty much washed VHS out of the system—at this point, we've got it down to about 3 percent—we're assuming growth rates will be better." He estimated that VHS sales would total around $475 million, compared with roughly $17.3 billion for DVDs.[55] In August, Twentieth Century Fox announced that *Star Wars: Episode III—Revenge of the Sith* would become the first major studio film to forgo circulation on VHS.[56] By the end of the year, Disney had abandoned VHS production, and Warners followed suit in early 2006. VHS was about to become a niche product.[57]

In early December 2003, a series of entertainment conferences was held in New York, attended by corporate executives and media investment analysts.

Speaking a few weeks after the release of the *Towers* extended edition and a week before *Return* appeared in theaters, one executive with more than a passing interest in those films singled out New Line for praise. "'A lot of the focus is on rising costs. Investment in special effects and film production has gone up. But revenue has risen faster,' Time Warner chief financial officer Wayne Pace said as he heaped praise on Warner Bros. and New Line early in his luncheon speech. 'Homevideo—DVD—is the largest driver of profits.'"[58] Although filmmaking made up only a small portion of the huge company, the *Harry Potter* and *Rings* series were important factors in helping Time Warner limp back toward prosperity after its problematic merger with AOL.

Measured by total revenues, the amount of money going back to the studio once theaters, stores, and distributors have taken their share, DVDs dominate the film industry. In 2004, studios' revenues totaled $45.0 billion, of which $21.0 billion came from home video, $7.4 billion from rentals of films to theaters, and the rest from fees paid for showings of the films on pay and free television.[59]

Bob Shaye could not have known all this back in mid-1998, when he greenlit Jackson's project. At that point DVDs had been commercially available for only about a year. He was probably interested primarily in a film franchise. The unexpectedly rapid rise of DVDs and their importance to studios' bottom lines meant, as *Variety* put it in mid-2003, that "booming DVD sales are adding muscle to the franchises." New Line's own *Austin Powers: International Man of Mystery* had made $53.9 million in its entire U.S. theatrical run. Its DVD brought in $54.9 million on its first weekend. And apart from direct income, DVDs can, as Hollywood quickly realized, create a much higher awareness of a film and build anticipation for a sequel.[60] With *Rings*, the release of the theatrical DVDs for each of the first two parts in August, followed by the extended editions in November, clearly fed interest for the succeeding parts. The rising box-office totals for each successive *Rings* film only confirmed the trend.

On 14 October 2005, TheOneRing.net ran a poll that asked: "Are you tired of any of the LotR movies yet?" The "Never!!" option garnered 87.8 percent of the votes, followed by "Slightly" at 5.9 percent. "Yes, totally sick of them" was the option for 1.4 percent of respondents.[61] New Line probably will rerelease *Rings* theatrically someday, perhaps simply to let fans see the extended versions on the screen, perhaps to celebrate an anniversary of the trilogy's premieres. The audience will certainly be there. Still, it will be on DVD and the formats that succeed it that most people will rewatch or discover *Rings*.

CHAPTER 8

Interactive Middle-earth

This is far more important than who gets the rights
to make the lunch boxes or the action figures.

JOHN MASS
William Morris Agency

WHEN THE EXTENDED DVD VERSION of *Return* came out in late 2004, millions of fans lamented that *Rings* was finally over. Millions of other fans, however, saw no end to adventures in Middle-earth. They were absorbed in what
will almost certainly, in terms of the amount of time eyeballs spend glued to
screens, be the biggest territory of the *Rings* franchise: the video games.

The licensed film-based games have been designed and produced by the
largest publisher of video games in the world, Electronic Arts. The first two,
"The Lord of the Rings: The Two Towers" and "The Lord of the Rings: The
Return of the King," hit store shelves about a month before the respective
parts of the film appeared in theaters. (The games' names appear in quota-
tion marks to differentiate them from the italicized film titles.) According
to Mark Skaggs, the executive producer of the later game "The Battle for
Middle-earth," "We'll continue to make games as long as people want to buy
them."

By the end of the film the Ring is destroyed and the various plotlines are
closed, so how can the games continue indefinitely? Stories that are part of
franchises need to go beyond the limits of the movies, so the problem is to
find new narrative material to develop. In expanding *Rings,* the games' designers chose to emphasize not the Ring, but the continent of Middle-earth,
the races that inhabit it, and the battles in which they participate. The fourth
game's title, "The Battle for Middle-earth," signals that approach. For gamers

who have not seen the film, Middle-earth will be primarily associated not with heroic Hobbits on a quest but with warriors and monsters locked in combat. "The Battle for Middle-earth" was the first EA game to center not on characters but on armies and strategies. The games of the franchise have not simply adapted Tolkien's tale. They have expanded his imagined world into a site for interactive play.

Here again the film's making coincided with major changes in technology, marketing, and merchandising. From 1999 to 2003, when *Rings* was shot and released, the business relations between the video game and film industries were changing rapidly, and advances in technology were making games look and sound more like movies.

COMPETITION OR CONVERGENCE?

Are the game and film industries fiercely competing with each other? Certainly the popular and trade press seem to think so. Coverage tends to treat their relationship as a race for money that the game industry is now winning. For years magazines and newspapers have told us that video games now make more money than films take in at the box office. As early as 1993, a *Time* survey of the business claimed: "Videogames rake in $5.3 billion a year in the U.S. alone, about $400 million more than Americans spend going to the movies." In 1999, *Variety* declared, "Showbiz certainly sat up when the videogame industry took in $6.3 billion last year—within a hair's breath [*sic*] of the $6.9 billion that the majors collected at the box office in 1998."[1]

In fact the game industry has not grown more lucrative than Hollywood filmmaking. Another *Variety* report on the respective incomes of the two businesses suggests why this myth has arisen: "Last year [2001] the [video game] biz surpassed the film industry's B.O. earnings for the first time, collecting $9.4 billion in revenues, thanks to new consoles from Microsoft and Nintendo, along with the continued success of Sony's PlayStation 2."[2] The "higher" income for the video game industry comes from lumping sales of the games themselves together with those of the consoles and other hardware used to play them. Not surprisingly, such creative comparisons originate with gaming-industry representatives. *Newsweek* reported on activity at the annual E3 (Electronic Entertainment Exposition): "In 2001, consumers snapped up $9.4 billion worth of game software and hardware—up 43 percent from the previous year—led by Sony's world-beating PlayStation 2. Noting that the game industry had once again outstripped Hollywood's box-office revenues, the head of Sony's U.S. computer-entertainment division, Kaz Hirai, says his next target is the $18 billion home-video industry."[3] A more mean-ingful comparison would be the annual income from gaming software and the combined film total from the theatrical box office, home video, and television rights. As of 2004, software accounted for $6.2 billion, about two-thirds of the total $9.9 billion income of the video game industry.[4] (Hardware was down that year in anticipation of the rollout of a new generation of gaming platforms in 2005 and 2006.) That year all means of film distribution, not counting the hardware used to view films in various formats, brought in $45 billion in revenues.[5] Clearly the film industry remains far larger and will be winning this "race" for a long time.

No doubt the game sector of the entertainment business is growing, and no doubt, too, the two industries are struggling for the leisure time of an expanding population of gamers. All the same, film and game companies have many reasons to cooperate. They are becoming more dependent on each other. They often are partners within the same franchises, with the films promoting the games, and the games promoting the films. They also depend on much of the same technology, and some personnel move freely between the two industries. "Convergence" has become the buzzword for describing the course of the two industries.

Just as film production budgets have spiraled upward in recent decades, the cost of creating new games has accelerated. As game companies have become more successful, competition among them grows. Each generation of more powerful and flexible consoles requires more elaborate games, which means higher investments. In 2001, the average cost to develop a new game was about $5 million; by 2004 it had reached $15 million. Unlike the big Hollywood studios, most game companies are not subsidiaries of large conglomerates. Their stock prices rise and fall with the fortunes of their blockbuster titles. Such financial pressures have driven the game industry, like the film industry, to rely increasingly on proven products that foster franchises: either original titles that spawn sequels ("Halo," "Grand Theft Auto") or licenses for adaptations, mostly based on sports and movies. The ten best-selling video games for 2003 were all sequels or film adaptations.[6]

Some of the biggest game makers got that way by gravitating toward licensing films, especially big franchise titles. Activision, which hovers around the number two rank in the industry, moved from northern California to Santa Monica in 1992, putting it closer to Hollywood. More than any other major firm, Activision has seen its growth fueled by movie titles, including the "Spider-Man" series and DreamWorks animated features like "Shrek" and "A Shark Tale." In late 2005, when Activision extended its DreamWorks contract through 2010, *Variety* commented, "With the vidgame business moving toward a model closer to Hollywood's in which big franchises drive profits, publishers have been snapping up long-term rights to the most valuable licenses."[7]

In contrast, Electronic Arts (EA) achieved dominance in the field largely through sports titles, notably the "Madden NFL" series, and these accounted for about a third of the company's revenues in 2004.[8] But by then EA had titles in seventeen sports categories, with diminishing possibilities for expansion in that area.[9] The success of its "Rings," "Harry Potter," and "James Bond" franchises, according to Neil Young, executive producer of the "Rings" games, helped EA "balance its portfolio," blending in more movie-based and original titles. As he explains:

> If you think about how EA has to grow to be the next great entertainment company instead of just the best game company, we have to move further along the continuum of intellectual-property ownership. It's our objective ultimately to be creating intellectual properties that would move into other media—that would move into film, move into television, move into books. Just like the film studios' motivation is to move to games, to own game companies.

He does not envision EA actually producing films, but it would increasingly provide the bases for franchises rather than licensing them from other media.[10]

Games are becoming more like films, and at least some films more like games. Technology strongly links the two media. Computer-generated imagery offers an obvious overlap, as does digital sound; THX, originally a sound-certification system for movie theaters and mixing studios, added a set of standards for game mixing studios in 2003. Many newer game consoles can play DVDs. And members of film casts and crews now commonly participate in the creation of the associated games. When in 1995 the game industry broke away from the Consumer Electronics Show in Las Vegas and started the E3, it moved the event to Los Angeles in order to be near the film industry. June 2006 saw the launch of a joint event that brought representatives of both industries together, the Hollywood and Games Summit.[11]

Most obviously, movies are adapted into games, and, rarely, games into movies. When it comes to adaptations, film studios so far have the advantage. Hollywood does not depend on games as a major source of material. As of December 2005, only fifteen game-based films had been released in the United States, with an average domestic gross of about $36 million; only two—*Lara Croft: Tomb Raider* and *Mortal Kombat*—had taken in more than $70 million domestically. (The *Pokemon* film series is often listed as a video game adaptation, but the franchise began as a TV series.) Keith Boesky, head of ICM's video game division, points out, "Not every game deserves to be a film. But Hollywood is buying, and video game companies are trying to get writers into games so they can have stronger characters, some kind of plot to adapt." Yet because games gross less than movies, most game firms cannot afford what established film writers expect to be paid. The result is that more scripts come from television writers than from film writers.[12]

Some big game companies, however, are increasingly competing with each other in acquiring licenses to adapt movies. Film companies' huge libraries contain potential video game sources. During 2004 and 2005, older titles were released or announced: "Fight Club," "Predator," and "Scarface"; "Tim Burton's The Nightmare before Christmas"; a "Dirty Harry" series; "The Godfather"; and the "Evil Dead."[13] In early 2005, Pascal Bonnet, director of licensing for Ubisoft North America, told a reporter that "the balance of power rests with studios because of the size of their catalogues and attendant franchise power. 'It is a bidding war between the major publishers, five to seven [software publishers] worldwide trying to get the worldwide rights. And it's going to get tougher.'"[14]

Competition for attractive titles has driven up licensing fees. In 1995 a game firm might have paid a few hundred thousand dollars for a minor title and $2 or $3 million for a major one. By early in the new century, the game rights for big franchises like "James Bond" and "Harry Potter" were reportedly going for more than $10 million.[15] The result was significant ancillary income for the film studios. By 2005, a hit title's license and royalties could generate around $40 million for a studio.[16] (Such a sum, though significant, would not be a huge portion of a film's ancillary income. To keep things in perspective, the WB network reportedly paid in the neighborhood of $160 million to hold the broadcast rights for the *Rings* trilogy for ten years.)

Convergence does not just mean that films are adapted into games. With the huge leaps in the power of consoles and PCs, designers can aspire to create games that look more like movies. The technical convergence could not really begin as long as games were two-dimensional, with locales like mazes ("Pac-Man") or landscapes scrolling as the action moved perpetually sideways ("Super Mario Brothers"). In the mid-1980s, a game based on a movie license might involve only two people, one to write the code and one to do the graphics, and their work might occupy a few weeks.[17] Increases in computing power permitted simple 3-D graphics, notably in "Doom" (1993), which helped establish the first-person shooter genre; in "Doom" the player controls a character that interacts with an immersive environment. Also in

1993, "Myst" popularized the CD-ROM as a software format, helping make CD-ROM drives standard features of PCs.

The turning point came in 1995–96, with the fifth generation of game consoles. Nintendo 64 and Sony's PlayStation were more powerful than PCs— and were considerably cheaper at a point when most home computers were owned by families with annual incomes over $45,000. During the second half of the 1990s, more complex games hinted that interactive imagery might someday match films in simulating movement through three-dimensional space: "Super Mario 64" (1996), "Tomb Raider" (1996), "Final Fantasy VII" (1997), and "The Legend of Zelda: Ocarina of Time" (1998). Most crucially, "GoldenEye 007," based on the James Bond film and released in 1997, marked the first popularly and critically acclaimed game adapted from a movie. That year and 1998 saw other successful film-based games: "Toy Story," "Die Hard Trilogy," "A Bug's Life," "Star Wars: Rebel Squadron," and "Mission: Impossible." Those were the years of *Rings*' preproduction at Miramax and its move to New Line.

These early games did not incorporate stars' voices or images; studios seldom shared designs or CGI files with game makers. Sounds and images were usually created from scratch. The first words heard in a video game were synthesized umpire calls in a 1980 arcade game, "Major League Baseball." In 1982, "Spike" had a single line, using the voice of an employee in the game developer's office. It was not until games moved onto CD-ROMs that high-quality vocals were possible. Even then programmers, amateurs, or minor actors might record the dialogue. The original "Grand Theft Auto" (1997) used people hired in a pub near the designer's Scottish headquarters. The situation had changed considerably by 2004, when the "Grand Theft Auto: San Andreas" entry in the series included vocal performances by Samuel L. Jackson, James Woods, and Peter Fonda.[18] As recently as 2000, it was considered noteworthy that Kate Mulgrew, who had played Captain Kathryn Janeway in various *Star Trek* series and films, voiced her character in the game "Star Trek Voyager: Elite Force."[19] Things changed quickly, and in 2002 Tobey Maguire and Willem Dafoe reprised their movie roles for the "Spider-Man" game. The following year Arnold Schwarzenegger agreed to have his voice and likeness used in "Terminator 3: Rise of the Machines."

By 2004, the *Hollywood Reporter* could remark, "In case anyone still doubts that video games can attract the best of Hollywood, Activision confirmed Wednesday that Jim Carrey has reprised his role as Count Olaf in its tie-in to Paramount Pictures' upcoming feature film 'Lemony Snicket's A Series of Unfortunate Events.'" Carrey spent a single day in the recording studio, undoubtedly for a handsome fee. Not only were actors discovering that video games could be lucrative, but any lingering stigma attached to participation in them faded when Marlon Brando played Don Corleone once more for the "Godfather" video game, Clint Eastwood agreed to participate in a "Dirty Harry" series, and Sean Connery, believing his grandchildren's claims that games are cool, voiced James Bond for "From Russia with Love."[20] The practice has hardly become universal, however. The "Harry Potter" games have been a huge hit despite the lack of participation by any of the films' actors—though the fourth one, "Harry Potter and the Goblet of Fire" (2005) was the first to make the characters resemble the actors.[21]

Along with performances, the music in video games was being upgraded. Earlier games had gotten by with synthesized music, but full orchestral sound tracks entered games when stars did. In 2003, Christopher Lennertz's score for EA's "Medal of Honor: Rising Sun" was the first to be recorded with union musicians, eighty-eight of them. Lennertz was among a growing number of young composers who, without winning fame in other areas of music, found themselves able to write, perform, and record long orchestral pieces. In November of the same year, celebrated film composer Danny Elfman created the title theme for the video game "Fable" (released 2004). EA's music executive, Steve Schnur, told an interviewer, "Can you imagine if they put out the last 'Matrix' film and it had a Casio [keyboard] as the score? Can you imagine if the last James Bond film came out and the score was done by an in-house composer in Century City? We really need to elevate [game music] to another level." Some games have generated their own CDs. *Rings* composer Howard Shore wrote another epic orchestral score for the Korean online video game "Soul of the Ultimate Nation" (still without an announced launch date as of late 2006), with a sound track CD released in 2006. Many pop songs have also been commissioned, and games threaten to replace radio as the medium for introducing them to young people. In 2003, 40 percent of gamers said that they had bought CDs by bands they had first heard in games. Players seem more impressed by music than by star voices, since so much of the mood of a game can be manipulated by its score.[22]

Apart from George Lucas, who had long housed an interactivity department in his Skywalker Ranch facilities, most directors avoided any involvement in games. In 2004 director Stephen Sommers, who had been disappointed with the game version of *The Mummy* (2000), got involved in the making of the game for his feature, *Van Helsing* (where his credit simply reads "Very special thanks"). As of 2005, John Woo had established his own game studio, Tiger Hill Entertainment, and well-known directors like John Singleton (making "Fear and Respect" for Ubisoft), George A. Romero, John McTiernan, and Bryan Singer were all working on game projects not based on their films. In October 2005 it was announced that Steven Spielberg would collaborate on three original games for EA. These were all intended to spawn franchises, with Spielberg having the option to help create each subsequent title. Both Spielberg and EA had ties to the University of Southern California, the director through the School of Cinema-Television and the games firm through its sponsorship of a video game development laboratory there.[23]

Perhaps the most important facet of the convergence process comes in the area of CGI and other digital technology that the two media share. The same firms and personnel may work on both games and films. Young sees game-film convergence as real: "If you look at, for example, the art pipeline for building a game, it's essentially the same as the art pipeline for doing visual effects or building a CG animated movie. If you look at the population of artists in this studio, I'd say 60, 70 percent of them have worked at some point in the visual-effects, feature-animation, CG-animation business." Some prominent names in the film world have also contributed to games. Oscar-winning effects expert Stan Winston designed creatures for three video games, while Mark Lasoff (*Titanic*) was hired as the senior art director of EA's new Los Angeles facility. Richard King, sound editor on *Master and Commander: The Far Side of the World,* designed the track for Flying Lab's online game "Pirates of the Burning Sea."[24] When Activision renewed its DreamWorks contract in 2005, it based a group of employees in Glendale, where DreamWorks Animation is located, to collaborate with the studio.[25]

One technique of CGI in particular links games and films: motion capture. Motion capture is accomplished by attaching sensors to various parts of a moving being or object. These are digitally read and synthesized into a moving wire-frame figure, which is ultimately rendered with texture and color. In 1992, Acclaim created a mo-cap studio to record martial arts fights for its first "Mortal Kombat" game. New software developed during the late 1990s for the "Final Fantasy" series made the technique more effective for use in films.[26] The Weta Digital team working on *Rings* pushed the technology further to create Gollum, sometimes using mo-cap on sets during filming rather than only in a special studio.

Members of film teams have occasionally participated in motion capture for games. "Rise to Honor," a 2003 game loosely derived from Jet Li's films, included voice work and mo-cap stunts performed by Li, who also brought in martial arts choreographer Cory Yuen to direct the mo-cap sessions. For the game based on *Star Wars: Episode III—Revenge of the Sith* (2005), the film's stunt coordinator and star Hayden Christensen worked with the developers to replicate the light-saber battles.[27]

Unsurprisingly, game companies are increasingly using Hollywood-style marketing campaigns, with their attendant higher costs. One new tactic involves press junkets. Stars who lent their voices to video games had initially been reluctant to do more than sit down with a few key entertainment reporters. Vin Diesel was an early exception, attending many publicity events for "The Chronicles of Riddick: Escape from Butcher Bay" (2004). In February 2005, EA staged a press event for its forthcoming "Godfather" title in New York's Little Italy, with Robert Duvall and James Caan appearing.[28] As big games become more like event movies, stars will undoubtedly find themselves with even more junkets to attend.

Despite all this convergence, however, films and games are not going to merge or to compete until one drives the other out of existence. In the franchise age, it makes no sense to eliminate a media product when one can induce some consumers to purchase a theater ticket, a DVD, and a game. Game makers often stress that their adaptations are not simply clones of the original movie. Universal Interactive's CEO, Jim Wilson, described taking care not to duplicate the original plotline:

> "I don't want to do 'See the movie, play the game,' because we know how the movie ends," Wilson says.
>
> He points to "The Thing" [2002] as an example of how the approach works. The survival-horror game, which is winning buzz in the enthusiast press, starts after the movie ends. It functions almost like the sequel that was never made, expanding fans' experience of the pic.
>
> "It's absolutely to build the franchises, to extend the franchises," Wilson says. "Consumers don't want a rehash of a movie."[29]

Within a franchise, games act as publicity for films and films for the games. MGM discovered through exit polls for *The World Is Not Enough* (1999) that a new generation that had never seen the early James Bond films or read Ian Fleming's books got introduced to the character via the EA games and started going to the new films.[30]

Brad Globe, the head of DreamWorks' consumer products area, suggests how games can be important ancillaries to films beyond the income they generate:

> I would say that the interactive component of merchandise is the single most important part of the program now. Once you have millions of games out

there and the kids are playing, it reinforces the brand. Unlike T-shirts and toys, these games capture the essence of the storyline and the personality and characters: you're interacting with them, they're coming to life. It's an extension of the movie experience.[31]

As John Mass says, the video games are the most important component of a franchise's licensed products.

Mass is a senior vice president of the consulting division of the William Morris Agency. In the early 1990s that agency, along with other big firms like International Creative Management, United Talent Agency, and Creative Artists Agency, all added "new media departments" to handle employment of their actors, writers, and directors to work on video games. That move no doubt helped accelerate the convergence process.[32]

MIDDLE-EARTH IN CYBERSPACE

Tolkien's novels were already popular and influential within geekdom when video games were developed. Back in the 1970s, rooms at the Stanford Artificial Intelligence Laboratory were labeled with place-names from Middle-earth, and the vending machine was dubbed the Prancing Pony. In a Tolkienesque spirit, that lab devised "Adventure" (aka "ADVENT"), the precursor of elaborate fantasy games such as "Myst," "Quake," and "Ultima."[33] From early on in the development of the fledgling technology, minor games based on Tolkien's novels were devised, such as "The Hobbit" (1982) and "War in Middle Earth" (1989, both from Melbourne House). Many other games created fantasy worlds influenced by Middle-earth, but no major software publisher took on *Rings* until New Line was building its film franchise. At that point two deals were made that would lead to parallel, competing video games, one series based on the book, the other on the film.

In December 2001, Vivendi Universal Games, a subsidiary of Vivendi Universal Publishing, announced that Saul Zaentz's Tolkien Enterprises had granted it licensing rights for video games based on the original book. VU Games' subsidiary, Universal Interactive, would develop three games corresponding to the three volumes of the novel. In March of the following year, VU Games further announced that another subsidiary of VU Publishing, Sierra Entertainment, would develop a game based on *The Hobbit*.[34] Universal Interactive's Game Boy version of "The Fellowship of the Ring" appeared in late October 2002, with versions for other platforms following.[35] In December, VU revealed that a third game, "War of the Ring," was in development. The firm shipped two new games a week apart in late 2003: "War of the Ring" on 4 November and "The Hobbit" on 11 November. That autumn VU canceled its game based on the second part of Tolkien's novel, to have been called "The Treason of Isengard," citing quality problems. None of the completed games sold particularly well, being overshadowed by their film-based rivals.

The other deal became public in October 2000, when the trade press reported that EA had acquired the film-based *Rings* game rights from New Line. The negotiations between the two firms did not involve Jackson or any of the filmmakers, already a year into principal photography. The rumored price was in excess of $10 million, which would have put it on the level of the "James Bond" and "Harry Potter" licenses.[36] According to Neil Young, however, the fee was lower than for "Harry Potter," since the rights to the book and the film had been split. For an open-ended game series, being limited to the films could create a serious problem—one that EA would face years later.

Rather than starting with a game to coincide with the release of *Fellowship,* the firm launched its series with "The Two Towers" in late October 2002. This happened to be the same week that Vivendi Universal's "Fellowship" game came out (under its Black Label Games subsidiary), no doubt sowing confusion among parents shopping for Christmas presents. Also confusingly, "Towers" included scenes and story elements from the first film, which did not have its own EA game.[37]

EA had not released a "Fellowship" game of its own in 2001 to coincide with the release of the film's first part because of organizational problems. "Honestly," explains Young, "the first year of development for the game for us—it predates my arrival in the franchise—was kind of troubled. So I think we would have loved to have had a game out with *Fellowship,* but it wasn't to be from a development standpoint." The license was shifted from one part of EA to another, where it came under Young's purview.

Although the *Rings* game license had been considered highly desirable, EA had no way of knowing whether Jackson's *Fellowship* would succeed— particularly since fantasy was still viewed as an unpopular genre. EA planned so that even if *Fellowship* failed, the "Towers" game would at least break even and they could drop the series. EA didn't build the game from scratch. Instead, planners took the underlying design from an existing game and created a new one around it. Mark Skaggs recalls: "We did say, 'Well, let's go ahead and repurpose an engine.'" Like New Line, EA found its cautious expectations wildly exceeded when *Fellowship* became a hit. In our interview in August 2004, Young described the financial results:

Plate 1. The press junket for *The Return of the King* world premiere included interviews in a beautiful setting, the national museum Te Papa. *Left to right:* Barrie Osborne, Ian McKellen, Orlando Bloom, John Rhys-Davies, Sean Astin, Billy Boyd, Elijah Wood, Richard Taylor, and Mark Ordesky. (Photograph © Keith Stern, courtesy McKellen.com.)

Plate 2. Mount Sunday, one of the trilogy's most remote locations, with a view from behind the set of the Golden Hall of Medulseld. The mountain ranges surrounding "Edoras" were not added by CGI. (Photograph © Ian McKellen, courtesy McKellen.com.)

Plate 3. The "party field" at the beginning of New Line's Cannes party. (Courtesy Judy Alley.)

Plate 4. John Howe, *Gandalf Returns to Bag End*. (© 1994 John Howe, reproduced courtesy of HarperCollins Publishers.)

Plate 5. Howe's Bag End exterior replicated in *The Fellowship of the Ring.*

Plate 6. The "Aragorn" Boeing 767300 went into service in January 2003. (Courtesy Air New Zealand.)

Plate 7. Electronic Arts' "The Battle for Middle-earth" video game centers around a map of the continent. (Courtesy Electronic Arts.)

Plate 8. Fighting outside Minas Tirith in "The Battle for Middle-earth" video game. (Courtesy Electronic Arts.)

Plate 9. Park Road Post balanced state-of-the-art facilities like this sound-mixing studio . . .

Plate 10. . . . with comfortable, elegant surroundings, as in this corridor outside the three mixing studios. (Photographs of plates 9 and 10 courtesy Park Road Post.)

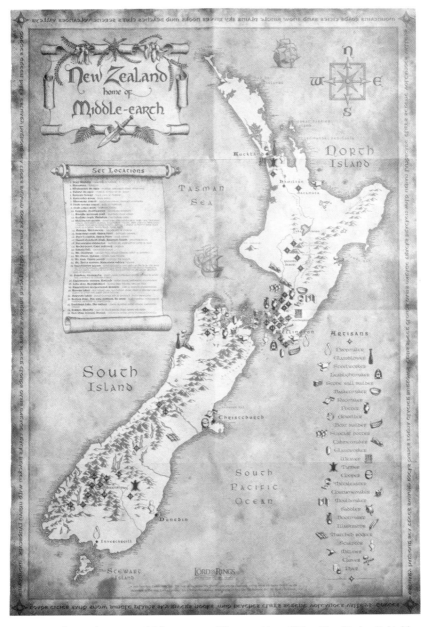

Plates 11 and 12. *This page and following page:* The two sides of Film New Zealand's highly successful promotional map. (Courtesy Film New Zealand. Photographs by Mark Ambrose.)

The first game, the business model worked at about 600,000 units, and it sold 6.5 million units to date, and it's still selling. Our original forecast for "Lord of the Rings," ahead of the movie craziness, was about $35 million, and we probably will generate at a gross revenue standpoint, by the time everything is done, probably about $500 million, so it was conservatively forecast.

(This estimate is for the entire game series as it was envisioned at the time. EA took over the book-based game license after it reverted to Tolkien Enterprises nearly a year after Young's remark, so the total revenues will be even higher.)

Both VU's "Fellowship" and EA's "Towers" games were well reviewed, but according to Young, "Towers" outsold its rival eightfold. Indeed, the firm nearly doubled its profits for the last quarter of 2002 based on its games linked to the James Bond, *Harry Potter,* and *Rings* franchises.[38]

Rings helped revolutionize the way that games are made from films. "Usually here's how games based on movies get made," Young explains. "You interface exclusively with the licensing arm of the distributor—the movie studio. Maybe you get a script. You might get some photos from the set. If you're lucky you might get a cuddly toy or a cup. If you're really lucky, you might get a visit to the set." With studios holding game designers at arm's length, the result could not closely mimic the look and story of the films. EA's licensing contract with New Line allowed the game company extensive access to the movie's assets, and the team of filmmakers cooperated in providing them. ("Assets" here means any items created for the film, from an Alan Lee drawing to a snippet of digital sound effects to a Gondorean helmet.)

For the first game, those assets were fairly simple. From early in 2002, Weta Digital was supplying such things as the digital skeletons for the people and creatures, as well as the digital doubles that were created for the actors. These were then rendered in a simplified form for "Towers" (figure 27). Weta's Matt Aitken describes the process:

We'll supply them with a digital double that'll be a hundred times more complex than what they actually want for their game player, but they're getting an asset that has been tested onscreen, so it's very valuable to them, and we're very happy to do it. We want the quality of the games to be as good as possible, to match the look of the films. We don't want them to have a stab at creating something that looks like a *mûmakil.* We'd rather just send them a *mûmakil,* and they've got that to work with, and there are no issues of scale or dimension or any of those things.

Figure 27. Aragorn in Electronic Arts' "The Two Towers" video game. (Courtesy Electronic Arts.)

Merchandising coordinator Judy Alley initially provided designs and plans as photocopies; later she could send most assets as digital attachments. Early on the EA designers were provided with scripts and with scans of the continuity snapshots taken on set. Later they were able to request that such objects as the actual armor and weapons used in the film be sent so that the game designers could study details like texture.

Getting such extensive access to a film's assets was so unusual that there was no system in place for handling requests. When Nina Dobner came on board as director of partner relations in April 2002, requests were being sent from EA to Alley in a haphazard way. As Dobner recalls, "We'd find out that two or three people in the organization would request the same thing, and they were getting pretty frustrated that maybe they'd sent an asset and one part of our organization knew we had it but another part of the organization didn't know that we had it." Dobner devised a request form and began tracking all assets herself. In October 2002, EA was allowed to create an office, which functioned for about a year, in the Three Foot Six building. Initially requests were routed to New Line for approval, but as the sheer volume of requests swamped its office, the process began to move more directly between EA and the filmmakers.

Inevitably there were tensions between EA and the filmmakers, not through any ill will, but because the two industries' aims and time constraints were so different. The main problems arose from two factors: the game makers' need to obtain assets that in many cases had not yet been created and the filmmakers' concerns about spoilers.

Video games typically take from eighteen months to two years to create. Although a film may languish in development hell for years, the actual period of its production is typically six to eighteen months. The film's story lines, designs, sound track, and other elements may not be in final form by the time the game producers need them. A film-based game aims to come out at about the same time as the movie, primarily to take advantage of the fact that film studios usually have much bigger budgets for advertising than do game firms. Skaggs calls this double-duty use of publicity "the whole franchise effect": "All the marketing and advertising and everything hits for the films, and people walk into the store, Best Buy or something, and they go, 'Oh, look, there's the thing I just saw advertised a thousand times on TV or in the movies. Wow, I want it!'"

In the case of films released in December, the game will ideally come out sooner to catch the Christmas buying season. EA's first two "Rings" games came out on 21 October 2002 and 3 November 2003, more than a month before the mid-December releases of the film's second and third parts. To hit those dates, the games had to be finished in August and September, respectively, since copies had to be tested in-house, approved by Barrie Osborne and New Line, and sent to Sony, Microsoft, or Nintendo for tests on their consoles. All that can consume a month, and the manufacturing process takes another. This schedule exacerbated the problem of getting access to film assets. The filmmakers could work much closer to the premiere date. While New Line approved the "Return" game on 5 September 2003, the film's final version was not locked down until 16 November, with the world premiere taking place in Wellington on 1 December.

At times the need for assets proved a logistical nightmare. Judy Alley's job was to archive the production's props, drawings, photographs, and other assets and also to respond to requests by the licensees by retrieving and sending those assets or images of them. The style guides provided the information required by most of the licensees, so the bulk of the requests came from EA. Because the game came out before the film, says Alley,

> They were asking *constantly* for assets that we didn't yet have, and in the beginning it was this sort of disbelief: "Well, you *must* have them." We work very close to the mark, we simply do not have this yet, and they're saying, "Well, you *have* to—obviously it's a big thing in the film," and we say, "Yes, well, we haven't started on it yet." So that was a huge challenge with them.

The request form reproduced here reflects the problems both teams faced (figure 28). As of 12 June 2003, in the midst of the stars' pickups for *Return,* EA wanted an excerpt of the recorded voice of the "Mouth of Sauron" (the character who emerges from the Black Gate when the army of the West challenges Sauron as part of its ploy to draw attention away from Frodo and Sam as they struggle toward Mount Doom). The priority is given as "medium," even though the recording for the game was little more than a week away. Alley showed me this form when I first interviewed her at the end of September 2003, saying that these vocals still had not yet been recorded. The "Mouth of Sauron" was included in the game without benefit of the actor being able to mimic Bruce Spence's voice. This character was excised from the film's theatrical cut, though his scene made it into the extended version.

Another dimension of the scheduling dilemmas resulted from the fact that Jackson kept changing the film. Basic plot elements sometimes were not available to the game makers. Alley recalls:

> They would come and ask what they thought was this obvious question: "So how is the film going to end?" and even at this date [30 September 2003] I can say, "Well, we don't know yet. *We* don't know yet. It could change at any time." Often they'd ask for information about battles and who did what, and [the answer] was always prefaced by, "At the moment, as far as we know, *this* is probably going to be happening." But, you know, it so often changed.

For such reasons, games can't fully reflect the films on which they are based.

Apart from all these difficulties, EA faced the fact that all three parts of *Rings* were released within the space of twenty-four months—a total period not much greater than the usual production time for a single video game. The initial design work on "Return" was done in early September 2002, almost exactly a year before New Line approved the finished game. Young admits that this deadline limited the first two games. "It was a big deal, because it meant that we essentially had to produce high-quality software on a *very* compressed schedule. If you think about what the games are, they're like an action-reel highlight of film of the actual movies themselves, and I think given more time, the games would have had different dimensionality."

Providing assets for the video games sometimes distracted the cast and crew during the hectic process of trying to finish the film. Coproducer Rick Porras, who helped coordinate the film team's contributions to the "Return" game, describes dealing with EA under the circumstances:

LOTR Asset Request Form # 212

Asset Name   Mouth of Sauron Vocals
Asset Format   AIFF (or WAV or SDII) on CD or DVD
Film & Scene #   Film 3

Requested By   Don Veca
Purpose   For reference for the sound alike for that character

Date Requested   6/12/03
Date Required   6/21/03
Priority: medium

Description
- Some reference as to what the mouth of sauron sounds like. Any reference is fine but we need this for the sounds alike ADR recording at Electronic Arts so that we can match as near as possible the voice of the character. These sound alike recordings are scheduled for the end of next week so the deadline is reasonably tight.

- We are requesting what you are recording on set as the ADR is not going to be on time for us.

Exclude
Where applicable, use this area to note similar assets we have, (including partner asset # if you have it) and areas you know not to be relevant.

Figure 28. Electronic Arts request form #212, for a vocal sample (12 June 2003). (Courtesy Electronic Arts.)

Understandably they're wanting to get their hands on as much as possible. So it was a tough thing for us, because on the one hand we wanted the games to be as great as possible, because we love games, and it's exciting for a good game to be out there, and let's face it, it doesn't hurt. If anything, it helps future ticket sales on the films. *But,* on the flip side, it was definitely yet another taxing thing, another thing on Peter's plate, another taxing thing on the different people.

Employees at Weta Digital, for example, might have to stop work on shots related to the film to deliver elements needed by EA. Actors returning to New

Zealand for film pickups might find themselves whisked to a sound studio and having, with minimal preparation, to record new dialogue for the games. Porras pitched in to help direct some of those recording sessions.

Aside from this, the moviemakers faced problems with spoilers. Any licensed game that comes out before its film risks giving away designs and plot points. As with fan spies and unofficial Internet sites, the amount of attention focused on every aspect of *Rings* made the risk of spoilers particularly acute. The same short list of design secrets that Jackson had decreed for Internet postings also applied to the games. His insistence that Gollum's appearance not be revealed dictated the structure of the games, with "Towers" focusing on Aragorn, Legolas, and Gimli; it begins with Aragorn's arrival at Helm's Deep, followed by flashbacks to earlier events. The original merchandising coordinator, Alyson McRae, describes Jackson's concerns:

> He thought, and probably had good reason to believe, that in the past a lot of this merchandising and franchising stuff had led to the release of stuff, leaks and stuff getting onto the internet, and so he was very nervous about that, and it made it hard for people like Electronic Arts. It had an impact on them as well, and they had to work hard at building a relationship, to make sure that people understood that.

While Gollum simply did not appear in the "Towers" game, EA was permitted to use Shelob for "Return"—provided that the company designed a giant spider that didn't resemble the one in the movie. Dobner describes the result: "We designed a Shelob, submitted it for approval, and they said the Shelob that we'd guessed was too much like the Shelob in the movie, so they wanted us to change the colors to look less like the ones in the movie." With Jackson absorbed in making the film, the responsibility for approving what elements made it into the games devolved upon producer Barrie Osborne, aided on "Return" by Porras.

Whatever problems the conflicting purposes of the game and film crews created, Jackson put a good face on the subject in the few interviews where he mentioned the games at all. In one he focused on the extensive use of film assets: "One of the exciting things about the EA games and what I've been seeing in the models as they've been built is the great replication of our sets and our characters."[39]

Apart from having access to film assets, EA hired some of the same talent that had worked on *Rings* to create further links between the games and the movie. These people included mapmakers and calligraphers, as well as motion-capture experts and stunt doubles. Most valuable for publicity were the main actors who lent their voices and appearances. Nowadays actors' contracts may contain clauses specifying that their images and recorded voices as used in films will also be made available to game companies. New recordings, however, were not included in the actors' contracts with New Line, and EA negotiated with their agents to arrange separate agreements. Some actors quickly priced themselves out of the game series: Viggo Mortensen and Orlando Bloom asked for higher payments after "Towers" and, when they were not forthcoming, declined to work on "Return." Several of the other stars participated. (Average actors' fees for games were then in the $40,000 to $60,000 range, though this may not have applied to the "Rings" games.)[40]

Ian McKellen ended up doing double duty on the games, both voicing Gandalf and providing the narration for the first two titles. According to McKellen, his deal with EA helped compensate for the relatively low payment that the actors had received for being in *Rings*. Once *Fellowship* was a huge success, New Line, as had become the custom in Hollywood, offered those actors a bonus (albeit reluctantly). Bonuses were not forthcoming for the second or third films, however. McKellen recounts: "Finally the deal done with *me*—I don't know about the other actors—was that, in exchange for agreeing to do all this extra stuff, I would be paid a hefty bonus which probably, all in all, added up to nearly as much as I was paid for doing the film." Dobner confirms that "the merchandising was looked at as a way that [the actors] would make the most of what became really iconic roles." McKellen's recordings proved to be worth the investment, since his participation was frequently mentioned in publicity and reviews.

Part of the major leap in complexity and realism between the first two games resulted from the use of motion capture done by some of the performers who had worked on the film. In September 2002, husband-and-wife stunt team Kirk Maxwell and Sharon James were approached by EA about the possibility of working on "Return."

Kirk Maxwell had started out in Auckland, setting up a team of stunt people made up of friends and relatives who were athletes and martial artists. That group became the core of the *Rings* stunt team. Maxwell was picked to be Viggo Mortensen's stunt double and during the long Helm's Deep shoot took over as swordmaster when Bob Anderson left. In 2003 he became the stunt coordinator during the marathon six months of pickups for *Return*. Sharon James was a body builder and stunt player who had, like many of the *Rings* crew, gained her experience on the TV series *Xena: Warrior Princess* and *Hercules: The Legendary Journeys*. For *Rings*, she started out playing generic Orcs during principal photography and was picked by Weta Digital to perform on the motion-capture stage. An expert with computers, she eventually became one of the main choreographers and designers for mo-cap, including the movements used in the Massive crowd scenes.

By the time Maxwell and James were approached by EA about the games, they had two years of experience creating mo-caps that would blend seamlessly into live-action footage. Maxwell recalls, "We were talking about the fact of, well, we've done all this stuff in mo-cap. All these guys are very well experienced at it, and wouldn't it make more sense to use the doubles to give it the exact same feel? All the fights would be the same." Steve Gray, the senior development director on the second game, had initially visited Weta Digital to talk about using existing digital assets, including mo-caps. He ended by also hiring Maxwell and James and others of the film's team to create additional moves for the games. The couple gave up offers of stunt work on *The Last Samurai* and headed for EA's Vancouver motion-capture studio. (For years EA had been employing mo-cap to reproduce sports moves precisely, as with highly accurate renderings of Tiger Woods's golf swings.) Along with helping to animate the game's characters, the New Zealand group contributed to its "cinematics," short transitions between actual footage from the films and the animated, playable sections of the action. Maxwell and James were also able to help correct some details of design and plot that had been changed since the information had been provided to EA.

The "Towers" game had been made using standard animation, based more on mathematical formulas than on real movement, and some players and reviewers had criticized this. The idea was to improve "Return" by making the figures' actions more realistic, more like the film. This was achieved, yet the compromises that had to be made reveal the shortcomings of game media at that time. The memory capacity of the game had to be geared to the PlayStation 2, which meant limiting the number of movements any given onscreen figure could perform.

James would explain these restrictions to Maxwell, who choreographed the handling of swords, spears, and other weapons to fit within them. Weta made a duplicate set of weapons for use by the games stunt team, causing raised eyebrows at customs when Dobner took them to the States in her luggage. Maxwell says that the mo-caps using these weapons often involved "really long arcs with the swords and things like that, trying to get as many frames as they could, from the maximum range of movement so that they could then chop bits out of it to make it faster. They wanted it as fast as possible, but needed maximum range of movement."

James explains why this speed was desirable: "As soon as the player pushes the button, he feels he's got reaction. If they play the full 15, 20 frames [of each movement], it would be more like they're looking at a movie." Dobner confirms that the process is done because "people are a lot less patient in a video game." The speed of the figures' movement gives the player a greater sense of controlling the action—and fewer frames eat up less memory. The mo-cap for the game was done at 60 frames per second, then cut back to perhaps 30 frames, or occasionally as few as 15. Thus the action of the second game was closer to that of the film and yet deliberately departed from it as well. In Maxwell's view, "It's a false reality, but it's that transition between live action and the actual digital coverage. They need something there that's going to be fluid, to give it a seamless feel, and mo-cap is real, but it's digital, so it combines the best of both worlds." Clearly no matter how close games get to movies, action-oriented interactivity will long remain a key boundary between them.

THE GAMES

Jackson has always insisted that the three parts of *Rings* fit together into a single film; indeed, one could eliminate the credits and cut them together end to end and create a unified flow to the narrative. Not so the games. Each is more self-contained, and they fit into different game genres, with very different styles of playing. Their variety and the potentially endless possibilities for creating new combinations of characters and action reveal the expanding nature of a successful franchise. Each game incorporated filmic elements and extended the franchise beyond the action of the movies.[41]

"The Lord of the Rings: The Two Towers" (21 October 2002) is a single-player game that gives the option of controlling Aragorn, Legolas, or Gimli in a series of battles in Moria, Helm's Deep, and other locations from the film's first two parts. (A version for Game Boy offered a playable Gandalf, Frodo, Aragorn, Legolas, and Éowyn.)[42] One reviewer commented, "The gameplay feels as if you paused your DVD copy of *Fellowship,* stepped right into the middle of key battles as Aragorn, Gimli, or Legolas, and then pressed play. Exclusive *Two Towers* footage and Howard Shore's score make this hotter than the fires of Mount Doom."[43] Five hours of Shore's music, newly recorded voice-overs by Mortensen, Bloom, John Rhys-Davies, David Wenham, Elijah Wood, and McKellen and footage that did not appear in the film were used as selling points. (Other characters' voices came from material recorded for the trilogy.) The game innovated the technique of cinematics.

"The Lord of the Rings: The Return of the King" (3 November 2003) reflects the higher budget allocated after the success of *Fellowship*. Built from scratch rather than using an existing engine, it offers a more complicated set of options, with three lines of action: Gandalf's journey to Minas Tirith and defense of the city; Aragorn, Legolas, and Gimli's journey through the Paths of the Dead and participation in the battles that follow; and Frodo and Sam's progress toward Mount Doom. Each character is playable. The whole thing was stitched together, according to Young, around "the concept of Gandalf as the great architect of these events";[44] again, McKellen lent his voice, providing narration in addition to new dialogue. New recording sessions also included Christopher Lee, Wood, Billy Boyd, Dominic Monaghan, and John Rhys-Davies. EA's sound-mixing facilities had just received THX certification, and "Return" was the first game to be awarded a THX label (though not the first released). The game could involve one or two players, and it offered an online feature allowing two players to compete remotely, communicating through headsets.[45] "Return" was the first game for which members of the stunt team worked on new motion-captures, and it incorporated a more technically sophisticated moving viewpoint for the "camera" (a term that is used in game design despite the lack of an actual camera in production), partly by using motion capture on some actual camera operators performing various maneuvers. There is also greater interaction between the figures and their surroundings. Shore's music was again used.

The third and fourth games, "The Third Age" (2 November 2004) and "The Battle for Middle-earth" (6 December 2004), were released only about a month apart. Here EA entered the postfilm phase of the franchise. Aragorn was king; Gandalf, the main Elves, and Frodo had crossed the sea. What was left? Middle-earth itself—of which there was a lot more than was shown in the film. And gamers were interested in exploring it. An obstacle limited the possible new locales, however, as Skaggs explained to fans in an online Q & A session about "The Battle for Middle-earth":

BLAZING SADDLES: Will armies be able to travel to all parts of Middle Earth that weren't featured in the film?

MARK SKAGGS: You'll be able to go to parts of ME that were shown or referenced in the film and fight battles there. One of the things we know people want from B4ME is the opportunity to experience more of ME so we're doing what we can to deliver there. If the location was not shown/ referenced in the film, then because of license issues we won't be going there.[46]

Much of gaming depends on moving through locales and discovering hidden weapons, door releases, and other concealed devices, so players focus a great deal on maps. Indeed, programs exist to allow them to create their own maps where "mods"—modifications of the action or graphics in an existing game—can be played out. One of the main features of "The Battle for Middle-earth" is a large, detailed map of the continent, over which the player seems to fly in moving from one locale to another, à la Google Earth (plate 7). (A poster of the map comes enclosed in the game's official strategy guide.) Some of the locales, especially of the "ancillary battles," such as Druadan Forest or Halifirien or Rhûn, will not sound familiar to film fans. Some are glimpsed on the maps, and as Skaggs told me, "There are just *so* many, if you do like we did and really study the film for all the references and somebody mentioning this and what's happening there." Places rather than plot offer the main thread for extending the franchise in the games.

"The Third Age" game stressed the era in Middle-earth's history during which the film's plot occurs (or, more precisely, the prologue shows the battle that ended the Second Age, and the destruction of the Ring and Aragorn's coronation herald the end of the Third Age). Here again, though, travel and fighting were central, as the publicity summarized how the game "allows players to adventure through Middle-earth, building a party of heroes as they journey." "The Third Age" was the first role-playing game in the franchise. This means, as Skaggs describes it, that "you have your characters and heroes, and you move them through the world, and they get experience and abilities that then they use to fight all the bad guys and solve the puzzles or the problems that the world presents." The "heroes" here are not the Fellowship members, who all appear as "guests" in the game. The playable heroes are a group of original characters, apparently derived, in keeping with the license, from minor figures plucked from the backgrounds and given names: Berethor, a guard of the Citadel in Minas Tirith; Idrial, a female Elf warrior of Lothlórien; Elegost, a Dúnedain Ranger; Hadhod, a Dwarf; Morwen, an Éowyn-like Rohan female soldier; and Eaoden, a Rohan cavalryman. These characters travel through Middle-earth, at times encountering the Fellowship in scenes derived from the film and assisting them in combat.

"The Battle for Middle-earth" is a real-time strategy game. Rather than playing individual characters, gamers take one side or the other and guide the battles. The members of the Fellowship appear here as "heroes," as do Éowyn, Éomer, Théoden, Faramir, and Treebeard, but none of them acts as a continuing playable character with whom the gamer identifies. There are no other significant individual characters, but "units" of various groups, such as "Rohirrim archers" and "Rangers." Given that the action often appears in a high-angle, distant view (plate 8), there is little opportunity for identification with the characters, and the images recall those of epic battle films. Although some of the battles resemble those in *Rings,* the fact that the player can take either side creates alternate scenarios that are at times reminiscent of fanfiction. In the "Good Campaign," for example, Gandalf must survive the fight with the Balrog, while in the "Bad Campaign," the objective is often to kill the hero characters—creating quite a continuity problem if, say, Legolas dies in one battle and shows up, alive and fit, in the next.

"The Third Age" uses vocal material from the original recording sessions with Lee and Rhys-Davies, and McKellen did further vocal work for the game. Brad Dourif's voice was derived from film assets. Naturally the original characters are voiced by actors who were not in the film. Lee and McKellen did further recording sessions for "The Battle for Middle-earth." From early January to late March 2004, Kirk Maxwell and Sharon James returned to California to work on "The Third Age," where their main task was to devise fighting strategies and moves that would distinguish the various cultures and races involved in the battles. Thereafter they were back in New Zealand, working on *King Kong,* both film and game. As of late 2005 they had moved to the Bahamas, where Maxwell was at work on the two *Pirates of the Caribbean* sequels, but he and James hope to work on both games and films in the future, possibly including more "Rings" titles for EA.

For its recent games EA has been on its own in generating images and sounds. In January 2004, as the *Rings* production ended, Alley notified all licensees that they needed to request any additional assets soon. As work on *King Kong* geared up, the props, drawings, and costumes from *Rings* had to be boxed up and stored. Dobner put together a final list of requests, and the last batch was delivered to EA at the end of February. Despite the ongoing nature of the games series, the lack of new material from that point on was not a problem. By then EA already had a huge number of assets from the film (nearly 300,000 digital items, Dobner estimates), and the entire movie existed for reference.

In July 2005, EA revealed that it had reached two major new licensing agreements for the "Rings" games series. The first extended its arrangement with New Line to the end of 2007, with an option to renew. The second was with Tolkien Enterprises, allowing EA finally to include characters, places, and objects mentioned in the book but not included in the film; it also was good through 2007 and renewable. Vivendi Universal had not released a book-based game since late 2003. The company's failure to "aggressively use its license" led to its being canceled and sold to EA.[47]

At the same press conference, EA announced two game projects that would exploit the new access to the contents of Tolkien's novel. The first, "The Lord of the Rings: Tactics" (11 August 2005) is a tactical-strategy game specifically for the PlayStation Portable. The gamer, choosing between leading the Fellowship and controlling the forces of Shadow, fights battles in locations from the novel and film "to determine the future of Middle-earth." "Tactics" allows play among up to five participants via WiFi. As before, the games put the emphasis on Middle-earth, with minimal links to the plot of the film.

The second, "The Battle for Middle-earth II" (November 2005), deals with areas of Middle-earth not used in the previous games, including the forest of Southern Mirkwood, where Sauron's lesser dark tower, Dol Guldur, was located; it also includes such northern locales as the Grey Havens (seen only at the end of the film), where sea battles occur, involving corsair ships of the type seen briefly in *Return* fighting against Elvish vessels. Legolas's father, Thranduil, King Dain, ruler of the Dwarves, and other characters from the books become major figures. The game's tagline on the official website is "The Middle-earth You've Never Seen" and in advertising, "With more lands, heroes and races, all Middle-earth is now at your command." Not quite all, since on 31 July 2006, EA announced that a new group of maps entitled "Aragorn's Journey: Map Pack 1" was available for Xbox, downloadable for purchase from the Xbox website.

"The Battle for Middle-earth II" was also available in a "Collector's Edition," including concept art, a new musical track, and a playable dragon that does not feature in the regular edition. The gaming industry had been doing special editions of this sort since the mid-1990s, giving them such labels as "Platinum Editions" or "Gold Versions." Mark Skaggs says that now such labels are chosen "to be more what people are used to, what they've been seeing more and more in the film business, you know, the director's edition, the collector's edition." More convergence.

In July 2006, EA announced another major *Rings*-based game project: another RPG entitled "The Lord of the Rings: The White Council," due to be released in late 2007.[48] EA's new Middle-earth might have a familiar feel, since both Alan Lee and John Howe were hired to do conceptual art for it. Characters that had been cut from the novel in adapting it for the film, such as Tom Bombadil, could be reinserted into the action. The film's actors continue to have the option of working for EA as well, as when Dobner and Mike Verdu (the series' new executive producer) held a recording session with Hugo Weaving in September 2005. Weaving contributed the voice for Elrond in "The Battle for Middle-earth II," and he also took over the narrating duties that McKellen had performed in earlier games.

In 2006, games manufacturers found that a hit movie didn't always spawn a comparably successful game. The game based on *The Da Vinci Code* did poorly, and even the one released alongside the third *X-Men* film was a disappointment. (Video games derived from hit animated films like *Cars* and *Over the Hedge* proved the only surefire nonfranchise products.) Games makers became more cautious about licensing summer blockbusters. They wanted, according to *Variety,* "major franchises that have a potential life far beyond that of a film release." *Rings* has proven such a franchise for EA, and for a studio like New Line that is lucky enough to launch a major game series, the rewards are great. Once the film series has finished, the later games don't have to be tied to the release schedule of each new theatrical release. The film studio may have spent time and effort cooperating with the creation of the early games in a series, but for the later entries, there is virtually no work involved and yet the royalties keep coming in. There are other advantages for the studio. *Variety* reporter Ben Fritz points out that it "allows the studio to keep *Lord of the Rings* in front of young audiences as it continues to exploit the franchise in other media."[49]

In the end, what impact has the *Rings* franchise had on the world of video games? Beyond helping raise EA's bottom line, the first two entries in the series set what Neil Young sees as a new approach—at least by EA—to film-based video games. In discussing the heavy use of film assets in creating the games, he said:

> "The Lord of the Rings" was unique in that regard. There's really only two games in the history of our medium that have had the degree of asset reuse or collaboration that happened on "Lord of the Rings." One is the "Lord of the Rings" games and one is the "Matrix" games. Now the "Matrix" games had much greater participation from the directors. But in terms of asset usage or reusage, I would say that "The Lord of the Rings" is second to none.
>
> Up until that point we hadn't done that on other projects. What "Lord of the Rings" showed us was, look, if we organize ourselves in this way, we're going to end up with a higher-quality piece of software at the end of the day. So why don't we start doing that on all the things we do?
>
> So now Nina Dobner is working on "Godfather"; she's working on "Batman"; she's working on this version of "Lord of the Rings" [i.e., "The Third Age"]—a bunch of licensed products that we have under development, essentially operating a similar process.

The technical developments of *Rings* have contributed to changes in video games. The handheld CGI work on the cave troll fights and the moving viewpoint of "The Return of the King" have been taken up. In early 2006 a commentator remarked, "The visual grammar of games and movies is bleeding into one. Glance at a TV trailer for 'Medal of Honor' and you'd think it was advertising *Saving Private Ryan.* Play 'Max Payne' and you're in *Sin City.* The scripting structure, production design, and lighting techniques are identical. Gaming's introduction of tricksy little touches like artificial handheld feel has lent a realistic edge to previously static and sterile worlds." ("Tricksy" is a Gollum-ism.)[50]

In general the "Matrix" games set a new level for filmmaker involvement, while the "Rings" games demonstrated how extensive the use of film assets could be. Blending those strengths would offer a leap forward for game-film convergence.

EA has continued to foster initiatives that will bring films and games closer together. In late 2004 the firm donated $8 million to create the EA Game Innovation Lab, a research facility housed in the Robert Zemeckis Center for Digital Arts in the University of Southern California's School of Cinema-Television. On 17 October 2005, EA's Los Angeles studio hosted the beginning of the first "Video Game Music and Sound Design" course, developed in collaboration with the Grammy Foundation. Some of this work may eventually contribute techniques and expertise to a *Rings*-based game far in the future.[51]

MIDDLE-EARTH IN YOUR POCKET

Rings would not seem to be a good candidate as a cell phone game. Not only would the image appear on a tiny screen, but most players spend an average of just over ten minutes playing a game on their phones and do so mainly to kill time. Of the types of games available for cell phones, film-based ones are the least popular. Nevertheless, in phone gaming, Hollywood has seen a new licensing possibility and another type of free publicity.

As with the Internet and DVDs, New Line turned to mobile gaming when it was a very young business. In mid-July 2001, the Finnish firm Riot Entertainment (Riot-E) announced that it had the exclusive worldwide rights to create and market wireless games for *Rings*. Riot-E had been formed in February of the year before and already had a reputation as the largest maker of games for cell phones. Its main earlier film-related games were based on

X-Men and *Bridget Jones's Diary*. At the time of the deal, the company claimed to have 110 million users through partnerships with mobile phone operators in several European and Asian countries. One "Rings" game was to be launched each year, timed with the releases of the three parts of the film. Riot-E did manage to bring its "Fellowship of the Ring" game out in Ireland, Germany, Spain, and some parts of Asia. The American release never materialized, and on 19 March 2001, three months after *Fellowship* was released into theaters, Riot-E declared bankruptcy.[52]

New Line soon formed a publicity partnership with Verizon. In exchange for exclusive rights to the games, developed by mobile-game provider Jamdat, Verizon agreed to provide publicity for *Towers* and *Return*, in both their theatrical and home-video releases. Jamdat provided an action game apiece for *Towers* (July 2003) and *Return* (December 2003), as well as a trivia game for each (2003 and 2004). Once the third film had been released, Verizon's deal ceased to be exclusive, and Jamdat began selling the games for all wireless phones. By the end of 2004, Jamdat had six games out, with, in addition to the four already mentioned, "Lord of the Rings: Pinball" (December 2003) and "Lord of the Rings: Trilogy" (December 2004).[53]

On 8 December 2005, another kind of convergence occurred when EA announced that it was buying Jamdat. EA had been trying with limited success to move into mobile gaming, and this deal suddenly put it into a highly competitive position in that growing market. It also brought together virtually all the *Rings*-based games in one firm.[54]

JACKSON GOES UBISOFT ON GAMES

Viewers sometimes wonder whether the anticipation that *Rings* would spawn video games influenced the filmmakers' design or staging decisions. According to Jackson, it did not, and stunt masters Maxwell and James have echoed that claim. A great deal of material, including most of the principal photography, had been generated for the film before the game deal was made. Indeed, all the evidence available to me suggests that during the filming, the games were seen as necessary and desirable, but they were ignored by most of the team. The production was complex enough, and worrying about the games could have been an impediment to filmmaking. A small number of people like Judy Alley, Barrie Osborne, and Rick Porras took over the task of dealing with EA. In contrast, the planning for the DVD supplements was clearly a paramount concern for Jackson and key members of his team from very early on.

Despite the heavy use of assets and talent from *Rings* in the production of the first two video games, there had been little creative input from the film's director. In July 2004 Jackson told me that despite being a gamer, he had never played "Towers" or "Return," not being fond of the "hack-and-slash" genre. Despite the games' success, both in sales and in prizes won, industry opinion has it that Jackson was in general not particularly happy with the way the "Rings" games had been handled.

Presumably as a result, Jackson approached the game for *King Kong* in a completely different way. Although several video game publishers were interested in the license, Jackson favored the large French firm Ubisoft.[55] Reportedly he had been impressed by the emotional depth of games by the company's developer, Michel Ancel, particularly "Beyond Good & Evil." Jackson talked with Universal, *Kong*'s producer, about approaching Ancel. They agreed, and in January 2004, while in Los Angeles for *Return*'s Oscar campaign, Jackson met with Ancel. Negotiations went forward, and by October 2004, Ubisoft officially announced that it would be manufacturing "King Kong," which would be based on a revamped version of the "Beyond Good & Evil" game engine and would premiere alongside the film.[56]

The deal gave Jackson and his team considerable creative control over the "Kong" game. In the planning stages, Ancel's team went to New Zealand and conferred with the filmmakers. Jackson says that he played the various levels as their initial versions were completed and sent comments. Echoing his approach on *Rings* to keeping fans informed, Jackson went on the Internet to answer questions about "Kong": "From day one we believed that close collaboration was essential to ensure that the game was a true extension of the film universe. We spent a lot of time during the preproduction phase of the game discussing key story points and gameplay elements. There has been ongoing communication throughout the entire process, and the team in New Zealand has had the ability to play game builds throughout." Although Jackson's team never went to the Ubisoft creative headquarters in Montpellier, France, the firm's representatives made two further visits to Wellington during the film's production. This time, planning for the game did influence the film, according to Jackson: "The creative process for gaming is actually very similar to filmmaking. You are really focusing on the story. What this has done is enabled us to really look at key scenes from both the cinematic and interactive perspectives and hopefully offer viewers the best of both worlds." Again assets were shared, but now the participation of the cast in doing voices was systematic and planned from the start. Quicktime scenes were sent for reference purposes, and the art department and Weta Workshop supplied concept art, to the point where Ubisoft was often able to skip doing its own concept drawings.[57]

The new control was financial as well as creative. Universal would split its share of the revenue from the game equally with Jackson.[58] The director no doubt benefited from his considerable clout in the wake of *Rings,* but the deal also reflected major changes in how Hollywood talent participate in the making of video games—changes that had been taking place during the years when Jackson's attention was riveted on making the trilogy. The most spectacular example of what filmmakers could hope to achieve in the world of video games had come with the release of "Enter the Matrix."

Larry and Andy Wachowski, codirectors of all three *Matrix* films, are avid gamers. They wanted to have a game for *The Matrix,* but in 1997 they could not find a publisher. Three years later, with the film an enormous hit, the brothers tried to induce Warner Bros. to create games to accompany the two sequels, but the studio was not interested. According to Joel Silver, a producer on all three films and "Enter the Matrix," the Wachowskis made a deal with the game designer Shiny Entertainment and allotted Warners a share of the revenue. The production budget was a hefty $21 million. The brothers wrote a 244-page script for the game, which picks up just before the action of the second film and runs parallel to it. The Wachowskis oversaw the development of "Enter the Matrix" and shot four extra hours of 35mm footage for it, one hour of which ended up being used.[59] No wonder Jada Pinkett Smith ("Niobe") found being in a wildly successful franchise complicated: "I'm confused about what script is what. I had three of them, and they all intertwined: the video game, the sequel, and the third movie."[60] "Enter the Matrix" was released on 15 May 2003, the day when the second film, *The Matrix Reloaded,* premiered at Cannes. By the spring of 2005, "Enter the Matrix" had sold nearly six million copies internationally. It had set the bar for directors participating in games based on their movies. The Wachowskis, by then two very rich men, were working on "The Matrix: Path of Neo," incorporating footage from all three films.[61]

During the announcement of the "Kong" game deal, Jackson stated, "By working closely with the development team, Ubisoft is enabling me to help shape the kind of gaming experience that I will be proud to associate with this new version of 'King Kong,' a story that began my lifelong love of film."[62] On 27 September 2006, Jackson announced that he had teamed with Microsoft to form Wingnut Interactive. Ken Kamins, Jackson's manager, declared, "The basic idea is to create a kind of interactive entertainment that's not games as we know it. Microsoft and Wingnut are going to attempt to figure out how to articulate that together." The first project would be a spin-off from the *Halo* film (itself adapted from a video game). The result, according to Jackson, would be "not quite a game, not quite a film."[63] Thus, as EA went on expanding Middle-earth without him, Jackson stepped into an era when directors can control far more of a franchise than the film at its center.

PART FOUR

The Lasting Power of the Rings

CHAPTER 9

Fantasy Come True

The time will soon come when hobbits
will shape the fortunes of all.

GALADRIEL
The Fellowship of the Ring

The Lord of the Rings is an independent film. A huge, expensive, and extremely successful independent film, to be sure, but independent nonetheless. People expect independent movies to have small budgets and play in art-house cinemas. Supposedly these films appeal to intellectual spectators who wouldn't dream of going to the latest blockbuster. Indie movies premiere at the Sundance Film Festival and break free of the conventions and constraints of Hollywood studio moviemaking. Independent films do not come as part of franchises, cost more than $100 million per part, and gross nearly $3 billion. Yet *Rings* did.

In the film industry, "independent" chiefly refers to the way a film is financed and distributed. A major studio has its own production budget and the ability to draw upon investments and loans to fund its films. It owns overseas branches that release and publicize its product. By contrast, an independent company typically raises a substantial portion of a film's budget by preselling the local distribution rights to firms in foreign countries. Much of the dealing over such rights takes place at the major international film markets, which, during the period when *Rings* was being financed and produced, were Cannes (held in May in the south of France), the American Film Market (late winter, Los Angeles), and MIFED (autumn, Milan). The easiest way to define an independent producer may simply be that it is a company that attends Cannes, the AFM, and MIFED as a seller.[1] New Line is such a company.

Officially the Independent Film & Television Alliance (IFTA), the trade group that produces the American Film Market (AFM), considers any film that obtains 51 percent or more of its financing outside the major studios to be independent.[2] Jonathan Wolf, executive vice president of IFTA and managing director of the AFM, adamantly confirms that *Rings* "was the most successful independent film three years in a row, and it *is* independent, and that's one of the things that even some people in our industry today won't accept." During the 2002 market, the American Film Marketing Association (as IFTA was then named) gave Bob Shaye its annual Lifetime Achievement Award. (Saul Zaentz had received the first award four years earlier.) In accepting he praised the AFM, where indies have "the opportunity to raise capital for films the old-fashioned way, by attracting buyers for them."[3]

The larger Hollywood independent firms can look a little like studios. *Variety* has referred to New Line and Miramax as "semi-indies" or "nominal indies."[4] As these phrases indicate, New Line is not a typical independent firm. Camela Galano, president of New Line's international releasing, has explained,

> The least understood part of New Line is that we still operate as an independent company. Yes, we are owned by Time Warner, but we still work very autonomously and have to finance films out of international [distribution]. On the other hand, we have corporate mandates that other independents don't have. We are not just a sales company taking a fee—it's our product. So we operate as an independent on the sales side but like a major on the distribution side.[5]

Variety recognized this fact in reporting on the upbeat tone of the 2004 American Film Market: "The celebratory air also highlights a number of AFMA member films up for awards, including Media 8's 'Monster,' Focus's 'Lost in Translation' and New Line's 'LOTR: The Return of the King.'"[6]

Although studios sink huge resources into blockbusters and tentpole pictures, they can absorb many weak films because income streams in from many other sources, from ancillary rights and television sales to DVD revenues and assets arising from large libraries of older films. Independents have much less of a hedge. These firms are vulnerable to a single slip. Artisan Entertainment released the most profitable film of the 1990s, *The Blair Witch Project.* Within two years, Artisan was drowning in debt, and its library was sold. In this context, Shaye's bet on not one but three blockbusters might well have seemed what it has been ceaselessly called—the riskiest movie gamble of all time.

The question is tantalizing. Would New Line have been shuttered, sold off, or absorbed into Warner Bros. if *Rings* had failed? Coproducer Rick Porras doubts that any such thing would have happened, and Wolf firmly denies it. After all, presales of foreign distribution rights and licensing of tie-in products had covered a substantial portion of the budget well before Film 1 was even finished. Wolf adds, "Too much going on there: a library, lots of other product. If Time Warner's desire was to be not only vertically integrated but as horizontally integrated as possible, they don't want to just close a business that's got a thirty-year history, so I would have been shocked. For one film? It's not *Cleopatra*."

Others, like agent Ken Kamins, think that Shaye was at serious risk of losing control over the company he had created. He recalls seeing Shaye at a party at the Sundance Film Festival of January 2001, looking devastated. He had just been forced to fire one hundred employees. "Of course if that first film didn't work," Kamins remarks, "New Line very quickly would have been looked upon as an industry joke, and the joke would have been that Films 2 and 3 were going to end up being the biggest TV miniseries in the history of TNT." That AOL Time Warner did force Shaye to fire those employees suggests how the situation might have developed had *Fellowship* flopped. New Line might well have survived, but only on a tight leash: further layoffs, strict caps on budgets, and curtailed control for Shaye and Michael Lynne. The firm that had, largely based on Shaye's judgment, released offbeat films ranging from *Teenage Mutant Ninja Turtles* to *Magnolia* might no longer be recognizable.

Even in early 2002, with *Fellowship* a hit, *Variety* seemed to assume that there was still a possibility that AOL Time Warner would sell New Line. Shaye, still smarting from the layoffs and major failures (*Town and Country, Little Nicky*), did not seem sure himself. "I hope and believe that we're on a good, strong, solid course right now," he was quoted in *Variety*. "I feel a lot of responsibility to our stockholders and to our international partners, who have stood by us through thick and thin. I was very unhappy when we couldn't deliver strong product. Movies like 'Lord of the Rings' make pay-back times." Perhaps someone at AOL TW contacted the magazine to set the record straight, for only a week later, *Variety* reported a rebound for New Line, with a recently announced plan to produce fourteen or fifteen films a year and a status as a major asset for AOL TW: "In the executive suites, New Line founder Bob Shaye—newly pumped up from the huge payoff of his 'Lord of the Rings' gamble—is exercising more hands-on involvement than he has in years."[7]

Rings' success could not have come at a better time. The merger with AOL in 2000 had proven a disaster for Time Warner, and in 2002 the conglomerate posted the largest annual loss in U.S. corporate history ($98.7 billion). The only good news was that its fourth-quarter revenue came in somewhat ahead of analysts' expectations. The cause was a 16 percent rise in the film wing, with the releases of *Towers* and the second *Harry Potter* film. *Variety* reported, "Now corporate execs are embracing New Line as a bright spot in an otherwise spotty balance sheet. The studio has been singled out regularly in AOL TW's earnings calls for praise over the past year."[8] It seems hard to believe that a relatively minor subsidiary of a huge conglomerate could have much impact on such a disastrous situation. Yet *Rings,* along with Warners' own *Harry Potter* and *Matrix* franchises, made a difference.

Something similar happened in 2003, when Time Warner eliminated the embarrassing "AOL" prefix. All its other units were gaining in revenue, and the corporation posted a full-year profit for the first time since the merger. While the average divisional gains for the fourth quarter were 6.9 percent, the film sector was the strongest, with a 17 percent rise, and this time there was no *Harry Potter* film. The main factors were strong DVD sales (led by the *Matrix* sequels), the unexpectedly large success of New Line's *Elf,* and the release of *Return.* By 2005, the *Rings* films were fading away as a major source of income after *Return*'s extended-edition DVD release in December of the previous year. In the second quarter, with DVD sales sagging and no big franchise film besides *Batman Begins* in release, Time Warner once again posted a loss. Its film revenue fell 15 percent, a figure comparable to the rises after each part of the trilogy appeared.[9]

The gambler had become a hero. By August 2004, when *Variety* named Shaye and Lynne its "Showmen of the Year," New Line had gained considerable autonomy. The new Time Warner CEO, Richard Parsons (promoted a week before *Fellowship* was released), had led the turnaround in the corporation's fortunes, and he enthused about the subsidiary's effects on stock prices. "If you have a property like New Line, which is just minting money, that obviously has a favorable impact with investors. I've always been a big believer in cash—free cash. And highly successful movie franchises like 'Lord of the Rings' produce lots of cash and that impresses investors." New Line still had to routinely justify its annual budget to Time Warner, but Lynne noted, "That budget comes basically from our request and not from their imposition on us. So we've never really had a confrontation. Since we are reasonable about what we request and we have a lot of experience at this point, it has always been approved." In 2005, Shaye and Lynne no doubt saw the irony in the layoffs of four hundred Warner Bros. employees, while this time New Line's staff remained intact.[10]

New Line did not abandon its early emphasis on comedies (*Wedding Crashers,* 2005) and low-budget franchise films like *The Butterfly Effect 2* and *The Texas Chainsaw Massacre: The Beginning* (both 2006). It has, however, widened its range and taken on a larger number of prestigious films than it could have in pre-*Rings* days. It also could afford the occasional big-budget sequel. After years of negotiations over Chris Tucker's pay for *Rush Hour 3,* in late 2005 the company finally announced that a deal had been struck, giving Tucker $20 million versus 20 percent and Jackie Chan $15 million versus 15 percent. The total budget was announced as $120 million, slightly more than each part of *Rings* had cost.[11] Such star power underscores just how much Shaye had saved by making the trilogy all at once.

In 1998, Mark Ordesky had become president of New Line's niche-film wing, Fine Line. When New Line acquired the *Rings* project in August of that year, however, Ordesky immediately became deeply involved in its production. Fine Line's releases slowed to a trickle during the years of the trilogy's making and distribution.[12] As a reward for his success, in early 2003 New Line promoted Ordesky to be the executive vice president and COO of New Line Productions, though he was still head of Fine Line. For New Line he was to oversee event pictures, especially potential fantasy franchises to replace *Rings.*

During 2003, Fine Line became more active, forming a codistribution deal with HBO. The two firms released *American Splendor* (2003), *Elephant* (2003), and *Maria Full of Grace* (2004), all critically acclaimed films. In 2004, Fine Line on its own acquired two imports, *The Sea Inside* and *Vera Drake.*[13] *The Sea Inside* gave New Line its first post-*Rings* Oscar when it won for Best Foreign Language Film, and both *Maria Full of Grace* and *Vera Drake* gained Best Actress nominations.

As an indication of New Line's growing prestige within the industry, in March 2004 one of the most respected directors in Hollywood brought a project to Ordesky. Terrence Malick, who had directed only three features in the past twenty-one years (*Badlands,* 1973, *Days of Heaven,* 1978, and *The Thin Red Line,* 1998), had just walked off a planned biopic on Che Guevara. Now he wanted to make *The New World,* dealing with the English colonization of America. New Line took on the project, to cost only a little more than $30 million, and released it on Christmas Day 2005. Combined with its previous February 2004 announcement that it would produce David Cronenberg's *A History of Violence* (2005), the acquisition of *The New World* led Shaye to boast that New Line was now attracting "the crème de la crème" of directors.[14]

With big projects like *The New World* on his plate, Ordesky bowed out of Fine Line in the autumn of 2004. For a time Fine Line became a specialty marketing label within its parent company rather than a separate firm.[15] That arrangement wasn't sufficient for New Line's ambitions, however, and in May 2005, at the Cannes Film Festival, New Line and HBO launched a joint venture, Picturehouse, which replaced Fine Line. Its president, Bob Berney, had been responsible for distributing two extremely successful independent films, *The Passion of the Christ* (2004) and *My Big Fat Greek Wedding* (2002), under his Newmarket banner. Picturehouse would annually release eight to ten films, some produced by New Line or HBO, some acquired on the independent market.[16] Its first release was Gus Van Sant's critically acclaimed *Last Days* (2005). In 2006 Picturehouse had its first significant box-office success with *A Prairie Home Companion,* reuniting New Line with director Robert Altman, whose *The Player* (1992) and *Short Cuts* (1993) had been distributed by Fine Line.[17]

At that same Cannes festival, New Line offered ten new films to foreign distributors. Rolf Mittweg, the firm's president of international distribution and marketing, declared, "It's the biggest Cannes slate we've had in the history of the company, and the first time we've had such a wide range of projects." Head of production Toby Emmerich credited the high number of releases in part to the fact that New Line no longer had to focus on *Rings.* He ebulliently compared New Line's upsurge in production to walking "into Barneys or Neimans, and you're in the mood, and you've got that credit card in your pocket."[18] The "credit card" was, of course, *Rings* profits.

During the years of the trilogy, New Line did well not just by independent-company standards but in relationship to the industry as a whole. In the period from 2000 to 2005, New Line was number one among distributors in terms of the ratio of its worldwide revenues to the total of its films' budgets. That ratio was 3.7, while those for the major studios were distinctly lower: 2.4 for the top-grossing firm, Warner Bros., 2.9 for Buena Vista, and 3.2 for DreamWorks, the second most profitable in the top ten. New Line's total revenue in 2003, the last *Rings* year, was $878.7 million, while for 2004 it fell to $303.2 million.[19] Once more, prudent aggression had paid off.

The trilogy's effects on New Line were obvious to industry insiders and the general public alike. The company's new situation was widely discussed in the trade and popular press. What was not so widely noted was the fact that, as an independent, New Line had brought in no fewer than twenty-five international distributors to share in the financing of Jackson's project. One of the most intriguing effects of the *Rings* phenomenon is that this blockbuster significantly benefited the international market for independent and non-English-language cinema.

Failure would take the cream of the distrib crop with it.
But if the pic succeeds, a tsunami of cash will sweep through
the coffers of these distribs, buoying up the whole
indie financing business.

ADAM DAWTREY
reporting for *Variety*, Cannes, May 2001

For an instant in the late 1990s, the market for independent films, both U.S. and foreign, seemed to be booming. High advertising income allowed European television channels to buy films, and money was coming in from home video. A string of German media companies launched IPOs and began paying large sums for distribution rights to independent films. But the overheated growth led to bankruptcies and mergers. By 2001, international producers offering films at markets found themselves forced to lower prices. *Variety* commented of the 2001 AFM, "After last year's boom time, when German IPO cash was flooding the halls of the Loews Santa Monica Hotel, and sales companies were reaping the benefits of overbidding and fierce competition for product, the 2001 mood is distinctly different."[20]

Other forces accelerated the downturn. In addition, mid-2000 saw the dotcom and telecom bubbles burst, sending the U.S. economy into a recession. The crises in the Brazilian economy at the beginning of 1999 and the Argentine economy in late 2001 affected those major Latin American markets. The World Trade Center terrorist attacks of 11 September 2001 disrupted independent dealing at the Toronto Film Festival (which had just begun when the attacks occurred) and the MIFED market (which was held shortly after). During these years the American dollar was also strong against most other currencies. Since international film acquisition deals at the markets were usually struck in dollars, this made it expensive for foreign distributors to acquire films. Add to this the fact that reality programming and a slump in advertising led to fewer independent movies being sold to television—traditionally a major outlet for local films, especially in Europe. The heady early days when video rental stores would stock copies of just about any title were over, and indie films could no longer depend on home-video sales to cover part of their production costs.

Jonathan Wolf, managing director of the American Film Market, sees these factors as contributing to yet another problem. Buyers of independent films, he says, became more cautious and cut back on their acquisitions. Typically these buyers would have been helping finance films through presales. With presales down, independent producers sought other ways of getting money to make their movies. Presales, however, had provided some indication of whether there was actually a demand for a specific film. A distributor had to be fairly confident that a film would sell in its market before pledging money for it. Other forms of financing didn't take demand into account.

One source of funds was the brief availability of large sums from the German media companies. Another was "gap financing." In this arrangement, the film hasn't yet sold to all territories, but on the basis of the existing presales, a bank extrapolates what the unsold territories will eventually bring and lends accordingly. Insurance companies also got into the business by offering policies to cover the risk of loss on a production, which encouraged producers to forge ahead without having enough presales to guarantee financing.

There were also soft-money sources. Some countries' tax funds allowed investors quick write-offs when they put money into film production. Other options were tax incentives, credits offered directly to film companies and designed primarily to bolster local production or bring in foreign projects for location shooting. Trying to lure film companies to spend money in their country or state, government agencies might also offer other forms of support, such as cheaper facilities, the unpaid use of military personnel, and help in building infrastructure like roads.

As a result of these other funding sources, Wolf says, during the late 1990s and into 2000, too many medium- and low-budget films were being made. These films weren't presold, and there was no way to predict whether anyone would buy them. "Now the sellers and the producers weren't making films on the basis of what the buyers said they would buy and then go make the film. They're making the film first and bringing it to market. So there was a glut of film that pushed down prices, and that caused a bit of a shakeup." That glut aggravated the downturn. Producers complained that they could no longer make presales to fund their projects. There were simply so many finished films available at deflated prices that distributors could fill their schedules without bothering with movies that hadn't been made yet.

As a result, many of the soft sources of financing dwindled. Fewer films were made and brought to the international markets. By the second half of 2002, buyers began to look at projects again, and the presale market began to recover. At that moment, *Rings'* income arrived. Probably the uptick would have happened in any case, but it's likely that the trilogy accelerated the movement back toward presales. Wolf thinks that the timing indicates that *Rings* was important: "The first film came out in Christmas 2001, and so the distributors starting by the summer of 2002 would have really started to see the full results of that, because the video would have gone out. Then you have it annually after that, so it *would* have started to have an impact on buying of films starting in mid- to late 2002 and going forward from there."

Additional factors fueled the recovery of late 2002. European advertising prices rose, leading to more sales of films for broadcast. In 2003, the dramatic decline of the dollar against the Euro and other currencies contributed to the independent market's recovery. Other big indie hits, chiefly *My Big Fat Greek Wedding* and *The Passion of the Christ* (both handled in some countries by the same distributors that had *Rings*), pumped money into the sector, as did rising DVD player and software sales in Europe.

Signs of strength were evident by early 2003. In covering the big spring markets, the trade journals attributed part of the recovery to *Rings*. The *Hollywood Reporter* commented on how rich some of the trilogy's distributors attending the AFM had become: "Marketgoers desperately needed some good news—and it came in the form of Baggins and the other members of his 'Rings' fellowship" (figure 29). A few months later, at Cannes, *Variety* reported that presales, the traditional, market-driven method of financing independent films, were coming back strongly in virtually every territory: "The global bonanza of 'Lord of the Rings' is playing its part in driving big-budget pre-sales." *Screen International* credited New Line with "buoying the indie market with *The Lord of the Rings*." By February 2004, sales space was sold out at the AFM. A few months later, attendance at Cannes was up 12 percent over 2003, and by 2005, some international distributors were so eager to make deals that they traveled to Los Angeles for pre-Cannes bargaining.[21]

Just who were these overseas distributors? What did they contribute to *Rings*' making, and what did they do with the profits that resulted?

Where the Money Came from and Went

New Line stuck to tried-and-true methods when it set out to secure the huge financing necessary for *Rings*. The task fell largely to Rolf Mittweg. Before he had taken over international distribution and marketing in 1988, New Line had sold films individually in each market. Mittweg shifted to a policy of output deals, usually meaning that a foreign distributor would contract to take all of New Line's films for a certain number of years. Minimum guarantees from such distributors could cover up to 70 percent of a film's production costs, and if a title ended up doing well in a territory, New Line would get a percentage of its income.

Figure 29. A caricature in the *Hollywood Reporter* shows Frodo tossing money to international distributors (probably Joel Pearlman of Roadshow Films, Australia; Trevor Green of Entertainment Film Distributors Limited, United Kingdom; and Hiromitsu Furukawa, Nippon Herald Pictures, Japan) visiting the American Film Market in early 2003. (© 2003 Victor Juhasz, reproduced courtesy of the artist.)

In late 1998 and into 1999, New Line happened to be negotiating or renegotiating output deals with foreign distributors. Twelve of these deals would run to the end of 2001, when *Fellowship* was released. Many were renewals with long-term partners, such as Entertainment in the United Kingdom, Aurum in Spain, Village Roadshow in Australia, and Metropolitan in France. Other participants, such as Kinowelt in Germany, A-Film in the Netherlands, and SF Film in Scandinavia, were new customers. The successes of *Rush Hour, The Wedding Singer,* and *Blade* in 1998 allowed New Line to bargain from a position of strength. *Rings,* acquired in August 1998, and not yet in principal photography, did not figure largely in the dealings.[22] The company still didn't have output deals in some territories—Japan, Italy, Benelux, and South Korea—and Warner Bros. Intl. handled most of its films in Austria, Switzerland, Eastern Europe, and Russia.[23]

Rings, however, was not like the other films in the output deals. In late 1999, Mittweg told twenty-five foreign distributors, many of them already regularly releasing New Line films, that those who wanted the trilogy would have to pre-buy all three parts, entirely sight unseen—despite the fact that many output deals ended after *Fellowship*'s release. The presales, he said, had to add up to roughly $160 million. *Rings* required a huge commitment. Moreover, New Line did not simply open the process and sell the rights to the biggest bidder in each country. Instead, it worked to obtain the best deal possible from its familiar distributors. Many of these were small firms and recent start-ups, nervous at the prospect of such a large, long-term investment—especially one that depended on an obscure director working in a country not known for filmmaking.

Mittweg wooed these distributors by sending them early drafts of the script and keeping them abreast of casting choices. Once principal photography had begun, some distributors' representatives were flown to New Zealand to tour the facilities and witness some of the filmmaking for themselves. Co-producer Rick Porras recalls running some of these tours, as well as encouraging a group of distributors who visited the set when he was directing the fight between Gandalf and Saruman. "I don't know who was behind it at the studio or who came up with the idea, but it was unique. I'd never worked on a movie before where we had investors and distributors coming and visiting the set or even visiting when we were in preproduction." As a result, he says, the distributors became enthusiastic about their share in the project: "Everybody likes to talk about the risk for New Line, but the Spanish distributor—it was the biggest thing they'd ever bought, and they had to buy all three movies at once. For everybody round the world—the distributors—they really took a risk with everyone. It was a shared risk, and they became like real supporters and patrons all in one."

At the Cannes Film Festival of 2000, Mittweg showed a twenty-minute trailer to the distributors. This looked nothing like the preview footage of a year later. The clips were mostly brief dialogue scenes, since none of the special effects had been finished. There was also a brochure packed with statistics on the popularity of Tolkien's books, aimed to demonstrate that this was not just a niche film for geeks. Deals were clinched with Nippon Herald (Japan), Metropolitan (France), Taewon (Korea), C + P (Benelux), and Nexo (Italy).[24]

Distributors for some of the biggest markets outside the United States paid substantial sums for *Rings* rights. The *Hollywood Reporter* put the figures for companies in major countries, such as Entertainment in the United Kingdom and France's Metropolitan, at roughly 7–8 percent of the total, which would be in the neighborhood of $20 million, "a figure nothing less than staggering in the relatively small-scale indie world." In early 2001, Lynne confirmed that *Rings* would have a budget of $270 million, but assured the press that New Line was risking only $60 million because $180 million had been covered via foreign presales, merchandising licenses, and tax incentives in New Zealand and elsewhere.[25]

Not only was the financial obligation high, but the international distributors had to wait a long time to see just what they had bought into. They finally found out at the Cannes preview screenings on 11 May 2001. *Variety* reported:

> It's hard to imagine a more relieved group of distribs gathered into one place than the collection who'd just finished watching a 26-minute film from New Zealand that cost $270 million.
>
> The enthusiastic response from distribs, exhibs and worldwide press to the screening of footage from New Line's "Lord of the Rings" at Cannes' Olympia theater means that foreign companies that bet the farm on the three-year franchise now have cause for confidence they'll recoup their investment—with coin to spare.

The same story quoted Mittweg, who had convinced those companies to make that leap of faith: "My Japanese distributor said he had a knot in his stomach for the whole year, and now it has dissolved."[26]

The impact that *Rings* had on its distributors around the globe is typified by one firm's life before and after investment. SF Film is the Danish branch of the venerable Swedish company AB Svenska Filmindustri, founded in 1919. The vertically integrated Svenska is now owned by Sweden's Bonnier AB, a

200-year-old, privately held media empire embracing around 150 separate companies. SF Film expanded in the summer of 1999 by opening branches in Denmark and Finland. (It already had one in Norway.) Mads Nedergaard, of the Copenhagen office, says that these branches needed some big hits in order to justify the expense of running separate outlets.

The Danish branch was small to begin with, with a staff of only around nine people. In 1998, New Line had signed a four-year output deal with the Swedish SF. Nedergaard recalls, "I think everybody knew that it was *Lord of the Rings* that was in that slate of movies, so you could argue that [that was] the reason why SF was so interested to get it." When the Danish office opened a year later, New Line was its only regular source for films. It released only five films in 1999 and seventeen in 2000. SF also bought some films from the newly founded Spyglass Entertainment. In 2000, Spyglass's second release, *The Sixth Sense,* provided SF's Danish branch with its first hit. It was *Rings,* however, that solidified the new company's success.

The trilogy was such a major release that SF Film expanded to twenty-three employees to handle it, rising to thirty-eight by the end. As Nedergaard points out, that allowed the company to distribute more films, since most of those people did not spend all their time on *Rings.* In 2001, the firm's releases rose to twenty-seven, then thirty in 2002, and around forty annually starting in 2003. To accommodate the growth, SF moved to new offices, a brick building a short way along the coast from the statue of the Little Mermaid, with a pleasant, sunny interior (figure 30). The offices doubled the firm's space, and SF was able to add a 35mm screening room. Over the trilogy's three years of release, it brought in 60 to 65 percent of SF's revenues, and the franchise effect made its profits an even higher proportion of the whole because advertising campaigns and other release costs were lower after the first film.

Another thing that SF needed early on was an output deal with a major Hollywood studio. Even before *Fellowship* was released, the very fact that SF had *Rings* impressed Twentieth Century Fox. For a decade Fox had distributed its films through the largest Danish company, Nordisk. Hollywood firms tend to check out new local distributors, however, hoping to negotiate more advantageous deals. Nedergaard believes, "Our results with *Lord of the Rings* more or less opened the door for a deal with Fox." The deal was struck in 2001, to begin in 2002. True, Fox could not yet know whether *Fellowship* would be a hit. Nedergaard explains, "But you go back to the Cannes party. They were also aware of what was coming." In fact, he adds, SF typically does not make a lot of money on Fox films, but they are glad to have "a steady flow of product."

Figure 30. SF Film's new headquarters in Copenhagen, made possible by the firm's *Lord of the Rings* income. (Courtesy SF Film.)

SF was not, however, focusing entirely on Hollywood. The other local news of the years 2001–3 was an upsurge in the popularity of Danish films. SF's parent company had been producing Swedish films since the silent era. "The general idea now," Nedergaard says, "is also, we should try to produce or buy Danish movies in Denmark. We're starting to do that. We are coproducing one movie and have been buying rights, over the last two years, to ten local movies. It's the same development in Norway and Finland as well—trying to diversify sources of films. . . . We have been using the money we made on *Lord of the Rings* to invest in local products." As of 2004, Danish films made up 22.3 percent of the total number released domestically—making it the world's ninth most successful country in the share of its own market that its productions control. In early 2005, SF Film purchased a substantial share of Tju-Bang Film, a small collective documentary production company, and plans to help expand it to produce both documentaries and fiction features.[27]

Four large firms handle nearly all of Danish distribution. Besides SF Film there are Warner Bros. (in association with a local company), UIP (Universal, Paramount, and Buena Vista), and the century-old Nordisk. Despite its recent founding and small beginnings, SF was the top Danish distributor in 2003 and number four in 2004 ("only half *Lord of the Rings*," as Nedergaard points out). In late 2004 Denmark's leading business newspaper placed SF on its list of the fifty fastest-growing companies of the past five years.

Rings had other effects in Denmark. A flurry of theater construction had begun in the late 1990s, especially after a German firm built three multiplexes. The Nordisk company, which controls approximately half of Danish exhibition, fought the invasion by constructing and renovating theaters. Then the slump in the entertainment industry began. Nedergaard says, "I have exhibitors telling me now, *Lord of the Rings* has saved our investment in our new cinemas. *Lord of the Rings* was just perfect for them, because it was the first year of their new leasing contracts."

The trilogy also helped lead Denmark's home-video market from VHS to DVD. SF had the video rights for *Rings*. According to Nedergaard, "It was right before the release of *Fellowship of the Ring* [when] the home-entertainment business started to talk about how now the DVD was really the new medium in home entertainment. It came a bit later here than in the States. I think that maybe also *Lord of the Rings* was one of the titles which was making the VHS completely die. I think we still have a big stock of *Fellowship of the Ring* on VHS, and *Return of the King* wasn't made at all on VHS." He adds that Danish video retailers were so impressed by the extended-edition DVDs that SF gained a much higher profile in the market.

Like New Line, SF took advantage of inexpensive Internet publicity. The firm saved money by not buying the files for New Line's official site to translate, figuring that most Internet-savvy Danes could read English. Instead, SF started a small site of its own, with a downloadable countdown clock and a link to lordoftherings.net. SF did not provide material to fan websites, as New Line did, but it issued press releases about new trailers on lordoftherings.net, and local newspapers covered these events. SF also was able to provide news items that New Line posted on its own site, such as the queen's attendance at the gala openings of all three films, and the premiere-based visits of Jackson, Viggo Mortensen, and Christopher Lee (whose wife is Danish).

Today SF's Danish branch is in good shape. Its strategy is to maintain two or three output deals as the "backbone" of the company, but also to buy individual films, including independent and European movies. In 2004, for example, SF obtained *Million-Dollar Baby,* a high-priced item that the firm could not have afforded without its *Rings* earnings.

Nedergaard sums up the impact of *Rings* on his company, pointing out that now Bonnier could see that its expanded film distribution wing was a good investment. "If we hadn't had *Lord of the Rings,* it would have been a much smaller company. Maybe we wouldn't even have been here at all. They are always opening and closing distribution companies in this region." He adds, laughing, "Our problem is, what do we do now? Now we just released the last DVD versions. The party's over!"

Other distributors used *Rings* money to produce local films. Videocine, the trilogy's Mexican distributor, sank part of the profits into its production activity. Korean producer and importer Taewon Entertainment has been making modestly budgeted genre films (*Married to the Mafia,* comedy, 2002; *Mr. Butterfly,* action, 2003; and *Face,* horror, 2004).[28]

A-Film, a small Dutch art-movie distributor founded in 1999 by San Fu Maltha and Pim Hermeling, branched out in other directions with its *Rings* windfall. At the Cannes festival of 2002, Maltha set out to build up a library of classics, acquiring a package that included such films as Fellini's *8 ½.* A-Film used them to start a DVD wing. Maltha also picked up some films for distribution—*Bend It Like Beckham, Intacto,* and *The Eye*—saying, "I would rather pay $50,000 or $60,000 for several smaller films than $300,000 for something bigger that I would also have to spend a lot of P[rints] & A[dvertising] on." In 2003, A-Film pursued the same strategy, releasing Lars von Triers's *Dogville,* Jane Campion's *In the Cut,* and Dutch director Robert Jan Westdijk's *Phileine Says Sorry.* That same year saw the company rise to the third position among Dutch distributors, with about two-thirds of its turnover coming from *Rings.* Late in 2004, A-Film announced plans to build ten art-house cinemas with eight to ten screens each around the country, suggesting that the impact of *Rings* on the independent cinema may be particularly deep and lasting in the Netherlands.[29] In August 2005, Maltha also announced that A-Film would finance Paul Verhoeven's *Black Book,* a European film that would mix characters speaking Dutch, German, and English. Its budget was $22 million, twice the cost of any previous Dutch film. Prominent at major film festivals in the autumn of 2006, it was highly successful when released in the Netherlands and became the country's candidate for a foreign-language film Oscar nomination. *Rings* was not mentioned in the press coverage, but A-Film surely would not have been in a position to undertake such a project without the expansion it enjoyed during the release of the trilogy. As Maltha pointed out, in 2004, even without *Rings,* his firm had taken 10 percent of the domestic market with films like *Bad Education, The Eternal Sunshine of the Spotless Mind, The Passion of the Christ,* and *Lost in Translation.*[30]

Rings distributors in larger markets tended to expand but go on handling independent films. Entertainment Film Distributors, a family-owned firm in the United Kingdom, had grown up during the video boom of the 1980s by releasing X-rated titles. A turning point came with a 1991 output deal with New Line. Films like *The Mask* and *Se7en* expanded the firm, and after releasing the trilogy, Entertainment topped a list of the British companies with the highest profit growth, having seen its take rise from £2.4 million in 2000 to £61.6 million in 2003. It put part of the money into a consortium that acquired the major Odeon cinema chain. Entertainment also began supporting small British productions and continued to release high-profile independents like *Gosford Park, Far from Heaven,* and *My Big Fat Greek Wedding.*[31]

Another family-owned firm, France's Metropolitan, had cemented its long-term relationship with New Line with the success of *Se7en.* At Cannes in 2002, Metropolitan was reported as "perhaps the most aggressive buyer among the 'Lord' distribs—but even that company was concentrating on cherry-picking smaller films." The firm continued to supplement its annual New Line releases with about a dozen films bought at international markets, such as *Hotel Rwanda,* the Korean import *Sympathy for Lady Vengeance,* and *Good Night, and Good Luck.*[32] Italy's Medusa, part of Silvio Berlusconi's media empire, was already that country's largest independent distributor. After *Rings,* Medusa continued its policy of producing and acquiring a wide range of product, from blockbuster Hollywood and Italian movies to international art films. In 2005, it released the sword-and-sandal epic *Keys of Heaven,* but at Cannes it acquired such fare as Altman's *A Prairie Home Companion* and Tom Tykwer's *Perfume.*[33]

Spanish distributor Aurum was in an anomalous situation. Despite being in the enviable position in 2002 of having no other films than the trilogy to release, it was owned by Zeta, a publishing house with little interest in the movie business. The speculation was that Aurum would be collapsed into Zeta once *Rings* ended. At the same time, however, the largest Canadian distribution firm, indie Alliance Atlantis, was looking to use some of its own *Rings* riches to branch into European distribution. In late 2002 it began looking at Spanish independent distributors, and Aurum's *Rings* deal (along with its subsequent releases of *My Big Fat Greek Wedding* and *The Passion of the Christ*) made it attractive. In May 2004, Alliance Atlantis bought Aurum (its second such acquisition, after British independent distributor Momentum). Thus, far from disappearing, Aurum again became a significant player in international distribution, and in the process Alliance Atlantis expanded its scope.[34]

Farther afield, Japan's long-established Shochiku, which codistributed *Rings* with Nippon Herald, emerged from a troubled period to enjoy revenue growth with the trilogy and some smaller hits. Village Roadshow Films of Australia vastly upgraded its video facilities to deal with the demand for the first *Rings* and *Harry Potter* movies. Hong Kong video distributor Deltamac was lucky enough to branch into the theatrical business with *Rings* as its first release, and it built up its distribution department with Miramax and New Line titles. Family-owned Pioneer Film Productions of the Philippines had started in 1986 by distributing a few Hong Kong action films each year. It slowly grew to handle films from American independents New Line, USA, Miramax, and others. It grew hugely as a result of releasing *Rings*.[35]

Given how widely the benefits from *Rings* were dispersed among its licensees, its brand partners, and its distributors, Galadriel's remark about Hobbits in the prologue seems prophetic. No doubt the fortunes of the trilogy's international distributors will fluctuate in the future, but the trilogy has allowed them to grow in impressive ways. The international art cinema has emerged the better for this "Hollywood" blockbuster.

WIZARDS ENCHANT HOLLYWOOD

Fantasy has traditionally been closely linked with the science-fiction genre. Specialty bookshops often deal in both, and video rental and sales racks typically have a combined sci-fi/fantasy section. Yet until recently, most fantasy films had, not without reason, been the butt of jokes.[36] Since the original *Star Wars* appeared in 1977, science-fiction films had frequently featured high on box-office lists. The first years of the new century, however, saw the balance tip in the other direction. As of February 2006, the ten all-time worldwide top-grossing films were *Titanic* (1997), *Return, Harry Potter and the Sorcerer's Stone* (2001), *Towers, Star Wars: Episode I—The Phantom Menace* (1999), *Shrek 2* (2004), *Jurassic Park* (1993), *Harry Potter and the Goblet of Fire* (2005), *Harry Potter and the Chamber of Secrets* (2002), and *Fellowship*.[37] Apart from the number-one film, *Titanic,* the rest are all fantasies or science fiction. Indeed, in the top twenty-five, the only other nonfantasy, non-sci-fi film is *Forrest Gump* (at twenty-one). Fantasy outnumbers sci-fi by fifteen to eight, though three of the fantasy films are big animated features. Take those away, and live-action fantasy still outruns live-action sci-fi twelve to eight.

Even more significant is the timing. Looking down the list, a drift from sci-fi to fantasy becomes apparent. Apart from the animated films, all twelve fantasies were released from 1999 onward (starting with *The Sixth Sense*). The four sci-fi films released from 1999 onward were all parts of series that had been established earlier: three sequels to *Star Wars,* one to *The Matrix.* No big new sci-fi franchises emerged, but five lucrative fantasy series appeared: *Rings, Harry Potter, Spider-Man, Pirates of the Caribbean,* and *The Chronicles of Narnia.* Eleven of the twelve live-action fantasies belong to these franchises (the exception being the earliest, *The Sixth Sense*).[38] Four of those franchises are ongoing (and *Rings* will presumably make a fifth, now that the production of *The Hobbit* has been announced). More are in the works. For an industry that had long depended on sci-fi for many of its biggest tentpole films, the shift was seismic.

Commentators were quick to notice the change. In late 2002, *Time* ran a pair of cover stories, on *Towers* and on fantasy. The latter commented, "The past quarter-century of American popular culture was ruled by the great mega-franchises of science fiction—*Star Wars, Star Trek, Independence Day, The Matrix.* But lately, since the turn of the millennium or so, we've been dreaming very different dreams. The stuff of those dreams is fantasy—swords and sorcerers, knights and ladies, magic and unicorns."[39] Jackson has expressed his delight at being able to boost fantasy in this way: "That for me is the proudest thing of these films—that I have taken a genre that I love, which Hollywood doesn't, and proved to them that it can be successful."[40] He also approved of fantasy apparently replacing science fiction to some extent: "It seems people are preferring stories more based in the real world. You know, still with the magic and still with a little bit of fantasy but not quite so artificial. I've always thought of science fiction being relatively artificial. I've never quite liked science fiction, to tell the truth. I've always preferred fantasy. Because fantasy feels more historical to me."[41]

There was more to the change, however, than financial success. There was prestige. Jackson perhaps aimed to make the trilogy do for fantasy what Kubrick's *2001* had done for science fiction—inject prestige into a previously despised genre. (In *Towers,* Gandalf's visions while dead look like an homage to the Stargate sequence of Kubrick's film.) Shortly after the release of

Return, Jackson spoke of the stress of finishing the trilogy: "My imagination was drying up, and that was freaking me out. So I used to go home and watch stuff like *JFK, GoodFellas, Saving Private Ryan*. Those movies are just wonderful examples of verve and imagination. They gave me a slap around the face. 'You know what your job is now—go back and do it.'"[42]

The fan press was naturally ecstatic over the results, but the intellectual press was often surprisingly respectful as well. The *New Yorker* carried an article that compared Jackson's trilogy favorably with Wagner's opera cycle. The same magazine's reviewer cited the beacons sequence and the "Shakespearean" moment of Éowyn revealing herself to the Witch King and declared that *Rings* was the first real epic in decades: "Jackson has revived a grand and unembarrassable quality that sustained moviemakers from Griffith to the heyday of David Lean: he has nerve." Just after *Return* came out, a writer for the cinephile journal *Film Comment* sketched out an academic analysis of *Rings*.[43]

The Oscars sweep for *Return* climaxed the recognition of fantasy. The television audience seemed to suspect that it would be a big night. Nearly forty-four million Americans tuned in, a huge jump from the thirty-three million of a year before. Sean Astin has recalled what Best Picture presenter Steven Spielberg said to him backstage, "You know how many kids around the world are happy right now because the Academy finally agrees with them and has the same sensibilities? They wanted it for *Star Wars*, they wanted it for Indiana Jones." When Astin asked if the Academy would honor science fiction and fantasy in the future, "Steven nodded. A smile crossed his bearded face; even now, in his mid-fifties, he looked like a kid. 'Yeah, I hope so.'"[44]

The moment also added a further touch of irony to the transfer of *Rings* from Miramax to New Line. In 2003, an unnamed executive at Disney was explaining why expensive R-rated films continue to be made, even though most of the biggest grossers are PG or PG-13: "You can't get directors of the caliber of Anthony Minghella [*Cold Mountain*], Martin Scorsese [*Gangs of New York*], and Quentin Tarantino [*Kill Bill*] to work on movies designed to get kids to buy toys and drag their parents to theme parks. And these are the directors who win Academy Awards."[45] Several months later *Return* snatched the golden statuettes away from the Disney/Miramax nominee *Cold Mountain*. It was the first blockbuster franchise film to win Best Picture.[46]

Although no other twentieth-century fantasy novel enjoys the high reputation of Tolkien's saga, there are some with considerable prestige.[47] Following the back-to-back successes of *Harry Potter and the Sorcerer's Stone* and *Fellowship*, Hollywood has not been slow in acquiring ambitious literary fantasy sagas. Two of the most obvious British series with crossover child-adult appeal were snapped up for development. In December 2001 the film rights for C. S. Lewis's seven-novel *The Chronicles of Narnia* series were purchased by Walden Media, a relatively new but powerful New York production company. (This happened early enough that any influence would have had to come from the success of J. K. Rowling's first *Harry Potter* novel.) On September 30, Walden announced a contract giving Disney a two-year first-look option on its projects. At the time there was no specific distribution contract on the *Narnia* films, then in development, but the potential seven features were seen as one of the deal's major attractions for Disney.[48] Disney released the first part, *The Lion, the Witch and the Wardrobe,* in December 2005, to great success, and a new fantasy franchise was launched.

In February 2002, less than two months after the release of *Fellowship,* New Line announced that it had optioned Philip Pullman's highly regarded three-novel series, *His Dark Materials* (the third of which, *The Amber Spyglass,* was the first children's book ever to win Britain's Whitbread Book of the Year Award). New Line signed the respected British playwright Tom Stoppard to write the screenplays (though he was later replaced). Toby Emmerich, New Line's president of production, declared, "Like Harry Potter or *Lord of the Rings,* it's one of those books that captures your imagination and just runs with it. . . . When *The Lord of the Rings* is over, hopefully we won't miss a beat."[49] New Line was systematically acquiring prestige fantasy projects, largely under the guidance of Ordesky. He declared that although many projects being pitched to the studio resembled *Rings* too closely, the evolution of the genre could be seen in projects he currently had in development. Apart from *His Dark Materials,* those were best seller *The Time Traveller's Wife,* the German children's fantasy *Inkheart,* whose author, Cornelia Funke, was at that point writing the series' third book (both films announced for 2008 release), and Susanna Clarke's *Jonathan Strange and Mr. Norrell* (no date announced).[50] All this was a far cry from *Nightmare on Elm Street.*

Fantasy films began to attract prestigious talent as well. The combined live-action/CGI version of *Charlotte's Web* (2006) took part in the trend toward major stars doing voice-overs for animated characters, assembling a remarkable cast that included Robert Redford, Julia Roberts, Steve Buscemi, Oprah Winfrey, John Cleese, and Thomas Haden Church. In September 2002, it was announced that Pulitzer Prize winner Michael Chabon (who declared that his new children's book, *Summerland,* had been inspired by the *Harry Potter* series), would collaborate on the screenplay for *Spider-Man 2.* He went from there to working on *Snow and the Seven* (planned for 2008) for Disney.[51]

The fantasy genre gained momentum. Book series aimed at children display echoes of *Harry Potter, His Dark Materials,* and *Rings.* Annie Sage and Mark Zug's *Septimus Heap, Book One: Magyk* (2005), *Book Two: Flyte* (2006), and *Book Three: Physik* (2006) seem to be *Harry Potter* for a younger audience. P. R. Moredun's *The World of Eldaterra, Volume One: The Dragon Conspiracy* (2005) concerns a fourteen-year-old boy on a quest in England, traveling through time to a parallel world and meeting Elves, Dwarves, Wizards, a talking bear, and "dangerous olorcs." More children on a quest appear in Emily Rodda's *Dragons of Deltora* series (beginning in 2004 and developing on the earlier *Deltora Quest* series, from 2001 on). A magic school and owls feature in Jenny Nimmo's series of Charlie Bone books, *The Children of the Red King* (2003, 2004, 2005, 2006); D. J. McHale's Pendragon series (2002–6) also echoes Harry Potter. Patrick Carman's trilogy *The Land of Elyon, Book 1: The Dark Hills Divide, Book 2: Beyond the Valley of the Thorns* (both 2005), and *Book 3: The Tenth City* (2006), mixes elements of Pullman (the heroine travels with a wolf) and Tolkien (a kindly white-bearded adventurer, a two-foot-tall man). Readers' reviews (often favorable) on Amazon.com reflect their recognition of these borrowings, but presumably such echoes aren't unwelcome.

Several book series have been optioned, acquired, or put into production. Miramax Books embarked on a series called *Artemis Fowl,* by Eoin Colfer (four books from 2002 to 2005), widely considered to be a direct imitation of the *Harry Potter* books.[52] A planned *Artemis Fowl* film was delayed by the contentious departure of the Weinstein brothers from Miramax in 2004. In 2005, Warner Bros. acquired the film rights to Kathryn Lasky's series *Guardians of Ga'Hoole,* an alternative-universe story about owls, for adaptation and began work on a CGI-animated feature. Teenage author Christopher Paolini's Tolkienesque best seller *Eragon* was adapted by Twentieth Century Fox and released on 15 December 2006, and once the second book, *Eldest,* appeared in 2005, both volumes were proclaimed as parts of "The Inheritance Trilogy."

With so much production of fantasies, oversaturation may lead audiences to sour on the genre. Fantasy is quite franchise-friendly, but a few spectacular failures of films might well spook producers. Still, with CGI technology increasingly accessible to individuals, more modest fantasy series like Robert Rodriguez's *Spy Kids* (launched in 2001) will most likely continue to be made. Subgenres like noir fantasies based on graphic novels, family-friendly animated features in the Pixar mold, and more series culled from classic children's literature may lend the genre enough variety that the legacy of *Rings* and its fantasy contemporaries will endure.

Jackson has often said that he was able to make *Rings* because the technology had finally caught up to Tolkien's vision. True, to some extent, but when pre-production commenced in 1997, some of the most important technology necessary for the film did not exist. The director had to get it developed for him, and the results will have a lasting impact on the way special effects are done.

A conversation with Richard Taylor, Daniel Falconer, and Ben Wootten at Weta Workshop put in perspective how much Jackson had demanded of his team:

TAYLOR: Stop for a moment and think: six years ago, when Pete came to us and said, "I want to do Gollum as a digital character," knowing where technology was six years ago. Gollum will one day act for twenty minutes of each of the films alongside the two lead actors of this movie and has to be totally credible, as plausible if not a better actor than them.

FALCONER: And that's pre–Jar Jar and those other characters.

TAYLOR: What was out there at that point?

FALCONER: Very little in the way of digital characters. The special editions of *Star Wars* were just coming out, where they'd gone back in and added—but they were just digital animals, they weren't really characters.

TAYLOR: *Jurassic Park*. The dinosaurs.

FALCONER: Which again were creatures rather than characters.

TAYLOR: I think that's an amazing faith and just downright—

FALCONER: Bloodymindedness.

WOOTTEN: Oh, no, I think, on Peter's behalf, it's that and it's the fact that he just sort of said to himself, "What do I need to make this work? This is what I need. It's the only way I can see it being done, so we need to do it."

TAYLOR: He's always pushed technology to the absolute limit of its abilities, because his mind can visualize solutions beyond what the equipment has achieved at this point.

The other demand that Jackson made was that soldiers in crowds would move as individuals. He pointed to the animal stampede in *The Lion King,* where all the creatures move in similar ways, being replicas generated from a few figures. Taylor recalls his request: "OK, you solve it. Come up with some technology."

During the work on *Rings,* several software innovations solved small-scale problems, such as putting leaves on trees or ripples into the Mirror of Galadriel. Technicians created the effect of handheld camera following an animated creature in the cave troll fight. The splendid "helicopter" shots swooping around the towers of Orthanc and Barad-dûr showed that miniatures could be the center of attention for a shot, not just background decor.

Technology was devised to meet the two demands that Jackson had made back in 1997, and additional breakthroughs that he had not envisioned came about as well. Two programs have had a considerable impact on subsequent filmmaking. The crucial subsurface particle-scattering technique used to make Gollum's skin so realistic was not a program but an approach to applying existing theoretical knowledge, and Weta shared that approach with specialists within the film industry. The Massive program allowed for the replication of motion-captured extras to create crowd scenes where the individual figures all had distinctive movements. From 1996 to 1998, Steve Regelous developed the program for Jackson. Regelous kept the rights to Massive in exchange for giving Weta unlimited use of it. The program, which went on sale to the industry in December 2003, has been adopted by major effects companies including Rhythm & Hues, which used it on *The Lion, the Witch and the Wardrobe.*[53]

Far less attention has been given to an equally important innovation, a selective digital grading program that was still nameless when Peter Doyle, who helped develop it, convinced Jackson to use it on *Rings.* Digital color grading was a new technology, having been innovated for *Pleasantville* (1998) and *O Brother, Where Art Thou?* (2000). A film could be scanned, manipulated as a "digital intermediate," and scanned back onto negative film stock. In *O Brother,* an autumnal yellow color was added to many scenes shot in lush green landscapes. The process was expensive, had many technical limitations, and involved a great deal of trial and error. (A comparison of that film with the Rivendell scenes of *Fellowship* indicates how far the technology had come in such a short time.) Doyle's system, custom-designed for *Rings,* improved on the earlier technology considerably, gaining in complexity and controllability. The system allowed for color grading to be used selectively for only one object or area within a shot. By dragging and shaping a loop around the area on the computer screen to be changed, Doyle's team could tweak the color in a face without altering the surroundings or subtly add a pool of sunlight to one area of the frame to draw the eye. This software was later named 5D Colossus and marketed to the industry in early 2002. When I asked Barrie Osborne what important effects *Rings* might have on the industry, he immediately mentioned its extensive use of digital intermediates.[54]

To special-effects artists and technicians, it was *Rings'* imaginative mixture of traditional and cutting-edge techniques that was most significant. In the opinion of Ned Gorman, visual effects producer at ILM, "If we learned one thing from Peter Jackson's the *Lord of the Rings* trilogy, it's that you can achieve great success by mixing different techniques." Stan Winston, multiple-Oscar-winning effects specialist, agrees: "He used techniques that we had all seen before—just never put together in quite that way. He mixed up digital matte paintings, men in makeup, digital characters, miniatures. He had the vision to use those tools to tell an amazing story."[55] The joints between the various types of effects sometimes showed in *Rings,* but Jackson continued to push his team; when *King Kong* came out, broad consensus had it that they had achieved the first "seamless" effects-heavy movie. The technical developments come so quickly in the digital age that in a few years *Rings* will no doubt look a bit dated. Still, like George Lucas, Steven Spielberg, and James Cameron, Jackson has achieved films that represent a great leap forward in the technique of moviemaking.

CHAPTER 10

———

Right in Your Own Backyard

He's doing the same thing that all the moguls did
in the thirties. He's getting all the tools under
one roof, because when you have that,
if you use it wisely, it's very efficient.

ALEX FUNKE
ASC, visual effects director of photography, *Rings*

OVER THE PAST TWENTY YEARS, digital technology has transformed the film industry. Its impact can be seen in the vast additional revenues from DVDs, the inexpensive publicity offered by the Internet, and the spectacle made possible by computer-generated imagery. Less obvious are the ways in which new technologies have fostered large-scale production in countries that formerly had minor film industries. For many decades, California has been the center of filmmaking. "Hollywood" equals the movies—at least the big movies that have dominated world screens. Since the 1920s, successful directors from abroad have come to make films in Hollywood. Money and fame were significant attractions, but for many of them, the opportunity to work in the world's best-equipped studios was the lure. To be sure, American productions have also been shot abroad for decades, mainly to exploit exotic locales, cheaper labor, and government tax incentives. Yet the other aspects of filmmaking, preproduction and especially postproduction, have depended on studio departments and support companies, most of which are located around Los Angeles.

Back when editing was being done manually and special effects created photographically, companies that handled such tasks needed extensive physical facilities. These were mostly clustered in or near the American studios or in a few large production centers in other countries. With the rise of digital technology for editing, special-effects work, sound mixing, and the like, it has become possible to build substantial postproduction facilities in places that previously had offered few if any such services. Peter Jackson's Wellington infrastructure has proven that a huge production like *Rings* can be almost entirely created in a country with only a minuscule film industry.

The rise of "Wellywood" announces a worldwide trend. For the first time since Hollywood established its dominance during World War I, it risks being dethroned as the center of the filmmaking universe. Countries with small or essentially nonexistent industries have built or are planning digital postproduction facilities. As more successful films like *The Matrix* and *Rings* are produced in such spots, the feasibility of moving entire productions outside the United States will become increasingly obvious to film financiers. Overseas producing centers may offer additional advantages such as lower labor costs, favorable exchange rates, and spectacular, unfamiliar scenery of the type we see in *Rings*. No one center will grow up to claim Hollywood's dominance. Instead, big-budget filmmaking will be dispersed internationally.

NEW ZEALAND, HOME OF MIDDLE-EARTH

The Lord of the Rings has been like one big rolling tourism promotion for New Zealand.

PRIME MINISTER HELEN CLARK
Air New Zealand interview

In 2004, shortly after the announcement that Peter Jackson would direct *King Kong*, Kiwi expat Roger Wadham, an aspiring director living in Los Angeles, noticed that the large globe outside Universal's theme park did not include New Zealand. He contacted the studio and pointed out the irony of its producing the epic in a country that apparently did not exist. Studio executives dismissed his request that New Zealand be added. Naturally Wadham started an Internet site and petition, and after Universal received hundreds of protests, it agreed to make the addition. Jackson's filmmaking had literally put New Zealand on the map.[1]

Perhaps no film has had as much impact on the country in which it was made as *Rings* had on New Zealand. The short-term and long-range effects on its national economy, on its film industry, and even on its culture in general are astonishing.

Initially New Line was reluctant to publicize the fact that the trilogy was being made in New Zealand, thinking it better to keep the locales part of an unknown fantasy world. Once the actors started enthusing to interviewers about the wonders of this pristine, remote land of four million people, previously famous for sheep, rugby, and Sir Edmund Hillary, the cat was out of the bag. New Zealand became Middle-earth to millions of fans who previously wouldn't have been able to locate it on a map.

The most immediate benefit to the country was in direct spending. More than 95 percent of the roughly $330 million film was made in New Zealand. From preproduction in 1998 to the completion of the *Return* extended version in early 2004, the project employed more than 22,000 people. Lumberyards, caterers, restaurants, hotels, and other businesses saw their sales soar. When I was in Queenstown in late 2002, the driver of the cab I hailed at the airport told me that the taxi service she worked for was responsible for transporting the exposed *Rings* footage each day from the shooting locations to the airport, from which the materials were shipped to Wellington for processing. The overall spending in New Zealand is probably impossible to calculate, but a government-commissioned study published in April 2002 estimated that about 74 percent of the production, postproduction, and labor costs of the trilogy had been spent within the country, totaling NZ$352.7 million. Investment in feature-film production had risen from NZ$16 million in the year ending 31 March 1999, to NZ$308 million in the year ending 31 March 2001.[2] Work on the trilogy's theatrical and DVD versions continued for about three more years.

Nor was this a onetime, short-term investment. The film left Wellington with world-class filmmaking facilities and the country with a pool of artisans and technicians who had learned or honed their skills on one of the biggest, most complex movies ever made. The tourism industry rose to become the country's number-one export. The government was quick to recognize the significance of the film and to use it to raise New Zealand's profile abroad. Overall, the filmmaking team's achievement left New Zealanders with a completely different view of their country's potential.

Set-jetting

Jason Bragg, the owner of Wellington Rover Tours, recalls that one day shortly after *Fellowship* was released, he was taking a group on his standard drive around the city. When they reached the park atop Mount Victoria, where the Hobbits' first encounter with the Black Riders had been shot, Bragg pointed in that general direction, as he usually did, and mentioned the filming. One tourist asked if they could visit the site. Bragg recalls, "I thought, why not? So we just walked down the hill and around the corner, and there was Frodo saying, 'Get off the road!' Not really, obviously, but you could just see the location in front of you. I was quite shocked. And the person I was with was just, 'Wow, this is great!'"

After seeking out other recognizable locations, in July 2003 Bragg created the Rover Rings Tour. Driving his only vehicle and offering the tour two or three times a week, he was unable to meet demand. In December and again in April 2004, he added a guide and another vehicle. From that point the two employees each ran a daily *Rings* excursion while Bragg handled the city tour. He estimates that Rover Rings brings in about 60 percent of the company's revenues.

To the thousands of fans who have visited New Zealand and the millions who would love to, it may seem strange that savvy Kiwi tour operators failed to leap immediately at the chance to profit from the film. To some extent the cautious approach might have stemmed from what many New Zealanders themselves see as a general lack of entrepreneurial spirit in the country. Bragg says, "Most New Zealanders were a bit blasé about it. Even today, people come up to me, and I tell them that we do *Lord of the Rings* tours. They're like, 'What?' They can't believe there's any such thing."

Despite its beautiful setting and surroundings, before *Rings* Wellington was not considered as attractive a tourist destination as are the endless pristine mountains and lakes of the South Island. The Queenstown area, with its many *Rings* locales, had long been a magnet for hikers, skiers, and lovers of bungee jumping and jet-boating. I visited twice, in early December 2002 and mid-November 2004, to trace how the city's tour companies that offered *Rings*-related packages fared in the wake of the trilogy. The changes were dramatic.

For years Robert and Jane Rutherford, owners of Glenorchy Air, have offered small-plane trips over the Southern Alps and Milford Sound. Prior to principal photography on *Rings,* Robert flew location scouts around the island and later carried cast and crew members to inaccessible spots.[3] After Film 1 came out, he recalls, there was little sense among the Queenstown tourist businesspeople of how much impact the film could have. Indeed, he thinks there was some suspicion that *Rings* tours could steal business from other Queenstown activities. Nevertheless, in May 2002, the couple began planning the "trilogytrail" tour. When I talked with them in early December of that year, just before *Towers'* release, they estimated that their business was up only 10 percent.

The Rutherfords also mentioned that *New York Times* travel writer James Brooke had just visited the area, including taking a flight with Glenorchy Air.

Figure 31. The vehicles that *The Lord of the Rings* bought: Robert Rutherford with Glenorchy Air's second, larger plane, named for the trilogy, and the Remarkables (aka the Misty Mountains) in the background. (Photograph by the author.)

Late in December, it and other local companies received a huge boost when Brooke published two major stories describing the places seen during the flight and stressing how recognizable they were from the film.[4] These and other travel articles on New Zealand as Middle-earth fueled a burst of demand. In September 2003, the Rutherfords purchased a second, larger airplane, christening it in honor of the film that paid for it (figure 31). They also added two vehicles to offer land tours to *Rings* fans and other tourists nervous about flying.

Although Dart River Safaris has not developed a specifically *Rings*-centered tour, as early as mid-2000 its manager, Hilary Finnie, added a brief mention of the film to publicity materials. *Rings* was still being filmed in the area, but already there were a few inquiries about location tours. In the year after *Fellowship* came out, business rose 20 percent. When I first visited, Dart River Safaris was quartered in a modest set of offices at the back of a downtown building. In May 2003, the company opened a storefront on one of the main streets, selling licensed *Rings* merchandise as well as tickets for its tours. In late 2004, its new manager, Kerry Walker, told me that business had spiked with each *Rings* release and had risen steadily overall.

Dart River doesn't plan to offer a dedicated film-related tour, since its clientele are not hard-core *Rings* fans but people who come for the jet-boating and enjoy seeing a few *Rings* locations along the way. Another Queenstown

Figure 32. Two new "Safari of the Scenes" Land Rovers with personalized license plates, GRIMAS and EOWYNS. (Photograph by the author.)

company, Nomad Safaris, took a different tack. When David and Amanda Gatward-Ferguson bought the company in 1994, it had a staff of four and owned three aging four-wheel-drive vehicles. After Film 1 appeared, they immediately planned a tour around *Rings* locations, adding the Safari of the Rings to their offerings in May 2002. In December, when I first met them, they were running the business out of a small house. They had just purchased a new Land Rover, the first vehicle intended specifically for the *Rings* tour. Their business was up that year by about 30 percent.

By late 2004, Nomad Safaris also had a shop, down the street from Dart River Safaris. The fleet of vehicles numbered 20, 16 of which were used for the *Rings* tours, and the firm had 37 employees (figure 32). David estimated that their business had risen by more than 500 percent in the intervening two years, based partly on tours and partly on sales of *Rings* merchandise. The number of hard-core film fans had declined, but the number who had simply seen the film and been inspired to visit its beautiful landscapes had grown. In June 2004, David started expanding the shop, hoping to use autographed posters and other memorabilia from the film to give it a museum element (though he has to keep declining offers from fans eager to buy the displays).

Later the tour name was changed to "Safari of the Scenes" to reflect the fact that other films had been shot on location in the area.

Lest anyone picture Land Rovers of costumed *Rings* geeks filling these tours, the operators say that there are actually few of them. Many nonfans take these tours because they visit some of the most scenic spots in the area. Robert and Jane Rutherford have escorted several costumed groups that recite dialogue on the sites. Robert recalls, "I know one lady who's a professor of English at the University of London came out with a sword and a cape, so that gives you some idea." Bragg says he encounters fewer tourists dressed as denizens of Middle-earth, "Generally only the Japanese."

The exception to the pattern is Red Carpet Tours, based in Auckland, which started operating its "Middle Earth Tours" in 2002. These twelve-day trips cover the North and South Islands intensively and are aimed at serious fans of the film and the spouses or friends they drag along. The tours usually involve 18 to 25 people, though in late 2003 a group of 160 embarked on a journey that included visiting Wellington for the world premiere of *Return*. Vic and Raewyn James spent six months of 2001 preparing the tour. They ran across the story of Erica Challis's trespassing notice, served by New Line when she was traipsing through the countryside spying for TheOneRing.net. Challis had often guided visitors who knew her through the website to some of the shooting locations. "It was so much fun, I thought, 'I wish there was a way of doing this properly and having tours come out and showing them around.'" The call from Vic James seemed like a dream come true. She became a consultant for Red Carpet and helped design the tour.

When James called the farmer whose land had served as Hobbiton, the bulldozers were about to level it. New Line at that point was opposed to tours and insisted on destroying all the buildings on the locations. Since the farmer was interested in cooperating on such a tour, the studio finally agreed that the blank white backings of the Hobbit holes could be left after being stripped of their facades. Tourists proved happy to visit even these ghosts of Hobbiton.

These small companies could not afford to obtain a license from Tolkien Enterprises, and the Tolkien Estate made it clear that the author's name was not to be associated with the tours. The various firms consulted lawyers and cautiously chose names. Challis and James had hoped for "Tolkien Tours," but they settled on "Red Carpet." Similarly, the Rutherfords used "trilogy-trail" because it does not refer to Tolkien or the film—though they have never encountered anyone who didn't immediately recognize that the tour involved *Rings*. So far they have all managed not to cross the line with their advertising, though some have been asked to take images off their websites. If tour

Figure 33. Kaitoke Regional Park added signs directing the visitor to the wooded area where some of the Rivendell sets were built. (Photograph by the author.)

operators were initially cautious in seizing the opportunity offered by *Rings,* their success taught others to be more ambitious. Even before *The Lion, the Witch and the Wardrobe* was released, Canterbury Sightseeing was accepting bookings for its "Through the Wardrobe Tour" of locations in the Christchurch region.

Many tourists visit *Rings* locations on their own. Kiwi *Rings* enthusiast Ian Brodie's surprise best seller, *"The Lord of the Rings" Location Guidebook,* published in late 2002, helps them find these sites. Virtually all the locales have been returned to their original state, and relatively few of them are marked by signs or other information (figure 33). They are sometimes difficult to recognize even with Brodie's directions, so he included precise latitude and longitude information for enthusiasts equipped with GPS devices.[5]

Jason Bragg points out that in the overall picture of tourism, serious *Rings* devotees are still a niche market. For him the film is "just a massive billboard of New Zealand. All these millions of people have seen the movie, and they're not coming here because they want to go on a *Lord of the Rings* tour but because New Zealand is beautiful, and that's what Peter's shown."

One little-known effect of the *Rings* film was to boost the national museum, Te Papa, which originated the international touring exhibition based on the trilogy (pp. 197–98). The museum had opened as recently as 1998, and although it had mounted a few small touring exhibitions, the *"Lord of the Rings* Motion Picture Trilogy—The Exhibition" was put together on a much larger scale. Indeed, Te Papa had not had a separate department for touring exhibitions. The *Rings* project allowed the museum to develop a touring exhibitions business unit and appoint Az James to manage it, working with one other full-time employee and another working half-time. When I talked with James in June 2004, Te Papa had six exhibitions touring and four in development, including two on the scale of the *Rings* event. These exhibitions draw mainly upon the museum's own holdings.

According to James, "Te Papa before wasn't known within the touring exhibitions area, and now our brand is out there and people understand that we can deliver a professional exhibition product. *Rings* has been very much to do with that." Just as this franchise blockbuster film strengthened international independent and foreign-language markets, it has given a higher profile to New Zealand culture and history.

A Five-Minute Drive

One of the most unlikely aspects of the local film industry's growth is the small size and considerable isolation of the country. People outside the southwest Pacific Rim region tend to think of it as situated somewhere near Australia. Certainly Australia is its nearest large neighbor, but to fly from Auckland to Sydney takes three hours. Wellington lies on the southern coast of the North Island. Although it is the capital of New Zealand (with nearly 400,000 people), it is distinctly smaller than Auckland (with about one million).

Until the 1990s, there was very little filmmaking infrastructure in New Zealand. Money was scarce, coming mostly as subsidies provided by a government agency, the New Zealand Film Commission. In the pre-*Rings* era, the country's successful filmmakers went abroad as soon as possible—Jane Campion, Vincent Ward, Lee Tamahori, Geoff Murphy, and Andrew Adamson being the most prominent émigrés. Jackson, however, wanted to stay and make his movies in Wellington. He also liked to keep close control over every phase of filmmaking, from scripting and design to special effects and sound mixing. That meant making his movies far away from the supervision of Hollywood producers. The only way to do all this was to build his own film industry.

Back in the early 1990s, when Jackson was beginning to create the group of companies that would eventually make *Rings,* Miramar was a suburb in decline. It had been a small industrial area surrounded by neighborhoods of relatively modest houses. The factories and warehouses had started closing down, and thus they were available for conversion into filmmaking facilities, temporary or permanent. The map shows the southeastern suburbs of Wellington: Miramar, Seatoun, and Rongotai. Jackson and Fran Walsh lived in Miramar at the time he started creating his filmmaking companies. Most of those companies are located in Miramar, though a couple of departments are in nearby Rongotai, adjoining the western side of the airport a short distance southwest of Miramar.

Jackson owns part or all of several coordinated companies, each of which adds distinct services to the filmmaking process.

- Wingnut Films (Miramar). Jackson's production firm has produced all his films since his first feature, *Bad Taste,* in 1987.

- Three Foot Six Ltd. (Miramar). This is the production company formed specifically to make *Rings;* it was housed in a rented office building near the airport. It ceased to exist at the end of 2003 and was replaced by Big Primate Pictures for *King Kong.*

- Weta Workshop (Miramar, with a miniatures department in Rongotai). A design and physical-effects company, the Workshop constitutes half of Weta Ltd., which is co-owned equally by Jackson, Richard Taylor, and Jamie Selkirk. (The weta is a giant cricket indigenous to New Zealand.)

- Weta Digital (Miramar, with a facility in Rongotai). A computer-graphics firm that forms the other half of Weta Ltd.

- Stone Street Studios (Miramar). This is Weta's filmmaking headquarters (including the art and costumes departments), used for much of the interior and backlot filming of *Rings.*

- The Film Unit, Ltd., which as of 1 January 2005 became Park Road Post (old building, Lower Hutt; new building, Miramar). This postproduction company, with laboratory, editing, and sound-mixing facilities, is wholly owned by Jackson.

Apart from these companies, *Rings* also depended heavily upon another firm:

- The PostHouse AG (Miramar; now closed). A branch of a German-based postproduction firm, it was responsible for the selective digital color grading of *Rings.*

Meshed together, these facilities can handle all phases of filmmaking.

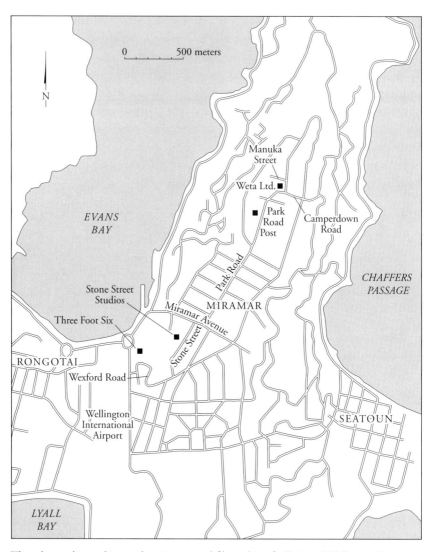

Though not clustered in one location, several filmmaking facilities in "Wellywood" are located within a short drive of each other in Wellington's Miramar suburb, 2002. (Adapted from Wellington City Council map.)

Wingnut Films was the first of the companies that Jackson owned. It moved into its current headquarters in 1996, when he bought a ten-bedroom house in Miramar.[6] It had been built in 1916 by one of the biggest landowners in the area. Initially Jackson and Walsh lived in the house while using it as the Wingnut offices. They later moved to the Seatoun area, but the Miramar house remains the company's headquarters.

Three Foot Six, the temporary production company set up for *Rings,* was housed in a rented building that had been a pilots' school. The building became home to a hodgepodge of production offices, sound-design rooms, the photo and drawings archives, and, temporarily, offices for people like Nina Dobner of Electronic Arts and Michael Pellerin, producer of the extended DVD supplements (figure 34). Walking along its corridors in the autumn of 2003, one was startled at intervals by loud roaring noises as office doors opened and closed. Each room contained someone working on the track for a bit of the Battle of the Pelennor Fields. With the dissolution of Three Foot Six at the end of 2003, the production base was consolidated into the other facilities.

Jackson's first step toward owning filmmaking facilities came with the buildup of Weta Ltd., a company formed in partnership with two filmmakers who had previously worked with him on his early features. Jamie Selkirk, apart from editing and coproducing most of Jackson's films, became the informal business manager of Weta. He also oversees the Stone Street Studios. Richard Taylor and Tania Rodger had been running a small physical-effects company out of their apartment. Their collaboration with Jackson began in 1990 with the design of the director's second feature, *Meet the Feebles,* for which they contrived the puppets.

The production of *Heavenly Creatures* in 1993 to 1994 set Jackson, Selkirk, and Taylor on the path to an expansion that ultimately made the production of *Rings* in New Zealand possible. Initially Weta was devoted simply to physical effects. The three partners bought an entire city block, including an old pharmaceuticals plant and a small ice cream factory. The pharmaceuticals facility was turned into the Camperdown Studios, the headquarters of Weta. Crucially, *Heavenly Creatures* involved the team's first use of CGI, with a single computer to make thirty special-effects shots. In 1994, Weta split into Weta Workshop and Weta Digital.

Taylor continued to focus on physical effects and ran the Workshop (also owned by his partner, Tania Rodger), which had seven departments: production, design, prosthetics, creatures, armor, weapons, and miniatures. The Workshop's original building housed most of its activities, but once the pro-

Figure 34. Three Foot Six's offices, across the road from the airport, Wellington. The Stone Street Studios are on the other side of the ridge, below one of the flight paths. (Photograph by the author.)

duction of *Rings* began, the miniatures department was housed in a large warehouse down the street. During the work on *Return*, the lease for the building expired. Yet another old factory in the nearby Rongotai district was being used as a blue screen stage, but it was essentially a huge open space. Alex Funke explains,

> We could define how we wanted the work spaces to be. This was very unusual, because usually you're moving into a space, you basically take it as it comes, and just live with it. But in this case we were actually able to define the size of the stages we wanted, certain things like mezzanines for lighting from and so forth, control of smoke, that sort of thing. In a sense we were able to build the perfect world for shooting miniatures—all the things under one roof.

The other half of the original company, Weta Digital, upgraded to fifty computers for *The Frighteners* (1995). The success of that film's effects—if not its box-office results—was what led the Jackson team to consider *Rings*. During the trilogy's production, Weta Digital expanded enormously. Much of its new computing capacity was stored in powerful hard drives housed in racks rather than in desktops. By the end of the production of *Fellowship*, Weta Digital had about 700 of these processors (in addition to the desktops being used by the individual filmmakers), providing 13 terabytes of hard-disk storage; 135 terabytes of material had been backed up on tape. By the end of *Re-*

turn, Weta had some 4,200 of these processors, with 120 terabytes of hard-disk storage and more than 500 terabytes of data backed up. During the making of the film, any of the hundreds of employees working at an online computer had access to every stored image and sound. The hard-disk space available during the making of *The Frighteners* had been a mere 1.6 terabytes.

Despite its enormous new capacity, however, Weta Digital simply could not finish all the CGI shots before each *Rings* deadline. Some sequences were subcontracted to other CGI firms in New Zealand, Australia, and the United States. In *Fellowship,* these were fairly important special effects, such as the flood at the Fords of Bruinen, animated by Digital Domain. Two years later, the subcontracted work was mostly routine, such as adding digital matte paintings to backgrounds.

Thanks to *Rings,* Weta's processing power had expanded nearly a hundredfold, and the company was one of the most sophisticated special-effects houses in the world.

Before *Rings,* Jackson shot his films in the same way that other Kiwi filmmakers did: partly on location and partly in rented factories and warehouses that would temporarily be converted into movie stages. Hard as it is to believe, *Rings* was made in a country that did not have a single soundproof stage suitable for motion picture filming.[7] Jackson realized, however, that he could not continue to work only in makeshift rented facilities for *Rings.* In 1998, Taylor called him with the news that an old paint factory was for sale. Jackson has described touring that factory with Taylor and Selkirk:

> A huge space. It would make a fantastic studio; it could be a drive-on lot, there was room enough for two, maybe three stages. In spite of the fact that we couldn't afford it, we went to have a look. The site was impressive; we immediately thought of what we could do—how we could best use the space to build sound stages, prop stores, wardrobe and make-up rooms. It was perfect for our needs.[8]

The three partners went ahead and bought the facility, taking out loans to do so. Part of the cost was also raised by selling the ice cream factory that had been acquired as part of the Weta Ltd. complex.

By the time *Rings* was made, the Stone Street Studios held three filming stages, none of them soundproof, along with the usual departments that one would find in a studio in 1930s Hollywood (figure 35). There are makeup and wardrobe areas near the stages, and the main buildings house lighting and construction areas, as well as offices. There is an art department in a build-

Figure 35. Studio A at the Stone Street Studios, with the last standing set for *The Lord of the Rings,* October 2003. (Photograph by the author.)

ing adjacent to the complex. The backlot was essentially a parking area bordered on two sides with a huge blue and green screen. Although much of the film was shot in these studios, so many sets were constructed simultaneously and so many units were filming that several factories and warehouses in the Wellington area also had to be rented in the traditional Kiwi fashion.

In the popular and technical press, a great deal of attention has been focused on the two halves of Weta, but another vital part of Jackson's buildup of Wellington's filmmaking facilities has been The Film Unit. Formed in 1945 by the Department of Tourism, it had been sold to TVNZ, the government-owned national television channel. In 1994 it became a separate business unit of Avalon Studios, the television facility in Wellington. It contained one of two film laboratories in the country, and it was the only film facility that could also provide sound production services and a full range of other postproduction services. In 1998, it was put up for sale, and the main prospective buyer was an Australian postproduction company that would probably have removed all the equipment to upgrade its own facilities. Had The Film Unit been scavenged and shut down, New Zealand filmmakers would have had to ship all their footage abroad for postproduction. CEO Sue Thompson believes that without the combined work of Weta Digital, the PostHouse, and The Film Unit, it would have been impossible to make the film on schedule. Jackson describes the situation:

> Basically it would mean that there would be no postproduction facilities here in New Zealand, and we'd have to go to Australia to mix our films. So it was at that point that I thought, "God, the only thing I can do to stop it is to try to buy it!" We obviously didn't have the levels of income in those days that we do now because it was a year or two before *Rings.* So we just scratched together loans and mortgages and various things and bought it.

"We" are Jackson and Walsh, who purchased the entire Film Unit themselves. At the time the price was estimated to be between NZ$1 million and NZ$3 million.[9] This purchase was taking place at about the same time that Jackson and his business partners were buying the factory that would become the Stone Street Studios, so the couple went into considerable debt during this period. Clearly these investments were as much a gamble for them personally as producing three features at once was for New Line.

During the production and postproduction of *Rings,* Jackson expanded The Film Unit enormously, adding a sophisticated Telecine machine and a huge state-of-the-art Euphonix sound-mixing console to the existing building. Despite the high cost, the technical upgrade worked. In 2000, the company had handled postproduction for films with a combined total budget of NZ$900 million, and Thompson declared herself "thrilled" with the way the investment was paying off.[10] The country's production is sporadic, however, and 2002 was a down year, with no New Zealand feature films made except on digital video. "It was dreadful, absolutely dreadful," Thompson says. "In fact, if *Lord of the Rings* hadn't happened, we would not be in business."

The Film Unit's building, which Jackson rented, was located in Lower Hutt, a town north of Wellington. Unfortunately, it was a thirty-minute drive from Jackson's other companies in Miramar, in a building that he describes as "a very government sort of 'Soviet bloc' feeling place." Selkirk recalls Jackson's solution. "Pete's always been, 'The closer you can get to home, the better.' The concept of having to drive out to The Film Unit . . . 'Uh, I don't think we'll do that. We'll move The Film Unit into town.'" In December 2002, Jackson announced the transfer.[11]

The result is an enormous, modern postproduction facility just down the road from Weta. The company was renamed Park Road Post in honor of its location. The new building, which quadrupled the firm's space, was designed by Jackson's regular art director, Dan Hennah, in a style evoking Frank Lloyd Wright. Park Road Post contains three digital sound-mixing studios, one housing the original Euphonix mixing desk and the others with new ones, making it a world-class facility (plate 9). These studios were completed—just barely—in time for use on *Return*.[12] Producer Mark Johnson, touring the country as he considered filming *The Lion, the Witch and the Wardrobe* there, visited in September 2003. He recalls, "We saw the mixing studio, which was unlike anything I've ever seen before." Later many offices with sound and editing equipment were laid out in long corridors, interspersed with kitchens and fireplaces in a rectangular building around a garden and fountain, and there is a block of apartments for visiting filmmakers. The laboratories are at the back of the building.

Jackson says that he is hoping to lure not just Hollywood but also Asian and Australian projects to do postproduction in the new building. Sound facilities around the world, he points out, tend to have much the same equipment. "It's actually the same desk that they mix on. It's the same speakers. There's really no difference. So the difference ultimately becomes the environment and the comfort level. So I just said, right from the beginning, I said, 'Listen, if I'm a filmmaker wanting to make a decision to come and mix in New Zealand, I'm going to be basing that decision on how comfortable it is, not on the desk that they've got'" (plate 10). For crews away from home for months on end in a distant country, comfort can indeed make a difference. *Variety* noted a trend in that direction in early 2005: "Post-production houses have gone positively posh as they try to out-luxe each other. In place of cinderblocks and day-old bagels, filmmakers are now likely to find personal chefs, tapas, and daily wine tastings. With pro-level tools now available on desktop computers, the big houses have to offer something special—and that something is luxury."[13]

Another facility, the PostHouse, belonged not to Jackson and his partners but to a German company that had developed an innovative technique for selective digital grading (pp. 280–81). Once Jackson's team signed on, the PostHouse established a branch office in Wellington. It was set up in an old warehouse down the street from Weta's headquarters and across from what became the new Film Unit building. The film's supervising digital colorist, Peter Doyle, had helped devise the program and adapt it to the production's needs. He acted essentially as the head of a studio department, attending daily production meetings to report progress, along with the various Weta Digital and Film Unit department heads.

Once *Return* was finished, the PostHouse's branch shut down, and Doyle went off to work on *Harry Potter*. Weta Digital added equipment designed for similar grading of digital intermediates. The renamed Park Road Post filled the gap by adding its own digital-intermediate department, though its equipment is designed mainly for quicker, simpler grading of films without special effects. Colin Hope, hired to train its staff, had a twenty-year career, including grading Peter Gabriel's music videos and training the colorists working on the second *Star Wars* trilogy. With Weta Digital and Park Road Post's new equipment, Jackson's facilities included all the cutting-edge technology needed for *King Kong* (which Doyle returned to color-grade).

The cost of building Park Road Post and upgrading the other facilities has not been revealed, but it surely runs into many tens of millions of dollars. In early 2004, when the building was well under way, Jackson told a reporter:

> Every time I've made a film, I've tended to pour any fees or profits I've earned back into my filmmaking infrastructure. In the old days, the money was modest, so we bought a tin shed and called it a studio. . . . Now, on the back of *The Lord of the Rings'* success, I've built my dream postproduction facility. I built it for the most selfish of reasons: I wanted my films to have the best soundtracks in the world, and I wanted it to be five minutes from my house![14]

The sound-editing and sound-mixing Oscars won by *King Kong* (which went to the same teams that had won the same awards for *Towers* and *Return,* respectively), indicate his success.

Film industries can be very good for a small country, for all the reasons that we have seen in *Rings'* benefits to New Zealand. Money flows in from larger countries, often in substantial quantities. Local talent gain skills and experience. Tourism may rise, if the country is lucky enough to become strongly associated with a popular film. Filmmaking is less harmful to the environment than many industries, especially if the production crew returns every location to its original condition.

Until recently, most countries outside Europe and North America could hope that filmmakers from abroad would visit and film on location and perhaps in some basic indoor filming facilities. Postproduction, however, would go on back in the United States or London or some other major filmmaking center. All the major CGI companies were in America.

There are different sorts of offshore shooting. The most straightforward is going on location. A film set in a distant place might actually be shot there.

Part of *Bridget Jones's Diary: The Edge of Reason* was filmed in Thailand. Countries stand in for other countries, as when *Around the World in 80 Days* (2004) used Thailand as itself, China, and India.[15] The term "runaway" production gets used loosely, sometimes to refer to any film made abroad. It is hard to find a definition, but the man who produced *The Matrix* in Sydney and *Rings* in Wellington presumably would be as well qualified as anyone to explain it. According to Barrie Osborne,

> I would say a runaway production would be a picture that's set in New York or Chicago or Los Angeles — or the United States — that was done over in a different country because it was cheaper to do over there. I did *Matrix,* and originally Larry and Andy [Wachowski] wanted to do it in Chicago. It was too expensive. We found a way to make it in Australia, and it worked out well. But in a sense, that would be what you'd call a runaway production, and a picture like *Lord of the Rings* I would not call a runaway production. It was a picture conceived by Peter Jackson, and he's a New Zealander who wanted to make his movie at home with his normal crew, so here we are in New Zealand.

Where runaway productions go often depends on a combination of finding suitable locations for the particular film at hand, a favorable exchange rate, a pool of skilled, often nonunion labor, a cooperative government bureaucracy, and, ideally, some sort of governmental financial incentive.

Wellywood Tours

New Line initially wanted the postproduction work for *Rings* to be done in the United States. The firm was convinced that creating something as complex as Gollum in CGI was impossible in Wellington. A crucial player in the drama was Carla Fry, the firm's president of physical production. In August 1998, as lawyers were thrashing out the Miramax–New Line transfer, Fry flew to Wellington to assess the facilities. She was impressed enough to report that the work, challenging though it was, could be handled there. Coproducer Rick Porras calls her the "unsung hero" of the *Rings* film and credits her with being decisive in winning New Line over to Jackson's terms.[16] When New Line's press release appeared on August 24, it included the news that the entire production would be made in New Zealand.

As further reassurance, in early 1999, the Weta Digital team agreed to a schedule of what were termed "milestones," significant CGI programs and tasks that they would complete within a specific time frame. If a deadline was missed, the work would be moved to the established effects houses in the

States. Such a proviso was not unique to *Rings;* other technically innovative films involve similar measures of capability.

"Grove," a piece of code developed by Matt Aitken and used to create foliage on trees and the Ents, was tested in four stages—animation, modeling, dynamics, and rendering—from July to September 1999. Both the Balrog and the Fell Beast went through model, shader, and motion phases due at intervals beginning April 12. The Massive program, motion-capture methods, variations of Elves and Uruk-hai for the army scenes, and above all the early phases of the development of Gollum were scheduled through 1999. Weta met every deadline.

Throughout the long production, however, skepticism and worry built, not just at New Line but among the foreign distributors, owners of big theater chains, and producers of ancillary products. Some of them were brought to Wellington for on-set visits, and there was a standard tour of the facilities. Jackson or Taylor often led these, but if they were unavailable, others took over, including Rick Porras. Investors got the full treatment, Porras says, visiting the set if any shooting was under way, being shown into the little picture palace at Weta to see some footage, strolling through Weta Workshop's design and maquette rooms, and ending in a studio typically occupied by a large miniature under construction. A quick stop at Weta Digital allowed visitors to see special-effects shots in the early stages of creation. Virtually everyone visited the art department, which had lined a corridor with a gallery of conceptual art and designs, running in order through the film. The Hennahs were the guides here. Chris describes the gallery as "a walk through the movie, and you'd walk down one side of the hall and back down the other side, and you had the whole trilogy." Dan adds, "That conceptual artwork—Alan Lee and John Howe, of course—was a *major* revelation to a lot of people."

Merchandising coordinator Alyson McRae recalls showing distributors around. "They were extremely excited, very impressed with what they saw." Taylor and his young designers at Weta Workshop were particularly good spokespeople for the project, enthusiastically showing off their work. "Richard would lay out all the weapons," McRae says. "They would have everyone working, and these groups would go through, and you could just see people's jaws dropping when they understood that seven to nine different cultures each had to have that level of detail worked out." Jane Johnson of Harper-Collins (publishers of both Tolkien's novels and the film's licensed tie-in books) went to New Zealand convinced that *Rings* was unfilmable. "When I turned up in New Zealand to wander around Weta Workshop, it was like walking into Middle-earth."[17] There was no finished special-effects footage to show off, however, and it was not until the Cannes preview of 2001 that all these people could get a real sense of what they had bought into.[18] Still, seemingly no one who took such a tour went away unconvinced that Jackson's team could handle *Rings*.

Life after Rings

After *Rings* was finished, the expansion continued for a while. In 2004, an immense soundproof stage was built at the Stone Street Studios. It was first used during the filming of *King Kong*. Jean Johnston of Film Wellington helped lobby to obtain NZ$2 million to help pay for the stage because, as she explains, "It's not just for Peter Jackson. It's for the industry."

Weta Workshop has been the most independent firm in the group of Miramar companies. Once the design work for *Rings* was largely over, Taylor pursued his own strategy of diversification in order to keep his staff continually employed. Several of the designers and sculptors were assigned to creating the *Rings* busts and other Sideshow Weta collectibles. Once those were finished, a new distributorship through Dark Horse was arranged for comparable *Kong* products. The Workshop has also created collectible figures tied to *The Lion, the Witch and the Wardrobe,* the Muppets, *Superman Returns,* and a video game, "Hellgate: London." Such products will presumably be a long-term part of the firm's business. Taylor has organized subsidiaries to take the firm into other areas. Weta/Tenzan manufactures "chainmaille" for filmmaking (used in *The Lion, the Witch and the Wardrobe* and *Kingdom of Heaven*). Weta launched its new publishing arm, Weta Worlds, in 2005, with a tie-in book for *King Kong*. The venture provided another opportunity for Weta's designers to work in areas besides filmmaking.[19]

Weta's primary new venture, however, has been in the area of children's television. In 2004, Weta Workshop was able to buy back the ice cream factory that had been sold to raise the money to buy the Stone Street Studios. The converted factory was turned into a real-time motion-capture stage for use on *Jane and the Dragon,* an animated children's series backed by a Canadian television company. Weta has also added its own IT department, equipped with the same sort of computers and processors as Weta Digital, but on a smaller scale.[20]

By 2005, the Miramar facilities had reached maturity. The companies that were created or expanded to make *Rings,* along with the additional equipment and facilities enabled by the funds that it generated, cover the entire range of filmmaking, from pre- to postproduction. And they all lie within five minutes' drive from Jackson's house in Seatoun.

Jackson sometimes speaks of his buildup of filmmaking facilities on the Miramar Peninsula as selfish. "We're hoping that if they come up to a standard that can do a *Lord of the Rings* or a *King Kong,* then they'll be usable facilities for other filmmakers—anyone, whether they're New Zealand filmmakers, Australian filmmakers, American filmmakers. But my involvement in it is really based on very selfish reasons." Few of the people who have benefited from the employment and upskilling that Jackson's filmmaking has provided would agree with that characterization.

Jackson and his partners have tried to make their state-of-the-art facilities available to New Zealand filmmakers. When The Film Unit moved into its luxurious new headquarters and became Park Road Post, the charges for services went up. Jackson specified, however, that New Zealand films would be billed at the old scale. He wants to make Weta services available as well. "Computer effects are very expensive, but wherever we can do them very cheaply, a few shots for New Zealand films, we try and do that. Sometimes even for free, just to help Kiwis out." Taylor confirms that Weta Workshop does much the same thing. "It's very important that it doesn't come over that we're fleecing our foreign clients, because we're not! [laughs] We have a very, very fixed overhead and a small profit that we charge on all the work, and when we do New Zealand films, the profit is put to one side, as long as we cover our overheads. To try and get companies to make film effects in New Zealand." The first local film to call upon the Workshop's services was *Black Sheep,* a New Zealand–Korean project made following a recent coproduction agreement (and with postproduction work by Park Road Post). The Workshop also helps local filmmakers create pitch packages by supplying illustrative material.

Although Jackson was again taking a chance by building such facilities, especially the lavish Park Road Post, he seldom mentioned the fact. Talking with an interviewer for the New Zealand trade magazine *Onfilm,* however, he explained the risk: "I'm taking a gamble because I'm building a post production facility that I know is not financially viable in New Zealand—I'm being foolhardy in what I'm doing in some respects, and I'm hoping like hell that, by presenting a world-class mixing facility and laboratory and digital grading and all the video post production, it'll be attractive to films from outside of the country—like Asian movies, some Australian movies, perhaps."[21]

Satellites, Fatpipes, and iPods

In early 1999, a young man whose main qualification was a natural bent for technical "stuff" got a part-time job at Three Foot Six, doing mundane jobs like connecting people to the Internet or e-mail and troubleshooting PC problems. Five years later he was still there, running the newly formed IT department. As far as Duncan Nimmo is aware, *Rings* was the first film with an IT department.

Nimmo's first "nonmundane" job was setting up a system that allowed Jackson to direct one filming unit and watch on a bank of monitors what was happening at locations where other units were shooting. Within Miramar, long cables could simply be run between buildings, but units in remote mountain locations in the Southern Alps were another matter. With the help of Sue Bridger, who handled the Three Foot Six account of Telecom, the country's principal telecommunications company, Nimmo put in place a satellite transmission system. Now video footage could be sent to Jackson's monitors, and the filmmakers could use their cell phones and Internet in most locations.

As *Fellowship* was being postproduced, footage or sound often needed to be sent somewhere—to New Line in Los Angeles for approval, to Jackson in London when he was consulting with Howard Shore. Such material went the old-fashioned way, either by courier or by e-mail. But shipping musical tracks via courier from London to Wellington often bumped up against deadlines, and when Jackson reviewed files on his laptop, he had to discuss them with the Wellington team by phone. It was far from ideal. Barrie Osborne started investigating much faster ways of sending sound and image materials. Film 1 had been relatively simple, but Films 2 and 3 had far more effects shots to be checked, and Osborne anticipated delays. He decided to set up a dedicated network. But New Line had never allowed such sensitive material to be sent via fiber-optic cable, and no more luscious a target for fan hacking could be imagined. The network had to be closed and utterly secure. As Milton Ngan, digital operations manager for Weta, explains, "Big businesses have these big, private dedicated lines all over the place. It's just that the size and length of this pipe was perhaps bigger than anyone had ever attempted before."

Bridger proposed a ten-megabyte dedicated system linking Wellington, Los Angeles, and London. The network was known to everyone on the production as the Fatpipe. Lucky timing played a role again. The Internet bubble had recently burst, and much of the broadband capacity on the Internet was suddenly lying idle. "It was just a *gift!*" Nimmo explains. "This thing should have cost hundreds and hundreds of thousands of dollars, but because of the success of the first film, they wanted our business, and they really gave it to us at an extraordinarily low price." The Fatpipe was hooked up initially at Weta Digital in March 2002, and eventually the closed Miramar system expanded to include all the main filmmaking facilities.

How did a *Rings* file start out in Wellington and travel via the Fatpipe to London? Weta Digital and Three Foot Six's offices had outlets from the local system. From there, the Fatpipe ran to Auckland, and signals were switched onto the Southern Cross Cable, which had become operational in November 2000. The cable extends to Palo Alto, California. From there the signal hopped across the United States via a series of local systems with which Telecom had arrangements. Reaching New York, it was switched to a cross-Atlantic cable and ended up at a company called Sohonet in London, which would transfer it to a local cable. There were not many options for the point of arrival, but there was an outlet at Pinewood Studios. While Jackson was in London, Nimmo's job was to go to Pinewood and download material from Wellington onto a removable firewire drive and hand-carry it to Jackson's house in Slough. To do so, he used an iPod, which could hold the entirety of *Towers* or *Return* in simple, unrendered form. On one occasion, he was chased through the streets by thieves intent on stealing his iPod. He escaped, and one can only imagine what his pursuers would have thought of the bizarre images that they would have found had they succeeded.

Jackson would not give final approval to an effects shot until he could see it projected in 35mm. For *Towers,* effects footage was sent over the Fatpipe as high-resolution jpg files and printed onto film at a laboratory in London. The procedure stretched the limits of the system, however, and for Film 3 couriers once again carried film reels to London for approval.

The Fatpipe also could help out with editing. Jackson took all the shots he thought he would need to London with him. Still, Nimmo recalls one instance where Jackson was having a problem linking a sequence. Having a remarkable memory, he recalled one take made long ago on Mount Ruapehu. They were able to request that particular shot from Wellington and have it within hours to insert into the scene.

The key use of the Fatpipe, though, was for videoconferencing. Ngan's team devised a remote-control system whereby Jackson at his end and the special-effects team at the other could watch the same footage at exactly the same time. Aitken describes how the conferences worked:

> It looks like you're playing a Quicktime movie yourself on your computer. He's seeing the same thing as we are, and there's a shared pointer so that we can indicate areas of the screen, which is important. Then there's a little picture of Peter in an armchair at the bottom corner of the screen, and he's got a little picture of a bunch of people around a conference table on the corner of his screen. That's a live feed, so he can wave his arms around and show us things.

The system proved a major improvement over phone discussions.

The Fatpipe was not absolutely essential. Nimmo says that the film could have been made without the dedicated network. "It would have been done differently," and he adds, "It would have been a great deal more expensive." Similarly, Bridger suspects that Films 2 and 3 might well not have been finished in time had it not been for the Fatpipe.

Rings was crucial in setting up this infrastructure. As Sue Thompson says, "It's *very* expensive and really could not have been done off the back of any other thing apart from *Lord of the Rings*." Once the system was in place, it or variations of it could be used for other films. The same videoconferencing system ran between Los Angeles and Wellington when Weta Digital created 300 effects shots for *I, Robot*. The Film Unit and Warner Bros. tailored a similar system for *The Last Samurai*. As the technology becomes easier to use, however, Fatpipe systems will eventually make it routine to send film material around the world in digital form.

Upskilling

Rings had a huge impact on the people who worked in all these facilities and used these technologies. Through them, lessons learned will affect the future of the New Zealand film industry. In the past, successful filmmakers accepted work abroad, and government funding was modest. Those staying behind had little opportunity to gain experience on complicated projects. The industry's output had been primarily documentaries and commercials, with a few low-budget features each year. *Rings* brought a new standard of film work to a minor producing country. Ken Saville, second unit sound recordist for *Rings* and head of the Wellington branch of the New Zealand Film and Video Technicians Guild, estimates that the skilled labor available for film in New Zealand increased tenfold over the course of the project. Selkirk reckons that the trilogy's biggest impact on the nation's film industry is "definitely the talent pool," especially in art department, digital effects, and stunt work. Weta Digital hired many animators from abroad who sat side by side with Kiwis, passing on their expertise.

Most people working on *Rings* were New Zealanders, but the country lacked experienced technicians in areas like sound mixing and sophisticated special effects. Some of the top people in those fields were brought in. Alex Funke, visual effects director of photography for *Rings,* came from the United States in 1999 to create the miniatures department that was so crucial to the trilogy's epic quality. He found few Kiwis with experience in miniature photography. As he explained:

We had to set up a school to teach motion control, because there were only one or two qualified motion-control people in the country, and they were already working on the movie. We basically taught a small cadre of people, the same ones we still have working here [on *King Kong*], how to use this particular motion-control system. The rest of the crafts they pretty well learned simply by doing.

Funke had worked on major, effects-heavy films like *The Abyss* and *Total Recall*, so the miniatures team were learning from one of the most experienced people in the business.

Production designer Grant Major assesses the pre- and post-*Rings* film industry. Before *Rings*, there were small local films and big foreign ones. For the big films, the producers would typically bring in their own department heads. Major had been in the industry for twenty years and never worked on any big projects. Crews, he says, could pick up experience on the level of building and dressing sets. In his opinion, "*The Lord of the Rings* changed that overnight, really. People now can come here and bring on people like myself— I would like to think—and gaffers and people with higher skills." The same went for postproduction staff. Sue Thompson says of the sound crew who worked on *Rings*, "The experience, the breadth of skill has just increased at an exponential rate."

Some of the personnel on *Rings*, including Major, had had formal training. Supervising art director Dan Hennah had a degree in architectural drafting and had been in the industry since 1981. Marjory Hamlin, the on-set prosthetics supervisor, had studied makeup for three years and had worked on such films as *Mad Max beyond Thunderdome*, *The Piano*, and *Heavenly Creatures*. Nancy Hennah, whose parents, Chris and Dan, were in the art department, decided to go into makeup. For her, "Basically the reason I went to do makeup training is because I heard that Peter Jackson was going to be making *The Lord of the Rings*."[22] She attended Greasepaint in London because of the lack of makeup schools on the required level of sophistication in New Zealand. Many of the film's crew members, however, had worked their way up through the industry without such training.

With few feature films being made in New Zealand, television had been an important source of skills in the pre-*Rings* period. Ken Saville had started as a sound recordist in television and radio in 1979 and learned as an apprentice on the job. He first dealt with film when shooting local news on 16mm and moved into freelancing during a brief upturn in Kiwi filmmaking in the early 1980s. Jamie Selkirk had had no training when he got a minor technical job with the national TV station in Wellington. A car accident sidelined his plans to become a camera operator, so he went into editing and became part of Jackson's core team early on, with *Bad Taste.*

Most television production was strictly local fare, but New Zealanders got a chance to observe American methods when Pacific Renaissance Pictures shot hundreds of hours of *Hercules: The Legendary Journeys* and *Xena: Warrior Princess* (both 1995) in and around Auckland. The producers could draw upon a small pool of experienced workers who had learned their crafts on *Shortland Street* (1992 on), the most popular Kiwi soap opera. In Ruth Harley's opinion, "It is productions like *Shortland Street, Hercules* and *Xena* that have generated the skill base that could create *Lord of the Rings.*"[23] The main jewelry designer for *Rings,* Jasmine Watson, had gone straight from art school to *Hercules* and *Xena,* and Mary Maclachlan, Weta Workshop's senior model maker, had attended film school and then worked on those series and *The Frighteners.* Major had worked on two *Hercules* TV movies. Stunt performer Kirk Maxwell did not work on either series, but most of the team he assembled for *Rings,* including Sharon James, had.

The most prominent of the *Rings* crew members who had worked on the two series was Ngila Dickson, who explains, "When I came on board *Lord of the Rings,* I really felt to refer to *Xena* in any way was a very bad thing because it was seen as kind of tacky, fast-turnaround television. I view it in a completely different way. I think that all of those people who worked on those series learned invaluable skills that actually helped them survive through the enormous difficulties of something like *Lord of the Rings.*" *Hercules* and *Xena* were made simultaneously, with episodes for each shot in alternation—a hectic approach that Dickson believes helped prepare crew members for the need to come up with solutions and changes on short notice during their later three-at-once *Rings* experience. She disagrees with the resistance to American influence among many Kiwi filmmakers. "I am completely opposite to that, because what I have seen is the extraordinary upskilling in the Kiwi crews through that contact." Dickson set up a training system that assigned inexperienced crew members to the tasks for which they showed the most aptitude. Eventually she took people from her staff to work on *Rings.*

Then there is the Peter Jackson approach to training, which is basically: just do it.[24] He has been making films since he was a child, discovering by trial and error how to create props, prosthetic makeup, and special effects. Of *Rings* he says, "Every time you step onto a film set, every day you're going to film school. Every day there's things to learn."[25] Like Jackson, Richard Taylor grew up making his own toys and models. The experience led to a career, one that linked to Jackson's during *Meet the Feebles*. Taylor made on-the-job training the philosophy of Weta Workshop. He takes on inexperienced but promising kids interested in design, crafts, and movies, sets them loose in the Workshop, and lets them grow into the job. Of the 158 people who worked there during the height of *Rings,* only 28 had any experience in film or television. Jean Johnston sums up the sense of confidence that *Rings* instilled in its crew: "After working on something like *The Lord of the Rings,* you can work on anything, really, can't you?"

New Zealand has long had a problem with brain drain, its talented and educated young professionals leaving for the United States, England, or Australia for better employment prospects. One might expect that with *Rings* on their résumés and Oscars on their mantelpieces, some of the more prominent crew members would leave for places where more filmmaking goes on. Granted, they would face green-card restrictions and union regulations in the United States, but there is a subtler reason for staying. As New Zealanders, they love working where they are and have few urges to enter the L.A. rat race. Grant Major has worked abroad for a couple of years but says, "Most people live here and have families here and all that sort of stuff, and, I think, live here for reasons other than professional."

The attraction of Miramar has partly to do with the beauty of the country, but it owes a lot as well to the friendly, unpretentious, enthusiastic way these people work. Jackson says that no matter how busy he is, he sets aside a certain amount of time to be with his children. He bought half a dozen houses on the same road on the Miramar peninsula so that his main designers and writers could be neighbors. During the shoot, instead of hiding away in luxurious trailers, the stars ate with the crew. Simone Flight, of Tourism New Zealand, who ushered some New Line executives on a tour during the shooting, vividly recalls Christopher Lee, in his Saruman outfit, eating lunch off a paper plate in a crowded mess tent. The cast, enchanted with all this, frequently refer in interviews to the production team as having become a family.

The attractions are particularly clear to those who have worked extensively in Hollywood. Funke summed up the way the Miramar companies are run: "It's a very humane group of people. Richard is very humane with his people. Peter's very humane with his people. They're very much concerned not only about excellent work and getting the job done but about the fact that the people are actually being treated right—which unfortunately I can't say for a lot of Hollywood." Jackson inspires intense loyalty, too, as is evident from the names that appear again and again in the credits of his films. Rick Porras recalls that in July 1998 Jackson and Walsh came to his engagement party, even though they were leaving for Hollywood the next morning with the pitch tape, knowing they had little chance of finding a new producer for *Rings*. "No one at that party knew that they were leaving the next day and that they had this mountain to climb, that it was a make-or-break moment for them. Not a hint," says Porras, adding, "They had me for life at that point. I basically will do whatever I can for them for the rest of my life, personally and professionally."

Like the fans, the *Rings* team created an immersive, participatory community. For these people, including Americans like Funke, the appeal lies not only in a neighborly working and living environment but also in the chance to develop a larger enterprise. As Harley puts it, "They're all engaged in building something."

REBRANDING A COUNTRY

The national government was remarkably quick to recognize the possible advantages that *Rings* could bring to the country as a whole. The notion of using the trilogy as a way to promote New Zealand in general originated with Paul Voigt, the investment director for the screen production industry at Investment New Zealand. In June 2001, he contacted the prime minister and some key government officials and laid out some suggestions. On 11 July, Prime Minister Helen Clark (also minister of the arts) visited Weta Workshop to make an announcement: NZ$9 million were being allotted for leveraging off two big events, the America's Cup and *Rings*. Over the years, as the success of the trilogy and its beneficial effects on the country became apparent, further allocations were made—especially when the world premiere for *Return* was secured for Wellington:

2001/02 NZ$1,468,500

2002/03 NZ$1,470,000

2003/04 NZ$4,600,000[26]

This money was in addition to funds allocated by various agencies. Activities funded by the national government included parties and dinners in various foreign cities, coinciding with the three parts' premieres; advertising supplements in the main English-language trade journals (*Variety, Hollywood Reporter,* and *Screen International*); and various local promotional projects.[27]

Clark appointed Pete Hodgson, member of Parliament and associate minister of foreign affairs and trade, to organize the government's participation. Journalists quickly dubbed him "The Minister of *The Lord of the Rings*," a position many have wrongly assumed is official. Hodgson explains that there have been two aims in leveraging *Rings*. One is the obvious promotion of tourism and the film industry.

> The second reason that taxpayers' money is being deployed is that New Zealand is doing something a little unusual, which is that it's looking to rebrand itself. The world image of New Zealand is that it's a rather lovely, rather quiet, rather sweet place with an awful lot of sheep. Whilst that's true to an extent or even to a large extent, it's by no means all the truth, and *Lord of the Rings* is proof of that, because it's the largest cinematic undertaking in world history.

The expenditure was not high, but Hodgson points out that "it is most unusual for a country to put any money at all into having the country use a movie to rebrand itself." The rebranding involved promoting sectors of the economy that were environmentally safe, such as technology, tourism, and creativity, especially filmmaking.

Investment New Zealand

The government agencies that worked together were organized by Voigt. He and Hodgson established a relationship with New Line that permitted them to use the slogan "New Zealand, Home of Middle-earth" without paying a licensing fee. In effect, New Zealand and New Line became promotional partners, probably the first time a Hollywood studio has made such a deal with a country. Other agencies were part of the team effort: Tourism New Zealand, the New Zealand Film Commission, and Film New Zealand. Although it is a private company, Air New Zealand, as the national carrier, was included. Never having leveraged off a film before, Voigt based his campaign on his work around the America's Cup, the Millennium, and the Sydney Olympics of 2000.

Once all the relationships were in place, one of Investment NZ's main activities was to host parties and meals at embassies and consulates in major international cities around the premieres of the three parts and around the Academy Awards presentations. For example, the *Towers*-related parties started on 5 December 2002 in New York, just before the world premiere. On 9 December there was a lunch at New Zealand's embassy in Paris, the day before the European premiere. Other events were held over the next week and a half in Los Angeles, London, again in New York (a reception for film industry officials, attended by Prime Minister Clark, New Zealand's U.S. ambassador, and Elijah Wood), with further parties in Toronto, Seoul, Madrid, Wellington, Auckland, and Singapore. New Zealand food and wine were served, and guests received gift bags containing *Rings*-themed mouse pads, bags, scarves, shirts, books, and DVDs, and the *Rings*-themed postage stamps issued by the New Zealand government. Later events were held in Hong Kong, Beijing, Berlin, Milan, and New Delhi.[28] Dinner parties in Los Angeles two days before the Oscars were instituted during the years when *Rings* was nominated and have continued as an annual event.

Voigt considers the production of *Rings* a transformational moment for New Zealand. When I talked with him in November 2004, there were four or five domestic features being made at budgets of NZ$15 to $20 million. "People would think they were lunatics five years ago if they'd said we're going to be making these movies in New Zealand that *are* New Zealand movies."

Tourism New Zealand

Pete Hodgson makes clear the determination of the government to link *Rings* with New Zealand as firmly as possible. "One of the trick questions is 'Where was *Star Wars* made?' And if you ask around, you'll get a variety. You'll get Nevada or Morocco, you'll get all sorts of answers. And we didn't want anyone to be in any doubt about that for New Zealand."

Initially some people in Tourism New Zealand were dubious about leveraging off the film. What if the country ended up being associated with a flop? But Voigt was pushing his plan, and the staff, though some were initially reluctant, eventually came on board.

As originally conceived, "New Zealand, Home of Middle-earth" was seen by New Line as a slogan for use within New Zealand. The studio was skeptical about the idea that linking the trilogy with that country would benefit it significantly, dismissing the fact that all the actors were praising New Zealand enthusiastically in interviews. Simone Flight, Tourism NZ's Los Angeles public relations manager, suspects that they might have believed that Jackson was backing the tourism initiative to gain publicity for his new filmmaking complex. In September 2001, after a meeting in New York failed to go well, Gregg Anderson, manager of the Los Angeles office, asked one studio executive to assess why. She replied that, as a PR person herself, she knew he was just saying the nice things that he was paid to say about his country. He immediately told Flight that she needed to take New Line's marketers to New Zealand.

Tourism NZ, in conjunction with Investment NZ, invited senior New Line marketing and promotional executives to spend a whirlwind week in New

Zealand. In May 2002, with Flight as their escort, the executives stopped at Auckland for meetings with Investment NZ, had a set visit and facilities tour in Wellington, and made a brief stay in Queenstown. As happened so often with visiting journalists and film company officials, the executives were bowled over. Flight recalls, "They were working on [*Rings*] on a daily basis, but none of them had visited New Zealand, so the stuff that the talent were saying— it was just, 'Oh, it's Peter Jackson telling them to say this. They're saying this to keep Peter happy or whatever.' But they got down here and they realized that the country was as beautiful as the talent was saying." A luxury lodge in Queenstown and various tour operators donated their services, realizing the potential payoff. Flight also took the executives to Te Papa for a meeting about the proposed exhibition, helping to convince them that the museum was capable of mounting such a show.

The Los Angeles branch of Tourism NZ handled most of the publicity and other activities. The producers of the making-of documentaries were contacted to ensure that they included mentions of New Zealand. Press junkets to Wellington were arranged for each of the New Zealand premieres, with the participants also taken around to experience other parts of the country. Local tour operators would take these journalists around for free. Around Oscar time, Tourism NZ would put up billboards, linking beautiful views with the film (figure 36). The agency also made the arrangements for the trips to New Zealand won through the sweepstakes run by New Line and its promotional partners. Finally, the staff also contacted travel agents, giving them information about filming locations and encouraging them to mention *Rings* in connection with New Zealand.

In March 2004, tourism became the country's biggest single export earner (replacing dairy products), and it has increased its lead since. How big a factor was *Rings?* Impossible to say, but for George Hickton, CEO of Tourism New Zealand,

> There's no doubt in my mind that it's been a factor in the awareness of New Zealand. When you ask how many people came to New Zealand specifically because of *Lord of the Rings,* you don't get a very high answer. But you get extraordinary knowledge around the world of people who are aware that the film was made in New Zealand. So I think what's happened is, it's enabled us to convert that interest into tourism results.

Hickton also points out that seeking *Rings* locations has lured people to areas of the country previously not much visited.

Figure 36. A Tourism New Zealand billboard referring to *The Lord of the Rings* outside Los Angeles Airport in February 2004. (Courtesy Tourism New Zealand.)

Certainly many people know that New Zealand "is" Middle-earth. Children writing letters to the characters address them there. An English twelve-year-old wrote to:

> Frodo and Legolas
>
> Address: Unknown
>
> Please help this get to somewhere in New Zealand

A nine-year-old in Edinburgh addressed a note:

> Samwise Gamgee
>
> 3 Bagshot Row
>
> Hobbiton
>
> New Zealand

Both reached the actors portraying these characters.

The number of hits on Tourism NZ's website indicates that there was a

TABLE I
Tourism New Zealand Website (NZ.com) Monthly Hits, 2001–2005

Month	2001	2002	2003	2004	2005
January	n/a	121,894	238,652	300,625	316,195
February	n/a	96,521	193,677	309,395	281,124
March	52,723	103,287	200,753	386,192	318,816
April	64,132	106,736	195,663	320,591	307,678
May	108,491	119,642	203,567	240,395	306,706
June	67,146	93,665	184,795	205,846	284,291
July	73,909	105,789	202,355	195,430	256,646
August	86,515	117,739	225,957	221,609	326,107
September	73,563	123,715	242,742	254,595	333,166
October	79,166	141,814	278,864	294,296	378,872
November	75,617	149,411	264,620	304,481	369,624
December	84,099	145,376	249,071	256,676	301,655
Total	765,361	1,425,589	2,680,716	3,290,131	3,780,880
Percentage of Increase		86	88	23	15

SOURCE: Tourism New Zealand (2006). Reproduced by permission.

spike in readership directly after the release of each part of the trilogy (see table). *Rings* at least had the effect that Hickton hoped, raising people's awareness of New Zealand as a desirable vacation destination. A stab at an estimate of *Rings'* impact on tourism came in the annual International Visitors Survey conducted in 2003. Officials added questions about whether departing visitors knew the film had been made in New Zealand and to what extent seeing *Rings* had influenced their choice of it as a destination. Eighty-nine percent had heard of the film, and 89 percent of those knew that it had been shot in New Zealand. Seven percent of those who knew where the film had been made said that was one factor in their decision. Of those 7 percent, 2,300 said it was their sole reason; for 5,100 it was the main factor; for 69,000 it was a major factor. Based on the average amount spent per person, these tourists injected just over NZ$40 million into the nation's economy.[29] In a country where tourism accounts for around 14 percent of the gross domestic product and employs roughly 10 percent of the workforce, the contribution was small but significant. The survey did not take into account the exceptional occasion of the *Return* world premiere, which drew in NZ$201

million (US$130 million) and generated news coverage that reached an esti-
mated 400 million people.[30]

In 2004, the annual staff poll by travel-guide publisher Lonely Planet picked
New Zealand as the top destination a second year in a row. Editor Don George
called the double win "extraordinary," crediting it to "a perfect storm of spectacular pristine scenery, hospitable citizenry, compelling culture, perceived
geo-political safety and free global big-screen advertising—courtesy of *Lord
of the Rings*."[31]

Film New Zealand

This agency's brief is to draw production from abroad into New Zealand. It
began operating in the early 1990s and incorporated in 2001. At that time its
annual funding of NZ$400,000 was committed only until mid-2003.

Like other cooperating government agencies, Film NZ was quick to exploit the publicity possibilities offered by *Rings*. At the Cannes event of 2001,
the agency handed out a beautiful two-sided map, with one side depicting
New Zealand as "Home of Middle-earth," with the shooting locales marked
(plate 11), and the other displaying the country as "Studio New Zealand,"
with lists of other films and an emphasis on facilities (plate 12).

One crucial endeavor by Film NZ was to standardize rules and regulations
for filmmaking across the country. The regional film promotion branches were
brought together to devise the "Film Friendly Protocol." Susan Ord, of Film
NZ, explains the situation before the protocol: "If you had three or four different locations over three or four different territorial areas, you might find that
your consents and your permissions process were entirely different. In fact, I
would argue that there are people who've been in the New Zealand film industry for twenty years who say, 'God, we've been asking that for thirty years!'"
Hayden Taylor adds, "With *The Lord of the Rings,* they're now recognizing
that film is a viable—and a large—industry that they have to cater for."

James Crowley, who arranged the locations for *The Lion, the Witch and the
Wardrobe,* believes that *Rings* paved the way to making access easier with both
local governments and local landowners. "We're not using any of the same
locations, but I think that people are generally excited about it—maybe more
than they would have been before those movies. Just having experienced it,
and I suppose it being a good experience, they see it as something that they
want to be part of." For its size, Film NZ achieved a high profile in the *Rings*
years, attending more overseas locations fairs, putting out several impressive
booklets of information for filmmakers, and building up its website—which
received 500 percent more hits after Film 1 came out.

In the summer of 2003, the government made a major step toward luring production from abroad. A controversial tax scheme that had provided an undisclosed amount of support to *Rings* had been eliminated, and New Zealand faced the prospect of competition from other countries that were putting in place various tax incentives to draw in offshore production. After pressure from within the industry—including urging from Jackson—the government passed the Large Budget Screen Production Grant, giving big productions from abroad that spent a certain percentage of their budget in New Zealand a 12 ½ percent tax rebate. The measure was rushed through to some extent because the producers of *The Chronicles of Narnia: The Lion, the Witch and the Wardrobe* were currently considering New Zealand as a place to shoot. Producer Mark Johnson says that he and others involved helped the government in terms of comparisons with the similar Australian scheme already in place. Was the production grant a factor in luring *Narnia* to New Zealand? "Absolutely," he says.

So far the grant scheme has been a success. In 2005 rebates totaling $33.3 million were given to producers, including $16.6 million for *King Kong* and $10.3 million for *The Lion, the Witch and the Wardrobe*. In early 2006, the grant was renewed to 2009.[32]

When I first visited in October 2003, the future funding of Film NZ was in doubt. In 2004, the agency was restructured as a trust. It was funded more substantially, and its board was reorganized to include more practicing film producers. Its success in helping to bring in both large and small productions from abroad has been crucial in the continuing health of the country's filmmaking.

The New Zealand Film Commission

The New Zealand Film Commission is the flip side of Film New Zealand, responsible for fostering domestic production, investing in projects, and selling the results abroad through its distribution wing, New Zealand Film. Back in 1986, the commission had launched Jackson's professional career by putting money into *Bad Taste*. In August 2002, Dr. Ruth Harley, the agency's CEO, pointed out that the commission had put a total of NZ$5 million into five of the director's early films, while the amount of money brought into the country by *Rings* was three times the commission's total film investments since its founding in 1978. Though the NZ Film Commission did not invest in *Rings,* its marketing and sales chief, Kathleen Drumm, found that the dramatic success of the Cannes 2001 preview of the trilogy raised the profile of other Kiwi films. "We were able to leverage opportunities for them through the exposure that *The Lord of the Rings* had in the marketplace. Deals were being struck along the lines of, 'If you let me have *Braindead* and *Bad Taste*, I'll also take . . . '"[33]

The production of *Rings* and the growth of the filmmaking infrastructure also drew back talented directors who had gone overseas to work. The NZ Film Commission found itself funding projects by the makers of classic Kiwi films. Roger Donaldson, whose *Sleeping Dogs* (1977) and *Smash Palace* (1981) launched the modern era in New Zealand cinema, achieved some success in the United States with such films as *No Way Out, Cocktail*, and *The Bounty.* He returned home and directed *The World's Fastest Indian* in late 2004; it sold well internationally and was released in 2005. Vincent Ward (*The Navigator,* 1988) had also worked in the States, making *Map of the Human Heart* (1993) and *What Dreams May Come* (1998). He returned to New Zealand during the *Rings* period and, after a long and troubled production, managed to finish his historical drama, *River Queen* (2005). Geoff Murphy (*UTU,* 1983; *The Quiet Earth,* 1985) worked abroad mainly on TV movies and as a second-unit director. He returned to New Zealand to direct the second unit on *Rings,* most notably filming scenes on the plains of Rohan. With a combination of private and NZ Film Commission funding, he directed a feature, *Spooked* (2004).

It was not just directors returning to New Zealand. Skilled filmmakers of all sorts came back. Jean Johnston says that as *Rings* was getting under way, Film Wellington was getting e-mails from people who had gone abroad for work and to pick up skills: "'I hear it's really cool back there. Are there any jobs?' So we've got quite a few back." Mara Bryan, who had been special-effects supervisor for James Bond films *The World Is Not Enough* (1999) and *Die Another Day* (2002, directed by Lee Tamahori, another Kiwi expatriate), went to Auckland to work for the country's second-biggest effects house, Oktobor.

During the trilogy's production, there had been fear among local filmmakers that *Rings* and other big projects would drive labor costs up and squeeze domestic activity out. By late 2004, that fear seems largely to have disappeared as people in the film industry realized that the two types of movies could coexist. During the late period of *Rings'* production, the NZ Film Commission was funding younger directors' work as well, such as Greg Page's first feature, the modestly budgeted zombie film *The Locals* (2003), and a British coproduction, Brad McGann's *In My Father's Den* (2004). Jean Johnston points out that while Film Wellington, a local agency for facilitating filmmaking, was helping on *Rings,* two Kiwi features, *Stickman* and *The Irrefutable Truth about Demons,* were also made in the city. The national government's restructuring of the various agencies supporting filmmaking provided more funding for both Film NZ and the NZ Film Commission. In late 2005, when I talked with Harley at the American Film Market, New Zealand Film had three films on offer for international distributors: *50 Ways of Saying Fabulous, River Queen,* and *The World's Fastest Indian.* She saw both local and offshore filmmaking as healthy. "We've had a great year. Probably the best year in our history." A few months later, Toa Fraser's first feature, *No. 2* (made for NZ$5 million), won the World Cinema Audience Award at the 2006 Sundance Festival and was picked up for American distribution by Miramax. Later that year Air New Zealand sponsored a gala screening of it at the London Film Festival. Fraser declared of the big films made in New Zealand, "The blockbusters have been phenomenally helpful for people like us trying to get a film made. I embrace the blockbusters and the Hollywood back lot as long as we can use it to tell our own stories."[34]

And New Zealanders were going to see local films. In previous decades, recalls Joe Moodabe, CEO of Village Sky City Cinemas, a chain that includes 40 percent of the country's screens, "There were exceptions, but New Zealand films were a tough sell." Now he is happy to book them, and the chain even put money into *Sione's Wedding* (2006), which also had NZ Film Commission money. *Sione's Wedding,* retitled *Samoan Wedding* abroad, helped sustain the level of Kiwi filmmaking into 2006. *Variety* gave it an enthusiastic review and declared it "an instantly exportable comedy." That same year, Robert Sarkies, director of the popular and critically lauded first feature *Scarfies* (1999), was finally able to make a second, *Out of the Blue* (starring *Rings*' Karl Urban), also praised by *Variety.*[35] New Zealand films were no longer rarities in international festivals and art cinemas, and it was apparent that the upturn in Kiwi filmmaking fortunes had well outlasted the trilogy's immediate effects.

Harley points out that many of the country's earlier, less popular films were made on small budgets, and the enhanced financing of the commission has contributed to improving the quality to the point where both Kiwi and international audiences want to see the local product.[36] Tim Coddington, production manager for *The Lion, the Witch and the Wardrobe,* credits *Rings* with doing more than helping build the infrastructure and draw investment: "We've got the government recognizing the film industry as a real industry, where before they didn't pay much attention to it at all. It was something that people sort of did 'over there.'"

Harley sees *Rings*' legacy in filmmakers' altered attitudes. "It's changed things enormously. It's changed people's sense of what's possible and their sense of ambition."

Wellington

Tim Cossar, CEO of Positively Wellington Tourism, the local agency charged with promoting business and leisure travel to the city, has nothing but praise for Jackson and his decision not to go abroad. He describes attending a luncheon in Melbourne, Australia, in an effort to sell Wellington as a site for conferences. "We had fifty quite influential conference organizers there that we were talking to, and the one common thread in the whole thing was *Lord of the Rings*. We could never have afforded to pay for that. Now it's like an invisible thing." Similarly, in September 2004, when a hundred Australian travel writers did hold a conference in Wellington, Cossar says, they all wanted to visit *Lord of the Rings* sites and Jackson's studio: "We can use it as an entrée to introduce them to the rest of what the city has got to offer."

Based on hoteliers' reports on how many of their guests have come to Wellington for *Rings*-related tourism, he estimates that the trilogy draws NZ$4 to 5 million into the city each year. In late 2001 and early 2002 (New Zealand's summer), in the midst of a sharp drop in worldwide travel in the wake of 9/11, Auckland, with the America's Cup, and Wellington, with the Te Papa *Rings* exhibition, were the only places in the country where tourism did not decline.

The world premieres of the first two parts of *Rings* had taken place in big cities: London (*Fellowship*) and New York (*Towers*). From early on, however, many of the filmmakers and local government officials had hoped to secure the third world premiere for Wellington, despite its relatively small population. At the national premiere of *Towers*, Jackson maneuvered Mark Ordesky to the microphone, telling the crowd that Ordesky wanted to announce the venue of the *Return* world premiere. Trapped, Ordesky had little choice but to declare enthusiastically, "Wellington, New Zealand!"

The premiere was not a done deal, however. New Line was willing to fly the stars to Wellington, as they would have done whatever the premiere venue was. The studio demanded that the city provide a world-class theater for the event, since any large city that it might have chosen would already have such a facility. The Embassy Trust, of which Peter Jackson and Fran Walsh were trustees, had been established some years earlier to raise the millions of dollars needed to restore a faded 1924 picture palace. An agreement between the city council and the trust anticipated that the city would take over ownership of the theater upon completion of fund-raising and restoration work unless the trust raised enough capital to pay for almost all the project. That, however, was never seen as likely.

The prospect of a world premiere, however, had made the restoration of the theater more urgent. From March to May 2003, it became public that the city had agreed to underwrite the work for up to NZ$7 million in case the trust's appeal failed. The city's financial involvement was controversial, and three times the city council debated the extent of both the restoration project and the city's support. New Line threatened to move the world premiere to Los Angeles. Finally, in late May, the council settled on NZ$4.5 million, and New Line officially announced that the world premiere would be in Wellington. Even then the financial problems were not over. In late October, only four weeks away from the premiere itself, the Embassy Trust revealed that it had raised only $540,000, a fraction of what was needed. By that stage, it was clear that only modest additional sums could be raised. Most of the re-furbishment had already been done, and it was assumed, in line with the earlier agreement between the trust and the council, that the city would take ownership of the Embassy. That takeover took place in August 2004, well after the premiere. In the autumn of 2005, Village Sky City Cinema, whose CEO, Joe Moodabe, had commented on the rising interest in New Zealand films, undertook the management of the theater.[37]

The city's move to pay for what might be seen as New Line's event was somewhat controversial. I talked with Mayor Kerry Prendergast in October 2003, shortly before the city took over refurbishment of the Embassy. She had remained supportive of the trilogy from the start, believing that the outlay for the premiere would be far exceeded by the economic benefit to Wellington. Already, Prendergast pointed out, Jackson's new companies in Miramar had created around three thousand jobs. The city council had been among the agencies commissioning the report on *Rings'* impact on New Zealand, as far back as April 2002, in anticipation of the inevitable resistance by some to the city's involvement.[38] The advance estimate was that the premiere would bring around NZ$7 million to the city, in addition to the NZ$5 million annual spending by tourists. The media coverage of the event would be the equivalent of NZ$25 million in advertising.

Prendergast declared, "There was huge support from Wellingtonians for what was NZ$1.8 million we put in our plan to help pay for the event this year." (This would not include the Embassy refurbishment.) That does seem to have been the case. During my month in Wellington, I talked with cab drivers and others about whether they approved of the city's expenditures on *Rings*. Only one had any objections to it, and many had stories of doing jobs like driving a forgotten prop out to a location shoot. Apparently so many people in the city and the country as a whole had at least in some small way seen a financial benefit to themselves that the council's claims would seem reliable. There was much talk at the time about the impending decision by producers of *The Lion, the Witch and the Wardrobe* as to whether to shoot the film in New Zealand, and claims about the country becoming a film-making center were plausible.

Kiwis also took an enormous amount of pride in the trilogy. To New Zealanders, *Rings* is a Kiwi film. Susan McFetridge, of Investment New Zealand, was employed by Roadshow Films, the trilogy's local distributor, at the time of the film's releases. She says:

> It created a huge boom in moviegoers, because I think every New Zealander felt it their patriotic duty to go and see *Fellowship of the Ring*. They kind of claimed it, and New Zealand having the small population that it does, a lot of people have some kind of connection to it, whether that was because it was shot near where they lived, or they were an extra on the film, or they knew someone that had worked on it.

The world premiere of *Return* in Wellington, on 1 December 2003, was an extraordinary event, with 100,000 people lining the streets to cheer the actors and filmmakers (figure 37). The various New Zealand agencies that had worked to leverage the film cooperated to bring hundreds of journalists for a press junket, and after the screening a huge government-sponsored party took place at Te Papa. Air New Zealand arranged a low-level flyover of the city by its "Frodo" plane, but the idea proved so popular that it was extended over the entire country, giving many schoolchildren their first view of a 747.[39] *Variety* titled its coverage of the Los Angeles American premiere two days later, "Outwellington'ed."[40]

Rings had made Jackson a national hero. In 2001, shortly before *Fellowship*'s release, he was voted "Wellingtonian of the Year." "Film director" showed up for the first time in a survey of the ten most respected professions. The prime minister led a cheering crowd in the Embassy Theatre watching on live television as *Return* swept the Oscars (figure 38). One reason Jackson was so admired was that his success was not perceived as having changed him. For a few months after the Academy Awards, he left one of his Oscars in his kitchen window, so that Wellingtonians could see it and tour guides driving past could point it out to fans.[41]

Paul Voigt stresses how broad the legacy of *Rings* has been: "To us the biggest would still be the rebranding of the country, followed by the film benefits and then tourism." The ripple effect has reached out into other areas. Before the

Figure 37. The street in front of the Embassy Theatre on 1 December 2003. The marquee supports a Fell Beast and Nazgûl created by Weta Workshop. (Photograph © Keith Stern, courtesy McKellen.com.)

trilogy, for example, Stansborough Fibres was a small firm striving to find a niche on world markets for its handwoven wool cloth. Once Stansborough was discovered by Ngila Dickson's team, the company was commissioned to weave cloth for *Rings,* including the gray Elvish cloaks that figure so prominently in the action. Scarves and similar cloaks went on sale as licensed products, but Stansborough also developed a high-end line of woolen products. Owner Cheryl Eldridge declared: "You can't put a price on walking up Fifth Avenue and seeing one of our garments in Donna Karan. We've hit the top end of the market in Australia, the UK and the US; we've opened a market in Italy and are working in Germany at the moment." She concludes, "The New Zealand image and *TLOTR* all helps. It's a real benchmark for us in terms of public profile. We're very lucky to be part of something as exciting as this."[42]

Rings also gave a boost to New Zealand's aspirations to develop its digital technology sector. Steve Regelous's Massive software has been widely used within the industry and is sold from its headquarters in New Zealand (with a Los Angeles branch). Less well known is a program created by *Rings* sound

Figure 38. After *The Return of the King* swept the Oscars, Deputy Principal Jill Holmstead had the idea for the students (ages nine and ten) at Miramar North School to create a banner for each of the eleven categories. Their banners were hung on central Miramar lampposts on 12 March 2004, not far from the Stone Street Studios. (Photograph by the author.)

editor John McKay. Developed for the trilogy, Virtual Katy (named for production assistant Katy Wood) allows sound tracks to be automatically changed to synchronize with images as they are reedited—a task that had been highly labor intensive when done by hand. One set of changes that took 6.8 hours to accomplish manually on *Rings* could be reduced to 3 minutes and 35 seconds.[43] The company is based in Wellington, with sales agents in several countries. Both programs are widely used within the film industry. In Voigt's opinion, New Zealand's creative and technical spheres in areas outside filmmaking have gained more confidence in their abilities to take on projects on an international level.

WELLYWOOD IN A GLOBAL AGE

Unquestionably Jackson and his colleagues have created a remarkable infrastructure and landmark films, and they are committed to continuing to work in New Zealand. The question is whether they can generate enough domestic films and bring in enough foreign projects to keep that expensive infrastructure busy.

Park Road Post inherited The Film Unit's large existing clientele. The Film Unit had worked on such major productions as *Vertical Limit, The Last Samurai,* and *Cast Away,* but it can attract a bevy of smaller productions like *Without a Paddle* (2004) as well as steady business from natural history films, TV series, short films, and commercials, from both New Zealand and abroad. Weta Digital, however, with its huge computing power, cannot keep working up to nearly its capacity with small films. After *Rings* it launched into work on some complex sequences, totaling around 300 shots, for *I, Robot* and some minor effects for *Van Helsing.* Those jobs provided three or four months of business. Milton Ngan says, "We're always on the lookout for more work, but we have to balance that out against the needs of Peter's next production." At one point of downtime between *Rings* and *Kong,* raw processing power, which costs thousands of dollars a month to keep running, was leased to other businesses or organizations on a short-term basis. Once *Kong* was ready to begin, other work was impossible. Even a facility like Weta Digital cannot handle two big projects at a time—one reason the firm did no effects for *The Lion, the Witch and the Wardrobe,* even though Weta Workshop provided the design, armor, and weapons for it.

By 2006, Weta Digital had clearly become part of the stable of high-end effects companies regularly called upon to work on major productions. In the summer of 2006, the *Hollywood Reporter* discussed how Twentieth Century Fox had been hard-pressed to make its 26 May release date for *X-Men: The Final Stand*: "The studio paid dearly to get elaborate visual effects from about six FX houses, including Weta Digital, finished in time." Weta created 178 shots for *X-Men*, most of them included in the climactic Alcatraz battle. Of the twelve companies that contributed effects to the film, Weta was second only to Hydraulx, which made 188 shots.[44]

In the wake of *Kong*, Jackson took on a number of effects-heavy projects, though he kept their schedules remarkably flexible, perhaps to allow for the possibility of Weta accepting commissions for other effects work. As early as April 2004, Jackson and Walsh began negotiations to personally acquire the rights to Alice Sebold's best seller, *The Lovely Bones*. They purchased them in January 2005, though a complete rough draft of the script was not completed until the summer of 2006. With no production or distribution company lined up, Jackson had no deadline for delivery of the completed film. A more intimate project than the blockbusters that filled the producer/director's slate, *The Lovely Bones*' depiction of a dead girl in heaven might still require effects comparable to the ones Jackson and Walsh had added to *Heavenly Creatures*.

In late 2005 Jackson and Walsh agreed to executive produce the movie adaptation of the video game "Halo," which would be made in New Zealand using the Miramar facilities. The pragmatics of keeping expensive facilities going and hundreds of employees in work presumably took precedence over Jackson's disinclination to produce films he was not directing. In early 2006, Walden Media, Beacon Pictures, and Revolution Studios announced that a children's fantasy novel, *The Waterhorse*, would be adapted into a film on the scale of *The Lion, the Witch and the Wardrobe*. It would start filming in New Zealand in May and would have its special effects done by Weta Workshop and Weta Digital.[45]

Beyond this activity, Jackson continued to acquire projects. In September 2006 there came a flurry of announcements. First he revealed that he would produce *Dambusters*, a remake of a British World War II film from 1954, *The Dam Busters*. Christian Rivers, storyboard and special-effects artist for *Rings*, would make his directorial debut. Although Universal and StudioCanal would cofinance the film, there was no deadline attached. About a week later Jackson made public his personal acquisition of Naomi Novik's "Temeraire" series of fantasy novels based on dragons fighting in the Napoleonic Wars. No details, including the schedule and whether Jackson would direct, had been planned. As we have already seen, at the end of the month Microsoft and Wingnut announced that they were teaming to create a games firm, Wingnut Interactive, though no specific projects were mentioned.[46]

While all this was happening, the 11–17 September issue of *Variety* carried a cover story on MGM's resumption of blockbuster production after its recent sale to Sony. Among the projects that chairman and CEO Harry Sloan described was "one or two installments of 'The Hobbit,' which Sloan hopes will be directed by Peter Jackson." Jackson quickly gave two major interviews on websites, declaring himself open to offers and even discussing briefly some ideas for adapting Tolkien's novel. Whether or not Jackson would be involved, the franchise had been revived.[47]

The Miramar filmmaking companies face increasing global competition as technology like the Fatpipe used for *Rings* makes sending sounds and images around the world faster and cheaper. The Large Budget Screen Production Grant scheme has already benefited big films like *The Last Samurai* and *The Lion, the Witch and the Wardrobe,* but other governments can offer incentives, too. Various tax breaks are available not only from countries but now from individual American states trying to lure Hollywood productions out of California. Even with the Large Budget scheme, the rise in New Zealand's currency in 2004 demonstrated how quickly a competitive advantage can shrink.

Jackson was not the first or only director to create a complete range of production facilities. George Lucas has done so at his Skywalker complex outside San Francisco and more recently at the Letterman Digital Arts Center in the Presidio. In his hometown of Austin, Texas, Robert Rodriguez has built a miniature version of an entire studio by exploiting new digital technologies that permit various tasks of postproduction like sound mixing, editing, and CGI work to be done on a home computer. Jackson has the distinction, however, of having built his filmmaking domain on an impressive scale without having previously produced a hit, so in some ways the accomplishment is more impressive. The director himself became a star as a result of *Rings'* success, and his reputation as a maverick against the Hollywood system gives Wellywood a high international profile.

In a more mundane way, however, new communications technology and the wide availability of sophisticated CGI equipment means that other complexes capable of handling entire film productions are being built or planned in far-flung locales. As more and more complexes combining shooting stages and modern postproduction facilities are built in countries around the world, Wellywood and all such centers will find themselves facing more competition for offshore productions.

Before *Rings, The Matrix* had been made in such a center. Sydney had sophisticated studio facilities at Fox Studios Australia, part of Rupert Murdoch's media empire. Many of the special effects were done by Australian companies, including Animal Logic, a firm housed within the Fox Studios. (Animal Logic also created a few effects for *Rings.*) Fox Studios Australia further demonstrated its capacity to host large-scale, technically complex productions at any stage from script to screen with *Moulin Rouge!* and the final two *Star Wars* episodes. More complexes of this sort, with postproduction technical abilities, will be built around the globe.

South Africa, for example, long a destination for location shooting because of its low costs, has made a move toward creating a large, state-of-the-art complex with eight soundstages and "digital production facilities." Dreamworld Film City, spearheaded by producer Anant Singh, was initially proposed in 2002 and planned to be built in 2005 and opened in early 2006. The government approved the plan in early 2004, and one of the backers claimed, "With this studio we could have made 'Lord of the Rings.'" The government added a rebate incentive scheme in July, hoping to lure in foreign projects. (With 40 percent unemployment, the country saw film as a possible boost to its economy.) Building began in August, but legal challenges and a lengthy study of the environmental impact brought it to a temporary halt. Finally, in August 2006 the project was officially launched, with building on the first phase to begin in early 2007. Four soundstages would be operable by 2008, but the rest of the infrastructure, including the postproduction facilities, would take even longer.[48] Similarly, Rotterdam is building an enormous media center, due to open in 2007, with facilities for many small companies, including animation, postproduction, and special effects.[49]

Other, older centers of production can add effects facilities to enhance their existing infrastructure. London's effects houses have lately been luring business away from even the biggest American firms. Cinesite, owned by Kodak, is based in Soho and was responsible for special effects in *Charlie and the Chocolate Factory, Harry Potter and the Goblet of Fire,* and *The Hitchhiker's Guide to the Galaxy* (all 2005). *Variety* declared in late 2004 that "U.S. shops like ILM and Digital Domain are being squeezed like never before by fast-rising competition from abroad, especially London."[50] In May 2006 Digital Domain was sold to an investment group. The high-pressure schedule demanded by effects-heavy films like *War of the Worlds* and *King Kong* (both 2005) necessitated big effects houses to outsource the more mundane tasks relating to digital effects to firms in places like India, Malaysia, and Singapore.[51]

As of 2006, a number of Asian countries were developing a significant postproduction sector. The success of South Korean cinema, which claimed about half of the domestic market, made the country a leader in the area. Hong Kong's leading CGI firm, Centro Digital Pictures, worked on both of Quentin

Tarantino's *Kill Bill* films (2003, 2004) and on Stephen Chow's successful export, *Kung Fu Hustle* (2004). The ease with which digital technology will make it possible to scatter postproduction tasks around the globe is exemplified by Zhang Yimou's *Curse of the Golden Flower* (2006), which had its digital intermediate scanned at Oriental Post (Bangkok), its sound and color grading done by Soundfirm (Australia and Beijing), and its special effects created by The Moving Picture Company (London) and Centro (Hong Kong).[52]

The traditionally sophisticated French postproduction sector initially suffered from the growing international competition (including firms like Weta Digital), but it is on the rise again. Buf Compagnie (founded in the mid-1980s) has contributed effects shots to *Harry Potter and the Goblet of Fire, Batman Begins,* and *The Matrix Revolutions.* Luc Besson's company, Digital Factory, provides state-of-the-art editing and sound facilities, and, like Park Road Post, includes "luxury lodging." Eclair created the digital effects for Jean-Pierre Jeunet's *A Very Long Engagement* and contributed postproduction services to films like Oliver Stone's *Alexander* (2004) and Spielberg's *Munich* (2005).[53]

With such an enormous investment in the new filmmaking infrastructure of New Zealand, Jackson and his team are well aware of the increasing competition as other production centers are built or expanded. The New Zealand dollar rose sharply during 2004, and Sue Thompson says she doubts whether at that point the trilogy would have been funded to shoot there. She emphasizes that the appeal for film projects to come in from abroad is not wholly dependent on currency fluctuations. "What we're finding is that the [South African] Rand's gone down, Romania and Czechoslovakia offer extremely cheap labor, which we cannot and will not compete with." Instead, Thompson says, New Zealand's strengths are in its diversity of landscapes, the flexibility of the newly upskilled workforce, and the quality of the new facilities. "One of the impacts of *Lord of the Rings* on The Film Unit as a facility was that their rigid quality standards and expectations of perfection have made The Film Unit a much better laboratory than it was four years ago." Voigt also considers the newly expert labor pool key: "I know that for *Cold Mountain* in Romania, they basically had to train them from the word go."

Whether for cost savings or to find a technically sophisticated set of facilities with skilled labor, more and more films are being shot outside the United States. Increasingly, they will be postproduced in the new CGI facilities that will be created, whether in traditional producing centers like Prague or places, like Wellington, that have little prior history of filmmaking.

This move abroad is not a vague threat beginning to take shape. It has already made a very significant dent in Hollywood-based production. In 2005, a study commissioned by the Screen Actors Guild and several other entertainment-industry craft organizations laid out the extent to which the making of films in other countries had cost those working in the traditional center of movie-making. Since 2000, feature film production abroad had cost the United States 47,000 jobs per year and roughly $23 billion in economic benefits. Although from 1998 to 2005 the total amount of spending on theatrical production had grown 30 percent, the American share dropped from $3.9 billion to $3.4 billion, a decline of 14 percent. During the same period, production spending abroad had gone from $1.6 billion in 1998 to $3.8 billion, a rise of 135 percent. The United States share of theatrical production income fell spectacularly, from 71 percent in 1998 to 47 percent in 2005. The study concludes that the American and California governments may have to introduce the sorts of tax and other incentives that other countries have had to resort to for years. For the first time since World War I, Hollywood is having to struggle to maintain its place as the Mecca of the filmmaking world.[54]

What will happen to Hollywood if more and more filmmaking moves abroad? I asked Osborne whether an increasing number of fully equipped production centers around the globe could lead to the point where there was very little production still happening in the United States. He replied, "Potentially that could happen. It's an interesting problem and a thorny one. My gut feeling is that it's somewhat cyclical. It depends on the strength and weakness of the American dollar. I think union regulations to some extent can chase production overseas." In particular, the Screen Actors Guild's attempts to protect American performers through regulations on their work overseas could backfire. "Right now the U.S. has a hold on the center of the financial organization of movies, and once you chase away the advantage of putting a movie together in L.A. away from the U.S., you've really lost the game, I think."

Jonathan Wolf, of the American Film Market, declares, "The studios produce only so that they can continue to distribute. They'd get out of the production business tomorrow if they were guaranteed a steady flow of product." With the spread of filmmaking centers, that steady product flow might well come from abroad. Perhaps the Los Angeles area eventually will be more centered on financing and distributing films than on physically making them. As *Rings* shows, an epic film not only can be made more cheaply abroad, but even, in the right circumstances, can be made better.

With so much stress being put on Jackson's commitment to New Zealand, I asked him if, had the *Nightmare on Elm Street* script he worked on back in 1991 been produced, he would have moved temporarily to Hollywood. He responded, "Yeah. From memory all the talk at that point was to shoot it there. And I had no track record at all, so you can't really insist on shooting in New Zealand." Given how things developed, the fact that Jackson's contribution to New Line's fading horror franchise never got made was another stroke of luck in the unlikely series of events that led to the making of *The Lord of the Rings* and to all its unimagined consequences.

FRANCHISES AND FILM ART

By now it should be clear that film franchises are not simply a sign that Hollywood's creative well has run dry. Franchises are a deliberate economic strategy aimed at maximizing the monetary worth of a studio's intellectual property. But do franchises have positive or negative effects on the world of filmmaking?

Some might claim that the modern franchise film is so commercialized that it blends into a mishmash of branded products and ceases to have a distinct cultural identity. I don't think there is any reason to believe this. The film is the center of the franchise, the product without which the others could not exist. Modern media culture has hardly confused us so much that we can't distinguish the movie from the products that surround it. Arguably people today are far more savvy than earlier generations about the economic connections between the entertainment they consume and the related items that they buy. Besides, when we enter a theater, we still see the film on a screen, isolated from all the related items for sale in stores or given away in fast-food restaurants or available on the Internet. A moviegoer can choose to ignore all the other commercial products generated by a franchise and simply concentrate purely on the film itself. Yet even a moviegoer who embraces those products, playing the licensed video game and wearing branded clothing, can still recognize viewing the film as a distinct experience.

Another, more serious claim has been that globalization and the domination of world screens by big-budget Hollywood movies increasingly stifle diversity of filmmaking and homogenize what audiences have available to see. One can always find evidence to bolster such a belief, but one can equally find evidence to refute it—suggesting that the truth lies somewhere in between. Certainly Hollywood films consistently make up about half of what people watch on cinema screens around the world. Yet even in this franchise age, a great variety of films occupy the other half. Only two months before I finished writing this book, the Oscars for 2005 films were handed out. In the Best Animated Feature category, a quintessentially British film, *Wallace & Gromit: The Curse of the Were-Rabbit,* won against a film by a long-revered

Japanese animator (*Howl's Moving Castle*) and another by a Hollywood eccentric (*Tim Burton's Corpse Bride*). A diverse trio, despite the fact that these three films were distributed in the United States by DreamWorks, Disney, and Warner Bros., respectively. (Hollywood is happy to distribute just about any kind of film, however unusual, providing that it makes money.)

The growing split between high-budget event movies and independent films also argues for diversity. Four of the five Best Picture nominees for 2005 were small independents, and even *Munich* was a relatively low-budget, personal project for Steven Spielberg. America is getting its first chain of art-house multiplexes with the formation of Sundance Theaters by Robert Redford. Independent and foreign-language films have their own cable channels. In general, a greater variety of films is available to most viewers than in the past. DVDs have made previously obscure or rare films of every historical period easily available. Film festivals have proliferated, providing a major separate type of venue for works that otherwise would not be shown outside their own countries. Nations that currently can boast of healthy film industries include South Korea, Iran, and Denmark, and if they eventually decline, others will arise. Most people may simply ignore all these options, but such developments would not have occurred were there not a significant market for alternatives to Hollywood tentpole films.

The Lord of the Rings is certainly not a typical film franchise. Still, it should caution us against making sweeping assumptions about franchises as such. *Rings* proved a boon for overseas distributors and their local film industries. Fans created their own multifaceted culture around this highly commercial project. And the trilogy has left in its wake a confident, skilled group of filmmakers in a small, isolated country. All these effects and more suggest that there's more to franchises than meets the eye. The best of them can even, as Peter Jackson would say, be fun.

NOTES

INTRODUCTION: Sequel-itis

1. Rayner Unwin, *George Allen & Unwin: A Remembrancer* (Ludlow: Merlin Unwin, 1999), 96–97.

2. Alynda Wheat, "What to Watch," *EW* (17 Dec. 2004): 75.

3. Glen Schaefer, "B.C. Boy Became Lord of the Brush," *Canada.com* (17 June 2005): www.canada.com/vancouver/theprovince/news/etoday/story.html?id=320c 446e-76ca-4a17-a0d9–33f582a109fd&page=1.

4. To the best of my knowledge, there were three such recordings, all issued by Caedmon: "Poems and Songs of Middle Earth" (TC 1231, 1967), "J. R. R. Tolkien Reads and Sings His The Hobbit and The Fellowship of the Ring" (TC 1477, 1975), and "J. R. R. Tolkien Reads and Sings His The Lord of the Rings: The Two Towers/ The Return of the King" (TC 1478, 1975). The first includes Donald Swann performing his song cycle, "The Road Goes Ever On." The latter was published as a book by Houghton Mifflin in 1967 and in a revised edition in 1978.

5. Ethan Gilsdorf, "Lord of the Gold Ring," *Boston Globe* (16 Nov. 2003): www .boston.com/movies/articles/2003/11/16/lord_of_the_gold_ring.

CHAPTER 1: Prudent Aggression

1. Melissa J. Perenson, "Director Peter Jackson Proves to Be the Lord of *The Fellowship of the Ring*," *SciFi.com* (2001): www.scifi.com/sfw/issue244/interview.html.

2. Humphrey Carter, ed., *The Letters of J. R. R. Tolkien* (Boston: Houghton Mifflin, 1981), 274.

3. Ibid., 260–61, 270–71.

4. Rayner Unwin, *George Allen & Unwin: A Remembrancer* (Ludlow: Merlin Unwin Books, 1999), 107–10, 128–30.

5. See Denis O'Dell, *At the Apple's Core: The Beatles from the Inside* (London: Peter Owen, 2002), 90–94, 103–4; Tony Bramwell, *Magical Mystery Tours: My Life with the Beatles* (New York: Thomas Dunne, 2005), 250–51.

6. Unwin, *George Allen & Unwin,* 130.

7. A good overview of Zaentz's career was published as a supplement, "Legends and Groundbreakers: Saul Zaentz," by *Variety* (23–29 Sept. 2002): B1–B10. When I began my research, all the trademarks that Tolkien Enterprises claims were listed on its website, www.tolkien-ent.com/new/index.html; this list has since been removed, but the Middle-earth Role-playing Community has posted it: www.merp.com/legal/telist.

The second half of *Rings* was made as an animated TV movie, *The Return of the King,* by Rankin/Bass Productions in 1980. The firm had also done a TV adaptation of *The Hobbit* in 1977.

8. Information on *Bad Taste* comes primarily from Ken Hammon, "The Making of Bad Taste," *The Bastards Have Landed* (n.d.), tbhl.theonering.net/badtaste/cast_Hammon_makingof.htm; and Simon Beattie, "My Wonderful Career," *Evening Post* (Wellington) (19 Dec. 2001): 11.

9. Ron Magid and David E. Williams, "New Zealand's New Digital Age," *American Cinematographer* (Aug. 1996): 55; Mark Cotta Vaz, "*The Frighteners:* The Thrill of the Haunt," *Cinefex* (Sept. 1996): 35; Jody Duncan, "The Beauty in the Beasts," *Cinefex* (Aug. 1993): 56, 60.

10. Gavin Edwards, "Lord of the Oscars," *Rolling Stone* (4 Mar. 2004): 33.

11. "*The Lord of the Rings: The Fellowship of the Ring,*" *Variety.com* (19 Dec. 2001): www.variety.com/index.asp?layout=studiosystems&ss_view=s_s_project&mode=allcredits&project_id=124580.

12. There was remarkably little press coverage of the *Rings* project in its pre–New Line days. Ain't It Cool News, a fan website, reported the possible Miramax pull-out in "Lord of the Rings!!! Does Miramax Lack Nerve?" (23 Feb. 1998): www.aintitcoolnews.com/display.cgi?id=682.

13. "*The Lord of the Rings: The Return of the King,*" *Creative Screenwriting* (Jan./Feb. 2004): 63.

14. James Stewart, *Disney War* (New York: Simon and Schuster, 2005), 301, 303.

15. Peter Biskind, *Down and Dirty Pictures: Miramax, Sundance, and the Rise of Independent Film* (New York: Simon and Schuster, 2004), 245. See also Garry Maddox, "Director Nearly Lost the 'Ring,'" *smh.com* (14 Mar. 2005): www.smh.com.au/article/2005/03/13/1110649055497.html?oneclick=true.news.bbc.co.uk;1/hi/technology/4333871.stm.

16. Benedict Carver, "Turnaround Paving Roads to Success," *Variety.com* (5 Aug. 1999): www.variety.com/story.asp?l=story&a=VR1117750089&c=13.

17. Ian Nathan, "*The Lord of the Rings:* The Untold Story," *Empire* (Jan. 2005): 122.

18. For Jackson's own description of Miramax's conditions, see his appearance on *The Charlie Rose Show* (22 Feb. 2002).

19. "New Line: Indie Unit of AOL TW Sticks to Its Roots Despite *Lord of the Rings* Windfall," *VDM* (22 Apr. 2002): 11. See also Josh Young, "Lights! Camera! Bigamy?" *EW* (11 July 1997): 13, and Dan Cox, "New Line, Rock on the Block," *Variety* (22–28 July 1996): 10.

20. Bill Higgins, "AFMA Raves over Shaye," *Variety.com* (22 Feb. 2002): www .variety.com/story.asp?1=story&a=VR1117861242&c=13.

21. Dan Madsen, "A Fine Madness," *LotRFCOMM* (Oct.–Nov. 2003): 51.

22. Patrick Goldstein, "A Studio Executive Tries His Hand at Wizardry," *Los Angeles Times* (11 Dec. 2001): F4.

23. *The Charlie Rose Show* (22 Feb. 2002).

24. Madsen, "A Fine Madness," 52; David Ansen and Jeff Giles, "The New Visionaries," *Newsweek* (9 Feb. 2004): 69.

25. I am grateful to Peter Jackson for giving me permission to watch the pitch tape, entitled *The Lord of the Rings* (produced by Wingnut Films), and to Jamie Selkirk for arranging a viewing at Park Road Post (7 Dec. 2004).

26. Goldstein, "A Studio Executive Tries His Hand at Wizardry," F4.

27. Jess Cagle, "Lure of the Rings," *Time* (2 Dec. 2002): 89.

28. Madsen, "A Fine Madness," 52.

29. John Forde, "Force of Hobbit: Conquering Cannes, Mining Moria and Partying at Hobbit Height," *E!Online* (15 May 2001): www.eonline.com/Features/Specials/ Lordrings/Word/010515.html.

30. John Yeabsley and Ian Duncan, *Scoping the Lasting Effects of "The Lord of the Rings": Report to the New Zealand Film Commission* (Wellington: New Zealand Institute of Economic Research, April 2002), 5.

31. "Page to Screen," *Bravo* (Dec. 2002).

32. Brett Pulley, "Hollywood's New King Kong," *Forbes* (5 July 2004): 108.

33. The $310 million figure appears in Keith Collins, "A Brief History," *Variety* "Showmen of the Year" Supplement (23–29 Aug. 2004): 26; Paul Voigt, in his "*The Lord of the Rings* Trilogy—Leveraging 2001–2004—Final Report" (Investment New Zealand, 5 Sept. 2004), says the trilogy cost "more than US$320 million"; $350 million was the figure I encountered most often: Justin Oppelaar, "New Line's Billion Dollar Bet," *Variety* (20–26 Jan. 2003): 11; Stewart, *Disney War,* 304; and Sharon Waxman, "Triumph of 'The King' in Hollywood," *International Herald Tribune* (2 Mar. 2004): 12.

34. In an interview done shortly after the release of *Fellowship,* Jackson compared its roughly $90 million budget with that of *Pearl Harbor,* which was made for $150 million. Based on the size of the cast and the number of effects shots, he estimated that *Fellowship* would have cost $180 million to make in the United States. Multiplying that by three gives $540 million, almost exactly the figure that I have suggested for the trilogy's theatrical versions based on the comparison with *Titanic.* See

Scott Collura, "Lord of the Cinema Rings—Part Two," *Cinescape.com* (8 Jan. 2002): www.cinescape.com/0/Editorial.asp?aff_id=08&this_cat=Movies&action=page&obj _id=32054#.

35. Goldstein, "A Studio Executive Tries His Hand at Wizardry," F5.

36. David Rooney, "The Brothers Grim," *Variety.com* (13 June 2004): www.variety .com/story.asp?1=story&a=VR1117906352&c=1019. This passage was not included in the print version of this article.

37. Peter Jackson on *The Charlie Rose Show* (22 Feb. 2002).

38. This press release and, indeed, the entire News section have been removed from the film's official website. The press release is archived on some fan sites, however, and on Ain't It Cool News it is accompanied by Harry Knowles's introduction. See "LORD OF THE RINGS. . . . It's Official!!!!!!!!!! This will be a day long remembered in the annals of geek history!!!" AICN (24 Aug. 1998): www.aintitcoolnews.com/display.cgi?id=1960.

39. "Peter Jackson Answers THE GEEKS!!! 20 Questions about Lord of the Rings," AICN (31 Dec. 1998): www.aint-it-cool-news.com/lordoftherings2.html.

40. Sean Astin, *There and Back Again: An Actor's Tale* (New York: St. Martin's, 2004), 103–4.

41. The fullest information on shooting locations is provided by Ian Brodie's *The Lord of the Rings Location Guidebook,* rev. ed. (Auckland: HarperCollins, 2003).

42. Dana Harris, "Rings' Fling Brings Payday," *Variety* (25 Feb.–3 Mar. 2002): 32.

43. Steve Galloway, "Innovative Voices," *HR* (Nov. 2002): 18.

44. "Sunday Morning Shootout," *American Movie Classics* (Feb. 2004).

45. Cagle, "Lure of the Rings," 89.

46. "New Line: Indie Unit of AOL TW Sticks to Its Roots Despite *Lord of the Rings* Windfall," *VDM* (22 Apr. 2002): 11.

47. Mittweg referred in his letter to *Armageddon,* a fifty-five-minute rough cut of which had been previewed for reporters at Cannes in 1998. That film went on to considerable success, but the Cannes screening was something of a disaster, with reporters laughing and Bruce Willis afterward trading testy words with them at the press conference.

48. Forde, "Force of Hobbit: Conquering Cannes, Mining Moria and Partying at Hobbit Height."

49. This nonglare version of the shot can also be seen on the back of the theatrical version *Fellowship* DVD box, as well as in magazine ads for the DVD and other products.

50. Nathan, "*The Lord of the Rings:* The Untold Story," 128.

51. Adam Dawtrey, "Will 'Lord' Ring New Line's Bell?" *Variety* (21–27 May 2001): 66.

52. Arathorn II, trans., "The Canal+ Interview with PJ," TORN (11 May 2001): www.theonering.net/archives/cannes/5/08.01–511.01.

53. For an evocative, detailed account of the party by one of the webmasters who

attended, see Calisuri's "Yesterday I Dreamt I Was in Middle-earth," TORN (14 May 2001): www.theonering.net/perl/newsview/11/989879749 and "I Dreamt I Was in Middle-earth . . ." (Part II), (20 May 2001): www.theonering.net/archives/cannes/5.12.01–5.20.01; for photos of the party (and one of Ian McKellen during the press junket), see www.theonering.net/scrapbook/oldsource/Ringer_Spy_Elfstone; for pictures of the party pass and the contents of the swag bag, see www.theonering.net/movie/cannes2001gal03.html.

54. Quickbeam, "The Spectacular Cannes Footage," TORN (1 Sept. 2001): green books.theonering.net/quickbeam/files/090101.

55. Dan Cox and Jill Goldsmith, "Inside Move: Body Count at New Line," *Variety.com* (31 Jan. 2001): www.variety.com/storyasp?1=story&a=VR1117792997 &c=13.

56. Dana Harris and Adam Dawtrey, "Can B.O. Postman 'Ring' Twice?" *Variety* (26 Nov.–2 Dec. 2001): 1.

57. Goldstein, "A Studio Executive Tries His Hand at Wizardry," F5.

58. Unless otherwise specified, all box-office figures are from www.boxoffice mojo.com.

59. The brief release of the extended version of *Fellowship* in December 2003 as a lead-up to the release of the third part brought its domestic gross to $314,776,170.

60. Don Groves and Adam Dawtrey, "Hogwarts & Hobbits in Global Grab," *Variety* (11–17 Feb. 2002): 1.

61. Jonathan Bing and Timothy M. Gray, "Kudoscape Shifts," *Variety* (3–9 Mar. 2003): 73.

62. See the beginning of "The Passing of an Age" on the second disc. Lest anyone think that this was simply a publicity stunt, New Line would never have voluntarily agreed to this so far in advance and with the financial details unresolved. During the spring of 2003, negotiations over such issues as who would pay for the renovation of the Empire Theatre became so heated that both New Line and the city of Wellington threatened to cancel the event.

63. Around 64 percent of the gross for all three parts of *Rings* came from outside the United States and Canada, a relatively high percentage even in an age when foreign markets have become more lucrative for American films. As of April 2006, on a list of top-grossing films domestically, *Return* was number 8, *Towers* number 12, and *Fellowship* number 17. Worldwide they appear at number 2, 4, and 10, respectively. In figures adjusted for inflation, the domestic ranking for the trilogy falls to 48, 57, and 72, with *Gone with the Wind* still number 1 (and *Titanic* number 6). In an industry where tens of thousands of films have been released, those figures still seem fairly respectable.

64. Even *Entertainment Weekly*, which accurately predicted virtually all of the winners, put *Return*'s chances at a screenplay Oscar at only 14 percent, fourth behind *Mystic River, Seabiscuit*, and even *American Splendor*. "And the Precious Goes to . . . ," *EW* (27 Feb. 2004): 33.

65. "Bets Are Off on Rings Finale," *Guardian Unlimited* (25 Feb. 2004): film
.guardian.co.uk/oscars2004/story/0,14064,1155756,00.html.

66. Sheigh Crabtree, "Tech Wizards Feted with Oscars," *HR* (17–23 Feb. 2004): 73.

67. "Showmen of the Year: Bob Shaye & Michael Lynne," supplement to *Variety*
(23–29 Aug. 2004).

CHAPTER 2: Not Your Father's Tolkien

1. "AV Club," *The Onion* (17 Apr. 2002): www.theonionavclub.com/avclub3814/
avfeature_3814.html.

2. Louis Menand, "Goblin Market," *New York Review* (17 Jan. 2002): 8–9.

3. Frank Ahrens, "'Rings' Has Two Targets," *washingtonpost.com* (19 Dec. 2001):
www.washingtonpost.com/ac2/wp-dyn/A62589–2001Dec18.

4. J. R. R. Tolkien, *The Lord of the Rings,* fiftieth anniversary edition (Boston:
Houghton Mifflin, 2004), xxiv.

5. Recently Warner Home Video has released a five-DVD set of MGM "Motion Picture Masterpieces" (2006), which lacks *Romeo and Juliet* but has *Pride and
Prejudice, David Copperfield, A Tale of Two Cities, Treasure Island,* and one nonlit-
erary item, *Marie Antoinette.*

6. See, for example, Nina Rehfeld, "The Next Reel," *GreenCine* (18 Dec. 2002):
www.greencine.com/article?action=view&articleID=62&.

7. David E. Williams, "All Hail the King," *Cinefantastique* (Feb./Mar. 2004): 26.

8. David Bratman, "Summa Jacksonica: A Reply to Defenses of Peter Jackson's
The Lord of the Rings Films, after St. Thomas Aquinas," in *Tolkien on Film: Essays on
Peter Jackson's "The Lord of the Rings,"* ed. Janet Brennan Croft (Altadena, CA:
Mythopoeic Press, 2004), 29, 43. Bratman assumes that New Line was willing to risk
just about any amount of money on *Rings* and that Jackson perversely passed up his
opportunity to exploit that for all it was worth and adapt the novel as literally as
possible.

9. First two quotations from the "Weta Digital" section (track 15) of the second
supplemental disc, *Fellowship* EE DVD; the last two are from director's and writers'
audio commentary on disc 2 of the film in the same edition, during the Cave Troll
and Balrog scenes.

10. *Return* EE DVD supplement, disc 4, track 2, "Music for Middle-earth."

11. Richard Taylor, designers' commentary, *Return* EE DVD, disc 1, track 35.

12. Stephen Galloway, "Best Picture," *HR* (Mar. 2003): 14.

13. "A Change of Hobbit," *Cinefantastique* (20 Nov. 2003): http://64.5.52.62/
%7ecfqcom/nuked/modules.php?name=News&file=article&sid=103.

14. Mike Hodgkinson, "Elf Portrait," *Arena* (Jan. 2003): 150. Bloom also com-
pares his character to a samurai in Iain Blair, "Orlando Bloom: Legolas," *Total Film*
(Jan. 2003): 65.

15. Guy Haley and Jayne Dearsley, "101 Reasons Why You *Must* See *The Two Towers*," *SFX* (Oct. 2002): 72; Iain Blair, "Ian McKellen: Gandalf the White," *Total Film* (Jan. 2003): 56; Ian Nathan, "It Is a Dark Time for the Rebellion," *Empire* (Jan. 2003): 104. For similar quotations using the word, see Richard Galpin, "Hot Thespian Action," *Arena* (Jan. 2003): 142, and Christelle Laffin, "'Le seigneur des anneaux': La saga continue," *Premiere* (France) (Oct. 2002): supplement, p. 4.

16. See especially the Gandalf cover, *Empire* (Jan. 2003).

17. Nathan, "It Is a Dark Time for the Rebellion," 104.

18. John Forde, "Force of Hobbit: Out of the Closet with Hobbits, Elves and Wizards," *E! Online* (1 June 2003): www.eonline.com/Features/Specials/Lordrings/Location/000601.html.

19. Peter Jackson, "My Favourite Location," in Ian Brodie, *"The Lord of the Rings" Location Guidebook,* rev. ed. (Auckland: HarperCollins, 2003), 119. Jackson makes similar remarks in the "New Zealand as Middle-earth" section of disc 3 of the *Towers* EE DVD.

20. Examples of journals devoting whole issues to extensive, informed explication of *Rings* are *"Le Seigneur des Anneaux," Dossiers Secrets* (Oct.–Nov. 2004) and *"Der Herr der Ringe: Die Rückkehr des Königs," Blockbuster* (2003).

21. Jan Stuart, "Script Magic," *Newsday.com* (23 Mar. 2003): www.newsday.com/templates/mis/printstory.jsp?slug+ny%2.

22. *"The Lord of the Rings: The Return of the King," Creative Screenwriting* 11, 1 (Jan./Feb. 2004): 62.

23. Dan Madsen, "The Storytellers," *LotRFCOMM* 18 (Dec. 2004–Jan. 2005): 28–29.

24. See www.theonering.com/movies/changes_index.cfm. As of October 2005, Ancalagon's list is still on The One Ring.com, though it has been revised to reflect its status as a historical document.

25. Nina Rehfield, "The Next Reel," *GreenCine* (18 Dec. 2002): www.greencine.com/article?action=view&articleID=62&.

26. The director's/writers' commentary track on the *Return* EE DVD discusses some of these changes and some others: Frodo sending Sam home, track 27; why Arwen is dying because the Ring has not been destroyed, track 30; the fact that Éowyn is not disguised as a male soldier named Dernhelm, track 34; and Gimli saying that the Army of the Dead should not be released from their pledge, track 55. A major interview with the three writers, "The Lord of the Rings: The Return of the King," in *Creative Screenwriting,* includes their rationales for other changes: why Gollum falls into the Crack of Doom because Frodo is fighting him rather than because he is simply capering about in joy over having the Ring at last (p. 67); why the scene of the Gondorean and Rohirrim troops fighting outside the Black Gate is intercut with the scene of the Ring's destruction (p. 67); and why the character of Gothmog was considerably expanded (p. 64). Jackson talks about the addition of Lurtz in Jon B. Snyder, "Update with Peter Jackson," *LotRFCOMM* 1 (Feb.–Mar. 2002): 20.

27. Kathy A. McDonald, "Philippa Boyens," *Variety.com* (12 Oct. 2000): www
.variety.com/story.asp?l=story&a=VR1117787647&c=13; "Page to Screen," *Bravo*
(Dec. 2001).

28. See, for example, Linda Segar, *Making a Good Script Great* (New York: Dodd,
Mead, 1987), 160.

29. In his book *Everything Bad Is Good for You: How Today's Popular Culture Is
Actually Making Us Smarter* (New York: Riverhead, 2005), Steven Johnson argues
that modern film, TV, video games, and other narrative forms have actually become
more cognitively challenging than in earlier years, citing the large number of characters in *Rings* as part of his evidence (126–27).

30. Scriptwriting expert Christopher Vogel has discussed some of the unconventional aspects of *Fellowship*'s narrative in "Running Rings around Hollywood,"
Scriptwriter (May 2002): 18–20.

31. Peter Jackson, director's/writers' commentary track, *Return* EE DVD, disc 2,
track 75.

32. Annie Collins and Jamie Selkirk, postproduction commentary track, *Return*
EE DVD, disc 2, track 17.

33. See Peter Krämer's "Would You Take Your Child to See This Film? The Cultural and Social Work of the Family-Adventure Movie," in *Contemporary Hollywood
Cinema,* ed. Steve Neale and Murray Smith (London: Routledge, 1998), 294–311.

CHAPTER 3: Handcrafting a Blockbuster

1. Dan Madsen, "A Fine Madness," *LotRFCOMM* 11 (Oct.–Nov. 2003): 55.

2. Lawrence French, "Looking over Middle-earth," *Starlog* (Feb. 2004): 58.

3. Cast commentary, *Return* EE DVD, disc 1, ca. 30 minutes.

4. In his documentary on the making of *The Frighteners,* he remarked, in something of an understatement, "I don't regard storyboards as the Bible." Peter Jackson,
The Making of "The Frighteners" (director's cut, Universal, 2005).

5. Grant Major, designers' commentary, *Return* EE DVD, disc 1, track 29.

6. Smilin' Jack Ruby, "Tales from the Junket Circuit: *The Return of the King,* Part
Five," *CHUD.com* (16 Dec. 2003): www.chud.com/news/dec03/dec17junket.php3.

7. Ian Nathan, "Peter Jackson," *Empire* (Jan. 2004): 89.

8. Charles Lyons and Dana Harris, "New 'Rings' Master," *Variety.com* (22 May
2001): www.variety.com/story.asp?l=story&a=VR1117799902&c=18; "New Line Cinema Names Russell Schwartz President, Domestic Theatrical Marketing," New Line
Cinema (22 May 2001): www.newline.com/press/2001/0522_schwartz.shtml. Technically, Schwartz did not take over until 1 June, but he, rather than Nimziki, was
present at Cannes in mid-May for the preview and party.

9. Jody Duncan, Don Shay, and Joe Fordham, "State of the Art: A Cinefex 25th
Anniversary Forum," *Cinefex* 100 (Jan. 2005): 105.

10. Kevin Goetz (Culver City), e-mail message to the author (18 Nov. 2005).

11. David Bordwell, *The Way Hollywood Tells It* (Berkeley: University of California Press, 2006), 58–59.

12. Humphrey Carter, ed., *The Letters of J. R. R. Tolkien* (Boston: Houghton Mifflin, 1981), 248.

13. See plates 25, 41, 45, 46, and 47 of *Pictures by J. R. R. Tolkien* (Boston: Houghton Mifflin, 1979).

14. E-mail message to the author from René van Rossenberg (Leiden) (3 Nov. 2004): www.tolkienshop.com.

15. Sketches and paintings by Lee, Howe, and other artists appear in three uniform volumes assembled by Gary Russell: *"The Lord of the Rings": The Art of "The Fellowship of the Ring"* (Boston: Houghton Mifflin, 2002), with the parallel volumes appearing in 2002 and 2003. See also Alan Lee, *"The Lord of the Rings" Sketchbook* (Boston: Houghton Mifflin, 2005).

16. The various *Rings* film tie-in books reproduce only the sketches and drawings made specifically for the film. Some of the Lee and Howe paintings that I am describing here have been reproduced so often that it is impossible to cite all instances. Apart from Houghton Mifflin's various illustrated editions of the novel, Lee's and Howe's paintings are most readily available in these sources (all part of the book-based franchise that I mentioned in the introduction): *"The Lord of the Rings" Poster Collection: Six Paintings by Alan Lee* (1991; London: HarperCollins, 1999); *Myth & Magic: The Art of John Howe* (London: HarperCollins, 2001); *John Howe: Sur les terres de Tolkien* (Nantes: Office régional culturel de Champagne-Ardenne and Librairie l'Atalante, 2002); *Realms of Tolkien: Images of Middle-earth* (New York: HarperPrism, 1996); and *Tolkien's World: Paintings of Middle-earth* (London: HarperCollins, 1992).

17. Francis K. Lalumière, "Conceptual Artist Alan Lee," *LotRFCOMM* 1 (Feb.– Mar. 2002): 54.

18. Calisuri, "Cannes Footage: Detail," *TheOneRing.net* (17 May 2001): www .theonering.net/archives/cannes/5.12.01–5.20.01.

19. Smilin' Jack Ruby, "Tales from the Junket Circuit." "PJ Approved" stamps appear in the graphic design of the "clipboard" holding the DVDs in *King Kong: Peter Jackson's Production Diaries* (Universal, 2005).

20. This and many of the other aspects of design that I discuss here are treated in great detail in the supplements to the three extended-version DVD sets.

21. Nicole Curin-Birch, "Precious Metals," *Air New Zealand* (Dec. 2003): 14, 17.

22. Carolyn Enting, "Creating Middle-earth," *Variety* (16–22 Dec. 2002): 28.

23. Peter Lobard, "Aged to Perfection," *LotRFCOMM* 15 (June–July 2004): 46.

24. Designers' track, *Return* EE DVD, disc 1, track 14.

25. Dan Madsen, "Riding into Cinematic History," *LotRFCOMM* 11 (Oct.–Nov. 2003): 35.

26. Quoted in Carla Atkinson, "Elven Armor and Weaponry," *LotRFCOMM* 8 (Apr.–May 2004): 55.

27. Chris Smith, *"The Lord of the Rings": Weapons and Warfare* (Boston: Houghton Mifflin, 2003), 119.

28. See Galadhorn, "Mazarbul Wall Inscriptions: Languages in the *Lord of the Rings* Movies" (n.d.): http://home.planet.nl/~raas0056/mazarbul/, and links in Ryszard Derdzinski, "Other Inscriptions" (n.d.): www.elvish.org/gwaith/movie_otherinscr .htm. Salo's contribution is linked on the latter page as "Gabil gund Mazarbul" (30 Nov. 2002).

29. His book *A Gateway to Sindarin: A Grammar of an Elvish Language from J. R. R. Tolkien's "Lord of the Rings"* appeared in 2004 (Salt Lake City: University of Utah Press).

30. Daniel Falconer discusses his collaboration with Salo in devising the weaponry designs in "The Languages of Middle-earth," *LotRFCOMM* 3 (June–July 2002): 20–21.

31. From three e-mail messages, 23, 25, and 29 March 1999. My thanks to David Salo for providing me with the relevant excerpts from these messages and for John Howe's permission to quote from the ones he wrote.

32. For a very technical account of the software and hardware used for *Rings*, see Barbara Robertson, "The Big and the Sméagol," *Computer Graphics World* (Jan. 2004): egw.pennnet.com/Articles/Article_Display.cfm?Section=Articles&Subsection=Display &Article_ID=196304.

33. Sheigh Crabtree, "AMPAS Sci-Tech Taps 9 for Nods," *HR* (13–19 Jan. 2004): 61.

34. Catherine Lopresto, "Mailbaggins," *LotRFCOMM* 8 (Apr.–May 2003): 9.

35. Steve O'Hagen, "A Lust for Life," *SI* (3 June 2005): 8.

36. Arthur De Vany, *Hollywood Economics: How Extreme Uncertainty Shapes the Film Industry* (London: Routledge, 2004), 6.

37. *Return* EE DVD, disc 4, "The Passing of an Age," supplement.

CHAPTER 4: Flying Billboards and FAQs

1. Stephen Galloway, "Where the Money Went," *HR* (20–26 May 2003): S-9–S-10, S-12.

2. Angela Phipps Towle, "They're with the Brand," *HR* (18–24 May 2004): S-10.

3. "Chrysler and New Line Home Entertainment Announce Promotion DVD and VHS Release of 'The Lord of the Rings: The Two Towers,'" *Yahoo! Finance* (21 Aug. 2003): biz.yahoo.com/prnews/030821/deth004_1.html.

4. Frank Ahrens, "'Rings' Has Two Targets," *washingtonpost.com* (19 Dec. 2001): www.washingtonpost.com/ac2-wp-dyn/A62589–2001Dec18; and Gordon J. Paddison, "Designing the Marketing Program for The Lord of the Rings," in Rafi A. Mohammed, Robert J. Fisher, Bernard J. Jaworski, and Gordon J. Paddison, *Internet Marketing: Building Advantage in the Networked Economy* (Boston: McGraw-Hill/Irwin, 2004), 600–601. For images of Burger King products and information on

other partnership activities, see "The Lord of the Rings: Fellowship of the Ring," *Hollywood FYI* (6 Aug. 2002): www.hollywoodfyi.com/lordoftherings.html.

5. Tehanu, "How Many 'Lord of the Onion Rings' Jokes Have You Heard?" TheOneRing.net (16 Nov. 2001), www.theonering.net/perl/newsview/1/1005952352; for New Line's press release announcing the partnership, see "Return of the Burger King?" TheOneRing.net (31 May 2001), www.theonering.net/perl/newsview/8/991317186.

6. Minorbird, "Final LOTR Flight," TORN (24 Oct. 2004): www.theonering .net/archives/main_news/10.21.04–10.27.04.

7. "Star Wars," *Variety* (30 Aug.–5 Sept. 2004): 1.

8. Wilson Dizard Jr., *Old Media New Media: Mass Communications in the Information Age* (New York: Addison Wesley Longman, 2000), 1, 82, 89.

9. Edward Jay Epstein, *The Big Picture: The New Logic of Money and Power in Hollywood* (New York: Random House, 2005), 82–84. See the *Columbia Journalism Review* online's "Who Owns What" pages for extensive listings of entertainment industry conglomerates and their holdings: www.cjr.org/tools/owners/.

10. *The Entertainment Weekly The Lord of the Rings Ultimate Viewer's Guide* (May 2004).

11. Epstein, *The Big Picture,* 33–34.

12. Nicole LaPorte and Bill Higgins, "Clash of the Kudos," *Variety* (10–16 Dec. 2004): 1, 67.

13. Geoffrey Macnab, "The PR Campaign" (brackets in original); Denis Seguin, "The Persuaders"; and Geoffrey Macnab, "The Critics," all *SI* (19 Nov. 2004): 23, 25.

14. Dan Madsen, "Update with Peter Jackson," *LotRFCOMM* 18 (Dec. 2004–Jan. 2005): 18.

15. Costa Botes, "The Making of *The Lord of the Rings: The Fellowship of the Ring,*" program, *Telecom 33 Wellington Film Festival 2004* (Wellington: New Zealand Film Festival Trust, 2004), 123.

16. Tehanu, "LOTR Behind the Scenes," TORN (9 June 2004): www.theonering .net/perl/newsview/8/1094504331. The same program was shown in various New Zealand cities, with Tehanu seeing it in Auckland in June.

17. Thomas K. Arnold, "New Line Refreshes 'Rings' with 3 New DVD Packages," *HR* (22 June 2006): 21.

18. Arden returned to make several making-of promotional films for *King Kong.* See the company website, www.ardenentertainment.com/news4.html.

19. None of these programs has been released on DVD.

20. My thanks to Roxane Gajadhar for helping me sort all this out via e-mail (16 Apr. 2006).

21. Philip Wakefield, "Movies: One DVD to Rule Them All," *stuff* (7 Jan. 2005): www.stuff.co.nz/stuff/0,2106,3149931a1860,00.html.

22. Ty Braswell, "In Search of QEIB: Gordon Paddison Interview," *Imedia Connection* (8 May 2003): www.imediaconnection.com/scripts/printver.asp; Aliya Stern-

stein, "New Line Online," *Variety.com* (22 Aug. 2004): www.variety.com/article/VR1117909436?categoryid=1757&c=1.

23. One press swag bag associated with *Return* included a copy of the third volume of Tolkien's novel (with a cover photo of Viggo Mortensen as Aragorn); a paperback copy of Brian Sibley's tie-in book, *The Lord of the Rings: The Making of the Movie Trilogy; The Lord of the Rings: The Return of the King Photo Guide* (aimed at children but providing a handy rundown of the plot for reporters); Jude Fisher's *The Lord of the Rings: The Return of the King Visual Companion;* a PlayStation 2 version of "The Lord of the Rings: The Return of the King" video game; a CD of the film's sound track; a licensed Wrebbit "Perfalock Poster Puzzle" of Gollum; a small action figure of Sharku on a Warg (actually from *Towers*) by Play Along; a folder containing miscellaneous press information; and a pink suede bag containing a bottle of Very Irresistible Givenchy, a perfume that featured Liv Tyler in its publicity.

24. Michael Learmonth, "Jolie's Junket Jangle," *Variety* (20–26 June 2005): 6; Mike Goodridge, "Summer Madness," *SI* (17 June 2005): 7.

25. For a detailed description of press junkets using *Legally Blonde 2* and *Terminator 3* as examples, see Dade Hayes and Jonathan Bing, *Open Wide: How Hollywood Box Office Became a National Obsession* (New York: Hyperion, 2004), 193–235.

26. Sean Smith and David Ansen, "Picture Perfect," *Newsweek* (31 Jan. 2005): 48.

27. Nicole Curin-Birch, "Picturing Success: Philippa Boyens," *Air New Zealand* (Dec. 2003): 73.

28. Bernard D. McDonald, "*The Lord of the Rings: The Two Towers,*" *Pavement* 56 (Dec. 2002/Jan. 2003): 86.

29. Smilin' Jack Ruby, "Tales from the Junket Circuit: The Return of the King, Part One," *CHUD.com* (11 Dec. 2003): www.chud.com/news/dec03/dec11junket.php3. Ruby extensively transcribed his recording of the interviews, and this five-part series provides a good sense of what such events are like. The *Texas Chainsaw Massacre* comparison comes from the fact that New Line had distributed it two months earlier.

30. *King Kong: Peter Jackson's Production Diaries* (Universal Studios Home Entertainment, 2005), disc 1, 26 November 2004 track.

31. *The South Bank Show* (A LWT Production for Granada, 2004).

32. Margy Rochlin, "A Night Out with: Middle Earth [*sic*] Ambassador Ian McKellen," *NYTimes.com* (24 Dec. 2003): www.nytimes.com/2003/12/14/fashion/14NITE.html?ex=1072535906&ei=1&en=1cf7cd4624961906.

33. Quoted from a 2003 interview by Epstein in his *The Big Picture,* 305.

34. Melissa J. Perenson, "King of the Ring," *Sci Fi* (Feb. 2004): 47.

35. Sean Smith, "Steely Man," *Newsweek* (12 Sept. 2005): 67.

36. Melissa J. Perenson, "Shire Reckoning," *Sci Fi* (Feb. 2004): 50; Kevin Fitzpatrick, "Up Close and Personal: A Day with the Stars," *LotRFCOMM* 2 (Apr.–May 2002): 43.

1. Kathy A. McDonald, "Gordon Paddison, New Line Cinema," *Variety.com* (1 Aug. 2000): www.variety.com/index.asp?l=story&a=VR1117784472&c=1009.

2. The site itself is gone, but its index page is reproduced in Craig E. Engler's review, "Sci-Fi Site of the Week," *Sci-Fi.com* (1998): www.scifi.com/sfw/issue67/site.html.

3. John Leland, "The *Blair Witch* Cult," *Newsweek* (16 Aug. 1999): 44–49.

4. Patrick Goldstein, "Hollywood Is More Than Just Browsing," *Los Angeles Times* (25 June 2000): members.tripod.com/VanTassell/article/la06252000.html; Ann Donahue, "Season on the Brink," *Variety.com* (15 Oct. 2000): www.variety.com/index.asp?layout=ev_print_story&articleid=VR1117787784&categoryid=17.

5. The site www.lightsoutentertainment.com no longer exists.

6. See www.theonering.net/perl/newsview/8/1032296044.

7. This posting is no longer on the site, which lost its 2003 archived news through a computer problem. These images were immediately posted on other sites.

8. Harry Knowles, "Lord of the Rings: The Two Towers Special Preview Trailer," AICN (25 Mar. 2002): www.aintitcoolnews.com/display.cgi?id=11838.

9. "A Sneak Peak at the TTT Trailer," Tolkien Online (24 Sept. 2002): www.theonering.com/articles/7449,1.html. I do not wish to imply that these reactions are unique. Numerous sites appealing to fans of various genres (e.g., Hong Kong martial arts films) have similar lists of comments with strings of exclamation marks.

"Tolkien Online—The One Ring" has since changed its name to The One Ring, not to be confused with TheOneRing.net.

10. "Peter Jackson Answers THE GEEKS!!! 20 Questions about Lord of the Rings!!!" AICN (30 Aug. 1998): www.aint-it-cool-news.com/lordoftherings.html; "Peter Jackson Answers THE GEEKS!!! 20 Questions about Lord of the Rings!!!" AICN (31 Dec. 1998): www.aint-it-cool-news.com/lordoftherings2.html.

11. "Stuntman Wins Name Suppression—for Now," *Onfilm* (Aug. 2000): www.onfilm.co.nz/editable/Onfilm_0800a.html.

12. Ian Pryor, unable to obtain the cooperation of the filmmakers, became a spy to obtain information on *Rings* for his unauthorized biography, *Peter Jackson: From Prince of Splatter to "Lord of the Rings"* (New York: Thomas Dunne, 2003). His account in chapter 14, "Spies in Middle-earth," gives a vivid sense of the travails undergone by such spies.

13. New Line's main site, www.newline.com, also carried publicity for the film, as well as housing the official shop. Other AOL Time Warner websites cooperated as well. Here I am focusing on sites where significant amounts of specific, unique material were generated for the franchise.

14. That link has been replaced by a link to "Official Conventions," leading to the website of Creation Entertainment, licensed by New Line to put on commercial fan cons.

15. Scott Edelman, "Taken by Tolkien," *Sci Fi* (Feb. 2003): 6.

16. For more on the early Internet campaign, see Erik Davis, "The Fellowship of the Ring," *Wired* (Oct. 2001): 119–33.

17. Dana Harris, "'Rings' Wizard Weaves Web of Magic," *Variety* (16–22 Dec. 2002): 8.

18. Davis, "The Fellowship of the Ring," 128.

19. Todd McCarthy, "'Lord' Rings Up Internet Users," *Variety.com* (11 Apr. 2000): www.variety.com/story.asp?l=story&a=VR1117780448&c=13.

20. See, for example, Rick Lyman, "Movie Marketing Wizardry: 'Lord of the Rings' Trilogy Taps the Internet to Build Excitement," *New York Times* (11 Jan. 2001): B1.

21. Gordon J. Paddison, "Designing the Marketing Program for *The Lord of the Rings*," in Rafi A. Mohammed, Robert J. Fisher, Bernard J. Jaworski, and Gordon J. Paddison, *Internet Marketing: Building Advantage in a Networked Economy*, 2nd ed. (New York: McGraw-Hill/Irwin, 2004), 569–623. Information on lordoftherings.net not otherwise cited in my discussion here derives from this source.

Paddison had been on the cutting edge for the first edition as well (2001) when he assisted on a similar case study of his website for *Austin Powers: International Man of Mystery* (585–617).

22. Frank Ahrens, "'Rings' Has Two Targets," *Washingtonpost.com* (19 Dec. 2001), www.washingtonpost.com/ac2/wp-dyn/A62589–2001Dec18.

23. Ibid.

24. Mohammed et al., *Internet Marketing*, 607.

25. Ann Donahue, "Getting the Word Out on the Web," *Variety.com* (18 Sept. 2000): www.variety.com/story.asp?l=story&a=VR1117786213&c=1009.

26. University of Otago, "Profiles: John Forde," *Otago Infosheet: Communication Studies* (n.d.): www.otago.ac.nz/humanities/pdf_infosheets/Communication%20Studies.pdf.

27. The series is indexed at www.eonline.com/Features/Specials/Lordrings/contents_location.html. Forde describes his experiences as an extra in the 1 May 2000 entry.

28. Mohammed et al., *Internet Marketing*, 608.

29. "The Return of the King" (17 Oct. 2001): www.corona.bc.ca/films/details/lordoftherings3.html.

30. Carla Atkinson, "The Fan Club 'Family,'" *LotRFCOMM* 3 (June–July 2002): 6.

31. "MailBaggins," *LotRFCOMM* 8 (Apr.–May 2003): 9. The Shore interview had run in issue 5.

32. Typing its former address, www.lotrfanclub.com, links one to a *Rings* page on Fan Headquarters, a company offering discounts on various film and other brand merchandise (lotr.fanhq.com).

With the club's website now gone, the magazines remain as the main evidence of its existence. Though out of print, issues surface regularly on eBay.

33. *Lord of Misrule: The Autobiography of Christopher Lee* (London: Orion, 2003), 340.

34. There was a website devoted to Elijah Wood, but apparently he was not interested in it. His agent cooperated with it, but Wood later denied that it was his official site, and it closed at some point after the premiere of Film 1.

35. Forde, "Force" (1 Feb. 2000): www.eonline.com/Features/Specials/Lordrings/Location/000201c.html.

36. According to Stern, after McKellen.com went online in September 1997, it received 250,000 to 500,000 hits a month. Once *Gods and Monsters* and *Apt Pupil* appeared in 1998, the average rose to around a million. Anticipation of *X-Men* boosted the level to 2 million monthly hits in 1999 and early 2000, and the film's July 2000 release sent it to 4 million. Interest in *Rings* helped maintain the level at around 4 to 6 million through 2000 and 2001. The 19 December 2001 release of *Fellowship* led to an average 8 million hits for a few months, with the figure sinking back to 4 to 6 million for most of 2002. The same pattern, with slightly larger figures, followed the release of *Towers*. *Return*'s effects were "phenomenal," says Stern, "building beyond 10 million hits per month in the last quarter of 2003 and for 5 or 6 days after [the] release in Dec[ember] we greatly exceeded our capacity of about 20–25 million per month. The site had to be spread over four or five servers to try and distribute the traffic. The 20 million level endured through January 2004, then declined to 16 million in February and 10 million in March. By autumn of 2004, the site was housed on three servers and was steadily averaging 3 to 4 million hits a month."

A "hit," the standard measure of website traffic, consists of a user viewing one item (image or page). A single user may visit several pages on a site—especially one that has grown as large as McKellen.com.

37. *Parkinson,* BBC (13 Apr. 2003).

38. E-Post sections devoted to *Gods and Monsters* and *Richard III* were added within a month, along with the miscellany, "Bits and Bobs." A "Shakespeare" section followed later in the year. The only subsequent separate E-Post sections have been for *X-Men 3* (1 Mar. 2005) and *The Da Vinci Code* (21 June 2005). The latter film also has a brief diary, parallel to the Grey and White Books, in "Teabing's Chronicle," beginning 30 July 2005.

39. "Potjy" (clearly not a native English speaker) wrote a charming inquiry about this subject: "It's really surprised me that you do many writing for your website and answer fanmails too. It's certainly that you must live a very busy life. How can you have time for all this quite 'trivia' things, especially answering the fan mails? At first I think 'that cannot be "him,"' but the writing style is just right. :-)." McKellen responded with a brief summary of the process; see "E-Post Bits and Bobs" (24 Oct. 2002): www.mckellen.com/epost/m021024.htm.

40. "E-Post: The Lord of the Rings" (5 June 2001): www.mckellen.com/epost/LOTR/. The fact that a fan could ask such a question more than six months before *Fellowship*'s premiere suggests how familiar fans were with the visual material used in the extensive publicity.

41. Gillian Flynn, "Nobody Beats the Wiz," *EW* (18 Jan. 2002): 50.

42. Adam B. Vary, "Middle School," *EW* special forecast issue (2002): 108.

43. Harry Knowles, *Ain't It Cool? Hollywood's Redheaded Stepchild Speaks Out* (New York: Warner Books, 2002), 45, 47–50.

44. Ibid., 204–6.

45. Ibid., 61.

46. "To Kong or to Hobbit, That Is the Question," AICN (30 Oct. 1997): www.aintitcool.com/display.cgi?id=213; "Cool News: Lord of the Rings!!!" AICN (3 Nov. 1997): www.aintitcool.com/display.cgi?id=224.

47. AICN (23 Feb. 1998): www.aintitcoolnews.com/display.cgi?id=682.

48. "Dammit, Why the Hell Did They Do That?" AICN (14 July 1998): www .aintitcoolnews.com/display.cgi?id=1219). No sequel to *Total Recall* (1990) has been made, though there have been rumors of such a project.

49. "Peter Jackson Answers THE GEEKS!!! 20 Questions about Lord of the Rings!!!" AICN (30 Aug. 1998): www.aint-it-cool-news.com/lordoftherings.html. The second twenty-questions session had the same title (31 Dec. 1998): www.aint-it-cool-news .com/lordoftherings2.html.

50. "Quint's First 'Real' Report from RETURN OF THE KING Set! Much Better Than the One Moriarty Posted!!!" AICN (n.d., ca. 2 Sept. 2003): www.aintitcool .com/display.cgi?id=15594.

51. Jo McCarroll, "The Fellowship of the Ring," *Sunday Star-Times,* "The Lord of the Rings Souvenir Magazine" (2001): 12.

52. Many of these dates derive from a chronology, "TORN Notable Events Information" (11 June 2004) kindly drafted at my request by Jincey, longtime staff member of TORN.

53. Challis's lengthier reports are gathered at www.theonering.net/features/ exclusives.

54. Snatched candid photos and reports from clandestine eyewitnesses to the filming were posted. Even now one can get a flavor of those heady early days, when so little was known, by visiting TORN's "Spy Reports" archive. Unlike many sites, TORN keeps virtually everything it has posted in its archives (though sometimes undated). Some links in the news sections are dead by now, but many articles that have disappeared from the original source sites remain here.

55. Forde, "Force" (12 Jan. 2000): www.eonline.com/Features/Specials/Lordrings/ Location/000112.html.

56. Links to all five parts of "Where the Stars Are Strange" Green Books section, TORN (26–30 Nov. 2001) can be found at http://greenbooks.theonering.net/ quickbeam/.

57. Paddison, "Designing the Marketing Program," 611.

58. Goldstein, "Hollywood Is More."

59. Aliya Sternstein, "New Line Online," *Variety.com* (22 Aug. 2004): www.variety .com/article/VR1117909436?categoryid=1757&c=1; Ty Braswell, "In Search of QEIB:

Gordon Paddison Interview," *imediaconnection.com* (8 May 2003): www.imediaconnection.com/scripts/printver.asp.

60. Francis K. Lalumière and Jon B. Snyder, "Spinning The Lord of the Rings Web," *LotRFCOMM* 1 (Feb.–Mar. 2002): 72. This article also profiles two other major *Rings* fan sites.

61. Ben Fritz, "'Net Heads Finally Get Some Respect," *Variety* (12–18 Apr. 2004): 9.

62. "DVD Producer Saddled with Kong-Sized Task," *stuff* (29 Oct. 2005): www.stuff.co.nz/stuff/print/0,1478,3460107a1860,00.html.

63. "Behind the Scenes," *EW* (16 Dec. 2005): 69.

64. Tim Lucas, "*King-Kong—Peter Jackson's Production Diaries,*" *Video Watchdog* (May/June 2006): 59.

CHAPTER 6: Fans on the Margins, Pervy Hobbit Fanciers, and Partygoers

1. This modest page can still be viewed via a link at the bottom of the "Elijah" index page at http://lilithlotr.ejwsites.net/Elijah/birthday/birthday.htm. (Lilith is in the process of moving her site to www.lilithlotr.com, but the site should remain accessible via links.)

2. The letter is dated 1 January 1970. See Humphrey Carter, ed., *The Letters of J. R. R. Tolkien* (Boston: Houghton Mifflin, 1981), 404.

3. Rebecca Tushnet, "Legal Fictions: Copyright, Fan Fiction, and a New Common Law," *Loyola of Los Angeles Entertainment Law Journal* 17 (1997), reprinted on the author's website, www.tushnet.com/law/fanficarticle.html. Tushnet teaches at Yale's law school.

4. The *Fellowship* captions are at users3.evi.net/~eekfrenzy/captionspage/bad fotrprologue.html; the *Towers* ones were at public.www.planetmirror.com/pub/engrish/ttt_captions/index.htm, but on 3 February 2003, New Line sent a message calling them "unauthorized" and demanded that they be removed, even though parodies are clearly protected by the fair-use law. The owner took them down. New Line's letter can be read at home.online.no/~gremmem/engrish_ttt_captions/. The only place where I could find the *Towers* captions as of April 2006 is http://sleepygeek.org/stuff/mirror/engrish_ttt/. With luck by now New Line has found better things for its lawyers to do than harass its own fans. (The *Return* bootleg, though it contains equally amusing subtitles, never received this treatment.)

5. Susan Wloszczyna, "'Lord' of the Extras: Elfin Charmer Nets Fans," *USA Today* (6 Aug. 2002): D1. I am grateful to Iris Hadad for providing information on Figwit Lives! via a series of e-mail messages in April 2006.

6. Director/writers' commentary, *Return* EE DVD, track 9.

7. See detailed accounts, including an image of the card, on Figwit Lives! http://fanhq.com/TCG/Card.aspx?gameID=7&cardID=3829.

8. Kimberly Nordyke, "HBO on Board with 'Conchords,'" *HR* (11 Sept. 2006): 4.

9. Alex Keown, "N.C. Family's Thespian Peeps Are a Hit Online," *USA Today* (13 Apr. 2004): usatoday.com/tech/webguide/internetlife/2004–04–13-lordofthe peeps_x.htm. This story, written as an Easter feature for the local newspaper in Wilson, North Carolina, was picked up by the Associated Press; information on the background of the site has mainly been taken from this account and from my "interview" via e-mail with Genevieve Baillie (7 Oct. 2005).

10. In the true spirit of fandom on the internet, the Orlando Peep interview actually was written by Laura and posted on her E-Zine site, "The Penguin Files." It was "reprinted" in the interviews section on Peeps. See thepenguinfiles.tripod .com/id12.html.

11. For a good general summary of fanfiction, see en.wikipedia.org/wiki/ Fanfiction. A less up-to-date version of this entry containing a much-expanded timeline and additional links is at www.answers.com/topic/fan-fiction?method=5&linktext =fan%20fiction. *Rings* fanfiction zines (including some containing slash) are available at www.agentwithstyle.com/ and www.skeeter63.org/~silvablu/Spider_web/LOTR _zines.htm.

12. "Seek and Find," Stories of Arda (n.d.), www.storiesofarda.com/chapterview .asp?sid=2458&cid=9697; "A Light in Dark Places," www.livejournal.com/users/ talechallenge03/9612.html#cutidl; "On the Shores of the Sea," www.livejournal.com/ community/talechallenge15/2340.html#cutidl. Thanks to Marigold—obviously a Pippin fan—for her recommendations.

13. For those wishing to dip a toe in the ocean of fanfiction, a good place to start would be the Mithril Awards site (www.storiesofarda.com/chapterview.asp?sid= 2458&cid=9697). The Mithrils, the Oscars of fanfiction, have been awarded since 2003, and the lists of past winners and finalists link to the original fics—many of which are book-canon (and a few of which are adult oriented). The big fan sites like TORN and WOTR contain fanfiction sections that are mostly gen and often film-canon.

14. See Amy H. Sturgis, "Reimagining Rose: Portrayals of Tolkien's Rosie Cotton in Twenty-first Century Fan Fiction," *Mythlore* 93/94 (Winter/Spring 2006): 165–187, which includes an extensive bibliography. Sturgis is perhaps the most prominent historian of slash fiction focusing on the *Rings* novel and film.

15. One of the most influential early studies of slash focuses on *Star Trek* and other television-based fanfiction. See Henry Jenkins, *Textual Poachers: Television Fans and Participatory Culture* (New York: Routledge, 1992), 185–222. In 2004, slash came full circle and went mainstream with the release of German film and television director Michael "Bully" Herbig's *(T)Raumschiff Surprise,* an over-the-top *Star Trek* parody with the crew of the spaceship portrayed as gay.

16. Two introductory essays on *Rings* slash are Susan Booker's "Tales around the Internet Campfire: Fan Fiction in Tolkien's Universe" and Amy H. Sturgis's "Make Mine 'Movieverse': How the Tolkien Fan Fiction Community Learned to Stop Worrying and Love Peter Jackson," both in *Tolkien on Film: Essays on Peter Jackson's "The Lord of the Rings,"* ed. Jane Brennan Croft (Altadena, CA: Mythopoeic Press, 2004),

259–305. For a plausible explanation of the phenomenon of slash, see Catherine Salmon and Donald Symons, *Warrior Lovers: Erotic Fiction, Evolution and Female Sexuality* (2001; New Haven, CT: Yale University Press, 2003).

17. Amy Fortuna, "Least Expected: The Crownless Again Shall Be King," *Tolkien _Slash* (12 Mar. 2005): groups.yahoo.com/group/tolkien_slash/message/17249.

18. See www.warofthering.net/gallery/galleries/, www.squidge.org/~praxisters/lotr .html, and www.libraryofmoria.com/fanart/index.html.

19. See groups.yahoo.com/group/LOTR_RPS and groups.yahoo.com/group/ closer_than_brothers. Mirrormere can be found at avia.silverbloom.net/mirror/ index.php.

20. David Plotz, "Luke Skywalker Is Gay?" *Slate* (14 Apr. 2000): slate.msn.com/ id/80225#ContinueArticle.

21. "E-Post: The Lord of the Rings," McKellen.com (23 Dec. 2002): www .mckellen.com/epost/lotr/1021223.htm.

22. "E-Post: The Lord of the Rings," McKellen.com (16 June 2000): www .mckellen.com/epost/lotr/1000616.htm.

23. For an archive of TORN's polls, see www.theonering.net/theonering/polls.html. The two quotations are from the 31 October 1999 and 6 May 1999 polls, respectively.

24. For similar comments in a published interview, see Jon B. Snyder, "Update with Peter Jackson," *LotRFCOMM* 2 (Apr./May 2002): 25–26.

25. Bernard D. McDonald, "Barrie Osborne: The American Producer," *Pavement* 56 (Dec. 2002–Jan. 2003): 125.

26. "Newsmakers Q & A: Dominic Monaghan," *Newsweek* (12 Sept. 2005): 87; "Newsmakers Q & A: Elijah Wood," *Newsweek* (26 Sept. 2005): 71.

27. Kristina Johansson, e-mail to the author (6 Jan. 2005). My thanks to Kristina for sharing her knowledge of *Rings* RPS on the Internet.

28. Kristina Johansson, e-mail to the author (23 Feb. 2004).

29. Harry Knowles, *Ain't It Cool?* (New York: Warner Books, 2002), 57–58.

30. This invitation constituted an about-face for Warner Bros., which had initially sought to squelch Harry Potter fanfiction by intimidating owners of small websites. Henry Jenkins summarizes this early approach to fanfiction and the studio's subsequent change of attitude, as well as the more general issue of copyright and fan creativity, in his *Convergence Culture: Where Old and New Media Collide* (New York: New York University Press, 2006), 184–191. Jenkins's book deals with several key issues relating to fan culture and new media.

31. "Now on EW.COM," *EW* (29 July 2005): 8; "The Challenge," EA Games (n.d.): www.theonering.net/giveaway/contestEA.php; www.theonering.net/fanfilms/. (This site includes the winning entries.)

32. Devin Gordon, "Movies: Snakes on a What?" *Newsweek* (10 Apr. 2006): www .msnbc.msn.com/id/12112809/site/newsweek.

33. Larry Curtis and Nanette Morris, "A Towering Lineup," *LotRFCOMM* 8 (Apr.– May 2003): 12–14.

34. Thanks to Diane Greenlee for answering my questions (via e-mail, 20 Jan. 2004) about the line party and to the entire group for helping pass the hours and divert my attention from the fact that I was gradually losing all feeling in my toes. Thanks also to Ethan De Seife for purchasing a Trilogy Tuesday ticket for me while I was on the other side of the world doing research.

35. Gillian Flynn, "The Big Night," *EW* (12 Mar. 2004): 44. Brief footage from the third TORN party is included in the "Passing of an Age" supplement on the second disc of the *Return* EE appendixes.

36. Dianne Garrett and Bill Higgins, "Life of the Parties," *Variety* (8–14 Mar. 2004): 55.

37. Program notes, *Frodo Is Great . . . Who Is That?!!* in *Telecom 33 Wellington Film Festival* (17 July–1 Aug. 2004): 122. My thanks to Stan Alley for showing me a nearly complete version of his film.

38. Dan Madsen, "The 'Fellowship of 22' Celebrates the Oscars," *LotRFCOMM* 3 (June–July 2002): 11.

39. Tehanu, "Where to from Here?" TORN (29 Apr. 2004): www.theonering .net/features/notes/note22.html.

CHAPTER 7: Licenses to Print Money

1. Ian Markham-Smith, "Lord of the Rings Films and Products Set to Out-magic Even Harry Potter," *tdctrade.com* (28 Dec. 2001): www.tdctrade.com/imn/imn190/ films05.htm.

2. Simon Ashdown, "Merchandising the Trilogy," *KidScreen Magazine* (1 Jan. 2001): www.kidscreen.com/articles/magazine/20010101/30567; "Getting the Goods," *The Entertainment Weekly The Lord of the Rings Ultimate Viewer's Guide* (May 2004): 74; Gregg Kiday, "Return of the 'Rings' Merch," *HR* (28 Apr. 2004): 13.

3. For Richard Taylor's own anecdotal account of the development of the relationship with Sideshow and the approach to making the collectibles, see his "Merchandising," www.wetafx.co.nz/workshop/collectibles/merchandising.htm.

4. For coverage of the traditional sorts of *Rings* collectibles (i.e., with scant DVD coverage and none for video games), see George Beahm, *The Essential J. R. R. Tolkien Sourcebook: A Fan's Guide to Middle-earth and Beyond* (Franklin Lakes, NJ: New Page Books, 2004).

5. "Te Papa Strike Unusual Deal with Jackson," *stuff* (8 Dec. 2005): www.stuff .co.nz/stuff/0,2106,3504479a14297,00.html. The million-dollar estimate came before the exhibition's second Te Papa run.

6. For a fuller description, see "Movie Exhibit Dazzles Fans," *LotRFCOMM* 1 (Feb.–Mar. 2002): 8–9.

7. For photographs of the Marshes and other exhibits, see "Toronto Hosts Middle-earth," *LotRFCOMM* 7 (Feb.–Mar. 2003): 15–16.

8. Visions Con was one of the last big fan-run cons, and its organizers lost so much money that they had to give up in 1999. My thanks to longtime fan Emma Abraham for sharing her knowledge of cons. E-mail to the author (10 Dec. 2005).

9. Ring*Con's website is ringcon.de. For descriptions of the first two cons, see Ian Smith, "Ring*Con 2002 a Hit with Fans," *LotRFCOMM* 7 (Feb.–Mar. 2003): 16–18, and Ian Smith, "One Ring*Con to Rule Them All," *LotRFCOMM* 13 (Feb.–Mar. 2003): 12–16.

10. As of April 2006, descriptions of both Fellowship Festivals remain at www .aaaevents.co.uk. For brief mentions of Ring*Con and the Fellowship Festival's origins, see Ian Smith, "One of a Kind . . . The Lord of the Rings Fans," *LotRFCOMM* 18 (Dec.–Jan. 2005): 60–63.

11. On Creation Entertainment, see www.creationent.com and an interview with co-CEO Gary Berman, Alex Kingsbury, "Q&A with Gary Berman: Lord of the Rings Fans," *U.S. News & World Report* (21 Jan. 2006): www.usnews.com/usnews/ news/articles/060121/21lord.htm. Its eBay shop is at stores/ebay.com/CREATION ENTERTAINMENT.

12. Thomas K. Arnold, "Power Brokers," *HR* (13–19 July 2004): 26, 28.

13. For a thorough definition of Easter Eggs, see The Easter Egg Archive, http:// www.eeggs.com/faq.html.

14. Keith Collins, "A Brief History," Supplement: "Bob Shaye & Michael Lynne," *Variety* (23–29 Aug. 2004): 16–26; Samantha Clark, "New Line Stretches DVD Boundaries Again," *Video Business* (16 Apr. 2001): www.videobusiness.com/article/ CA620332.html?text=lord+of+the+rings.

Easter Eggs had originated early in the video game age, when Atari game designer Warren Robinett hid his name in "Adventures" in 1979. Jensen, "Videogame Nation," *EW* (6 Dec. 2002): 20–29.

15. Jennifer Netherby, "Universal Sales Eclipse $1 Billion in Fourth Quarter," *Video Business* (19 Dec. 2001): www.videobusiness.com/article/CA619242.html?text= lord+of+the+rings.

16. Jennifer Netherby, "DVD Outlook: The Cart before the Horse," supplement: "Showmen of the Year: Bob Shaye & Michael Lynne," *Variety* (23–29 Aug. 2004): 101–102.

17. Scott Hettrick, "Q&A: Juggling All Three Rings," *DVD-premieres.com* (29 Oct. 2002): www.dvd-premieres.com/HTMLNews/NewsQAKurtti-Pellerin.html.

18. Ibid.

19. Adam Dawtrey, "Will 'Lord' Ring New Line's Bell?" *Variety* (21–27 May 2001): 66.

20. Cristina Clapp, "Mastering Middle-Earth," *NewBay Media* (1 Apr. 2003): www.uemedia.com/CPC/printer_6561.shtml.

21. Matt Hurwitz, "One DVD to Rule Them All," *Videography.com* (6 Aug. 2004): www.uemedia.net/CPC/videography/article_9454.shtml; Hettrick, "Q&A."

22. Eric Moro, "It Takes Two Towers," *Cinescape* (3 Dec. 2003–4 Jan. 2004): 52.

23. Clapp, "Mastering Middle-Earth."

24. Michael Pellerin, e-mail to the author (28 Mar. 2006).

25. Daniel Frankel and Jennifer Netherby, "Studios Rein in DVD Control," *DVD Exclusive* (1 Nov. 2003): www.dvdexclusive.com/article.asp?=articleID=16Pellerin &query=pellerin.

26. Philip Wakefield, "Peter Jackson, Filmmaker," *Hollywood Reporter.com* (24 Feb. 2004): www.hollywoodreporter.com/thr/interviews/article_display.jsp?vnu_content_id=1000443007.

27. Scott Collura, "The Return of the Rings," *Cinescape* (Nov.–Dec. 2002): 89.

28. "Success Is at Hand," New Line information brochure sent to Kia dealerships, 2002.

29. Jennifer Netherby, "New Line Reveals a Trilogy of Rings Videos," *Video Business* (26 Mar. 2002): www.videobusiness.com/article/CA619007.html?=lord+of+the+rings.

30. "Dialogue with Peter Jackson," *HR* (24 Feb.–1 Mar. 2004): 13; Sam Andrews, "'Potter,' 'Rings' in Tight Race for U.K. 2002 Video Crown," *HR* (17–13 Dec. 2002): 66, 72; ad, *EW* (18 Dec. 2002): 84; Jill Kipnis, "'Rings' Lords over Vid Sales," *Reuters* (29 May 2004): www.reuters.com/newsArticle.jhtmljijsessionid=5GBJ3HLWHAE WWCRBAEZSFEY?type=topNews&storyID=5293049&pageNumber=1.

31. Jessica Wolf, "Playing with DVD," *Video Store Magazine* (27 May 2005): www .videostoremag.com/hers/html/breaking_article.cfm?_id=7581; brackets in original. DVD games were another new technology that New Line took advantage of. They had originated in 2002 with the release of Screenlife's "Scene It?" which spawned a successful series of dozens of games.

32. Mandy Brierly, "*Mulan:* Special Edition," *EW* (29 Oct. 2004): 56; "ew.com Poll 5," *EW* (15 Apr. 2005): 45.

33. David E. Williams, "All Hail the King," *Cinefantastique* (Feb./Mar. 2004): 22, 25.

34. I am grateful to Ian McKellen for showing me his copy of the compilation of these videos.

35. Scott Hettrick, "Warners Going Ape," *Variety.com* (4 Aug. 2005): www.variety .com/story.asp?l=story&a=VR1117927026&c=20; Gabriel Snyder, "It's a Jungle Out There," *Variety* (23–29 May 2005): 6.

36. For an account of Pellerin's work on the various *Kong*-related projects, see Anne Thompson, "DVD Producer Saddled with 'Kong'-Size Task," *HR* (28 Oct. 2005): www.hollywoodreporter.com/thr/columns/risky_business)display.jsp?vnu_content_id=100139145.

37. Scott Hettrick, "New Line Forges Steel DVD Deal," *Variety.com* (10 Nov. 2005): www.variety.com/article/VR1117932788?categoryid=20&cs=1.

38. Douglas Gomery, *The Hollywood Studio System: A History* (London: British Film Institute, 2005), 232.

39. *2002 Annual Report on the Home Entertainment Industry* (Encino, CA: Video Software Dealers Association, 2002), 14.

40. Dave McNary, "Disc-ord Ahead," *Variety.com* (23 Dec. 2003): www.variety .com/index.asp?layout=print_story&articleid=VR1117897581&categoryid=1066; Johnnie L. Roberts, "The Disc That Saved Hollywood," *Newsweek* (20 Aug. 2001): 30.

41. "Subtle Structural Changes Enrich Studios' DVD Windfall," *VDM* (7 Apr. 2003): 1.

42. Scott Hettrick, "A DVD Family Affair," *Variety.com* (11 Sept. 2002): www .variety.com/article/VR1117872675?categoryid=13&cs=1.

43. A comparable phenomenon seems to have occurred in Britain. *Fellowship* was the top-selling video of 2002, with 3.9 million DVD and VHS copies sold. *Harry Potter and the Philosopher's Stone* was second with 3.46 million. *Fellowship* led by a much higher margin in DVD sales, with 2.36 million versus 1.25 million for *Harry Potter,* while the latter led in VHS sales by 2.21 million to 1.57 million. See Sam Andrews, "Britain Sold on 'Rings' Video," *HR* (7–13 Jan. 2003): 10.

44. With *Rings,* New Line gave consumers another incentive to avoid VHS. The letterboxed widescreen versions of the extended editions (preferred by most fans to the full-screen versions) were released only on DVD.

45. I have calculated all the percentages given here from figures given in video sales and rental charts on www.boxofficemojo.com. See note 48.

46. *2003 Annual Report on the Home Entertainment Industry* (Encino, CA: Video Software Dealers Association, 2003), 2–3, 8–9.

47. In early 2006, *Newsweek* summarized an academic study of "the mystery of why people seemed more inclined to rent 'Two Weeks Notice' but dug deep to own 'Punch-Drunk Love'" and mentioned one of the customers whose habits were scrutinized: "Customer No. 303, who rented 'Phone Booth' but bought 'The Lord of the Rings: The Two Towers.'" Daniel McGinn, "Rent or Buy That DVD?" *Newsweek* (20 Mar. 2006): E4.

48. All DVD and VHS rental figures not otherwise cited are from www.boxoffice mojo.com/dvd/2002/sales, www.boxofficemojo.com/video/2002/sales/, www.box officemojo.com/dvd/2002/rentals.htm, and www.boxofficemojo.com/video/2002/ rentals.htm. During 2003, Box Office Mojo began offering only general "video rental" charts, not differentiating between VHS and DVD, making comparable percentages for *Towers* and *Return* impossible to obtain.

49. *2003 Annual Report on the Home Entertainment Industry,* 19.

50. "Blockbuster's situation was further exacerbated by a strong box office season this year and a plethora of juicy DVD titles for sale, such as 'Harry Potter' and 'Lord of the Rings.'" Meredith Amdur, "Blockbuster Rentals Drop as DVDs Gain," *Variety* (24 Feb.–2 Mar. 2003): 34.

51. Jill Goldsmith, "DVDs Spin Respect on Street," *Variety* (15–21 Dec. 2003): 6.

52. *2004 Annual Report on the Home Entertainment Industry* (Encino, CA: Video Software Dealers Association, 2004), 10.

53. *2005 Annual Report on the Home Entertainment Industry* (Encino, CA: Video Software Dealers Association, 2005), 7.

54. *2004 Annual Report on the Home Entertainment Industry*, 9, 13; *2005 Annual Report on the Home Entertainment Industry*, 13. The lower figure for *Return* probably stems from its extended-edition DVD being released about a month later than those of the other two parts, on 14 December; more of its earnings would have come in the following year.

55. Thomas K. Arnold, "Biz Expecting Record Q4 as DVD Optimism Returns," *HR* (4–10 Oct. 2005): 61.

56. Jennifer Netherby, "Fox Releases *Sith* on DVD Only," *Video Business* (26 Aug. 2005): www.videobusiness.com/article/CA6251599.html.

57. "Video Industry Adds Final Nails to VHS's Coffin," *SD* (Feb. 2006): 53.

58. Goldsmith, "DVDs Spin Respect on Street," 6.

59. *2005 Annual Report on the Home Entertainment Industry*, 11.

60. Carl DiOrio, "H'w'd: A Sequel Opportunity Town," *Variety* (16–22 June 2003): 1.

61. See www.theonering.net/cgi-bin/poll_SSI.cgi?keyword=sneef_20051014.

CHAPTER 8: Interactive Middle-earth

1. Philip Elmer-Dewitt, "The Amazing Videogame Boom," *Time* (27 Sept. 1993): 68; Marc Graser, "New Playground for Studios," *Variety* (17–23 May 1999): 9.

2. Marc Graser, "H'wood's New Big Game Hunt," *Variety* (1–7 Apr. 2002): 13.

3. N'gai Croal, "Now Video Vérité," *Newsweek* (3 June 2002): 43.

4. See Ben Fritz, "Stars Study Rules of the Game," *Variety.com* (16 Feb. 2004): www.variety.com/story.asp?l=story&a=VR1117900246&c=1009; "Video Games," *2005 Annual Report on the Home Entertainment Industry* (Encino, CA: Video Software Dealers Association, 2005), 16.

5. *2002 Annual Report on the Home Entertainment Industry*, 11.

6. Ben Fritz and Marc Graser, "Is the Game Getting Lame?" *Variety* (10–16 May 2004): 1, 69.

7. Ben Fritz, "Activision Extends Dream Deal," *Variety.com* (16 Nov. 2005): www.variety.com/story.asp?1=story&a=VR1117933104&c=13.

8. John Gaudiosi, "EA, ESPN Ink 15-Year Deal for Vid Games," *HR* (18–24 Jan. 2005): 69.

9. Duff McDonald, "Hollywood to E.A.: Bring It On," *Wired* (Aug. 2005): 77.

10. In the spring of 2006, EA ended its contract to do James Bond games, saying that it was limiting its licensed series and shifting toward a greater concentration on generating original games. Activision signed an agreement with MGM to make Bond games up to 2014. EA's commitment to the *Rings, Harry Potter,* and *Godfather* games remained firm. See Ben Fritz, "Action Traction," *Variety.com* (3 May 2006): www.variety.com/story.asp?1=story&a=VR1117942524&c=10.

11. Carly Mayberry, "Raising the Game," *HR* (29 June 2006): 6.

12. Marc Graser and David Bloom, "The New Game in Town," *Variety* (21–27 Apr. 2003): 59.

13. John Gaudiosi, "Game Makers Mining H'wood's Past," *HR* (14–20 Sept. 2004): 13; Gaudiosi, "Push to Play," *HR* (17–23 May 2005): 28.

14. Denis Seguin, "The Great Game," *SI* (25 Feb. 2005): 15.

15. Rex Weiner, "Vidgames Won't Play by Hollywood's Rules," *Variety* (20–26 Mar. 1995): 62; John Gaudiosi, "Double-Barreled Development," *Wired* (Aug. 2004): 60.

16. McDonald, "Hollywood to E.A.," 79.

17. Chris Green, "All Systems Go to Join the Convergence Game," *SI* (17 Mar. 2006): 7.

18. Tim Gnatek, "Giving Voice to Videogames," *New York Times* (4 Nov. 2004): www.nytimes.com/2004/11/04/technology/circuits/04voic.html.

19. Ann Donahue and Marc Graser, "Vidgames' Star Treatment," *Variety* (8–14 May 2000): 41.

20. John Gaudiosi, "Carrey Virtual for 'Lemony' Videogame," *HR* (23 Sept. 2004): 1; "The Must List," *EW* (Summer 2005): 51.

21. Chris Marlowe, "EA Has More 'Potter' Magic," *HR* (12–18 Apr. 2005): 4.

22. Dylan Callaghan, "For Love of the Game," *HR* (Jan. 2004): 13, 109; Susan Carpenter, "The Next Level," *Los Angeles Times calendar.com* (6 May 2004): www .calendarlive.com/printedition/calendar/cl-wk-cover6may06,2,3888812.story?coll=cl-calendar.

23. Laura M. Holson, "In the Land of Oscars, Rich Category Is Best Video-games," *New York Times* (10 Apr. 2004): A1; John Gaudiosi, "Straight to Videogame," *Wired* (Apr. 2005): 54; "Spielberg, EA Playing for 3 Titles," *HR* (18–24 Oct. 2005): 72; David S. Cohen and Ben Fritz, "Spielberg Gets In on Vidgame Action," *Variety.com* (14 Oct. 2005): www.variety.com/article/VR1117930926.html.

24. John Gaudiosi, "Soft Sell," *HR* (13–19 May 2003): S5; Fritz, "Stars Study Rules of the Game." "Pirates of the Burning Sea," an MMORPG (massively multiplayer online role-playing game), was announced at the beginning of 2003; its online date was still to be announced as of April 2006.

25. Fritz, "Activision Extends Dream Deal."

26. Philip Elmer-Dewitt, "The Amazing Videogame Boom," *Time* (27 Sept. 1993): 72; N'gai Croal, "Living in a 'Fantasy' World," *Newsweek* (21 Aug. 2000): 66.

27. Gaudiosi, "Soft Sell," S-5; Gaudiosi, "Push to Play," 30.

28. Fritz and Graser, "Is the Game Getting Lame?" 69; McDonald, "Hollywood to E.A.," 81. EA's event proved premature when later that year the company had to push the game's release back to early 2006.

29. David Bloom, "Viv U Fine-Tunes Its Playbook," *Variety* (20–26 May 2002): 24. The movie version of *The Thing* was directed by John Carpenter (1982).

30. Ann Donahue and Tim Swanson, "H'wood Hits Paydirt in Playtime," *Variety* (28–31 Dec. 2000): 74.

31. Sam Molineaux, "Playing to Win," *HR* (12 May 2004): S12.

32. John Brodie and Andy Marx, "Two Can Play This Game," *Variety* (27 Dec. 1993): 74.

33. Julian Dibbell, "Adventure," in *Supercade: A Visual History of the Videogame Age 1971–1984,* ed. Van Burnham (Cambridge, MA: MIT Press, 1996), 135.

34. During this period, Vivendi Universal owned Houghton Mifflin, the American publisher of Tolkien's works; on 31 December, VU sold Houghton Mifflin to a large investment conglomerate. See Meredith Amdur, "Next Chapter for VIV," *Daily Variety* (2 Jan. 2003): 1.

35. Some descriptions of these divisions and archive news items covering the history of these games is available at www.lordoftherings.com/us/news.jsp, although items I used in my summary have been removed.

36. John Gaudiosi, "Electronic Arts Circles 'Rings' Rights," *Variety.com* (11 Oct. 2000): www.variety.com/article/VR1117787541.html.

37. David Bloom, "Rival 'Rings' Vying for Vidgamers' Fingers," *Variety* (28 Oct.–3 Nov. 2002): 8.

38. David Bloom, "Vidgame Giant Plans L.A. Studio," *Variety.com* (29 Jan. 2003): www.variety.com/article/VR1117879706?categoryid=1009&cs=1.

39. John Gaudiosi, "Gamesters of Middle-earth," *Cinefantastique* (Dec. 2003/Jan. 2004): 42.

40. Geoff Keighley, "PayStation," *EW* (5 Mar. 2004): 18.

41. For those who, like me, are not gamers, the official strategy guides describe the games in minute detail and are copiously illustrated. These guides, by the way, are one of the few ancillary products that video games typically generate (although some games, like "Tomb Raider," led to T-shirts, posters, and other traditional sorts of merchandise). The two main publishers of such guides are Prima and Brady. See Dan Egger's *The Lord of the Rings: The Two Towers* (Roseville, CA: Prima, 2002); Maro De Govia, *The Lord of the Rings: The Return of the King* (Prima, 2003); Bryan Stratton, *The Lord of the Rings: The Battle for Middle-earth* (Prima, 2004); Maximus "Berserker" Zhang, *The Lord of the Rings: The Third Age* (Prima, 2004); and n.a., *The Lord of the Rings: The Battle for Middle-earth II* (Prima, 2006).

42. For a user's lengthy review of the Game Boy version, see Elbren, "From the Snows of Caradhras to the Plains of Rohan," *theonering.com* (16 Feb. 2003): www.theonering.com/articles/9485,1.html.

43. "These Got Game," *EW* (6 Dec. 2002): 30, 35.

44. Dan Jolin, "Let's Hunt Some Orc . . . ," *Total Film* 84 (Jan. 2004): 78. The notion of Gandalf as the "great architect" of the War of the Ring comes closer to the novel's structure than to the film's.

45. This online feature involved no extra charge. EA has never attempted to create an MMORPG for its "Rings" series. Such games can be very lucrative, since thousands of subscribers typically pay around fifteen dollars a month to participate (after an initial investment of perhaps fifty dollars for the software). They are also

expensive and risky to develop, and many announced games have never come to fruition. A few very successful MMORPGs like "EverQuest," "Lineage," and "Final Fantasy XI" dominate the market ("Markets: More Online Game Projects Cancelled," *SD* [Sept. 2004]: 282.) "The Battle for Middle-earth" does contain an online feature that allows large groups to play, but it is not an RPG, and there is no subscription fee.

46. EA Games, "Community Chat Log #2 with Mark Skaggs," *eagames.com* (16 July 2004): www.eagames.com/official/lordoftherings/thebattleformiddleearth/us/subpage.jsp?src=chatwithmarkskaggs2.

47. "Electronic Arts to Make 'Rings' Games," *cnn.money* (25 July 2005): money .cnn.com/2005/07/25/technology/personaltech/electronic_arts.reut.

48. See the home page for "The White Council," www.ea.com/lordoftherings/thewhitecouncil/index.jsp.

49. Ben Fritz, "Game Biz Cools on Movie Tie-ins," *Variety* (18–24 Sept. 2006): 10, 13; Ben Fritz, "Electronic Arts Seals Monster Deal," *Forbes.com* (25 July 2005): www.forbes.com/digitalentertainment/2005/07/25/ea-tolkien-deal-cx_variety _0725lordoftherings.html.

50. Rob James, "Rise of the Machines," *Total Film* (Jan. 2006): 75.

51. Chris Marlowe, "USC Unveils Game Research Lab," *HR* (16 Oct. 2004): 27; Chris Marlowe, "EA, Grammy Foundation Add Class to Video Game Sounds," *HR* (30 Aug.–5 Sept. 2005): 8, 27.

52. Riot Entertainment, "Press Release 2001," *mobileinfo.com* (16 July 2001): www .mobileinfo.com/Press_Releases2000/Riot_July16.htm; "Game over for RIOT-E, after Two Years and EUR 20 Million," *Helsingin Sanomat* (20 Mar. 2002): www2.helsin ginsanomat.fi/english/news.asp?id=20020320.

53. Sara Wilson, "More to It Than Just Fun and Games II," *imediaconnection* (6 Mar. 2003): www.imediaconnection.com/content/2567.asp; Jamdat Web site, www .jamdat.com/JamdatWeb/Catalog/US/en/game/mobile/AllGamesView/platform Group-1/assetType-1.

54. The exception is an MMORPG based on *Rings*. Vivendi Universal had been trying to create one of these games, "Middle-earth Online." It was being developed for VU by Turbine, publishers of several successful MMORPGs, such as "Dungeons & Dragons." In May 2005, Turbine announced that Tolkien Enterprises had granted it exclusive rights to create MMORPGs based on the novel. It took over the "Middle-earth Online" project, renaming it "The Lord of the Rings Online: Shadows of Angmar." "Turbine Announces The Lord of the Rings Online: Shadows of Angmar," *Turbine Games* (10 May 2005): www.turbinegames.com/index.php?page_id=20& pagebuilder[module]=article&pagebuilder[display_item=4.

55. At the time, Ubisoft was the third largest independent games publisher in Europe and the seventh largest in the United States. By 2006 it had moved up to fifth in the U.S. market. See the Wikipedia entry, en.wikipedia.org/wiki/Ubisoft,

and the "Corporate Facts" page of the firm's Web site, www.ubisoftgroup.com/AboutUbisoft/Default.aspx?cpid=181.

56. Gaudiosi, "Push to Play," 30; "Peter Jackson's King Kong: King Kong Developer Interview I," *GameSpot* (8 Aug. 2005): www.gamespot.com/xbox360/action/kingkong; Peter Griffin, "King Kong Stomps Its Way to a Console Near You," *nzherald.co.nz* (20 Aug. 2005): www.nzherald.co.nz/index.cfm?c_id=6&ObjectID=10341574.

57. "King Kong Q & A: Peter Jackson Speaks," *GameSpot* (4 Aug. 2005): www.gamespot.com/news/2005/08/04/news_6130320.html; Dana Jongewaard, "King of Kong," *1up.com* (18 Oct. 2005): www.1up.com/do/feature?cId=3144789. Thanks also to Judy Alley for vetting this passage via e-mail.

58. Holson, "In Land of Oscars, Rich Category Is Best Videogames," A1.

59. Ibid.; Gaudiosi, "Soft Sell," S4–S5.

60. Daniel Fierman, "Caught in the Matrix," *EW* (18 Apr. 2003): 29.

61. Gaudiosi, "Push to Play."

62. John Gaudiosi, "Ubisoft to Ape New 'Kong,'" *HR* (12–18 Oct. 2004): 56.

63. Ben Fritz, "Lord of the Games," *Variety.com* (27 Sept. 2006): www.variety.com/story.asp?l=story&a=VR1117950837&c=18.

CHAPTER 9: Fantasy Come True

1. In 2004, the AFM switched to the autumn, putting an end to MIFED, which was not held after that year. As this shuffle occurred, buyers and sellers increasingly negotiated deals at festivals like Berlin, Toronto, and Pusan.

2. During the period when *Rings* was being produced and distributed, the Independent Film and Television Alliance was called the American Film Marketing Association; the name change occurred in June 2004.

3. Bill Higgins, "AFMA Raves over Shaye," *Variety.com* (22 Feb. 2002): www.variety.com/story.asp?l=story&a=VR1117861242&c=13.

4. Claude Brodesser, "Niche Pics Stoke Summer Heat," *Variety* (8–14 Mar. 2004): 53; Bob Marich, "Upscale Films Find Bigger Avenues, Payoff in Tight Indie-Distribution Arena," *VDM* (11 Aug. 2003): 5.

5. "The High Rollers," *SI* (30 Apr. 2004): 14.

6. Cathy Dunley and Sharon Swart, "Prize Fight," *Variety* (23–29 Feb. 2004): A1.

7. Dana Harris, "H'wood Maverick Shaye Still Does It His Way," *Variety* (18–24 Feb. 2002): A12; Dana Harris, "Rings' Fling Brings Payday," *Variety* (25 Feb.–3 Mar. 2002): 11.

8. "AOL TW Skids into Record Books," *HR* (4–10 Feb. 2003): 51; Justin Oppelaar, "New Line's Billion-Dollar Bet," *Variety* (20–26 Jan. 2003): 11.

9. "Time Warner Posts Profit for Full Year," *HR* (3–9 Feb. 2004): 65; Jill Goldsmith, "Time Warner Stock Socked by TV and AOL," *Video Business* (28 Jan. 2004):

www.videobusiness.com/article/CA615132.html?text=lord+of+the+rings; Susanne Ault, "Time Warner Has Red 2Q," *Video Business* (5 Aug. 2004): www.videobusiness .com/article/CA632835.html?text=lord+of+the+rings; Jill Goldsmith, "AOL Still Denting Time Warner," *Variety.com* (3 Aug. 2005): www.variety.com/article/VR 1117926953?categoryid=18&cs=1.

10. Adelia Cellini, "Indie in Practice and Spirit," Supplement, "Showmen of the Year: Bob Shaye & Michael Lynne," *Variety* (23–29 Aug. 2004): 16, 49; Pamela Mc-Clintock, "WB Hands Out 400 Pinkslips," *Variety.com* (1 Nov. 2005): www.variety .com/article/VR1117932140?categoryid=18&cg=1.

11. Michael Fleming, "Third 'Hour' Starts Clock," *Variety.com* (20 Nov. 2005): www.variety.com/article/VR1117933304?categoryid=13&cs=1.

12. Supposedly the concentration on *Rings* also led New Line to ignore some of its own acquisitions. For instance, Liliana Cavani's 2002 film, *Ripley's Game,* was slated for release in the United States but eventually went straight to cable and DVD.

13. Kevin Maynard and Nicole LaPorte, "Fine Line Divides Ordesky between Niche, Event Pictures," Supplement, "Showmen of the Year: Bob Shaye & Michael Lynne," *Variety* (23–29 Aug. 2004): 46.

14. Steve Chagollan, "Malick's Brave 'New World,'" Supplement, "Showmen of the Year: Bob Shaye & Michael Lynne," *Variety* (23–29 Aug. 2004): 28; David Hafetz, "The Two Towers," same, p. 99. New Line had previously distributed Cronenberg's controversial *Crash* (1996).

15. Dana Harris, "New Lineup at Artsy Banner," *Variety.com* (15 Sept. 2004): www .variety.com/story.asp?l=story&a=VR1117904780&c=13.

16. Ian Mohr, "Picturehouse Revs Up Specialty Biz," *Variety* (25–31 July 2005): 14; Minu Pak, "The Kid Stays in the Picture," *HR* (18–24 Oct. 2005): 20.

17. Gregg Goldstein, "Picturehouse Heats Up Thanks to 'Prairie' Fire," *HR* (7 Sept. 2006): 19.

18. Sharon Swart, "Get in Line: A Peek at New Line's Packed Slate," *Variety* (2–8 May 2005): B1.

19. "Film Production Budgets Soar," *SD* (May 2006): 133; Gina McIntyre, "Fantastic Voyages," *HR* (Aug. 2006): F-2.

20. Cathy Dunkley, "Indie Mood One of Caution for AFM," *Variety.com* (19 Feb. 2001): www.variety.com/story.asp?l=story&a=VR1117793788&c=1030. This story contains an excellent discussion of many of the factors involved in the downturn.

21. Stephen Galloway, "Hey, Big Spenders!" *HR* (Feb. 2003): 4; Don Groves and Adam Dawtrey, "Pre-sales Preempt Market Woes," *Variety* (26 May–1 June 2003): 11; Mike Goodrich, "The Cannes 101," *SI* (16 May 2003): 16; Robert Marich, "Rookie Exhibs Are All the Rage This Year," *Variety.com* (28 Feb. 2004): www.variety .com/story.asp?l=story&a=VR1117900932&c=1711; Stephen Galloway, "The Real Deal," *HR* (May 2005): 35; Sharon Swart, "Beach Blitz," *Variety* (2–8 May 2005): B6.

22. Benedict Carver, "New Line Firms Int'l Pacts," *Variety.com* (4 Nov. 1998): www.variety.com/story.asp?l=story&a=VR1117488103&c=13; Benedict Carver, "New Line Lines Up Global Distrib Deals," *Variety.com* (26 Mar. 1999): www.variety.com/ story.asp?l=story&a=VR1117492738&c=13. Kinowelt subsequently went into two years of bankruptcy, and at the last minute New Line arranged for *Rings* to be distributed by Warners in Germany. See "King of the Rings," *SI* (20 Feb. 2004): 17.

23. Carver, "New Line Firms Int'l Pacts"; Anthony D'Alessandro, "Global Conquest," *Variety.com* (22 Aug. 2004): www.variety.com/story.asp?l=story&a=VR 1117909433&c=1757; Dana Harris, "Rings' Winners Are Stingy Fest Spenders," *Variety* (17 May–2 June 2002): 7.

24. "Rings Lords It at Cannes," *Onfilm* (June 2000): www.onfilm.co.nz/editable/ lotr/onfilm_PJ_0600.htm; Adam Dawtrey, "Will 'Lord' Ring New Line's Bell?" *Variety* (21–27 May 2001): 66.

25. Galloway, "Hey, Big Spenders!" 4; "Rings Site New World Web Wonder," *Onfilm* (Feb. 2001): www.onfilm.co.nz/editable/lotr/onfilm_PJ_0201c.html. The discrepancy in the figures may result from the fact that not all deals for foreign territories had been closed.

26. Dawtrey, "Will 'Lord' Ring New Line's Bell?" 1.

27. "World Film Production/Distribution," *SD* (June 2005): 178; Jacob Wendt Jensen, "New Fruit: Denmark," *SI* (19 May 2006): 30. Danish films SF has released and/or produced to the end of 2005 are *Send mere slik* (2001), *Polle Fiction* (2002), *Midsommer, Til Højre ved den Gule Hund, Møgunger, Tvilling* (2003), *Den talende muse, Cirkeline* (2004), *Oscar og Josefine, Springet* (coproduced), *Between a Smile and a Tear, Strings, Den tyske Hemmelighed, Allegro* (coproduced), and *Swenkas* (2005).

28. "King of the Rings," 17.

29. Harris, "Rings' Winners Are Stingy Fest Spenders," 7; Marlene Edmunds, "Savvy Strategy Boosts Benelux Area Indies," *Variety* (17–23 Feb. 2003): 26; "DVDs: Europe's Precious," *SI* (13 Feb. 2004): 4; Patrick Frater, "On the Rights Track," *SI* (9 July 2004): 9; "The Netherlands," *SI* (12 Nov. 2004): 34.

30. Adam Dawtry, "'Black Book' Rewrites Rules and History," *Variety.com* (10 Sept. 2006): www.variety.com/story.asp?l=story&a=VR1117949751&c=1246; Robert Mitchell, "Book Launched," *SI* (29 Sept. 2006): 26; and Geoffrey Macnab, "Black Book Opens for Business," *SI* (19 Apr. 2005): 11.

31. Tim Dams, "Britain's Mystery Moguls," *SI* (20 Feb. 2004): 15–17; "Top UK Indie Thrives via New Line Tie, Rolls Dice w/Exhibition Diversification," *VDM* (17 Nov. 2003): 6; Tim Dams, "UK's Entertainment Sees Profits Leap on Back of *Rings,*" *ScreenDaily.com* (20 Feb. 2004): www.screendaily.com/print.asp?storyid=16428; Samantha Haque, "Lord of the Rings Firm Soars to Top of Profits League," *Times Online* (4 Apr. 2004): business.timesonline.co.uk/tol/article/business/1055474.ece.

32. Harris, "Rings' Winners Are Stingy Fest Spenders," 7; Charles Masters, "At Metropolitan, It's a Family Affair," *HR* (1–7 Mar. 2005): 8; Alison James, "France," *Variety* (10–16 May 2004): 38.

33. Melanie Rodier, "Quiet Power," *SI* (13 May 2005): 19–20; Nick Vivarelli, "Medusa Sets Wide-Ranging Slate," *Variety.com* (22 May 2005): www.variety.com/story.asp?l=story&a=VR1117923282&c=1884.

34. Harris, "'Rings' Winners Are Stingy Fest Spenders," 7; John Hopewell and Emiliano de Pablos, "Aurum Sees Shake-up Despite 'Rings' Success," *Variety* (16–22 June 2003): 14; Adam Dawtrey, "Momentum Ties Up w/Spanish Distrib Aurum," *Variety.com* (9 May 2004): www.variety.com/story.asp?l=story&a=VR1117904543&c=1246.

35. Mark Shilling, "Dynastic Dynamo," *SI* (20 Aug. 2004): 10; "Lord of the Warehouses: Village Roadshow Writes Happy Ending for IT Strategy," *NZSun.com* (29 July 2002): nz.sun.com/localpress/2002/07/2_print.html; "Hong Kong," *SI* (23 Jan. 2004): 41; "Pioneer," *VDM* (16 Dec. 2002): 11.

36. For a summary of the genre, see Adam Smith, "Fantasy Island," *Empire* (Jan. 2002): 70. For some reason, denigrating discussions of fantasy films have tended to ignore Tim Burton's classic contributions to the genre, notably *Beetlejuice* (1988), *Edward Scissorhands* (1990), and *The Nightmare before Christmas* (1993). Perhaps Burton's eccentric vision seems too inimitable to influence the genre significantly.

37. This ranking is based on figures not adjusted for inflation, but studio executives and the public do not think in adjusted dollars, and perhaps they are right. Shifts in taste and genre popularity probably mean that the fact that *Gone with the Wind* is still the highest-grossing film of all time is irrelevant for their purposes.

38. The summer of 2006 altered these figures only slightly. *The Pirates of the Caribbean: Dead Man's Chest* soared to number three, knocking *Fellowship* off the top ten to the eleventh position—and, ironically, relegating the first *Pirates* movie to number 26. *The Da Vinci Code* climbed to number 21, thus joining *Titanic* and *Forrest Gump* among the three nonfantasy, non-sci-fi films in the top 25.

39. Lev Grossman, "Feeding on Fantasy," *Time* (2 Dec. 2002): 90.

40. Dan Madsen, "Update with Peter Jackson," *LotRFCOMM* 5 (Oct.–Nov. 2002): 29.

41. Nina Rehfield, "The Next Reel," *GreenCine* (18 Dec. 2002): www.greencine.com/article?action=view&articleID=62&.

42. Gillian Flynn, "Best Director: Peter Jackson," *EW* (6 Feb. 2004): 92.

43. Alex Ross, "The Ring and the Rings," *New Yorker* (22 + 29 Dec. 2003): 161–165; Anthony Lane, "Full Circle," *New Yorker* (5 Jan. 2004): 91; Graham Fuller, "Kingdom Come," *Film Comment* (Jan.–Feb. 2004): 24–29.

44. Sean Astin, *There and Back Again: An Actor's Tale* (New York: St. Martin's, 2004), 307.

45. Edward Jay Epstein, *The Big Picture: The New Logic of Money and Power in Hollywood* (New York: Random House, 2005), 240–41.

46. *The Godfather* and *The Godfather Part II* both won Best Picture, but the first film was not intended as the foundation of a series, and at the time the films did not generate much in the way of licensed products.

47. Mervyn Peake's three *Gormenghast* novels are well respected, but the BBC had already made a lavish miniseries with a stellar cast based on the first volume, *Gormenghast,* broadcast in January and February 2000. Its ratings declined precipitously after the first episode, and a film adaptation seems unlikely.

48. Charles Lyons and Cathy Dunkley, "Disney Digs Walden," *Variety.com* (30 Sept. 2002): www.variety.com/article/VR1117873583?categoryid=13&cs=1.

49. Jonathan Bing and Dana Harris, "Fantasy 'Dark' Sparks New Line," *Variety .com* (11 Feb. 2002): www.variety.com/story.asp?l=story&a=VR1117860252&c=21; Michael Fleming and Dana Harris, "Stoppard to Pen 'Dark Materials,'" *Variety.com* (16 May 2002): www.variety.com/index.asp?layout=cannes2002_page&internal= cannes2002_story&articleid=VR1117867031&categoryid=1241&cs=1. Pullman's trilogy proved more difficult to adapt for the screen than Emmerich anticipated, and *His Dark Materials: The Golden Compass* is currently announced for a 2007 release.

50. Josh Spector, "Hollywood Roundtable," *Creative Screenwriting* (July/Aug. 2005): 63.

51. Dana Harris and Cathy Dunkley, "Scribe Nets Spidey Gig," *Variety.com* (19 Sept. 2002): www.variety.com/article/VR1117873068?categoryid=1236&cs=1.

52. Richard Lacayo, "Kids Are Us!" *Time,* international edition (9 Dec. 2002): 58, 60.

53. Adam Gifford, "Academy Award Literally a Dream Come True," *New Zealand Herald* (27 Feb. 2004): www.nzherald.co.nz/storyprint.cfm?storyID=3551553. See Massive's website for technical details and later versions and applications of the technology: www.massivesoftware.com. Massive wrought such a distinctive change in crowd scenes that reviewers associated it with *Rings'* style. One reviewer remarked of *Lion,* "The war itself, with its digital tumult, will look familiar to anyone who saw the *Lord of the Rings* films." Owen Gleiberman, "The Chronicles of Narnia: The Lion, the Witch and the Wardrobe," *EW* (16 Dec. 2005): 60.

54. I am grateful to Peter Doyle for giving me a demonstration of digital selective grading in the PostHouse, Wellington (2 Oct. 2003). A short supplement, "Digital Grading," on the *Fellowship* extended-edition DVD, briefly explains the system. Doyle has gone on to grade the third and fourth *Harry Potter* films, *Charlie and the Chocolate Factory,* and *King Kong.* For a summary of the early history and technology of 5D Colossus, see "5D Colossus Grades 3000 shots for The Lord of the Rings," *Digital Animators* (21 Jan. 2002): www.digitalanimators.com/articles/viewarticle. jsp?id=7442. The *Hollywood Reporter* chose 5D Colossus as one of the most significant new technologies in Debra Kaufman and Sheigh Crabtree's "10 Technologies That Will Change the World," *HR* (Nov. 2003): 64. (In mid-2003, the program was revamped as Lustre.)

55. Jody Duncan, Don Shay, and Joe Fordham, "State of the Art: A Cinefex 25th Anniversary Forum," *Cinefex* 100 (Jan. 2005): 36.

CHAPTER 10: Right in Your Own Backyard

1. Jo-Marie Brown, "Email Protest Puts NZ on Universal's Map," *New Zealand Herald* (5 Oct. 2004): www.nzherald.co.nz/feature/story.cfm?c_id=678&ObjectID=356319.

2. New Zealand Institute of Economic Research, *Scoping the Lasting Effects of "The Lord of the Rings": Report to the New Zealand Film Commission* (Wellington, 2002), 5–6.

3. See Robert Rutherford's own account in "Glenorchy Air's Involvement in the Making of the *Lord of the Rings* films," at www.trilogytrail.com/story.html.

4. James Brooke, "New Zealand Markets Itself as Film Land of the 'Rings,'" *New York Times* (31 Dec. 2002): C1, 4; Brooke's "A Long Journey Rewarded" was one of two long articles on the country spread over four pages of the *Times'* travel section (22 Dec. 2002): sec. 4, pp. 1–2, 6–8.

5. Ian Brodie, *"The Lord of the Rings" Location Guidebook* (Auckland: Harper-Collins, 2002). An expanded edition appeared in 2003, and a larger, more sumptuously illustrated version, presumably for armchair travelers, appeared in 2004.

6. Information on the Wingnut Films building comes from "Jackson Purchases Miramar Hostel," *Evening Post* (13 Feb. 1996), New Zealand Film Archive, "Peter Jackson" folder (page number not included).

7. There were two facilities with soundproof stages, South Pacific in Auckland and Avalon in Wellington, but these were relatively small and used almost exclusively for television production.

8. Peter Jackson, "Filming Three Tales at Once? A Little Madness Helps," *TORN* (16 Dec. 2001): www.theonering.net/perl/newsview/8/1008522263.

9. Simon Beattie, "My Wonderful Career," *Evening Post* (Wellington, 19 Dec. 2001): 11.

10. "Balancing the Complex Needs of the International Film Production Community," *Business of Film* (May 2001): 83.

11. "Jackson Bringing TFU Facility Closer to Home," *HR* (10–16 Dec. 2002): 75.

12. For a brief account of the building of these studios and views of them being used for mixing, see the track "The End of All Things" in "The Appendices Part Six," disc 4 of the *Return* EE DVD.

13. David S. Cohen, "The Post w/ the Most . . . ," *Variety* (11–17 Apr. 2005): 6.

14. Phil Wakefield, "The Post Is Clear," *HR* (24 Feb.–1 Mar. 2004): 22.

15. Borys Kit, "Filmmakers Go around the World in Thailand," *HR* (9 June 2004): 48.

16. Fry, who served as executive in charge of production, died in April 2002. Her importance to the project can be judged from the fact that in his speech upon win-

ning the Best Picture Golden Globe for *Return* in 2004, Jackson acknowledged three people: Saul Zaentz, Harvey Weinstein, and Carla Fry.

17. *A Filmmaker's Journey: Making "The Return of the King,"* supplementary disc of the *Return* theatrical DVD.

18. Even with *King Kong* there was a "credibility gap." Universal held the "King Kong Partner Summit," flying twenty-five heads of big theater circuits to be wined and dined and given a tour by Jackson. Josh Young, "The Slate," *VLife* (Oct. 2005): 78.

19. *The World of Kong: A Natural History of Skull Island* (New York: Pocket, 2005). "Weta Workshop" is credited as the author.

20. Tom Pullar-Strecker, "IBM Serves Up Dragon," *stuff* (26 Sept. 2005): www.stuff.co.nz/0.2106,3423084a28,00.html.

21. Nick Grant, "Interview with the Ring Master," *Onfilm* (Mar. 2003): www.archivesearch.co.nz/ViewEditorial.asp.

22. John B. Snyder, "Hobbiton," *LotRFCOMM* 1 (Feb.–Mar. 2004): 47; Francis K. Lalumière, "Put Your Best Foot Forward," *LotRFCOMM* 2 (Apr.–May 2002): 41; Julie Matthews, "Beyond a Touch of Makeup," *LotRFCOMM* 13 (Feb.–Mar. 2004): 51–52.

23. Matt F. Palmerton, "New Zealand: Home of Middle Earth," *Variety* (17–23 Dec. 2001), n.p.

24. Jackson's only formal training came in 1990, when he and Walsh attended Robert McKee's famous "Story Seminar." Costa Botes rightly says that Jackson's films after the seminar, from *Braindead* on, contain much more coherent, structured narratives. Costa Botes, "Made in New Zealand: The Cinema of Peter Jackson," *nzedge.com* (May 2002): www.nzedge.com/features/ar-jackson.html.

25. "The Charlie Rose Show" (6 Feb. 2004).

26. [Paul Voigt,] "The Lord of the Rings Trilogy—Leveraging 2001–2004—Final Report" (Investment New Zealand, 5 Sept. 2004), 2–3.

27. "Govt to Secure Spin-offs from The Lord of the Rings and America's Cup Regatta with $9 Million Funding Package," New Zealand government website (11 July 2001): www.beehive.govt.nz/Print/PrintDocument.aspx?DocumentID=12272.

28. "Lord, What a Promotional Schedule," *filmNZnews* (Dec. 2002): 4, www.filmnz.com/studionz/whatsnew/news/02-December.pdf; Voigt, "Final Report," "Annex One The Lord of the Rings 2003/2004: Monitoring Report of Activities."

29. See "Coming Back for More" and "Rings Set in Concrete," *Tourism News* (July 2004): 6–7; "Rings Bring Thousands of Tourists to NZ," *Marlborough Gazette* (5 July 2004): www.stuff.co.nz/stuff/marlboroughexpress/0,2106,2961,525a6422,00.html.

30. "'The Lord of the Rings' Boosts New Zealand," *USA Today* (25 Mar. 2004): www.usatoday.com/travel/news/2004-03-25-nz-tourism_x.htm; "Putting 'Middle Earth' on the Map," *Scoop* (4 June 2004): www.scoop.co.nz/mason/stories/PA0406/S000081.htm.

31. Anne Beston and NZPA, "NZ Tops Travel Poll Second Year in a Row," *New Zealand Herald* (2 Feb. 2004): http://xmb.stuffucanuse.com/xmb/viewthread.php ?tid=405.

32. John Drinnan, "Kiwis Reup Rebates to Attract Epics," *Variety.com* (3 Mar. 2006): www.variety.com/story.asp?l=story&a=VR1117939232&c=13.

33. "Cineposium a Real Confidence Booster," *filmNZnews* (Aug. 2002): www .filmnz.com/studionz/whatsnew/news/02-August.pdf; "Rings Fuels Catalogue Sales," *Onfilm* (Aug. 2001): www.onfilm.co.nz/editable/lotr/Onfilm_0801b.html.

34. Tracy Withers, "Hobbits, Witches, King Kong Lift New Zealand's Filmmakers," *Bloomberg.com* (10 Feb. 2006): www.bloomberg.com/apps/news?pid= 10000088&sid=aW8EgH9S9HVs&refer=culture.

35. Eddie Cockrell, "*Samoan Wedding*," *Variety* (18–24 Sept. 2006): 93; Dennis Harvey, "*Out of the Blue*," *Variety* (16–22 Oct. 2006): 62.

36. John Drinnan, "Local Pix Mint Green with Kiwis," *Variety* (20–26 Feb. 2006): 10; Phil Wakefield, "Restless Natives," *HR* (6 Mar. 2006): 20.

37. "Film Premiere under Threat," *NZCity* (30 Apr. 2003): home.nzcity.co.nz/ news/default.asp?id=31065&c=w; "Embassy Upgrade Thrills Capital," *nzoom.com* (8 May 2003): onenews.nzoom.com/onenews_detail/0,1227,188587–1–7,00.html; Steve Rendle and Tom Cardy, "Date Set for Return of the King," *stuff* (24 May 2003): www.stuff.co.nz/inl/print/0,1478,2495810a10,00.html; and Julie Jacobson, "Failed Fundraising Puts Rings Theatre in Public Hands," *stuff* (30 Oct. 2003): www.stuff .co.nz/stuff/print/0,1478,2709217a2202,00.html; Sandy George, "Village Skycity Takes Control of the Embassy," *ScreenDaily.com* (23 Oct. 2005): www.screendaily .com/print.asp?storyid=23823.

38. New Zealand Institute of Economic Research, *Scoping the Lasting Effects of "The Lord of the Rings."*

39. A brief passage in the *Return* EE DVD's "The Passing of an Age" supplement contains shots of the low-level flyover.

40. Bill Higgins, "Outwellington'ed," *Variety* (8–14 Dec. 2003): 79.

41. For a vivid description of the Embassy Oscar party, see "PM Joins Celebrations," *stuff* (2 Mar. 2004): www.stuff.co.nz/stuff/print/0,1478,2831958a11,00.html; Phil Bartsch, "Ring of Confidence," *Escape.com.au* (16 Apr. 2005): escape.news.com/ au/story/0,9142,15028174–38615,00.html. Positively Wellington Tourism sponsored Bartsch's visit.

42. Sharon Cuzens, "LOTR Spin-offs," *Bright* (Jan. 2004): www.virtualkaty.com/ company/press_releases/Jan_2004_NZTE_s_Bright_Magazine.pdf.

43. Nick Smith, "Sound Revolution Set to Make Millions," *National Business Review* (12 Mar. 2004): www.virtualkaty.com/company/press_releases/march_2004 _sound_revolution_nbr.pdf; "Virtual Katy Hits the Road Again," *National Business Review* (18 Apr. 2005): www.nbr.co.nz/home/column_article.asp?id=11804&cid =8&cname=News.

44. Anne Thompson, "Fox Got Bigger Hit, But WB Happy with Singer," *HR*

(18–20 Aug. 2006): 8; Jody Duncan, "Dark Phoenix Rising," *Cinefex* 106 (July 2006): 40.

45. Nicole Laporte, "Revolution Rides 'Horse,'" *Variety.com* (6 Feb. 2006): www .variety.com/article/VR1117937506?categoryid=13&cs=1.

46. "Jackson on Mission for 'Dambusters,'" *HR* (5–11 Sept. 2006): 68; Borys Kit, "Serpent Time for Jackson," *HR* (12–18 Sept. 2006): 53.

47. Jill Goldsmith and Nicole LaPorte, "When Harry Met Leo," *Variety* (11–17 Sept. 2006): 1; the first interview where Jackson reacted to the *Hobbit* announcement was the last of a five-part series where all of the director's new projects were discussed: "Quint Interviews Peter Jackson about His Next Fantasy Epic: Naomi Novik's TEMERAIRE Series!!!" AICN (12 Sept. 2006): www.aintitcool.com/node/30014; "Quint and Peter Jackson, Part II: THE LOVELY BONES!!!" (13 Sept. 2006): www.aintit cool.com/node/30037; "Part 3: Quint and Peter Jackson Talk HALO!!!" (14 Sept. 2006): www.aintitcool.com/node/30050; "Part 4: Peter Jackson and Quint Discuss THE DAMBUSTERS Remake!!!" (15 Sept. 2006): www.aintitcool.com/node/30076; and "Part 5: Quint and Peter Jackson Talk THE HOBBIT and a Potential Return to Low Budget Horror!!!" (16 Sept. 2006): www.aintitcool.com/node/30085. The second interview was for *Entertainment Weekly* online: Steve Daly, "Action Jackson," *EW.com* (24 Sept. 2006): www.ew.com/ew/report/0,6115,1538494_1_0_00.html and www.ew .com/ew/report/0,6115,1538494–2-2_1||233612|1_,00.html. Daly based an article on this interview: "Shire Circumstances," *EW* (29 Sept. 2006): 16.

As I finished proofreading this book, the situation concerning the *Hobbit* film remained in flux. On 10 January 2007, Bob Shaye declared that Jackson would not direct the film for New Line. A coolness had arisen between the director and the company over a lawsuit Jackson had filed to force an audit of the records concerning income from *Fellowship* and its ancillaries. With the production rights to *The Hobbit* due to revert to Saul Zaentz in 2009, New Line was under pressure to find a new director. However the situation develops, *The Hobbit* will eventually carry on the Tolkien-based film franchise. See "Shaye: New Line Blacklists Jackson," *Sci Fi Wire* (10 Jan. 2007): www.scifi.com/scifiwire/index.php?category=3&id=39462; and "Wingnut and Peter Jackson respond to Bob Shaye's tongue-lashings!!" AICN (10 Jan. 2007): http://www.aintitcool.com/node/31211.

48. Lauren Beukes, "Capetown Boomtown," *HR* (17–23 Aug. 2004): 19–22; "After Charlize," *Economist* (6 Mar. 2004): 58; Christelle De Jager, "S. African Film Complex Faces Delay," *Variety.com* (20 July 2005): www.variety.com/story.asp?l=story&a= VR1117926289&c=1043; Christelle De Jager, "Cape Town Studio Bows," *Variety* (21– 27 Aug. 2006): 10.

49. Marlene Edmunds, "City Seeks Starring Role," *Variety* (24–30 Nov. 2003): 14.

50. David S. Cohen, "Blighty Challenging U.S. f/x Companies," *Variety.com* (28 Dec. 2004): www.variety.com/story.asp?l=story&a=VR1117915509&c=19.

51. David S. Cohen, "'War' Is Hell for F/X Shops," *Variety* (22–28 May 2006): 3.

52. Liz Shackleton, "Mastering the Art," *SI* (18 Aug. 2006): 10–13.

53. Nancy Tartaglione-Vialatte, "French Post Bites Back," *SI* (16 Mar. 2006): 16.

54. The Center for Entertainment Industry Data and Research, "U.S. Runaway Major Feature Film Production Continues to Grow as More Countries Introduce Federal Tax Incentives, Continuing Study Shows," press release (30 July 2006): www.ceidr.org/CEIDR_News_3.pdf.

INDEX

A & E, 118

ABC, 110, 111, 118, 187

Academy Awards and nominations, 51, 331–32; AFMA films, 258; *Black Book*, 273; *The English Patient*, 23; *Godfather* films, 363n46; *Heavenly Creatures*, 21–22; infotainment, 110, 111; *King Kong*, 299; *Maria Full of Grace*, 261; R-rated films, 276; *The Sea Inside*, 261; *Vera Drake*, 261; Winston, 281; Zaentz films, 19

Academy Awards and nominations—*Rings*, 17, 52; Air NZ promotion, 108; fan parties, 185–87, 189–90; *Fellowship*, 204; Investment NZ parties, 312; Knowles prediction, 155; New Zealand location choice unchanged by, 309; press kits before, 123; *Return*, 20, 52, 218, 251, 258, 276, 299, 322, 324*fig*, 337n64, 365n16; technical, 51, 52, 97, 100; TORN April Fool's news, 159–60; Tourism NZ billboards, 313; *Towers*, 51, 186, 299

Access All Areas Events Ltd., 202

Acclaim mo-cap studio, 231

Ackerman, Forrest J., 18–19, 150

action figures, *Rings*, 11*fig*, 193–94, 197, 215

action scenes: battle styles, 61, 246; *Rings* film vs. novel, 59–60

Activision, 226–27, 229, 231, 356n10

actors: costs rising for sequels, 32–33; fame from franchised movies, 6; importance to viewers, 5; video games, 229–30, 232. *See also* stars; *individually named actors*

actors—*Rings*: action figures, 193–94, 197, 215; Cannes, 44, 45; casting, 8, 37, 57; DVD commentaries, 212; extras, 142, 170; family atmosphere with crew, 309; fan cons, 201–3; fanfiction effects, 182; fans admired by, 188; fan site photographs, 166; farewell videos, 217–18; interviews, 45, 61, 63, 81–82, 117, 126–30, 145, 212, *Plate 1*; mail from children, 314; New Zealand enthusiasm, 284, 312; *Rings* books not read by, 59, 83; stardom, 6, 33; straight, 179; stunt performers, 61, 138, 241–43, 246, 250, 308; video games, 238–46, 247; websites, 129, 139, 144–49, 159, 347n36. *See also individually named actors*

Adamson, Andrew, 290
ADR (automatic dialogue replacement), 148
The Adventures of Huckleberry Finn, 6
The Adventures of Tom Sawyer, 6
advertising, 105–6; international, 263, 265; Internet, 141, 154, 159, 161; magazine, 106; making-ofs, 113–14; video game, 237. *See also* infotainment; publicity and marketing
A-Film, Netherlands, 272–73
Ain't It Cool News (AICN), 133, 149–55, 183, 336n38; finances, 154, 159; Jackson and, 43, 83, 150, 181; New Line cooperation, 162; *Towers* trailer, 136
airlines. *See* Air New Zealand; Glenorchy Air
Air New Zealand, 107–9, 311, 319; "Aragorn" plane, *Plate 6;* Clark interview, 283; DVDs of *Rings*, 215; "Frodo" plane, 108, 322; making-of documentaries, 119
Aitken, Matt, 41–42, 235–36, 301
Alien, 84
Allen & Unwin, 1–2, 18–19, 84
Alley, Judy: Cannes, 40, 43, 44; merchandise, 196; video games, 236–38, 246, 250
Alley, Stan, 188
Alliance Atlantis, Canada, 198–200, 273–74
Altman, Robert, 72, 262
Amazon.com, 154, 159, 167, 178, 278
American Film Market (AFM), 257–58, 263–65, 266*fig*, 319, 330, 360n1
American Film Marketing Association (AFMA), 258, 360n2
America's Cup, 310, 311, 320
Ancalagon the Black, 68, 165, 339n24
Ancel, Michel, 251
Anderson, Bob, 57–58, 61, 241
Anderson, Gregg, 312
Animal Logic, 327–28
animated films: *Charlotte's Web*, 277; Oscars, 331–32; *Rings* flop (Bakshi, 1978), 2, 8, 12, 20, 25, 34, 55; *Rings* proposal (Ackerman, 1957), 18–19; video games, 248

Antonioni, Michelangelo, 19
AOL, 135, 141, 142, 215; Time Warner merger, 48–50, 140–42, 223, 259–60
Applause gifts, *Rings*, 194
Apple Films, 19
Arden, Dan, 114–19, 120
Armageddon, 336n47
Around the World in 80 Days, 300
Artemis Fowl, 278
art-house multiplexes, Sundance Theaters, 332
Artisan Entertainment, 258
artworks: *Rings*, 86–89, 341n16, *Plate 4;* sequels, 6–7; Tolkien fanart, 169–80. *See also* illustrators
Asia: distribution firms, 267, 268, 274; postproduction sector, 298, 303, 328–29. *See also* Hong Kong; Japan; Korea
Astin, Sean, 37; Academy Awards night, 276; fan party, 186; press junket for *Return* premiere, *Plate 1;* in press kit, 123; website, 145
Auckland, 290; America's Cup, 320; Fatpipe, 305; Investment NZ, 313; Maxwell, 241; *Narnia*, 162; Oktobor, 318; Pacific Renaissance Pictures, 308; Red Carpet Tours, 288; South Pacific, 365n7
audience: age, 9, 53–55, 74, 81; family, 6, 74, 143; gender, 9, 81, 142, 157–58, 160, 201–2. *See also* fan
Aurum, Spanish distribution, 273–74
Austin Powers, 31, 34, 49, 135, 206, 221, 223
Australia, 290; *Matrix*, 40, 300, 327–28; New Zealand brain drain to, 309; postproduction sector, 295, 296, 297, 298, 303, 327–28, 329; *Rings* crew from, 37, 38; travel industry, 320; Village Roadshow distribution, 267, 274
Avalon Studios, 296, 365n7
awards: AFMA Lifetime Achievement Award, 258; DVD, 216; Mithrils, 350n13; television shows, 110, 111, 276. *See also* Academy Awards and nominations

Back to the Future, 7
Bad Taste, 20–21, 28, 290, 308, 317–18
Baillie, Genevieve, 172–74, 189
Bakshi, Ralph, *Rings* animated film (1978),
    2, 8, 12, 20, 25, 34, 55
Ballantine, Tolkien tie-in products, 7, 10
Bangkok, Oriental Post, 329
The Bastards Have Landed, Jackson fan
    site, 159
Batman films, 3, 6, 31, 55, 81
"The Battle for Middle-earth" video
    games, 224–25, 244–48, *Plates 7,8*
Beacon Pictures, 326
Behind the Scenes: The Lord of the Rings:
    The Return of the King, 118
Beijing, Soundfirm, 329
Berlusconi, Silvio, 273
Berney, Bob, 262
Besson, Luc, 329
Beswarick, Jamie, 90
"Beyond Good & Evil" video game, 251
Beyond the Movie: The Lord of the Rings,
    117
Beyond the Movie: The Lord of the Rings:
    The Return of the King, 118
Big Primate Pictures, 291
billboards, Tourism NZ, 108, 313, 314*fig*
Bio Extra: The Lord of the Rings Trilogy, 118
Biography Channel, 118
Black Book, 272–73
Black Sheep, 303
Blade, 48–49, 53, 154, 206, 267
Blade Runner, 84, 86
The Blair Witch Project, 113, 134–35, 258
Blanchett, Cate, 8, 37, 117
Blockbuster, 219, 222
Bloom, Orlando: Cannes, 44, 45; fighting
    skills, 58, 61; press junket for *Return*
    premiere, *Plate 1;* in press kit, 121;
    stardom, 6, 33; video games, 241, 243
blooper videos, *Rings*, 217, 218
BlueTights.net, 164
Boesky, Keith, 228
Bogdanovich, Peter, 53, 55, 74
Bonnet, Pascal, 228
Bonnier AB, Sweden, 268–69, 272
books: children's, 1, 11, 277–78, 326; coffee-

table books, 87; Harper-Collins, 10–
    11, 194, 301; Houghton Mifflin, 10–
    11, 87, 117, 186, 194, 358n34; *"The*
    Lord of the Rings" Location Guidebook,
    289; sourcebooks, 195–96; tie-in
    books, 7, 10, 12, 87, 94, 95, 117, 194,
    301, 302, 341n16, *Plate 4*; video game
    strategy guides, 245, 358n41. *See also*
    Tolkien, J.R.R.
Booth, Melissa: Forde online reports, 142;
    junket interviews, 127, 131; on Ian
    McKellen, 148; press kit, 120; press
    release, 120; vs. spies, 135; TORN
    usefulness, 159
Booth, Nick, 188
Bordwell, David, 84
Borsellino, Mary, 177
Boston, Museum of Science, 199*fig*
Botes, Costa, 22, 114–19, 188, 210, 366n24
The Bounty, 318
box-office totals, 112. *See also* gross
Boyd, Billy, 77, 78, 186, 244, *Plate 1*
Boyens, Philippa, 17–18, 25, 83; Academy
    Awards for *Return*, 52; departure
    of film from novel, 68, 69–71, 72;
    directing, 38; DVDs, 212, 217; eBay,
    180; fan parties, 185; press junket, 126;
    Salo working with, 95; script length,
    77–78
Bragg, Jason, 284–85, 288, 289
Braindead/Dead Alive, 19, 21, 25, 58, 318,
    366n24
brain drain, New Zealand, 290, 306, 309
Brando, Marlon, 230
brands: film franchises, 5–6, 106, 125, 197;
    partnerships, 106–9, 215, 250, 274,
    311, 322; rebranding of New Zealand,
    310–11
Bratman, David, 59, 338n8
Bravo, 118
Bravo! Channel, Canada, 119
Bridger, Sue, 304, 306
Bridget Jones's Diary: The Edge of Reason,
    300
Britain. *See* United Kingdom
Broadway, Cliff (Quickbeam), 48, 156, 159,
    185, 186, 188–89

Brodie, Ian, 289
Brooke, James, 285–86
Bryan, Mara, 318
Buchhorn, Kathryn (Skybly), 143
Buck, Karina, 118, 119, 120
budget: advertising, 105–6, 141; *The Blair Witch Project*, 135; Dutch film, 272–73; Film NZ, 316; Miramax, 25–26, 27, 36–37, 40, 80; New Zealand domestic features, 312; New Zealand location, 31–33; *Rings* compared with *Titanic*, 33, 335n34; *Rings* Films 2 and 3, 37, 51, 96, 243–44; worldwide revenues in ratio to, 262. *See also* costs; finance; income
Buelles, Marcel, 200–201
Buena Vista, 214, 262, 271
Buf Compagnie, 329
Burger King, brands partnerships, 107
Burton, Tim, 3, 24, 130, 228, 332, 363n36

Caan, James, 232
calendars, *Rings* tie-in products, 10, 11*fig*, 136
Calisuri. *See* Pirrotta, Chris
Cameron, James, 23, 24, 33, 82
Campbell, Jonathan, 91
Camperdown Studios, 293
Campion, Jane, 290
Canada: Alliance Atlantis, 198–200, 273–74; Bravo! Channel, 119
Cañizares, Alberto G., 89
Cannes, 257–58; *Armageddon*, 336n47; international distribution, 40–41, 257–58, 262–63, 265, 268, 272–73, 301–2; *The Matrix Reloaded*, 252
Cannes preview—*Rings*, 8, 40–49, 119, 131, 208; domestic distributors, 269; exhibitions emulating, 198; Film NZ map, 316; international distributors, 40–41, 257–58, 268, 273, 301–2; Internet webmasters, 43, 48, 88–89, 184; New Zealand film industry benefiting from, 317; party, 42–48, 47*fig*, 126, 340n8, *Plate 3*; press, 32, 43, 44, 45, 126; in *Quest for the Ring* on Fox, 114; Shaye view, 40, 42, 43–44, 47, 79

Canterbury Sightseeing, 289
Carrey, Jim, 31, 32, 229–30
CBS, 110
CD-ROMs, games, 228–29
CDs, video game music, 230
cell phone games, 249–50
Centro Digital Pictures, Hong Kong, 328–29
CGI. *See* computer-generated imagery (CGI)
Chabon, Michael, 277–78
Challis, Erica (Tehanu), 134, 155–60; fan cons, 156*fig*, 201; fan parties, 185, 190; *Narnia* site, 162; New Line-Burger King partnership, 107; Red Carpet Tours, 288; trespassing notice, 157, 201, 288. *See also* TheOneRing.net (TORN)
Chan, Jackie, 261
Charlie Bone books, 278
Charlotte's Web, 277
Chercoeur, Bellemaine, 177
The Children of Húrin (Tolkien), 11
children's books, 1, 11, 277–78, 326. *See also* Tolkien, J.R.R.
Chow, Stephen, 329
Christensen, Hayden, 232
The Chronicles of Narnia, 275
The Chronicles of Narnia: The Lion, the Witch and the Wardrobe, 277, 319, 326; Canterbury Sightseeing's "Through the Wardrobe Tour," 289; Coddington, 319; collectibles, 197, 302; Crowley, 316; Internet fans, 162; Mark Johnson, 5, 162, 298, 317; Massive program, 280; New Zealand Large Budget Screen Production Grant, 317, 327; Wellington, 322; Weta Workshop effects, 325
"The Chronicles of Riddick: Escape from Butcher Bay" video game, 232
Cinesite, 328
Cingular, brand partnerships, 106
Claire, Cassandra, 178
Clark, Helen, 283, 310–11, 312
Clarke, Hannah, 188
Clarke, Susanna, 277

Cocktail, 318
Coddington, Tim, 319
Colfer, Eoin, 278
collectibles, 194, 196–97, 302; collector's edition DVDs, 207; Creation, 202–3; fan parties, 186; Knowles family, 149–50; Lilith of Sherwood, 167; of *Rings* crew members, 83. *See also* eBay; merchandise; Sideshow Weta; tie-in products
Collins, Annie, 74
color grading, 280–81, 291, 298–99
Columbia, 4–5
Comic-Con, 154, 167, 189, 200
Company Wide Shut, 208, 212
computer-generated imagery (CGI), 22, 30, 96–101; cost, 33, 51, 98–100; facilities, 294–95, 299; fantasy, 58, 60, 278; *The Frighteners*, 22–24, 294, 295; games and films, 227, 231, 249; "Grove" code, 301; *Heavenly Creatures*, 293; Hong Kong's Centro Digital Pictures, 328–29; Lord of the Peeps, 172; Massive program, 97, 280, 301, 323, 364n52; "milestones," 300–301; New Line press release, 36; *Rings* Films 2 and 3 budget, 51, 96; subcontracted, 295; Weta Digital capability, 41, 89, 96–98. *See also* digital technology; special effects
conglomerates, media, 4–5, 110
Connery, Sean, 230
conventions, fan. *See* fan cons
Cook, Randy, 185
Cordova, Carlene, 185, 186, 188–89
Corman, Patrick, 278
Cossar, Tim, 320
costs: advertising, 105–6, 141; cost-per-minute, 33; DVDs, 219; filmmaking facilities, 297, 299; independent films, 257–59; *Rings* production, 31–37, 80–81, 284, 335n33; *Rings* website, 141; special effects, 5, 27, 33, 51, 96, 98–100, 223; Tolkien Online, 161; VHS videos, 219, 222; video game production, 226, 241. *See also* budget

costumes: *Rings*, 63–64, 65, 79, 89, 91, 127, 323
council-of-elrond.com, 161–62
Creating Lord of the Rings Symphony: A Composer's Journey through Middle Earth, 118–19
Creation Entertainment, 201–3
crew: from abroad, 37–38, 306–7, 318; directing, 38, 78–79, 82, 318; family atmosphere, 309–10; Internet activity, 180–84; loyalty to Jackson, 37, 76, 81, 309–10; New Zealand film industry, 32, 37, 306–10, 318–19, 321, 326; straight, 179; Tolkien/*Rings* fans, 82–83; training, 307–9, 366–67n24; upskilling, 306–10, 329. *See also* Miramar
Criterion Collection, 207
crossovers, gen fics, 176
Crowley, James, 316
Cuarón, Alfonso, 3
Cunningham, Carolynne, 38
Curse of the Golden Flower, 329
The CW, 110

Dafoe, Willem, 229
Dambusters, 326
Dark Horse, 302
Dart River Safaris, 286–87
The Da Vinci Code, 248, 363n38
Dawtrey, Adam, 263
de Andres, Sherry, 170, 174
Decipher, 142–43, 172, 195–96
Deltamac, Hong Kong, 274
Denmark, SF Film, 268–72, 270*fig*
design, *Rings*, 75, 77–80, 86–101; detail and craftsmanship, 91–96, 93*fig*, 94*fig*; DVDs, 212–13; merchandise style guides, 194–95. *See also* digital technology; production; special effects; Weta Workshop
diaries, 163; Jackson (*King Kong*), 127, 163–64, 218; McKellen (*Rings*), 144, 145–47
DiCaprio, Leonardo, 125–26
Dickson, Ngila, 89; costumes, 63–64, 65, 79, 89, 91, 127, 323; press junket, 126, 127; television training, 308

Die Another Day, 318
Diesel, Vin, 232
Digital Domain, 295, 328
Digital Factory, 329
digital technology, 282–83, 327; games and films, 231–32; grading, 280–81, 291, 298–99; international filmmaking facilities, 326–29; IT departments, 302, 304–6; outsourcing, 328; *Rings* boost to New Zealand, 323–25; *Rings* design, 96–101. *See also* animated films; computer-generated imagery (CGI); Weta Digital
Dimension, 25
directing, 38, 78–79, 82, 318. *See also* Jackson, Peter
director's cuts, 208, 214, 216
"Dirty Harry" video games, 230
Disney: ABC, 110; animated films, 332; brand partnerships, 106; Disneyland, 111; expensive R-rated films, 276; franchise principle, 4; *Narnia*, 277; *Rings*, 25–27, 35; *The Sixth Sense* DVDs, 209, 214; *Snow and the Seven*, 277; video supplements, 206–8, 222; Walt Disney, 4, 111; Walt Disney Home Entertainment, 206–7. *See also* Miramax
distribution rights: *The Hobbit*, 23; independent films, 257–58, 262–74. *See also* international distribution; licensing rights
Dobner, Nina, 236–37, 246, 248; actors doing game roles, 241; Hugo Weaving recording session, 247–48; Shelob for "Return," 240; speed of game figures' movement, 243; Three Foot Six office, 236, 293; weapons through customs, 242
documentaries: about fans, 185, 187–90. *See also* making-of documentaries
Donaldson, Roger, 318
Don Quixote, 6
"Doom" video game, 228–29
Dority, Rose, 210
Dourif, Brad, 246
Doyle, Peter, 280, 298–99

Dragon Con, 189
Dragons of Deltora, 278
DreamWorks, 163, 205, 226–27, 231–33, 262, 332
Dreamworld Film City, 328
Drumm, Kathleen, 317
dubbing, Jackson's control over, 89
Duvall, Robert, 232
DVDs, 9, 204–23, 250; awards, 216; *Creating Lord of the Rings Symphony: A Composer's Journey through Middle Earth*, 119; director's cuts, 208, 214, 216; "The End of All Things" supplement, 211; extended versions, 106, 113–19, 143, 204–18, 271, 355n44; fan club charter members, 143; fan documentary, 189; *Fellowship*, 50, 117, 118, 119, 135, 136, 204–5, 208–9, 212–16, 220–21, 271, 355n43; games, 354n31; *Harry Potter*, 215, 221, 355n43; "Infinifilm," 205–6; international producers, 265, 271, 272; Internet, 136; Jackson, 211–18, 250; *King Kong*, 127, 163, 213, 218; making-ofs, 106, 113–19, 163, 204, 207, 210; menus, 212–13; "Motion Picture Masterpieces" (MGM), 338n5; New Line department, 207–23, 260, 354n31, 355n44; players, 106, 222, 265; rentals vs. sales, 219–22, 355–56n47; *Return*, 52, 60–61, 65, 77, 111, 118, 119, 210–17, 222, 224, 260, 271, 339–40n26, 356n54; *Rings* in both theatrical and extended versions, 51, 52, 115, 214, 223; *Rings* on cutting edge, 10; sales, 204, 205, 219–23, 265; *The Sixth Sense*, 209, 214; still images, 212; *Towers*, 106, 118, 119, 209, 215, 216, 222

E3 (Electronic Entertainment Exposition), 225, 227
E!, 111, 118
E! Online, 139, 141–42, 157
Easter Eggs, 205, 353n14
Eastwood, Clint, 230
eBay, 180; Creations shop, 202–3; Lilith of Sherwood collectibles, 167; *Rings*

animated film (Bakshi, 1978), 12; *Rings* press kits, 123

Ebert, Roger, 105, 110, 124–25, 129, 152

Eclair, 329

economy: New Zealand benefit from *Rings*, 284–87, 299, 306–12, 315, 316, 320, 322–23; New Zealand currency fluctuations, 32, 83, 327, 329; tax breaks for film production, 264, 317, 327, 330; Wellington, 321. *See also* finance; franchises; international economy; publicity and marketing

Edelist, Evan, 207

Edelman, Scott, 139–40

Einhorn, Stephen, 205

Eisner, Michael, 25–27, 35–36, 40

Eldest, 278

Eldridge, Cheryl, 323

Electronic Arts (EA) video games, 186, 194, 197, 224–53, 356n10; fanfiction contest, 183; Game Innovation Lab, 249; James Bond, 227–35, 356n10; in *The Lord of the Rings Fan Club Official Movie Magazine*, 144; MMORPG, 358n45; request forms, 236, 238, 239*fig*; "The Two Towers," 204, 224, 234–37, 236*fig*; "Video Game Music and Sound Design" course, 249. *See also* Dobner, Nina; Skaggs, Mark; Young, Neil

electronic press kits (EPKs), 108, 118–24, 122*fig*, 128

Elf, 27, 260

ELF con, 201, 202, 203

Elfman, Danny, 230

Embassy Theater, 320–22, 323*fig*

Emmerich, Toby, 262, 277

employees. *See* labor

"The End of All Things" supplement, 211

The English Patient, 23, 34

Entertainment Film Distributors, United Kingdom, 273

Entertainment Tonight, 110

Entertainment Weekly, 111, 183; DVDs, 216; *Harry Potter* fanfiction, 183; Jackson-fan connections, 163; McKellen.com, 147; Oscar fan parties, 187; *Return* Oscar predictions, 337n64; *Rings* special number, 111, 127

"Enter the Matrix" video game, 252

EPKs (electronic press kits), 108, 118–24, 122*fig*, 128

E-Posts, McKellen.com, 146–47, 179–80, 196, 347–48

Eragon, 278

erotic fanfiction, 175, 176, 177–82

Esgate, Patricia, 165

Estelio Ammen, 177

Executioners from Shaolin, 64*fig*

extras, *Rings*, 142, 170

Falconer, Daniel, 90, 93–94, 201, 279

family: audience, 6, 74, 143; Jackson family time, 309; *Rings* cast and crew atmosphere, 309–10; *Rings* fan club, 143; Tolkien novel family trees, 84

fan: fan clubs (general), 142–43; fanfilms, 183; Hollywood arrangements, 162–63, 165; marketing roles, 105, 107, 132, 135–64; New Line Cinema working with, 138, 139, 149–64, 165, 183–84; professional, 152; "textual poaching," 169. *See also* audience; fan cons; fanfiction; Lord of the Rings Fan Club; Tolkien/*Rings* fans

fan cons, 167, 174, 189, 200–203; Comic-Con, 154, 167, 189, 200; One Ring Celebration (ORC), 156*fig*, 183, 201–3, 202*fig*, 203*fig*, 218; Visions Con, 353n8

fanfiction, 169–83, 349–51; book-canon, 175, 350n13; crossovers, 176; erotic, 175, 176, 177–82; fanfiction.net, 176; femmeslash, 178; film-canon, 175, 350n13; FPS fics, 175, 179, 182; gen fics, 175–77, 350n13; *Harry Potter*, 176, 177, 183, 351n30; het fics, 175, 176, 177–79, 180; Mithril Awards, 350n13; *Rings*, 169–83, 349–50; romantic, 175, 176, 177–79; RPS fics, 175, 176, 179–80, 181–82; slash fics, 175, 176, 177–82, 351

fanfilms, 183

fantasy, 54, 57, 274–78; in all-time world-
    wide top-grossing films, 275; Burton,
    363n36; market, 9, 55–56; *Rings* as
    history rather than, 85–86, 90, 94;
    after *Rings* for New Line, 261, 277;
    Rings popular-genre conventions
    with, 57–59; slash fics, 179–80; and
    video games, 234
Fantasy Films, 19–20
farewell videos, *Rings*, 217–18
*The Father Christmas Letters/Letters from
    Father Christmas*, 11
Fatpipe, 304–6, 327
Fatty, 161, 162, 165
FedCon GmbH, 200–201
Fellowship Festival, London, 202
The Fellowship of the Ring, 2, 257, 363n38;
    Academy Awards, 204; action scenes,
    59–60; Baillies, 172; budget rise for
    Films 2 and 3 after success of, 37,
    51, 96, 243–44; clutter in Saruman's
    study, 92–93, 93*fig;* December release,
    48, 49, 51, 347n36; digital color grad-
    ing, 280–81, 291; digital technology,
    96, 98, 99*fig;* DVDs, 50, 117, 118, 119,
    135, 136, 204–5, 208–9, 212–16, 220–
    21, 271, 355n43; fan responses, 140, 145,
    166; film script, 25; *Gandalf Returns to
    Bag End* (Howe), 87, *Plates 4,5;* gross,
    50, 96, 220–21, 274, 337n63; Internet
    publicity, 141, 159, 347n36, 347n40;
    among literary adaptations, 57–59;
    making-ofs, 106, 117, 118, 119, 204;
    martial arts choreography, 64; Menand
    review, 54; merchandise, 173; Mines
    of Moria sequence, 41–42; mobile
    phone game, 250; New Line financial
    risks, 49–50, 259, 267–68; novel ap-
    pearance, 2, 18; number of significant
    characters, 72; postproduction, 42,
    304; premieres, 39, 126, 142, 145, 320;
    press junkets, 126, 131; press kit, 121,
    122, 122*fig; Quest for the Ring* pro-
    gram ads, 114, 117; role-playing game
    sourcebook, 196; screen savers, 174;
    special effects, 295; unconventional
    qualities, 72; *Vanity Fair* on set, 131;

VHS tape, 204, 220, 221, 271, 355n43;
    video game, 233, 234, 235
Fellowship of 22, 189–90
femmeslash, 178
fiction. *See* books; fanfiction
50 Ways of Saying Fabulous, 319
Figpeep Lives!, 174, 175*fig*
Figwit, 170–72, 171*fig*, 174, 178, 188
Figwit Lives!, 170–72, 171*fig*, 174, 188
Film and Video Technicians Guild, New
    Zealand, 306
film-canon fanfiction, 175, 350n13
Film Comment, 276
film festivals, 167, 273, 332; London, 202,
    319; Toronto, 263; Wellington (July
    2004), 116, 118. *See also* Cannes; Sun-
    dance Film Festival
film franchises, 4–7, 131–32, 331–32;
    brands, 5–6, 106, 125, 197; games
    most important to, 233; genres chosen
    for, 6; New Line interest in, 31–32,
    206, 223; *Rings* durability, 197; *Rings*
    franchise success, 7, 9–10, 18. *See also*
    collectibles; licensing rights; mer-
    chandise; sequels
film industry: adaptation rights for sale,
    34; DVD domination, 223; fan clubs
    created by, 142–43; "independent,"
    257; before infotainment, 109–10;
    Internet support, 154–55; layoffs, 49,
    259, 260; nations' healthy film indus-
    tries, 332; video game competition/
    convergence, 225–33, 237–41, 247–
    49, 251–52. *See also* crew; film fran-
    chises; film industry benefits from
    Rings; New Zealand film industry;
    production
film industry benefits from *Rings*, 9; digital
    technology transformations, 280, 282;
    foreign-language films, 9, 262–74;
    independent films, 9, 262–74. *See also*
    New Zealand film industry
Film New Zealand, 311, 316–17, 319, *Plates
    11,12*
The Film Unit, 44, 76, 187, 291, 296–98;
    Jackson ownership, 20, 44, 291, 297;
    The Last Samurai, 306; Park Road

Post, 291, 297–99, 303, 325; quality, 329

Film Wellington, 302, 318

finance: AICN, 154, 159; fan parties, 185, 186–87; filmmaking facilities, 44, 297, 299, 302; "gap financing," 264; by international distribution, 39, 258; Jackson and Walsh personal debt, 44, 297; New Line risks and successes, 29–40, 49–50, 80–81, 194–95, 258–62, 265, 267–68, 338n8; New Zealand government support, 310–25, 327; presales, 39, 259, 264–65, 267, 268; soft-money sources, 264; tax breaks for film production, 264, 317, 327, 330; Time Warner, 259–60; TORN, 159, 186–87; Wellington *Return* premiere, 321–22. *See also* budget; costs; economy; gross; Miramax; New Line Cinema

Fine Line, 28, 261–62. *See also* Picturehouse

Finkelstein, David, 184

Finnie, Hilary, 286

Fist of Fury, 62*fig*

5D Colossus, 280–81

Flight, Simone, 309, 312–13

Flight of the Conchords, 170, 172, 188

Fogelson, Alex, 112

Forbeck, Matt, 195–96

Ford, Harrison, 77

Ford, John, 56, 65, 73

Forde, John, 142, 145–46, 157

foreign distribution. *See* international distribution

foreign-language films, 56–57; A-Film, 272–73; cable channels, 332; *Rings* success benefiting market for, 9, 262–74; SF Film, 270–71

Forgotten Silver, 22, 114–15

Forrest Gump, 275, 363n38

Fortuna, Amy, 178

Fox channel, 114, 117

Fox Studios Australia, 40, 327–28. *See also* Twentieth Century Fox

Fox Trot, 69*fig*

FPS fics, 175, 179, 182. *See also* RPS fics; slash fics

France: Metropolitan distributors, 267, 268, 273; postproduction sector, 329; Ubisoft creative headquarters, 251. *See also* Cannes

franchises, 331; *Rings* novels, 10–12, 11*fig;* worldbuilding, 84. *See also* film franchises; licensing rights; tie-in products

Fraser, Toa, 319

French, Hayley, 115

The Frighteners, 22–24, 28; CGI, 22–24, 294, 295; laser discs, 114, 208, 214; making-of documentary, 114, 208

Fritz, Ben, 248

Frodo Is Great . . . Who Is That?!!, 188

"From Russia with Love" video game, 230

Fry, Carla, 300, 365n16

Funke, Alex, 37, 282, 306; menu shoot, 212–13; miniatures, 294, 306–7; on New Zealand's appeal, 309–10

Funke, Cornelia, 277

Gajadhar, Roxane, 119

Galano, Camela, 258

games: cell phone, 249–50; Decipher, 142–43, 172, 195–96; DVD, 228, 354n31; Parker Brothers, 215–16; *Rings*, 10, 11*fig*, 142–43, 195, 215–16; role-playing games (RPGs), 195–96, 245, 247, 357n24, 358n45, 359n54; trading-card games (TCGs), 172, 194, 195, 196, 197; trivia, 250. *See also* video games

Games Workshop, 186

Gandalf Returns to Bag End (Howe), 87, *Plates 4,5*

"gap financing," 264

Gatward-Ferguson, David and Amanda, 287

geek factor, 82–84. *See also* fan; Internet

Gelfman, Sam, 19

gender: *Rings*/Tolkien audience/fans, 9, 81, 142, 157–58, 160, 201–2; slash fic authors, 178; *Star Trek* audience, 142; Yahoo! groups profiles, 178

gen fics, 175–77, 350n13

Gentle Giant, 197

George, Don, 316

Giant apparel, *Rings*, 194

Gilsdorf, Ethan, 12

Glenorchy Air, 285–86, 286*fig*

globalization, 100–101, 331–32; films shot abroad, 100–101, 282–83, 299–300, 316–17, 328–31

Globe, Brad, 232–33

Godfather films, 7, 56, 363n46

"Godfather" video games, 228, 230, 232, 248, 356n10

Golden Globe Awards, 111

Gone with the Wind, 337n63, 363n37

Good Morning, America, 110

Gorman, Ned, 281

Gormenghast, 364n47

grading, digital, 280–81, 291, 298–99

"Grand Theft Auto" video games, 226, 229

Gray, Steve, 242

Greenlee, Diane, 184–85

gross: all-time worldwide top-grossing films, 274–75; *The Blair Witch Project*, 135; *Fellowship*, 50, 96, 220–21, 274, 337n63; *Gone with the Wind*, 337n63, 363n37; independent films, 257; international, 50, 252, 337n63; *Return*, 52, 274, 337n63; *Rings* (all three), 9, 33, 274, 337n63; target audience and, 74; top twenty-five, 275; *Towers*, 51, 105, 274, 337n63; video sales/rentals compared with film gross, 220–22. *See also* box-office totals; budget; income; profits; sales

Guardians of Ga'Hoole, 278

Gulf + Western, 4

Hadad, Iris, 170, 174

Halo film, 253

"Halo" video game, 226, 253, 326

Hamlin, Marjorie, 307

Harley, Ruth, 308, 309, 317, 319

Harper-Collins, 10–11, 194, 301

Harryhausen, Ray, 58, 60

Harry Potter films: in all-time worldwide top-grossing films, 274; directors, 3; DVD, 215, 221, 355n43; fanfiction, 176, 177, 183, 351n30; fantasy's status, 9, 275, 276–77; *Rings* competition

with, 49–50, 51, 57; Time Warner, 49–50, 183, 223, 260; VHS sales, 220, 355n43

Harry Potter novels (Rowling), 277, 278

"Harry Potter" video games, 227, 228, 230, 235, 356n10

Hawks, Howard, 56, 73–74

HBO, 261, 262

Heavenly Creatures, 8, 21–22, 28, 34, 293

Hennah, Chris: Cannes party, 42–47; exhibitions, 198; tours for investors, 301; training, 307

Hennah, Dan: Cannes party, 42–47, 126; DVDs, 210, 213; exhibitions, 198–200; Park Road Post, 298; real wood and leather props, 92; Tolkien fan, 83; tours for investors, 301; training, 307

Hennah, Nancy, 307

Henry, Louise, 202

Henson, Jim, 89

Hercules: The Legendary Journeys, 241, 308

Hermeling, Pim, 272

Der Herr der Ringe website, 200

het fics, 175, 176, 177–79, 180

Hickton, George, 313, 315

Hirai, Kaz, 225–26

His Dark Materials, 277, 278

The Hobbit: Ballantine paperback edition, 7; distribution rights, 23; film production, 109, 275, 327, 368n47; games based on, 233–34; Jackson involvement, 23, 327; novel appearance, 1; *Rings* as sequel to, 6; trademark ownership, 12, 19, 20

Hodgson, Pete, 310–11, 312

Hollywood, 282, 331–32; films shot away from, 100–101, 282–83, 299–300, 328–31; Miramar compared, 309–10. *See also* Academy Awards and nominations

Hollywood and Games Summit, 227

Hollywood Foreign Press Association (HFPA), 111

Hollywood Reporter, 112; horror film conventions, 61; "The Lord of the Onion Rings," 107; New Line's DVDs, 205; *Rings* DVDs, 215; *Rings* international distributors, 265, 266*fig*, 268; *Rings* negotiations, 19; *Rings* publicity interviews, 118; video games, 229; *X-Men: The Final Stand* release, 325–26

Holm, Ian, 45, 57, 80*fig*

Holmstead, Jill, 324*fig*

Hong Kong: action films, 274; Centro Digital Pictures, 328–29; Deltamac, 274; martial arts choreography, 61

Hope, Colin, 299

Hopkins, Bruce, 201

Hopkins, Mike, 210

horror film conventions, *Rings*, 60–61

Houghton Mifflin, 10–11, 87, 117, 186, 194, 358n34

Howe, John, 86–89, 95–96, 341n16; calendar illustrations, 10; *The Dark Tower*, 87–88; *The End of the Third Age*, 88; *Éowyn and the Nazgûl*, 87–88; *Gandalf Returns to Bag End*, 87, *Plates 4,5*; pitch tape drawings, 27; tours for investors, 301; video games, 247

humor, Tolkien-related, 169–74

Hydraulx, 326

illustrators: of Tolkien book franchise, 87–89; Tolkien as (children's books), 11. *See also* artworks; Howe, John; Lee, Alan

ILM (Industrial Light & Magic), 97, 281

Iluvatar, 161, 165

Imhoff, David, 197, 216

income: films vs. games, 225–26; Lilith's Lord of the Rings Site, 167; *Rings* film actors, 32–33, 37, 241; *Rings* franchise, 9; *Rings* video game actors, 241. *See also* gross; profits; sales

Independent Film & Television Alliance (IFTA), 258, 360n2

independent films, 257–74, 332; costs, 257–59; distribution, 257–58, 262–74; Internet publicity, 134–35; market benefited by *Rings* success, 9, 262–74; *My Big Fat Greek Wedding*, 262, 265, 274; Netherlands, 272; New Line, 50, 75–76, 258–62; *The Passion of the Christ*, 262, 265, 273, 274; presales, 39,

259, 264–65, 267, 268; *Rings*, 9, 75–76, 257, 258–59, 263–74; "semi-indies"/"nominal indies," 258

Industrial Light & Magic (ILM), 97, 281

infotainment, 109–33; press junkets, 79, 81–82, 125–32, *Plate 1*; press kits, 108, 118–24, 122*fig*, 123, 128. *See also* making-of documentaries; press; publicity and marketing; television

"The Inheritance Trilogy," 278

Inkheart, 277

In My Father's Den, 318

international distribution, 39, 193, 258, 265–74, 266*fig*; Cannes, 40–41, 257–58, 262–63, 265, 268, 272–73, 301–2; dubbing approval, 89; gross, 50, 252, 337n63; independent films, 257–58, 262–74; market benefited by *Rings* success, 9, 262–74; output deals, 265, 267, 269; presales, 39, 264–65, 267, 268; SF Film, 268–72, 270*fig*; tours of Wellywood, 267, 301; Universal, 24

international economy, 263–74. *See also* globalization; international distribution

international films. *See* foreign-language films

international postproduction facilities, 325–30

International Visitors Survey, 315

Internet, 133–64; Amazon.com, 154, 159, 167, 178, 278; AOL, 135, 141, 142; *The Blair Witch Project*, 113, 134–35; BlueTights.net, 164; box-office coverage, 112; cast and crew sites, 180–84; collapse of the bubble (2000), 154; Decipher products, 196; efficiency as marketing tool, 141; E! Online, 139, 141–42, 157; fan sites, 8, 68, 83, 132, 135–90; Fatpipe, 304–6, 327; Figwit Lives!, 170–72, 171*fig*, 174, 188; film departures from novels, 68, 69*fig*, 145; Film New Zealand, 316; "hits," 347n36; infotainment, 110; Jackson communications with fans, 83, 136–38, 151–52; *King Kong*, 153–54, 163–64,

Internet *(continued)*
218; languages invented by Tolkien,
95; line party organization, 184–85;
LiveJournals, 175, 178; The Lost in
Space Galaxy, 134; marketing cri-
tiques, 107; McKellen.com, 129, 139,
144–49, 159, 347, 347n36; MMORPG,
357n24, 358n45, 359n54; multipliers,
139, 160–64; New Line arrangements,
139–64, 182, 349–50n4; New Line
marketing pioneering, 134, 135; official
and sort of official sites, 139–49; official and unofficial sites, 133–34, 135,
139; parodies, 172–74, 349–50; pe-
riphery sites, 165–90; press junkets,
127; previews, 43, 48, 88–89; publicity
and marketing, 43, 123, 132, 135–36,
141, 159–64, 271–72, 347n36, 347n40;
quasi-sanctioned sites, 149–60; *Rings*,
135–90; SF Film publicity, 271–72;
spoilers, 133–34, 147–48, 153, 162, 181,
247; *Star Wars*, 133, 162; stolen tapes,
138; test screenings, 82; TheForce.net,
162; TheOneLion.net, 162; Tourism
New Zealand, 315*table;* video game
capacities, 244; Wadham petition,
283; Yahoo!, 133, 141, 178, 179. *See also*
Ain't It Cool News (AICN); eBay;
fanfiction; lordoftherings.net (official
website); TheOneRing.net (TORN)
Internet Marketing, 141
interviews: awards shows, 11; canned,
110; frequently asked questions, 125–
29; New Line employees, 30; press
junkets, 125–26
interviews—*Rings,* 58–59, 83; actors, 45,
61, 63, 64–65, 81–82, 117, 126–30,
145, 212, *Plate 1;* Cannes, 40, 45; costumes (Dickson), 63–64, 65; DVD,
211, 212; history rather than fantasy,
85–86; Jackson, 27, 29, 45, 51, 58–59,
83, 97, 116, 118, 126, 128, 143, 211, 240;
making-ofs, 114, 116, 117, 118, 119; in
New Zealand, 12–13, 81, 117, 126–28,
Plate 1; pitch tape, 27; press junkets,
79, 81–82, 125–32, *Plate 1; Rings* fan
club magazine, 143–44; Shaye, 34,

118; Taylor (Weta Workshop), 83–84,
85–86, 90, 96, 119; *Towers* as most
spectacular, 51; writers' decisions, 69–
70, 72, 83
Investment New Zealand, 310, 311–13, 322
Iraq war, 186
I, Robot, 306, 325
The Irrefutable Truth about Demons, 318
Italy, Medusa, 273
IT department: *Rings,* 304–6; Weta Work-
shop, 302

Jackson, Peter, 20–22, 327; *Bad Taste,* 20–
21, 28, 290, 308, 317; *Braindead/Dead
Alive,* 19, 21, 58, 366n24; *Dambusters,*
326; family time, 309; fan site potential, 163; film collectibles, 83; The
Film Unit, 20, 44, 291, 297; fluid
approach to filmmaking, 78–79; *Forgotten Silver,* 22, 114–15; *The Frighteners,* 22–24, 28, 114, 208, 214, 294;
fun, 73–74, 332; geek factor, 82–84;
generous with facilities, 303; "Halo,"
326; *Heavenly Creatures,* 8, 21–22, 28,
34, 293, 326; *The Hobbit* possibilities,
23, 327, 368n47; Knowles, 150–53,
154–55; laser disc collection, 114, 217;
The Lovely Bones, 326; loyalty of team
to, 37, 76, 81, 309–10; making-ofs,
114–15, 127, 208; maverick, 100; *Meet
the Feebles,* 21, 293, 308–9; national
hero, 322; New Zealand Film Commission, 317; New Zealand location
choice, 17, 37, 76, 283, 290, 300, 309,
320, 325, 330–31; *Nightmare on Elm
Street,* 28, 76, 330–31; Park Road
Post, 298; Seatoun house, 293, 302;
"Temeraire," 326; training, 308–9,
366–67n24; "Wellingtonian of the
Year," 322; Wingnut Films, 83, 86–87,
290, 293, 326; Wingnut Interactive,
252–53, 326. See also *King Kong*
Jackson, Peter—*Rings,* 2, 7, 17–18, 22, 53,
81, 327; Academy Awards nights, 51,
185, 186, 365n16; Cannes, 40, 41–44,
47–48; control, 89, 100, 101, 290;
debt, 44, 297; Denmark visit, 272;

design and production, 60, 75, 77–80, 82, 89, 92, 96, 98; DVDs, 211–18, 250; family atmosphere of crew and actors, 309; fan communications, 83, 136–38, 151–52; fan concerns about, 140, 151, 153; fan parties, 185, 187; fan sites, 149, 158, 159, 160, 163, 180, 181, 184; fantasy's success, 275; Fatpipe, 304–6; Figwit, 171–72, 188; film departure from novel, 68, 69; horror film conventions, 60–61; interviews, 27, 29, 45, 51, 58–59, 83, 97, 116, 118, 126, 128, 143, 211, 240; making-ofs, 26, 27, 28–29, 36–37, 87, 114–15, 117; merchandise style guides, 194; Miramar residence, 291, 293, 309; Miramax, 22, 23–30, 34–36, 76; movie rights, 19, 23–25; New Line, 12, 18, 29–37, 41, 51–52, 73, 76–77, 79, 82, 84, 87, 151–52, 338n8; New Zealand Large Budget Screen Production Grant, 317; pitch video, 12, 26, 27, 28–29, 36–37, 87, 309–10; press kit, 121; simplified complexity, 65; spoiler prevention, 134, 147–48, 240; Stone Street Studios, 295; stress of finishing trilogy, 275–76; vs. summary scenes or crawl title, 73; technological demands, 279–80; three parts fit together, 243; tours for investors, 301; turnaround, 26–29, 34–35; video games, 240, 250–53; Weta special effects, 96–97. See also *The Lord of the Rings* (films)

Jamdat, 250
James, Az, 198, 290
James, Raewyn, 288
James, Sharon, 241–43, 246, 250, 308
James, Vic, 288
James Bond films, 7, 53, 234; collectibles, 197; franchise as star, 6; special-effects supervisor, 318; Tamahori, 3, 318
James Bond games, 227–35, 356n10
Japan: animated films, 331–32; martial arts choreography, 61; Nippon Herald, 268, 274; *Rings* fans, 108, 288; Shochiku, 274

Jenkins, Henry, 169, 351n30
Jeunet, Jean-Pierre, 329
Johnson, Jane, 301
Johnson, Mark, 5, 162, 298, 317
Johnston, Jean, 302, 309, 318
Jolie, Angelina, 112, 125
Jonathan Strange and Mr. Norrell (Clarke), 277
Journey to Middle-earth, 118
junkets, press, 79, 81, 124–32, 313, *Plate 1*
Jurassic Park, 22, 274

Kaitoke Regional Park, 289*fig*
Kamins, Ken: Cannes, 43–45; Miramax, 23–28, 35, 36–37; New Line, 31, 36–37, 43, 259; New Zealand location, 76; Wingnut Interactive, 252–53
Katz, Marty, 28
Katzka, Gabe, 19
Kia Motors America, 214, 215
Kiesling, Mary, 143–44
Kill Bill films, 63, 276, 328–29
King, Richard, 231
King Kong: Big Primate Pictures, 291; color grading, 299; "credibility gap," 366n18; DVDs, 127, 163, 213, 218; games, 246, 251–53; Internet, 153–54, 163–64, 218; interviews, 127; Jackson diaries, 127, 163–64, 218; Knowles poster, 150; New Zealand, 283; New Zealand Large Budget Screen Production Grant, 317; original (1933), 20, 127, 150, 218; Oscars, 299; special effects, 281; Stone Street Studios, 302; stunt performers, 246; Universal, 23–24, 153–54, 163, 213, 252, 283, 366n18; Weta Digital, 325; Weta Workshop, 197, 251–52, 302
Knowles, Harry, 43, 133, 136, 149–55, 183, 336n38. *See also* Ain't It Cool News
KongIsKing.net, 163, 218
Korea: postproduction sector, 328; Taewon Entertainment, 272
Kubrick, Stanley, 19, 275
Kung Fu Hustle, 329
Kurtti, Jeff, 207–8

labor: from abroad, 37–38, 306–7, 318; layoffs in film industry, 49, 259, 260; upskilled, 306–10, 329. *See also* actors; crew

Ladbrokes betting chain, 52

languages: *Rings* dubbings, 89; Tolkien novels/film, 84–85, 94–96. *See also* foreign-language films

Lara Croft: Tomb Raider, 227–28

Large Budget Screen Production Grant, New Zealand, 317, 327

laser discs, 114, 204, 205, 206–7; *The Frighteners*, 114, 208, 214; Jackson collection, 114, 217

Laser Pacific, 208, 213

Lasky, Kathryn, 278

Lasoff, Mark, 231

Lasorsa, Matt, 116, 206

Lasseter, John, 207

The Last Samurai, 242, 306, 325, 327

Lean, David, 19, 276

Least Expected, 178

Lee, Alan, 86–89, 92; calendar illustrations, 10; fans loving, 186; making-of interviews, 119; menu shoot, 213; pitch tape drawings, 27; tie-in book paintings, 341n16; tours for investors, 301; video games, 247

Lee, Bruce, 61, 62*fig*

Lee, Christopher, 37, 144, 309; AICN, 153; Cannes interviews, 45; Denmark visit, 272; video games, 244, 246

Lee, Susie, 212

Lennertz, Christopher, 230

Leonard, J. P., 212–13

Lesnie, Andrew, 37, 51, 160

Lewis, C. S., 277

Li, Jet, 231

Library of Moria, 178, 179, 180

Licensing International shows, 194, 197

licensing rights, 4, 183; cell phone games, 249, 250; Decipher, 142–43, 195; film and video game convergence, 226–33; games, 228, 233, 234, 235, 246; New Line, 39, 50, 108, 139, 141, 142–43, 186, 193–223, 234, 246; Ring*Con, 200–201; *Rings* budget, 259; *Rings* fan

club, 139, 142–43; *Rings* merchandise, 39, 108, 141, 172, 173, 184, 186, 189, 193–223, 259; Tolkien Enterprises, 12, 20, 193, 233, 246, 288, 334n7, 359n54. *See also* distribution rights; tie-in products

Lieberman, Al, 165

Lights Out Entertainment, 136

Lilith of Sherwood, 166–68, 168*fig*, 189; Lord of the Rings Site (http://lilithlotr.com/), 166–67

line parties, 165, 167, 184–88, 189–90

The Lion King, 279

literary adaptations, 56–59; *Rings* departure from novels, 59–60, 68–74, 69*fig*, 75, 145, 180–81

LiveJournals, 175, 178

The Locals, 318

London: effects houses, 328, 329; Fat-pipe, 304–5; *Fellowship* premiere, 126, 142, 145, 320; film festivals, 202, 319; Greasepaint, 307

Lonely Planet, 316

Lord of the Peeps, 172–74

The Lord of the Rings—films: animated film (Bakshi, 1978), 2, 8, 12, 20, 25, 34, 55; animated film proposal (Ackerman, 1957), 18–19; behind-the-scenes talent, 37–38; broadcast rights, 228; budget before New Line, 25–26, 27, 36–37; casting, 8, 37, 57; costumes, 63–64, 65, 79, 89, 91, 127, 323; dailies, 79; departure from novels, 59–60, 68–74, 69*fig*, 75, 145, 180–81; Fatpipe dedicated network, 304–6, 327; genealogy, 21*fig*; historical significance, 8–9; horror film conventions, 60–61; independent film, 9, 75–76, 257, 258–59, 263–74; international distribution, 24, 39, 40–41, 89, 193, 257–58, 262, 265–74, 266*fig*, 270*fig*; martial arts choreography, 61–65, 62*fig*, 66*fig*, 83; Miramax, 22, 23–30, 34–36, 40, 67, 76, 80, 150, 229, 276; movie rights, 18–20, 22, 23–25, 34; music, 42, 60, 118–19, 121; New Line commitment, 8, 35–37, 40–41,

151, 229; New Line's financial risks, 29–40, 49–50, 80–81, 194–95, 258–60, 265, 267–68; New Zealand benefit from, 284–87, 299, 306–25; PG-13 rating, 74, 218; pitch video, 12, 26, 27, 28–29, 36–37, 87, 309–10; plot points that are given only once, 73; popular-genre conventions, 57–59, 75, 83; pre-production, 25–30, 34–35, 37, 279; Shaye's three-film gamble, 29–37, 258–59, 261; simplified complexity, 65–74, 75; stunt performers, 61; technological innovations, 10, 97–100, 225, 249, 279–81, 327; test screenings decided against, 82; three-part film version, 2001–2003, 2, 7, 17–18, 275–76; three parts shot at once, 2, 22, 31–33, 238–39, 308; trademark ownership, 12, 19, 20; in turnaround, 26–31, 34–36, 150; unconventional qualities, 72. *See also* Academy Awards and nominations; actors; budget; Cannes preview; design; DVDs; *The Fellowship of the Ring*; film industry benefits from *Rings*; gross; Internet; Jackson, Peter; making-of documentaries; production; publicity and marketing; *Return of the King*; tie-in products; Tolkien/*Rings* fans; *The Two Towers*

The Lord of the Rings (Tolkien)—novels, 6, 84–96; actors not having read books, 59, 83; Ballantine, 7; film departure from, 59–60, 68–74, 69*fig*, 75, 145, 180–81; forewords, 1, 55; franchises based on, 10–12, 11*fig*; Harper-Collins, 10–11, 301; history rather than fantasy, 85–86, 90, 94; illustrators, 87; reference volumes, 85; "richly realized world" of Middle-earth, 55–56, 84–96, 100; submission to publisher, 1–2; video games based on, 233–34. See also *The Hobbit*; Tolkien, J.R.R.; Tolkien/*Rings* fans

Lord of the Rings Fan Club, 139, 142–44; Decipher running, 142–43, 195; Fellowship of 22, 189–90; "Into the West" party, 187; *The Lord of the Rings Fan Club Official Movie Magazine*, 93, 100, 131, 142–44, 184, 189–90

"The Lord of the Rings" Location Guidebook (Brodie), 289

lordoftherings.net (official website), 140–41, 160; Danish link, 271–72; *Fellowship* screen savers, 174; making-of clips, 119; trailers, 135, 271–72

"The Lord of the Rings Online: Shadows of Angmar," 359n54

"Lord of the Rings: Pinball" mobile phone game, 250

"The Lord of the Rings Symphony" (Shore), 118–19

"The Lord of the Rings: Tactics" video game (11 August 2005), 247

"Lord of the Rings: Trilogy" mobile phone game, 250

"The Lord of the Rings": Weapons and Warfare book, 94, 95

"The Lord of the Rings: The White Council" video game, 247

Los Angeles: Air NZ, 108, 109; DVD production, 211; Fatpipe, 304, 306; *Fellowship* premiere, 126; filmmaking activities, 282, 330; games industry, 227, 231, 249; New Line office, 48, 304; press junket, 79, 127–28; *Return* premiere, 321, 322; Tourism NZ, 312, 313, 314*fig*; Universal's theme park, 283. *See also* Academy Awards and nominations; Hollywood

Los Angeles Times, 50, 152

The Lost in Space Galaxy, 134

The Lovely Bones, 326

Lucas, George, 149; DVDs, 216; franchise, 4, 84; Internet, 133, 162; Letterman Digital Arts Center, 327; Skywalker Ranch, 230, 327; video games, 230. See also *Star Wars*

Lustig, Branko, 100

Lynne, Michael, 77; Cannes preview, 48; financial risks, 39, 259, 268; pitch tape, 29; *Rings* commitment, 35; *Variety*'s "Showmen of the Year" (with Shaye), 52, 260

Maclachlan, Mary, 308

Madsen, Dan, 143

magazines: advertising, 106; celebrity-oriented, 111; fan (general), 174; game and film industries' competition, 225; *The Lord of the Rings Fan Club Official Movie Magazine*, 93, 100, 131, 142–44, 184, 189–90; *Newsweek*, 130, 182, 225, 355n47; *New Yorker*, 276; *Onfilm*, 303; *Time*, 225, 275; *USA Today*, 112, 131, 153, 170; *Video Business*, 216. See also *Entertainment Weekly; Hollywood Reporter; Variety*

Maguire, Tobey, 229

Mahaffie, John, 38

Major, Grant, 86, 94–95; Jackson approach to filmmaking, 78–79; New Zealand location, 309; "no-budget" approach to sets and other physical elements, 96; PJ stamp, 89; pre- and post-*Rings* film industry, 307; training, 308

"Major League Baseball" video games, 229

making-of documentaries, 113–19, 127, 207

making-of documentaries—*Rings*, 106, 108, 114–19, 204, 210, 211; *Behind the Scenes: The Lord of the Rings: The Return of the King*, 118; *Beyond the Movie: The Lord of the Rings*, 117; *Beyond the Movie: The Lord of the Rings: The Return of the King*, 118; *Bio Extra: The Lord of the Rings Trilogy*, 118; Botes, 22, 114–19, 188, 210; *Creating The Lord of the Rings Symphony: A Composer's Journey through Middle Earth*, 118–19; DVDs, 106, 114–19, 163, 204, 210; *Fellowship*, 106, 204; *Journey to Middle-earth*, 118; *Making the Movie: The Lord of the Rings*, 118; New Zealand mentions, 313; *On the Set: The Lord of the Rings: The Two Towers*, 118; *Page to Screen: The Lord of the Rings*, 118; *A Passage to Middle-earth: The Making of The Lord of the Rings*, 118; pitch to New Line Cinema, 26, 27, 28–29, 36–37, 87, 309–10; *Quest for the Ring*, 114, 117; *The Quest Fulfilled: A Director's*

Vision, 117; *Return to Middle-earth*, 117; *Welcome to Middle-earth*, 117, 119

Malick, Terrence, 261

Malik, Ernie, 126, 162

The Maltese Falcon, 7

Maltha, San Fu, 272–73

Map of the Human Heart, 318

maps: Middle-earth, 84, 245, 247, 316, *Plates 7,11,12*; Miramar, 292

martial arts choreography, 62*fig*, 64*fig*; *Rings*, 61–65, 62*fig*, 66*fig*, 83

The Mask, 31, 205, 273

Mass, John, 224, 233

Massive program, 97, 280, 301, 323, 364n52

The Matrix: films, 37–38, 40, 252, 260, 275, 300, 327–28; video games, 248, 249, 252

Maxwell, Kirk, 241–43, 246, 250, 308

Maya technology, 97

MCA (Music Corporation of America), 4

McDonald's, brand partnerships, 106

McFetridge, Susan, 322

McGann, Brad, 318

McHale, D. J., 278

McKay, John, 323–25

McKee, Robert, 366–67n24

McKellen, Ian, 8, 18, 33, 37, 80, 179; Academy Award nomination, 51; bobble-heads, 196; Cannes interviews, 45; costumes, 65, 91; diary, 144, 145–47; DVD commentary, 212; E-Posts, 146–47, 179–80, 196, 347–48; fan communications, 146–47, 179–80, 196; fan Lilith of Sherwood, 166, 169; fan parties, 185–86; interviews, 63, 64–65, 127–28, *Plate 1*; martial arts choreography, 63, 64–65, 66*fig*; McKellen.com, 129, 139, 144–49, 159, 347n36; preview after Cannes, 47–48; *Rings* books never read by, 59; Shaye birthday party (3 March 2000), 80*fig*; TORN meeting, 158; video games, 241, 243, 244, 246, 248

McKenzie, Bret, 170, 171*fig*, 172, 188

McRae, Alyson, 160, 194, 240, 301

McTiernan, John, 231

Medusa, Italy, 273

Meet the Feebles, 21, 293, 308–9

Menand, Louis, 54

merchandise, franchise, *Star Wars*, 4. *See also* tie-in products

merchandise, *Rings*, 193–223; action figures, 11*fig*, 193–94, 197, 215; Decipher, 142–43, 172, 195; at fan parties, 184, 186; *Fellowship*, 173; Internet sales, 159; licensed, 39, 108, 141, 172, 173, 184, 186, 189, 193–223, 259; Lord of the Peeps, 173; style guides, 194–95; swag bags, 47, 344n23. *See also* collectibles; DVDs; games; tie-in products

Metropolitan distributors, France, 267, 268, 273

Mexico, Videocine, 272

MGM, 5, 23, 56, 327; films in 1930s-1940s, 3, 56; games, 232, 356n10; "Motion Picture Masterpieces" DVD, 338n5

Mickey Mouse Club, 111

Microsoft, 252–53, 326

Middle-earth, 9–10, 63, 149; Air New Zealand to, 108, 109; battle styles, 61, 246; Cannes, 42–43, 46–47; Christopher Tolkien's edits, 8, 11; design, 75, 79, 86; fanfiction, 169, 176; fan party, 187–88; film departures from novels, 59, 68, 71; games, 224–25, 233, 244–48, 253, *Plates 7,8;* maps, 84, 245, 247, 316, *Plates 7,11,12;* New Zealand, Home of, 283–88, 311, 312, 314, 316, *Plates 11,12;* "richly realized world," 55–56, 84–96, 100; tours, 167, 284–89; *Welcome to Middle-earth*, 117, 119; Weta Workshop, 301

"Middle-earth Online" project, 359n54

MIFED, 257–58, 263, 360n1

Minghella, Anthony, 276

miniature photography, 294, 306–7

Miramar, Wellington, 290–99, 292*map*, 309–10; Fatpipe, 304–6, 327; Jackson and Walsh residence, 291, 293, 309; Miramar North School banners, 324*fig;* Park Road Post, 291, 297–99, 303, 325, 329, *Plates 9,10;* PostHouse, 291, 297, 298–99; studios and warehouses (general), 38, 89, 290–97, 302–4, 309, 321, 326–27; Wingnut Films, 83, 86–87, 290, 293. *See also* Stone Street Studios; Three Foot Six; Wellywood; Weta Workshop

Miramax: *Heavenly Creatures*, 34; independent films, 258, 319; *King Kong*, 24; *Rings*, 22, 23–30, 34–36, 40, 67, 76, 80, 150, 229, 276; Weinsteins leaving, 35, 278

Miramax Books, 278

Mithril Awards, 350n13

Mittweg, Rolf, 81–82, 336n47; international distribution, 39, 40, 81–82, 262, 265, 267

MMORPG (massively multiplayer online role-playing game), 357n24, 358n45, 359n54

mobile phone games, 249–50

Moloshok, Jim, 133, 141

Monaghan, Dominic, 182, 186, 189, 193, 197, 244

Moodabe, Joe, 319, 321

Moran, Eileen, 210

Moredun, P. R., 278

Mortal Kombat film and video games, 134, 205, 227–28, 231

Mortensen, Viggo, 37; art exhibition, 189; book signing (2002), 189; Denmark visit, 272; interviews, 129; *Rings* books not read by, 59, 83; stardom, 6, 33; stunt double, 241; video games, 241, 243

motion capture (mo-cap), 301; children's television, 302; video games and films, 231–32, 241–43, 244

Moulin Rouge, 328

movie rights: *Rings*, 18–20, 22, 23–25, 34, 234. *See also* distribution rights; international distribution; licensing rights

The Moving Picture Company, London, 329

Mr. and Mrs. Smith, 112–13, 125

Mr. Bliss, 11

MTV, 106, 111, 118

Mulgrew, Kate, 229

Mullane, Liz, 182

multipliers, Internet, 139, 160–64
Mulvihill, Mike, 116, 207–8, 213
Munich, 332
Murdoch, Rupert, 5, 327
Murphy, Geoff, 38, 290, 318
Murray, Sandy, 116–17
Museum of Science, Boston, 199*fig*
museums, *Rings* exhibitions, 119, 197–
    200, 199*fig*, 289–90, 313, 320, 352n5.
    See also Te Papa national museum
music: *Rings*, 42, 60, 118–19, 121; Swann,
    10; video games, 230. *See also* Shore,
    Howard
My Big Fat Greek Wedding, 53, 262, 265,
    274
"Myst" video game, 228–29

Narnia. See The Chronicles of Narnia
Nasmith, Ted, 10, 87
National Geographic Society, 117, 118,
    204–5
The Navigator, 318
NBC: Golden Globe Awards, 111; NBC
    Universal, 110
Nedergaard, Mads, 269–72
Netherlands, A-Film, 272–73
New Line Cinema, 17, 30–31, 83; *Austin
    Powers*, 31, 34, 49, 135, 206, 221, 223;
    Blade, 48–49, 53, 154, 206, 267; DVD
    department, 207–23, 260, 354n31,
    355n44; *Elf*, 27, 260; failures after
    1990s, 48–49; fans working with, 138,
    139, 149–64, 165, 183–84; financial
    risks and successes, 29–40, 49–50,
    80–81, 194–95, 258–62, 265, 267–68,
    338n8; Fine Line, 28, 261–62; inde-
    pendent films, 50, 75–76, 258–62;
    international distribution/Mittweg,
    39, 40, 81–82, 257–58, 262, 265, 267;
    Internet marketing, 134, 135, 163;
    Maria Full of Grace, 261; *The Mask*,
    31, 205, 273; *Mortal Kombat*, 134, 205;
    The New World, 261; *Nightmare on
    Elm Street*, 28, 30, 76, 277, 330–31;
    Picturehouse, 262; *Rush Hour*, 27,
    48–49, 206, 261, 267; *The Sea Inside*,
    261; *Se7en*, 205, 273; *Snakes on a Plane*,
    183–84; Time Warner, 28, 39, 49–
    50, 111, 140, 141, 223, 258–60; *Vera
    Drake*, 261; *The Wedding Singer*,
    48, 267. *See also* Lynne, Michael;
    Ordesky, Mark; Shaye, Bob
New Line Cinema—*Rings*, 8, 17, 18, 29–
    40, 76–80, 258–59; Academy Awards
    party, 187; brands partnerships, 106–
    9, 215, 250, 311; Cannes, 40–49, 79,
    208, 257–58, 268, 340n8, *Plate 3*;
    commitment, 8, 35–37, 40–41, 151,
    229; fan documentary, 188; Fatpipe
    dedicated network, 304; financial
    risks, 29–40, 49–50, 80–81, 194–95,
    258–60, 265, 267–68; independent
    films benefited by success of, 9, 262–
    74; international distribution, 24, 39,
    40–41, 89, 193, 257–58, 262, 265–74,
    266*fig*; Internet arrangements, 139–
    64, 182, 349–50n4; licensing rights,
    39, 50, 108, 139, 141, 142–43, 186, 193–
    223, 234, 246; making-ofs, 114–18;
    marketing offices, 123; merchandise
    style guides, 194–95; New Zealand
    links, 107–9, 283–88, 300, 310–25;
    no summary scenes/crawl title, 73;
    pitch video, 12, 26, 27, 28–29, 36–37,
    87, 309–10; *Return* premiere, 51–52,
    321; security, 138, 157–58; three-film
    gamble, 29–37, 258–59, 261; turn-
    around, 26–29, 34–36. *See also*
    budget; publicity and marketing
New Line Home Entertainment, 116, 119,
    204, 206
New Line Home Video, 205–6
news. *See* infotainment; Internet; news-
    papers; press; publicity and marketing
News Corporation, 5, 110
newspapers: advertising, 105; box-office
    coverage, 112; *Los Angeles Times*, 50,
    152; *New York Times*, 76, 285–86;
    video game and film industries'
    competition, 225
Newsweek, 130, 182, 225, 355n47
The New World, 261
New York: entertainment conferences,
    222–23; Fatpipe, 305; *Rings* merchan-

dise design, 194; *Rings* premieres, 126, 311, 320; Walden Media, 277

New Yorker, 276

New York Review of Books, 54

New York Times, 76, 285–86

New Zealand, 283–331; brain drain, 290, 306, 309; Challis travel articles, 155, 157, 190; currency fluctuations, 32, 83, 327, 329; Department of Tourism, 296; Film and Video Technicians Guild, 306; Film Commission, 20–21, 290, 311, 317–19; Film NZ, 311, 316–17, 319, *Plates 11,12;* finance for filmmaking, 310–25, 327; Home of Middle-earth, 283–88, 311, 312, 314, 316, *Plates 11,12;* Investment New Zealand, 310, 311–13, 322; Jackson location choice, 17, 37, 76, 283, 290, 300, 309, 320, 325, 330–31; Large Budget Screen Production Grant, 317, 327; *Rings* actors enthusiastic about, 284, 312; *Rings* benefit to, 283, 284–87, 290–300, 306–25; *Rings* fans approving of, 100; *Rings* interviews, 12–13, 81, 117, 126–28, *Plate 1; Rings* production, 31–33, 37, 38, 41, 76, 283, 293, 300; Telecom, 304; tourism, 284–89, 299, 311, 312–16, 320; tours of *Rings* locations, 167, 284–90, 320; TVNZ, 296. *See also* Air New Zealand; Auckland; Jackson, Peter; Queenstown; Te Papa national museum; Tourism New Zealand; Wellington; Weta Ltd.

New Zealand Film, 317, 319

New Zealand Film Commission, 20–21, 290, 311, 317–19

New Zealand film industry, 32; "Film Friendly Protocol," 316; Film New Zealand, 311, 316–17, 319, *Plates 11,12; Rings* crew from, 32, 37, 306–10, 318–19, 321, 326; *Rings* effect, 32, 283, 290–300, 306–12, 316–25; upskilling, 306–10, 329. *See also* Miramar; Wellywood

Ngan, Milton, 304, 325

Nielsen EDI, 112

Nightmare on Elm Street, 28, 30, 76, 277, 330–31

Nimmo, Duncan, 303–6

Nimmo, Jenny, 278

Nimziki, Joe, 81, 340n8

Nintendo 64, 229

Nippon Herald, Japan, 268, 274

Noble Collection, 186

Nomad Safaris, 287

Nordisk, 271

No. 2, 319

Novik, Naomi, 326

No Way Out, 318

O Brother, Where Art Thou?, 280

Oktobor, 318

Olssen, Jabez, 42

One Ring Celebration (ORC), 156*fig*, 183, 201–3, 202*fig*, 203*fig*, 218

OneRing.net. *See* TheOneRing.net (TORN)

Onfilm magazine, 303

Online Testing Exchange, 82

On the Set: The Lord of the Rings: The Two Towers, 118

Opening Soon at a Theater Near You, 110

ORC (One Ring Celebration), 156*fig*, 183, 201–3, 202*fig*, 203*fig*, 218

Ord, Susan, 316

Ordesky, Mark, 28–35, 36*fig*, 76–77, 79, 261; Air NZ, 108; Cannes, 43–45; fan parties, 185; fantasy projects, 277; Figwit, 188; Fine Line, 28, 261–62; Quint reports, 153; *Return* premiere, 52, 320, *Plate 1*

Oriental Post, Bangkok, 329

Osborne, Barrie M., v, 77; *The Matrix*, 37–38, 40, 300; runaway production, 300, 330

Osborne, Barrie M.—*Rings*, 37–38, 300; Academy Awards fan party, 186, 187; Cannes, 40–42, 44, 45, 46; Challis spying, 158; digital intermediates, 280–81; Fatpipe dedicated network, 304; Figwit, 188; "Frodo" plane, 108; Internet, 152, 181; making-of documentary, 117; New Line support,

Osborne, Barrie M.—Rings (continued)
80–81; publicity interviews, 119;
Return behind schedule, 211–12;
Return premiere, 189, Plate 1; video
game approval, 238, 240, 250; war
and martial arts inspirations, 61
Oscars. See Academy Awards and
nominations
Otto, Miranda, 201
Out of the Blue, 319
outsourcing: digital effects, 328. See also
"runaway" production/production
abroad

Pace, Wayne, 223
Pacific Renaissance Pictures, 308
Paddison, Gordon, 134–35, 140–42, 160–
62, 346n21; digital press kits, 120;
Knowles, 152, 154; Quint, 153; TORN,
159, 160
Page, Greg, 318
Page to Screen: The Lord of the Rings, 118
Pagono, Joe, 215
Paolini, Christopher, 278
Paramount, 4, 5, 219, 229, 271
Parker, Craig, 201
Parker Brothers, 215–16
Park Road Post, 291, 297–99, 303, 325, 329,
Plates 9,10. See also The Film Unit
parodies, Rings, 172–74, 349–50
Parsons, Richard, 260
parties: Cannes, 42–48, 47fig, 126, 340n8,
Plate 3; fan, 165, 167, 184–90
A Passage to Middle-earth: The Making
of The Lord of the Rings, 118
The Passion of the Christ, 74, 262, 265, 273,
274
Peake, Mervyn, 364n47
Peeps parodies, 172–74, 175fig, 350n10
Pellerin, Michael: DVDs, 114, 119, 163,
207–14, 218, 219; making-ofs, 114,
115–16, 119, 163; Three Foot Six
office, 293
Pendragon series, 278
Perenson, Melissa J., 131
Philippines, Pioneer Film Productions, 274
photography: miniature, 294, 306–7;

Rings, 38–40, 81, 115, 120, 142, 152,
157, 306–7
Picturehouse, 262. See also Fine Line
Pinewood Studios, 305
Pinkett Smith, Jada, 252
Pioneer Film Productions, Philippines, 274
The Pirates of the Caribbean films, 32, 246,
275, 363n38
Pirrotta, Chris (Calisuri), 155; Cannes, 43,
88–89; fan social gatherings, 156fig,
186–87; Sideshow's webmaster, 159.
See also TheOneRing.net (TORN)
Pitt, Brad, 112, 125
Pixar, 207
Planet of the Apes, 23–24
PlayStations, 225, 229, 242, 247
poems, Tolkien, 10, 11
Pokemon, 227–28
PolyGram, 27–28
popular genre conventions, 56–59, 75, 83
Porras, Rick, 38, 259; Cannes, 43; Carla
Fry, 300; DVDs, 209–10; loyalty to
Jackson, 309–10; making-of documentary, 26; New Line policy, 17, 81;
spoilers, 162; tours for investors, 267,
301; video games, 238–40, 250
Positively Wellington Tourism, 320
posters, 105; Rings, 10, 81, 245. See also
maps
PostHouse, 291, 297, 298–99
postproduction: budget, 51; crew, 38, 307;
DVD content, 74, 98, 127, 163, 210,
211, 218; facilities, 20, 76, 213, 282–83,
291, 296–99, 300, 325–30; Fellowship,
42, 304; The Film Unit, 20, 76, 291,
296–99; international facilities, 325–
30; King Kong diaries, 127, 163–64,
218; Laser Pacific, 208, 213; Park Road
Post, 291, 298–99, 303; PostHouse,
291, 298–99. See also digital technology; special effects
Powell, Lucy, 109
A Prairie Home Companion (2006), 262
premieres, 184; Fellowship, 39, 126, 142, 145,
320; Towers, 51–52, 108, 198, 311, 320.
See also Return of the King
Prendergast, Kerry, 321

presales, film, 39, 259, 264–65, 267, 268

press: Cannes, 32, 43, 44, 45, 126; electronic press kits (EPKs), 108, 118–24, 122*fig*, 128; fantasy taken seriously, 276; *Fellowship* review, 54; game and film industries' competition, 225; junkets, 79, 81–82, 124–32, 313, 322, *Plate 1;* New Line's financial risks and successes, 39–40, 49–50, 259, 262; swag bags, 47, 124, 344n23; Weta, 296. *See also* advertising; magazines; newspapers

production: "runaway"/abroad, 100–101, 282–83, 299–300, 316–17, 328–31. *See also* postproduction

production—*Rings,* 36–40, 41, 76–80, 86–96; costs, 31–37, 80–81, 284, 335n33; fan sites and, 138, 148–49, 180–81; New Zealand, 31–33, 37, 38, 41, 76, 283–84, 293, 300; photography, 38–40, 81, 115, 120, 142, 152, 157, 306–7; three parts shot at once, 2, 22, 31–33, 238–39, 308; tours for investors and executives, 267, 301–2, 309, 312–13. *See also* design; Wellywood; Weta Ltd.

products. *See* merchandise; tie-in products

profits: British Entertainment Film Distributors, 273; DVDs, 204, 219–23; fan cons, 201, 203; museum exhibitions, 198, 203; *Rings* franchise, 9; video games, 204, 225; video rentals, 219–22. *See also* gross; income; sales

publicity and marketing, 39, 55–56, 105–8, 114–20; brands partnerships, 106–9, 215, 250, 274, 311, 322; cost, 105–6, 141; DVDs, 214–15; electronic press kits (EPKs), 108, 118–24, 122*fig*, 128; fan roles in, 105, 107, 132, 135–64; fantasy, 9, 55–56; film shaping at same time, 123; Internet, 43, 123, 132, 135–36, 141, 159–64, 271–72, 347n36, 347n40; making-ofs, 106, 108, 115–19; press junkets, 79, 81–82, 125–32, *Plate 1;* Schwartz, 81–82; SF Film, 271–72; unwanted publicity, 112–13; video games/films, 232–33. *See also*

advertising, Cannes preview; infotainment; Internet; interviews; merchandise; posters; press; television; Tolkien/*Rings* fans; trailers

Pullman, Philip, 277

puzzles, *Rings*, 10, 11*fig*

Queenstown: *Rings* benefits to, 284–87, 312; *Rings* shooting, 145–46, 157, 284; tours, 285–87, 313

Quest for the Ring, 114, 117

The Quest Fulfilled: A Director's Vision, 117

Quickbeam. *See* Broadway, Cliff (Quickbeam)

The Quiet Earth, 318

Quint, 153–54

Raskind, Claire, 120, 131, 153

rating: PG-13, 74, 218; R, 74, 276

real-person slash (RPS), 175, 176, 179–80, 181–82

Red Carpet Tours, 167, 189, 288

Reeve, Daniel, 194, 195

Regelous, Stephen, 97, 280, 323

Regina, Michael (Xoanon), 155–56, 156*fig*

Reigel, Jim, 37

RenderMan, 97

research, Tolkien's invented world, 86

Return of the King, 2; Academy Awards, 20, 52, 218, 251, 258, 276, 299, 322, 324*fig*, 337n64, 365n16; action scenes, 59–60; Air New Zealand, 107–8, 322; behind schedule, 211–12; CGI shots (number), 96; costumes, 79; dubbing and subtitling for foreign premieres, 211; DVDs, 52, 60–61, 65, 77, 111, 118, 119, 210–17, 222, 224, 260, 271, 339–40n26, 356n54; Embassy Theater, 320–22, 323*fig*; end credit design, 213; fan parties, 187; Fatpipe, 305; Figwit, 170, 172; film version, 2, 51–52; gross, 52, 274, 337n63; Hobbit-scale jug, 77, 78*fig*; interviews, 79, 127, 131, *Plate 1;* Jackson stress of finishing, 275–76; Los Angeles, 321, 322; martial arts choreography, 66*fig*; mixing studio, 298; mobile phone game, 250; New

Return of the King (continued)
Line finances, 260; New Zealand
benefits from *Rings*, 310, 315–16; no
summary scenes or crawl title, 73;
novel appearance, 2, 18; premieres,
51–52, 320–22; press junket, 79, 127,
322, *Plate 1;* press kit, 123; Red Carpet
Tours, 167, 189, 288; swag bag, 344n23;
Te Papa national museum, 198, 322,
Plate 1; TORN, 187, 189; Trilogy Tuesday, 184; video game, 224, 237, 238,
240, 242, 243–44, 249, 251; Wellington location choice, for premiere, 51–
52, 320–22
Return to Middle-earth, 117
Revolution Studios, 326
Rhys-Davies, John, 128; farewell video,
217; ORC, 201; press junket for
Return premiere, *Plate 1;* video games,
243, 244, 246
rights: broadcast, 228; over fan websites,
183; *Rings*, 23–25, 34, 193, 228. *See also*
distribution rights; licensing rights;
movie rights
Ring*Con, 200–201, 203
Ringbearer.org, humor section, 169
Ringers: Lord of the Fans, 185, 189
Rings. See Lord of the Rings
Riot Entertainment (Riot-E), 249–50
"Rise to Honor," 231
River Queen, 318–19
Rivers, Christian, 326
Roadshow Films, 322
Robson, Scott, 142
Rodda, Emily, 278
Rodger, Tania, 293
Rodriguez, Robert, 278, 327
role-playing games (RPGs), 195–96, 245,
247; MMORPG (massively multi-
player online role-playing game),
357n24, 358n45, 359n54
romantic fanfiction, 175, 176, 177–79
Romero, George A., 231
Rongotai, Wellington, 291, 294
Roth, Joe, 25
Roverandom, 11
Rover Rings Tour, 285–88, 287*fig*

Rowling, J. K., 277
Royal Ontario Museum's *Towers* exhibi-
tion, 198–99
RPGs. *See* role-playing games
RPS fics, 175, 176, 179–80, 181–82
"runaway" production/production abroad,
100–101, 282–83, 299–300, 316–17,
328–31
Rush Hour, 27, 48–49, 206, 261, 267
Rutherford, Jane, 285–86, 288
Rutherford, Robert, 285–86, 286*fig*, 288
Rygiel, Jim, 185

Safari of the Rings, 287
Safari of the Scenes, 287*fig*, 288
Sage, Annie, 278
sales: brands partnerships, 106; DVDs,
204, 205, 219–23, 265, 355–56n47;
film presales, 39, 259, 264–65, 267,
268; New Zealand businesses during
Rings production, 284; *Rings* merchan-
dise, 194; video games, 225, 234. *See
also* gross; income; profits
Salo, David, 95–96
Sanders, Tim, 38
Sarkies, Robert, 319
Saville, Ken, 306, 307
Scarfies, 319
Schnur, Steve, 230
Schwartz, Russell, 81–82, 340n8
Schwarzenegger, Arnold, 23, 24, 229
science-fiction films, 274, 275, 276
Sci Fi channel, 113, 118
Sci Fi magazine, 131, 140
Scorsese, Martin, 276
Scott, Ridley, 100, 101
Screen Actors Guild, 330
Screen International, 112, 265
screen savers, *Fellowship*, 174
The Sea Inside, 261
Seatoun, Wellington, 291, 293, 302
Sebold, Alice, 326
security: *Rings* script, 195; *Rings* sets, 138,
157–58
Selkirk, Jamie, 74, 79, 306; *Bad Taste*, 20–
21, 308; DVDs, 210; The Film Unit,
76, 297; Oscar, 20; *Rings* books not

read by, 59; Stone Street Studios, 29, 76, 293, 295; training, 307–8; Weta, 76, 291, 293

September 11 attacks (2001), 263

Septimus Heap, 278

sequels: artworks, 6–7; film, 2–3, 4, 32–33, 206, 271

Serkis, Andy, 122, 127, 145

Servos, Stefan, 200–201

Se7en, 205, 273

Seven Arts, 4, 124

SF Film, Denmark, 268–72, 270*fig*

Shakespeare, William, 6

Shakespeare in Love, 24, 26

Shake technology, 97

Shalit, Gene, 110

Shaye, Bob, 27–35; AFMA Lifetime Achievement Award, 258; birthday party (3 March 2000), 80*fig; Variety's* "Showmen of the Year" (with Lynne), 52, 260

Shaye, Bob—*Rings,* 77, 223; *Batman/ Superman* parallels, 31, 55, 81; Cannes preview, 40–44, 48, 79; financial risks, 39, 50, 258–59; interviews, 34, 118; pitch video, 28–29, 36–37, 40; production visits, 79; rough cut viewing, 82; three-film gamble, 29–37, 258–59, 261

Shiny Entertainment, 252

Shippey, Tom, 118

Shore, Howard: Cannes preview, 42; *Creating Lord of the Rings Symphony: A Composer's Journey through Middle Earth,* 118–19; fan club magazine interview, 143–44; fan parties, 185; horror film conventions, 60; "The Lord of the Rings Symphony," 118–19; Oscar, 185; press junket, 127; press kit, 121, 123; rewriting and rerecording, 211, 214; video game soundtracks, 230, 243, 244

Shrek, 74, 222, 274

Sideshow Weta, 196–97, 302; DVD extras, 204–5; fan cons, 189, 201, 202*fig;* fan party sponsor, 185, 186; TORN link, 159, 185; webmaster Pirrotta, 159

Sierra Entertainment, 233

The Silmarillion (Tolkien), 11, 95, 169, 176

Silver, Joel, 40, 252

Sinclair, Steven, 25

Singer, Bryan, 164–65, 200, 231

Singh, Anant, 328

Singleton, John, 230–31

Sione's Wedding/Samoan Wedding, 319

Siskel, Gene, 110, 152

The Sixth Sense, 275; DVDs, 209, 214; international distribution, 269

Skaggs, Mark, 224, 234, 237, 244, 245

Skarratt, Peter, 42

slash fics, 175, 176, 177–82, 351

Slate, 179

Sleeping Dogs, 318

Sloan, Harry, 327

Smash Palace, 318

Smith of Wootton Major (Tolkien), 11

Snakes on a Plane, 183–84

Sneak Previews, 110

Snow and the Seven, 277

Sommers, Stephen, 230

Sony, 5, 23, 327; ads on AICN, 154; Cordova, 188; fan-generated publicity, 163; *Ringers: Lord of the Fans*, 189; video games, 225–26, 229, 237

Soria, Lorenzo, 111

"Soul of the Ultimate Nation," 230

Soundfirm, Australia and Beijing, 329

sourcebooks, 195–96

South Africa, filmmaking facilities, 328

South Bank Show, 127

Southern Cross Cable, 305

South Korea: postproduction sector, 328; Taewon Entertainment, 272

South Pacific, 365n7

Spain: Aurum distribution, 273–74; *Rings* distribution, 89

Spangler, Larry, 213

special effects, 2, 22; costs, 5, 27, 33, 51, 96, 98–100, 223; *Heavenly Creatures*, 22, 326; high-end companies, 325–26; international companies, 325–30; *King Kong*, 281; New Zealand film industry talent, 306–7. *See also* digital technology; Weta Ltd.

special effects—*Rings*, 2, 27, 41, 96–101;
    Cannes preview, 301–2; cost, 51, 98–
    100; crew from abroad, 37, 306–7;
    facilities, 294–95; innovations, 97–
    100, 279–81, 327; Weta, 25, 294–95,
    300–302
Spider-Man films, 106, 220, 221, 275, 277
"Spider-Man" video games, 226, 229
Spielberg, Steven, 150, 281; fun, 73–74;
    game projects, 231; *Jaws*, 4; *Jurassic
    Park*, 22; Lustig, 100; *Munich*, 332;
    Oscar presentation, 52, 276; Zemeckis
    mentor, 23
spies: *Rings* set, 135–38, 149, 153, 157–58,
    240, 345–46n12, 348–49n54. *See also*
    spoilers
"Spike" video game, 229
spoilers: Internet, 133–34, 147–48, 153, 162,
    181, 247; "nondisclosure agreements,"
    112, 147–48, 153; video games, 237,
    240. *See also* spies
Spooked, 318
Spyglass Entertainment, 269
Spy Kids, 278
staff. *See* crew
Stanford Artificial Intelligence Laboratory,
    233
Stansborough Fibres, 323
stars: at awards shows, 111; films affected
    by behavior of, 112–13; franchise film
    actors, 6; franchises as, 6. *See also*
    actors
Star Trek, 275; con organizer, 200–201;
    fan club, 143; franchise, 5, 6, 7; games,
    195; gender of audience, 142; slash
    fics, 177–78, 350n15; video games,
    229; worldbuilding, 84
Star Wars, 274, 275; Academy Awards
    nomination, 51; DVD, 222; fan club,
    143; Fox Studios Australia, 328; fran-
    chise, 4, 84; games, 195, 231–32; Inter-
    net, 133, 162; Knowles, 149–50
Starz Encore, 118
Stern, Keith, 129, 144–48, 159, 168–69,
    347n36
Stickman, 318
Stone Street Studios, 76, 291, 295–96;

photos related to, 294*fig*, 296*fig*,
    324*fig;* purchase, 295, 297, 302;
    Return, 210, 211–12; Selkirk, 29,
    76, 293, 295; soundproof stage
    addition, 302
Stoppard, Tom, 277
"Storytellers" archive, 177
StudioCanal, 326
stunt performers, *Rings*, 61, 138, 241–
    43, 246, 250, 308
Sturgis, Amy H., 350–51n14
Sundance Film Festival, 113, 134, 257,
    259, 319
Sundance Theaters, 332
Superman, 4, 31, 55, 81
Superman Returns, 130, 164, 200, 302
Svenska Filmindustri, 268–69
Swann, Donald, 10
Sweden, Bonnier AB, 268–69, 272

Taewon Entertainment, Korea, 272
Tales from the Crypt, 22
Tamahori, Lee, 3, 290, 318
Tarantino, Quentin, 150, 276, 328–29
tax breaks, for film production, 264, 317,
    327, 330
Taylor, Hayden, 316
Taylor, Richard, 76, 79, 279, 291, 293–94,
    309; collectibles, 197; fan parties, 185;
    geek factor, 83–84; interviews, 83–84,
    85–86, 90, 96, 119; *Meet the Feebles*,
    293, 308–9; merchandise style guides,
    194; Oscar, 185; press junket for
    Return premiere, *Plate 1;* after *Rings*,
    302; *Rings* DVD commentary, 60–
    61; *Rings* realism, 85–86, 90, 93, 96;
    Stone Street Studios, 295; tours for
    investors, 301; training, 308–9. *See
    also* Weta Workshop
technologies, 282; CD-ROMs, 228–29;
    Fatpipe dedicated network, 304–6,
    327; 5D Colossus, 280–81; games and
    films, 227–29, 249; *Rings* innovations,
    10, 97–100, 225, 249, 279–81, 327. *See
    also* digital technology; DVDs; special
    effects; video games
Tehanu. *See* Challis, Erica

television: advertising, 105; Avalon Studios, 296, 365n7; award shows, 110, 111, 276; cable, 110–14, 261, 262, 332; children's, 302; *Forgotten Silver*, 22, 114–15; *Gormenghast*, 364n47; *Hercules: The Legendary Journeys*, 241, 308; independent movies, 263; infotainment, 110–11; making-of documentaries, 113–14, 117, 118, 119; press junkets, 125; *Rings* fan party, 187–88; *Rings* press kits, 121; *Rings* promo films, 118; *Shortland Street*, 308; *South Bank Show*, 127; talk shows, 110–11; training ground, 307–8; TVNZ, 296; *Xena: Warrior Princess*, 63, 241, 308

"Temeraire," 326

Te Papa national museum, 289–90; *Return* premiere, 198, 322, *Plate 1; Rings* touring exhibition, 119, 197–98, 289–90, 313, 320, 352n5

"Terminator 3: Rise of the Machines" video game, 229

theaters: Embassy Theater, 320–22, 323*fig;* Sundance art-house multiplexes, 332; Weta "movie palace," 211. *See also* premieres

Theban Band, 179

TheForce.net, 162

TheOneLion.net, 162

TheOneRing.com, 155–56, 161, 339n24

TheOneRing.net (TORN), 134, 155–60; Academy Awards April Fool's news, 159–60; Academy Awards parties, 184–86, 189–90; Broadway, 48, 156, 159, 185, 186, 188–89; Cannes preview, 43, 48, 88–89, 184; community, 189–90; Cordova, 185, 186, 188–89; departures of films from novels, 180–81; fanfiction, 183, 350n13; Figwit Lives! link, 170; founders, 155–56, 156*fig,* 185; Jackson monitoring, 181; KongIs King.net, 163, 218; making-ofs, 116; merchandising, 159; New Line cooperation, 162, 185; polling "Are you tired of any of the LotR movies yet?," 223; *Return*'s world premiere in Wellington, 189; "Spy Reports" archive, 348–49n54; The One Peep parody, 174; unreleased materials, 136, 137*fig;* Xoanon (Michael Regina), 155–56, 156*fig. See also* Challis, Erica (Tehanu); Pirrotta, Chris (Calisuri); Thomas, Bill (Corvar)

"The Thing" (2002), 232

"The Third Age" video game, 244, 245, 246

Thomas, Bill (Corvar), 155, 156*fig,* 159, 185, 186

Thompson, Sue: crew upskilling, 307; Fatpipe, 306; The Film Unit CEO, 44, 58, 187, 297; New Zealand currency fluctuations, 329

Three Foot Six, 89, 291, 293, 294*fig;* dissolution, 291, 293; EA, 236, 293; Nimmo, 303–6

"Through the Wardrobe Tour," 289

THX, 227, 244

tie-in products, 259; books, 7, 10, 12, 87, 94, 95, 117, 194, 301, 302, 341n16, *Plate 4;* brands partnerships, 106, 107; calendars, 10, 11*fig,* 136; Comic-Con, 200; DVD players, 106; fans' concerns, 107, 194; film franchises (1920s), 4; Tolkien novels, 7, 10, 12. *See also* collectibles; licensing rights; merchandise

Tiger Hill Entertainment, 230

Time: cover stories on *Towers* and on fantasy, 275; game vs. film industries, 225

The Time Traveller's Wife, 277

Time Warner, 5, 28; AOL merger, 48–50, 140–42, 223, 259–60; *Entertainment Weekly*, 111, 183; *Harry Potter*, 49–50, 183, 223, 260; New Line, 28, 39, 49–50, 111, 140, 141, 223, 258–60; video supplements, 223; Warner Bros. Network (The WB), 110, 117, 228

Titanic, 33, 150, 274–75, 335n34, 337n63, 363n38

Tju-Bang Film, 271

Today show, 110

Tolkien, Christopher, 8, 11

Tolkien, J.R.R., 12, 54–56, 57, 86; children's books illustrated by, 11; drafts left at death, 11; making-of documentaries, 117; movie rights, 18–19, 34; poems, 10, 11; *The Silmarillion*, 11, 95, 169, 176; *Smith of Wootton Major*, 11; *The Tolkien Reader*, 11; tours, 288. See also *The Lord of the Rings* (Tolkien)—novels

Tolkien Enterprises: licensing rights, 12, 20, 193, 233, 246, 288, 334n7, 359n54; trademark ownership, 12, 19, 23, 193, 334n7

Tolkien Estate, 19–20, 288

Tolkien Online, 136, 155–56, 161

The Tolkien Reader, 11

Tolkien/*Rings* fans, 9, 53–56, 85, 165–90; age, 9, 53–55, 74, 81; Air New Zealand campaign, 108; Ancalagon the Black, 68, 165, 339n24; "communities," 189–90; concerns about film living up to books, 140, 148, 151, 153; crew of *Rings*, 82–83; departures of films from novels, 68, 69*fig*, 73, 145, 180–81; fanart, 169–80; fanfilms, 183; films about, 185, 187–90; fun, 74; gender, 9, 81, 142, 157–58, 160, 201–2; humor and parodies, 169–74, 349–50; Internet, 8, 68, 83, 132, 135–90; Jackson fan site, 159; Lilith of Sherwood, 166–68, 168*fig*, 189; making-ofs, 115; McKellen online communications with, 146–47, 179–80; Middle-earth realization, 88–89, 100; New Line/*Rings* team Internet cooperation, 138, 139, 149–64, 185; parties, 165, 167, 184–90; Peeps parodies, 172–74, 175*fig*, 350n10; research, 86; RL (real life), 184–90; tours in New Zealand, 167, 287–88; before video games, 233. See also fan cons; fanfiction; Internet; Lord of the Rings Fan Club; spies

Tolkien Sarcasm website, 169

Tolkien Society, 188, 200

Topps, 194, 197

TORN. *See* TheOneRing.net

Toronto Film Festival, 263

tourism, New Zealand, 284–89, 299, 311, 312–16, 320. *See also* tours

Tourism New Zealand, 106, 215, 309, 311–16; billboards, 108, 313, 314*fig*; Los Angeles, 312, 313, 314*fig*; website, 315*table*

tours: Glenorchy Air "trilogytrail," 285–86, 286*fig*, 288; Jackson Oscar, 322; journalists, 313; Queenstown, 285–87, 313; *Rings* investors and executives, 267, 301–2, 309, 312–13; *Rings* locations, 167, 284–90, 320; Rover Rings Tour, 285–88, 287*fig*; Te Papa *Rings* exhibition, 119, 197–98, 289–90, 313, 320, 352n5; Wellington Rover Tours, 284–85; Wellywood, 267, 300–302. *See also* tourism

Tower Records, 215

Toy Biz, 193–94

trademark ownership: fans and, 169; Zaentz's Tolkien Enterprises, 12, 19, 20, 23, 193, 334n7

trading-card games (TCGs), 172, 194, 195, 196, 197

trailers: Air New Zealand, 108; cost, 105; international distributors, 268; Internet, 135–36, 141, 271–72; press kit, 120–21, 123; *Return*, 212; *Towers*, 135–36

training, *Rings* crew, 307–9, 366–67n24

Transamerica Corporation, 4

"trilogytrail" tours, 285–86, 286*fig*, 288

Trilogy Tuesday, 184–85, 187–88

Tucker, Chris, 261

Turbine, 359n54

turnaround, 25; *Rings*, 26–29, 34–36, 150

Twentieth Century Fox: *The English Patient*, 23; *Home Alone*, 26; "The Inheritance Trilogy," 278; *Kingdom of Heaven*, 100; News Corporation, 5, 110; *Planet of the Apes*, 23; SF Film, 269; *Star Wars*, 4, 162, 222; *X-Men*, 6, 325–26. *See also* Fox Studios Australia

2001: A Space Odyssey, 84, 275

The Two Towers (Tolkien), 2; Academy Awards, 51, 186, 299; action scenes,

59–60; costumes, 65; digital technology, 96, 98, 99*fig;* DVDs, 106, 118, 119, 209, 215, 216, 222; fan parties, 184; Fatpipe, 305; film departure from novel, 70–71; gross, 51, 105, 274, 337n63; Internet, 135–36, 347n36; Kubrick homage, 275; Lee illustrations, 87; making-ofs, 117, 118, 119; marketing budget, 105; martial arts choreography, 64–65, 66*fig;* mobile phone game, 250; no summary scenes or crawl title, 73; novel publication, 2, 18; premieres, 51–52, 108, 198, 311, 320; press junkets, 126; press kit, 120–23, 122*fig,* 128; Sinclair script credit, 25; sourcebook, 195–96; video game, 204, 224, 234–37, 236*fig,* 240, 242, 243, 251
Tyler, Liv, 37, 45, 157

Ubisoft North America, 228, 231, 250–53, 359n55
UIP (Universal, Paramount, and Buena Vista), 271
United Artists, 4, 19, 23, 34
United Kingdom: Entertainment Film Distributors, 273; Whitbread Book of the Year Award, 277. *See also* London
United States: CGI firms, 295; crew from, 37–38, 306; economics of production abroad, 330. *See also* Los Angeles; New York
Universal, 4; *Dambusters,* 326; *King Kong,* 23–24, 153–54, 163, 213, 252, 283, 366n18; *Rings* international distribution, 24; theme park globe, 283; UIP, 271; video games, 232, 233, 252
Universal Interactive, 232, 233
Unwin, Rayner, 1–2, 18–20
Unwin, Stanley, 1–2, 18
UPN, 110
Upper Deck Company, 196
Urban, Karl, 93, 319
USA Films, 28, 81
USA Today, 112, 131, 153, 170
UTU, 318

Van Helsing video game, 230, 325
Vanity Fair, 131
van Rossenberg, René, 86–87
Variety, 112; Academy Awards/nominations/parties, 51, 187; award shows, 111; Blockbuster earnings, 222; box-office coverage, 112; Cannes preview of *Rings,* 268; Disney percentage of *Rings,* 35; DVD sales, 223; fan webmaster queries, 163; games and films, 225, 227, 248; infotainment, 110; international distribution, 263, 265; international effects houses, 328; *King Kong* restoration DVD, 218; lordofthe rings.net, 140; MGM blockbuster production, 327; New Line's financial risks, 39–40, 49–50, 259; New Zealand local films, 319; post-production houses, 298; *Return* premieres, 322; *Rings* casting, 37; "semi-indies"/ "nominal indies," 258; "Showmen of the Year" (Shaye and Lynne), 52, 260
Vera Drake, 261
Verdu, Mike, 247
Verhoeven, Paul, 272–73
Verizon, 250
VHS tapes, 204, 205, 206, 219–22, 271, 355
Viacom (CBS and UPN), 110
video: blooper, 217, 218; high-definition, 217; rentals vs. sales, 219–22, 355–56n47; *Rings* farewell, 217–18; VHS tapes, 204, 205, 206, 219–22, 271, 355. *See also* DVDs; laser discs
Video Business magazine, 216
Videocine, Mexico, 272
videoconferencing, Fatpipe, 305–6
video games, 9, 10, 224–53; Activision, 226–27, 229, 231, 356n10; actors, 229–30; "The Battle for Middle-earth," 224–25, 244–48, *Plate 7,8;* CD-ROMs, 228–29; cell phone, 249–50; Easter Eggs, 205, 353n13; film production convergence, 225–33, 237–41, 247–49, 251–52; "Halo," 226, 253, 326; ICM, 228; James Bond, 227, 228, 229, 230, 232, 234, 235, 356n10; *King Kong,* 246, 251; MMORPG, 357n24, 358n45,

video games *(continued)*
359n54; "mods," 245; music, 230; New
Line licensees, 194; PlayStations, 225,
229, 242, 247; RPGs, 195–96, 245,
247, 357n24, 358n45, 359n54; scheduling film/game production, 237–39;
special editions, 247; strategy guides,
245, 358n41; Ubisoft North America,
228, 231, 250–53, 359n55; VU Games,
233–35, 246, 358n34, 359n54; Wingnut Interactive, 252–53, 326. *See also*
Electronic Arts (EA) video games
Village Roadshow Films, Australia, 267,
274
Village Sky City Cinema, 319, 321
Vinet, Pierre, 120
viral marketing, 160–64
Virtual Katy, 323–25
Visions Con, 353n8
Vivendi Universal Games (VU Games),
233–35, 246, 358n34, 359n54
Voigt, Paul, 310–12, 322–23, 325, 329,
335n33

Wachowski, Andy, 252, 300
Wachowski, Larry, 252, 300
Wadham, Roger, 283
Walden Media, 277, 326
Walker, Kerry, 286
*Wallace and Gromit: The Curse of the Were-
Rabbit*, 7, 331–32
Walsh, Fran: Academy Award nights, 185,
186; Boyens hire, 25, 83; Cannes, 43–
44; debt, 44, 297; design process, 77–
78; directing, 38; DVDs, 212, 217;
family atmosphere with crew, 309–10;
fan parties, 185; The Film Unit, 44,
297; *The Frighteners*, 22; "Halo," 326;
Heavenly Creatures, 21, 326; *King
Kong*, 24; *The Lovely Bones*, 326;
Miramar residence, 291, 293; Mira-
max reducing *Rings* to single two-
hour feature, 26; New Line pitch,
27–28; *Rings* script, 25; Salo, 95;
Seatoun house, 293; simplified complexity, 65; training, 366–67n24
Ward, Vincent, 290, 318

"War in Middle Earth," 233
Warner Bros., 4–5; animated films, 332; fan
webmasters working with, 163; games,
252; *Guardians of Ga'Hoole*, 278;
Harry Potter, 183, 223, 351n30; *Home
Alone*, 26; international distribution,
267, 271; *The Last Samurai*, 306; lay-
offs (2005), 260; *The Maltese Falcon*,
7; *The Matrix*, 40, 260; press junket,
124; top-grossing, 262; video supple-
ments, 222, 223. *See also* Time Warner
Warner Home Video, 218
warofthering.net (WOTR), 136, 161, 162,
179, 350n13
The War of the Ring script, 25
"War of the Ring" video game, 233–34
The Waterhorse, 326
Watson, Jasmine, 308
The WB, 110, 117, 228
Weapons and Warfare, 94, 95
Weaver, Rebecca, 108–9
Weaving, Hugo, 247–48
Web. *See* Internet
The Wedding Singer, 48, 267
Weinstein, Bob, 25, 27, 35, 36*fig*, 278
Weinstein, Harvey, 23–27, 193; acknowl-
edgments, 36–37, 365n16; leaving
Miramax, 35, 278; *Rings* at Cannes,
45; *Rings* credits and profits, 35, 36*fig*;
Rings in turnaround, 26–27, 34,
35–36
Welcome to Middle-earth, 117, 119
Wellington, 12, 20–21, 25–26, 76, 290,
320–25; Avalon Studios, 296, 365n7;
Film Festival (July 2004), 116, 188;
Film Wellington, 302, 318; ice cream
factory building, 293, 295, 297, 302;
The Irrefutable Truth about Demons,
318; Positively Wellington Tourism,
320; *Rings* premieres, 51–52, 189, 237,
320–22, *Plate 1*; *Rings* press junkets,
79, 81, 126–28, 313, 322, *Plate 1*; Rongotai, 291, 294; Seatoun, 291, 293,
302; *Stickman*, 318; Wellington Rover
Tours, 284–85. *See also* Miramar;
Wellywood
Wellywood, 283, 292*map*, 325–31; tours,

267, 300–302. *See also* Miramar; Wellington; Weta Ltd.

Wenham, David, 243

Westerns, 56, 65

weta, giant cricket indigenous to New Zealand, 291

Weta Digital, 76, 89, 291, 293–95, 298–99; Fatpipe, 304–6; *I, Robot*, 306, 325; *King Kong*, 325; *Van Helsing*, 325; *The Waterhorse*, 326; *X-Men*, 325–26

Weta Digital—*Rings*, 41, 89, 294–95, 297; archive footage for publicity, 119; crew from abroad, 306; Fatpipe, 304–6, 327; "milestones," 300–301; mo-caps, 231, 242; pitch video, 27; postproduction DVD content, 210; preview at Cannes, 41–42; production, 36, 39, 41, 96–101; subcontracting, 295; tours for investors, 301; video games, 231, 235–37, 239–40, 242

Weta Ltd., 20–21, 22, 89, 291, 293; DVD recording sessions, 212; martial arts choreography, 65; "movie palace" decorated theater, 211; *Rings* costs, 33; *Rings* preproduction, 25, 26, 30, 37. *See also* Weta Digital; Weta Workshop

Weta/Tenzan, 302

Weta Workshop, 76, 89–94, 279–80, 291, 293–94, 303; Clark visit, 310; collectibles, 197, 302; Falconer, 90, 93–94, 201, 279; IT department, 302; "Kong" game, 251–52; Maclachlan senior model maker, 308; movie geeks, 83; *Return* premiere, 323*fig;* after *Rings*, 302, 325–26; tours for investors, 301; training, 309; *The Waterhorse*, 326. *See also* Sideshow Weta; Taylor, Richard

Weta Worlds, 302

What Dreams May Come, 318

William Morris Agency, 233

Willis, Bruce, 336n47

Wilson, Jim, 232

Wingnut Films, 83, 86–87, 290, 293, 326

Wingnut Interactive, 252–53, 326

Winston, Stan, 82, 231, 281

Wolf, Jonathan, 258, 259, 263–65, 330

Woo, John, 230

Wood, Elijah, 37; Air NZ, 108; fan club charter member, 143; fanfiction effects, 182; fan Lilith of Sherwood, 166; interviews, 127, 131, 145, *Plate 1;* One Ring Celebration, 203*fig;* overnight star, 33; parties, 312; video games, 243, 244; website devoted to, 347n34

Wood, Katy, 325

Woolf, Tony, 61

Wootten, Ben, 90, 279

workers. *See* labor

worldbuilding, 84. *See also* Middle-earth

The World Is Not Enough, 318

The World of Eldaterra, 278

The World's Fastest Indian, 318–19

www.of-the-shire.net, 143

Xena: Warrior Princess, 63, 201, 241, 308

X-Men, 6, 248, 325–26, 347n36

Xoanon (Michael Regina), 155–56, 156*fig*

Yahoo!, 133, 141, 178, 179

Young, Neil, 227, 234–35, 238, 244, 248

Yuen, Cory, 231

Zaentz, Saul, 12, 18–25; AFMA Lifetime Achievement Award, 258; *The English Patient*, 23, 34; Jackson thanks to, 365n16; *Rings* film rights, 20, 34; *Rings* production, 76; *Rings* turnaround terms, 27. *See also* Tolkien Enterprises

Zemeckis, Robert, 22, 23, 32, 38

Zeta, 273–74

Zhang Yimou, 329

Zug, Mark, 278

Text:	11/13.5 Adobe Garamond
Display:	Adobe Garamond and Perpetua
Indexer:	Barbara Roos
Cartographer:	Bill Nelson
Compositor:	Integrated Composition Systems
Printer and binder:	Sheridan Books, Inc.